Feminization of the
Labour Force

2

Europe and the International Order
Series Editor: Joel Krieger

Published:
Peter A. Hall, *Governing the Economy*
Judith Adler Hellman, *Journeys Among Women*
Joel Krieger, *Reagan, Thatcher and the Politics of Decline*
George Ross, Stanley Hoffmann and Sylvia Malzacher, *The Mitterrand Experiment*

Forthcoming:
Mark Kesselman, *The Fading Rose*
Andrei Markovits, *The West German Left*
David Stark, *Politics at Work in a Socialist Society*

Feminization of the Labour Force

Paradoxes and Promises

EDITED BY

*Jane Jenson, Elisabeth Hagen
and Ceallaigh Reddy*

Polity Press

First published 1988 by Polity Press
in association with Basil Blackwell.

Editorial Office:
Polity Press, Dales Brewery, Gwydir Street,
Cambridge CB1 2LJ, UK

Basil Blackwell Ltd
108 Cowley Road, Oxford OX4 1JF, UK

British Library Cataloguing in Publication Data
Feminization of the labor force : paradoxes
and promises — (Europe and the
international order).
1. Sexual division of labor. 2. Women
— Employment
I. Jenson, Jane II. Hagen, Elisabeth
III. Reddy, Ceallaigh IV. Series
331.4   HD6060.6

ISBN 0-7456-0548-6

Typeset in 10 on 11.5pt Times
by Alan Sutton Publishing Limited
Printed in Great Britain by T.J. Press Ltd, Padstow

Contents

PART III   THE POLICY PROCESS: PROMISES BROKEN OR
RENEWED?

PART IV   WOMEN'S IDENTITIES: INTO THE FUTURE

List of Contributors

Hugh Armstrong is Associate Dean, General Studies at Centennial College in Toronto, Canada. A sociologist, he is co-author (with Pat Armstrong) of *The Double Ghetto: Canadian Women and their Segregated Work* (McClelland and Stewart, 1984) and *A Working Majority: What Women Must Do For Pay*, (CACSW, 1983) as well as numerous articles in areas related to women's work, employment, and the state.

Pat Armstrong is an Associate Professor of Sociology at York University in Canada. She is co-author (with Hugh Armstrong) of *The Double Ghetto: Canadian Women and Their Segregated Work* (McClelland and Stewart, 1984) and *A Working Majority: What Women Must Do For Pay*, (CACSW, 1983) as well as several articles on women's work and social theory, and author of *Labour Pains: Women's Work in Crisis* (Women's Press, 1984).

Peter Albin is a Professor of Economics at the City University of New York and Director of the Center for the Study of Systems Structure and Industrial Complexity located at John Jay College in New York City. He is the author of *Progress Without Poverty* (Basic Books, 1978) and *Analysis of Complex Socioeconomic Systems* (Lexington, 1975) as well as many articles.

Eileen Appelbaum is an Associate Professor of Economics at Temple University. She is the author of *Back to Work* (Auburn House, 1981) and several recent articles on women and work. She has served as a consultant to the Office of Technology Assessment, United States Congress on several publications, including *Office Automation* (1985) and *International Trade in Services* (1986).

Isabella Bakker is an Assistant Professor of Political Science at York University in Canada. She has worked for the Organization of Economic Cooperation and Development (Paris) on a publication entitled *The*

Integration of Women in the Economy and has written several articles on the political economy of gender.

Veronica Beechey is a Senior Lecturer in Women's Studies at the Open University in Britain. She is the author of *Unequal Work* (Verso, 1987), co-author (with Tessa Perkins) of *A Matter of Hours* (Polity, 1987), and co-editor of *Women in Britain Today* (Open University Press, 1986) and *Subjectivity and Social Relations* (Open University Press, 1985).

Anni Borzeix works at the Laboratoire de Sociologie du Travail et des Relations Professionelles (Conservatoire National des Arts et Métiers), and is a member of the Centre National de la Recherche Scientifique. She is the author of *Syndicalisme et organisation du travail* (CNAM, 1980) and the co-author (with Margaret Maruani) of *Le Temps des chemises* (Syros, 1982), as well as numerous articles on the labor movement, collective action and work organization.

Harold Brackman is a visiting Senior Lecturer in History at the University of Missouri at Columbia. He teaches and does research in American social history, particularly on the topics of gender and ethnicity. He has published (with Steven Erie) 'The Future of the Gender Gap' in *Social Policy* (1986).

Anne-Marie Daune-Richard works in the Laboratoire d'Economie et de Sociologie du Travail in Aix-en-Provence and is a member of the Centre National de la Recherche Scientifique. She is the author of *Travail professionel et travail domestique. Etude exploratoire sur le travail et ses representations au sein de lignées féminines* (Petite collection CEFUP/ Document Travail et Emploi, Université de Provence/Ministère du Travail, Aix-en-Provence/Paris, 1984), and has an article in the collective book, *Le Sexe du travail* (Presses Universitaires de Grenoble, 1984), as well as several other articles.

Daniela Del Boca is an Associate Professor of Economics at the University of Turin in Italy. On the topic of women, family and the labor market she has published *Famiglia e mercato del lavoro* (Il Mulino, 1979), as well as articles in *Ricerche Economiche*.

Steven P. Erie is an Associate Professor of Political Science at the University of California, San Diego. He is the author of *Rainbow's End* (University of California Press, 1988) and co-author (with Martin Rein) of 'Women and the Welfare State: Potential for a New Progressive Alliance?' in Carol Mueller (ed.) *The Politics of the Gender Gap* (Sage, 1987).

Gisela A. Erler is a member of the 'Work and Family Life' Study Group at the Deutsches Jugendinstitut in Munich. She has been involved in research on women, work, and family, focusing on the family identity of women in different life situations. She is the co-author of West Germany's controversial 'Mothers' Manifesto' (1987), as well as *Frauenzimmer. In favor of a policy of sexual difference* (Wagenbach Verlag, Berlin, 1985).

Elisabeth Hagen is an economist who has studied the restructuring processes of American and Western European industry. She is affiliated with the Program on Science, Technology and Society at the Massachusetts Institute of Technology.

Jane Humphries is a Lecturer at the Faculty of Economics and Politics, Cambridge University, and a Fellow of Newnham College. Her research involves the study of the historical interaction between family structure and women's involvement in productive activities. She is the author of 'Women's Employment in Restructuring America: The Changing Experience of Women in Three Recessions' in Jill Routledge (ed.) *Women and Recession* (Routledge, 1988) and 'Women and Work' in *The New Palgrave: A Dictionary of Economic Theory and Doctrine* (Macmillan, 1987), as well as numerous other articles on women's work in the United States and the United Kingdom.

Jane Jenson is a Professor in the Political Science Department at Carleton University in Canada. She is the co-author (with George Ross) of *The View From Inside: A French Communist Cell in Crisis* (University of California Press, 1984) and an editor of *Behind the Lines: Gender and the Two World Wars* (Yale, 1987), as well as numerous articles on the women's movement and French politics.

Margaret Maruani works at the Laboratoire de Sociologie du Travail et des Relations Professionelles and is a member of the Centre National de la Recherche Scientifique. She is the author of *Les Syndicats a l'épreuve du féminisme* (Syros, 1979), *Mais qui a peur du travail des femmes?* (Syros, 1985), and co-author (with Anni Borzeix) of *Le Temps des chemises* (Syros, 1982).

Martin Rein is a Professor of Urban Studies and Planning at the Massachusetts Institute of Technology. He is currently involved in a comparative study of social policy of selected European countries and the United States. He is the author of *From Policy to Practice* (Macmillan, 1983), *Women and the Social Welfare Labor Market* (Wissenschaftzentrum, Berlin, 1985) and co-author (with Lisa Peattie) of *Women's Claims: A Study in Political Economy* (Oxford, 1983).

Jill Rubery is a Senior Research Officer and a member of the Labour Studies Group, Department of Applied Economics, at Cambridge University in Britain. Her research has dealt with the topics of women's employment and the labor market. She is the co-author (with C. Craig and E. Garnsey) of 'Payment Structures in Smaller Firms: Women's Employment in Segmented Labour Markets' (Department of Employment Research Paper no. 48), and (with J. Humphries) 'The reconstitution of the supply-side of the labour market: the relative autonomy of social reproduction', *Cambridge Journal of Economics*, and editor of *Women and Recession* (Routledge and Kegan Paul, 1988).

Mary Ruggie is an Assistant Professor of Sociology and Comparative Social Policy in the Graduate School of International Relations and Pacific Studies at the University of California, San Diego. She is the author of *The State and Working Women: A Comparative Study of Britain and Sweden* (Princeton University Press, 1984).

Barbara Sichtermann is a political economist and a freelance author. She is the author of *Femininity* (Policy Press, 1986) and *Frauenarbeit* (Wagenbach Verlag, Berlin 1987).

Ronnie Steinberg is an Assistant Professor of Sociology and Women's Studies at Temple University. She is the author of *Wages and Hours: Labor and Reform in Twentieth-Century America* (Rutgers University Press, 1982), editor of *Equal Employment Policy for Women: Strategies for Implementation in the United States, Canada, and Western Europe* (Temple University Press), and co-editor of *Job Training for Women: Research Perspectives and Policy Directions*.

Elisabeth Vogelheim is the Head of the Women's Department at the I.G. Metall headquarters in Frankfurt. She is the author of 'Mehr als nur ein organisationspolitisches Potential – Frauen und Gewerkschaften' in *Gewerkschaften auf neuen Wegen* (Marburg 1987), and editor of *Frauen am Computer* (Hamburg, 1984).

Preface

This book began as a Conference held at the Center for European Studies (CES), Harvard University in March 1986. The goal of the conference was to bring together researchers and labor activists from Europe and North America in order to assess the current situation of women in the labor force. In that initial exploration, it became clear that the previous two decades in advanced industrial economies had been marked by profound changes to the economy, to politics and in family relations. Not only were more women working, but they were doing so in different ways and, in fact, seemed to be located where economic restructuring was most likely to occur.

As a result, the questions asked at the 1986 Conference differed from those that might have been posed at a similar event held a decade earlier. No longer was the primary question one of women gaining access to the world of paid labor. The participants all agreed that had occurred. Instead, the concerns focused more on the impact of new technologies on the kinds of work women will do and especially on the growth of part-time employment, initiated by companies to cope with economic restructuring. Many conference participants saw too an increase in women's double burden coming from the politics of neo-productivism, which would cut back state supports for caring programs and push responsibility for such care back into the 'family', which has always really meant work by women. Yet, at the same time, some people saw new opportunities for the 'feminization' (or humanization) of work life and community, opportunities which depended, of course, on the willingness of political actors, including women themselves, to take up such projects.

The conference was, as so many like events at CES, based on the work of many more people than the editors of this book. Judy Leff participated from the very beginning as a co-organizer of the conference. We thank her profoundly for her ideas, her enthusiasm and her collegial support after the event. Abby Collins, in her role as Assistant Director of CES, was crucial to the initiation of the project and remained responsible for most of the organization of the conference. As so many others before us, we thank her for her labors. Carol Heim, Serenella Sferza and Stephen Wood, as Associates of the Center, provided much needed advice and help in contacting participants.

Financial support for the Conference came from the Center for European Studies, the Commission of the European Community (Bureau for questions concerning employment and equal treatment for women), the Council for European Studies, the French government, the German Marshall Fund of the United States, Marietta Lutz and Radcliffe College. Financial aid for the preparation of the manuscript was provided by CES and the Dean of Graduate Studies and Research, Carleton University.

Behind all these institutions are the real people who decide, and it is them as individuals whom we thank for their enthusiasm and concrete suggestions about our project, as well as expressing our gratitude for the institutional support. Finally, we must acknowledge the great help of all the people at the Conference, whose comments as chairpersons, discussants and participants, helped to shape the editors' understanding of the feminization of the labor force and of the possibility that there might be a book in it.

PART I

Introduction

1

Paradoxes and Promises
Work and Politics in the Postwar Years

Elisabeth Hagen and Jane Jenson

BASIC THEMES

One of the most dramatic changes in industrial societies in the postwar years has been the intensification of women's participation in the paid labor force. All over Europe and North America the number of working women has rapidly increased. Well over half of the adult women in most member countries of the Organization for Economic and Cultural Development (OECD) are now in the paid labor force. Their participation rate is, therefore, rapidly approaching that of men, which has been falling over the same period.

Women have, of course, always worked, performing paid labor as well as housework. Nevertheless, in most cases, working for wages tended to be temporary and discontinuous, usually confined to the times in women's lives when their family duties were lightest or to moments of national emergency when they were called on to substitute for men. Moreover, since their domestic activity did not qualify as 'work', and their participation in the paid labor force was considered marginal at best, the 'model worker' was a man with a dependent family.[1]

The last two decades have dramatically undermined the credibility of this model. No longer is it possible to assume that the norm is a traditional gender division of labor which assigns women exclusive responsibilities for childraising and domestic labor in exchange for economic support from their spouses. Nor is it possible to assume that the 'average worker' is a full-time male worker with a dependent family. Now more women work for wages essential to the income of the whole family (of which women increasingly are the head), yet they quite frequently have difficulty inserting themselves into the labor force full-time. Thus, the ranks of part-time workers and workers with temporary labor contracts are disproportionately feminized.

Therefore the assumptions that women are not waged and that the 'average worker' is full-time and male – assumptions which have dominated popular, political and state discourses for more than a century – must be replaced by a better representation of the realities of the labor force. There must be a recognition that both women and men compose the labor force, that work is gendered and not equitably distributed, and that the existence of gendered work has important consequences not only for employers and the state but also for the political action of organized workers.

Beginning in the early 1960s, in most countries two important changes occurred in the ways that women labor. First, not only did women enter the paid labor force in increasing numbers, but their attachment to employment became much more permanent. As a consequence, participation rates rose for all types of women, blurring differences which previously existed due to marital status, age, or number of children. Second, working women finally entered the public consciousness and became a subject of political debate and action. Male workers, employers, trade unionists and politicians all reacted – albeit in different ways in different places – to these phenomena.

This book is about responses to the feminization of the labor force in seven countries: Britain, Canada, France, the Federal Republic of Germany, Italy, Sweden and the United States. It has three major sections which explore, in turn, the current status of women in the labor markets of these countries, the policy responses of major social actors to the phenomenon of feminization, and finally the consequences of these social and economic changes in the ways that women construct their lives. All sections of the book stress three major themes.

The first theme is that there is a great deal of diversity in women's actual work experience. No clear trend has emerged that could adequately characterize the present status or the future of the female labor force. On the one hand, participation rates are rising everywhere, regardless of the responses of the major social actors. Thus, whether the context is one of social policies intended to keep women at home and hostile trade unions dominated by men, or one of social and labor market policies supportive of working women with organized labor enthusiastic about the emancipatory effects of paid labor, the statistical curves have climbed. Thus, sheer numbers reflect the importance of female workers to the economies of all advanced industrial societies. Moreover, the resilience of these participation rates during the years of economic crisis since the early 1970s demonstrates that women's paid labor is here to stay. In fact, it even suggests that in some cases businesses' success in maneuvering a way through economic restructuring may very well depend upon the employment of women.

Despite these profound alterations in the labor force, however, women are far from fully equal with men. Many work part-time or have dead-end jobs. Women as a group remain concentrated in a few, low-paid sectors of the labor force. Thus, women's 'willingness' to work part-time may make them attractive employees in an economy dominated by a growing service sector and undergoing technological change, as so many economies currently are; yet it leaves them with low incomes and an increased intensity of work. Moreover, nowhere has the division of domestic labor become equal. Women continue to bear the traditional double burden of paid and domestic labor.

There is also a great deal of diversity and complexity in the responses of the major social actors to these changes. In many instances the positions of employers, unions and the state have been inconsistent if not contradictory. In the early 1970s all three often encouraged women to enter the paid labor force. Employers saw in women an available source of labor, less expensive and more flexible than the traditional male supplies. Unions, influenced by the new women's movement of the late 1960s, devoted energy to the organization of women workers and ended some of their more egregious discriminatory past practices.[2] Finally, state labor market policies and the programs of the welfare state had intended (and unintended) effects. They encouraged women to undertake new training and shift out of some of the female job ghettos, and produced legislation in support of equal pay measures.[3] Nevertheless, recent economic and political changes, especially the growing popularity of neo-liberal ideologies among businessmen and politicians, have resulted in many instances of policy turnaround.

Women, however, have resisted efforts to turn the clock back. They themselves have refused to be reinserted into traditional roles, whether because they appreciate the emancipatory effects of greater economic self-sufficiency or because they can no longer count on support from a man's earnings. Many of them struggle to find new ways of living, thus constantly creating alternatives to old roles.

A second major theme involves the explanation of why the situation is confusing. A basic premise of the book is that there is no one-way relationship of cause and effect. Feminization is not a new variable affecting a set of fixed factors, like the organization of the labor market, trade union strategy, state policy, or other things. Rather, the relationship is reciprocal as all factors change simultaneously. In other words, at the same time as women's participation rates began to rise, the economies of the advanced industrialized countries were undergoing substantial structural changes. The increasing economic importance of the service sector and of part-time work meant that there were more jobs in sectors where women had traditionally been concentrated. Thus, female employment could expand. At the same time, however, since these structural changes occurred in the context of crisis and restructuring, they had negative effects for all workers, especially the ones who were the lowest paid, the least covered by legislative protections, and had the least seniority. Women were disproportionately located in such groups.[4] But whatever the specific patterns of benefit and loss, the important point to note is that the very process of response to economic crisis came to involve an increased dependence on high rates of female employment, which meant that some employers would be reluctant to see that source of labor dry up in the future.

At the same time, and somewhat ironically – given the increasing importance of women's employment – major political changes accompanied economic crisis and restructuring. A new conservatism, sometimes termed neo-liberalism, gained in popularity. Based on a rejection of the universalistic and egalitarian goals that motivated much of postwar politics, especially in countries where social democracy was influential, this political position promoted a return to individualism, a reduced social role for the state, and greater freedom for management in labor–management relations. Imbedded at the heart of neo-liberal ideology was an attack on women's newly-won positions in political rhetoric as well as in action. The earlier stress on programs to help women gain labor market and social equality with men declined and the effects of unequally structured and segmented labor markets were allowed to stand. Unions, which had often only just emerged as protectors of women's right to work, came under attack and lost some of the rights to collective bargaining and to the organization of the labor market that they had won in the postwar years. The rapidity with which these political changes occurred, as well as the existence of mobilized opposition to them in some countries, explains much of why the situation appears so confusing and as yet unsettled.

A third theme is that there are several lessons to be learned from the rapid feminization of the labor force over the last three decades. One is that it is necessary to rethink some of the basic categories available for analysing women's employment. Despite the fundamental alteration in the gender composition of the labor force, many analysts still make use of ones which in one way or another assume that the 'model worker' is a male with a dependent family. Women workers rarely appear at all in labor market theories. However, where they do, they are constituted as a separate category the boundaries of which are determined biologically and the characteristics of which are derived primarily if not exclusively from the traditional gender division of labor and particularly women's family responsibilities.[5] The authors represented in this book reject both the lack of attention to the specificity of women's labor market situation and the notion that such specificity is understood by exclusive reference to their family situation. Instead of trying to sketch the 'new woman worker', they attempt to show the complicated ways in which all social actors, including women themselves, both incorporate existing patterns of gender relations into their behavior and simultaneously – through their behavior under new conditions – innovate in the social construction of gender relations. In this way the authors demonstrate the importance of recognizing the gendering effects of labor markets and work experience.[6] Theory must, this book argues, take into account the variety of women's experience in the labor market.

A second lesson is that theoretical rethinking is only one aspect of a major social and political reassessment of women's employment. Over the last few decades employers, trade unions and the state have all changed – for better or for worse – the ways in which they discuss the labor force and women's place within it. Using these discourses they have constructed new ways of organizing the labor process, new strategies for labor–management negotiations and new state policies. These discourses have, in turn, created possibilities for women. There is a new openendedness to the proliferation of ways of constructing and reconstructing social identities. Women (and men, for that matter) may have more chance than ever to reshape their lives, in the productive as well as the reproductive, spheres. This means that they can create a variety of ways of living in the future, ways in which their workplace experience will play a crucial part.

TWO ECONOMIC REGIMES – THE BACKGROUND FACTORS

The economic basis of the feminization of the labor force lies in two distinct economic regimes.[7] The first was a period of economic growth and stability while the second was one of turmoil, economic crisis and restructuring. All the economies of the advanced industrial countries experienced these two periods and both of them had enormous effects on the composition and organization of the labor forces in those countries. From 1945 until the late 1960s the economies were characterized by a system of mass production, where economic growth depended upon stable demand in mass markets. This demand was sustained in part by governments increasing public expenditure when unemployment rose, so as to keep some money in people's pockets which they could then spend on consumption. The economic growth which occurred in these moments of a 'virtuous circle' between the mass consumption demands and mass production possibilities led to tight labor markets. In this way, the shortage of workers helped to draw more women into the paid labor force, where they could earn wages which the family needed to meet the costs of the mass consumption life style which was now within its grasp.

Female participation rates rose in all industrialized countries. In some – like the USA, Canada and Sweden – the increase was quite pronounced, since the initial postwar rates had been rather low. In those countries the rates increased above the average amount. In other countries – like France and Germany – participation rates rose only gradually, because they had started at a high level. Finally, even in Britain and Italy, where the starting point was low and the rate was slow, there was a substantial increase in women's share of the labor force. In other words, the trend was universal in the post-1945 years (see chapter 2, table 2.2, p. 19).

The Keynesian policies developed by most governments in the postwar years – those most commonly associated with the expanding welfare state – proved to be beneficial to women for several reasons. First, they provided the macroeconomic framework for growth and thus for an increased demand for labor. But in addition, they included a set of social policies, designed to maintain stable demand, which would then, it was believed, contribute to the maintenance of general social equilibrium. These social policies had many effects – some intended but even more unintended – on women. Several of the social services, including the provision of care for the elderly, childcare and other services for dependants, mitigated the traditional family responsibilities of women and allowed them to work outside the home for wages. Expanding educational facilities drew young women into higher education and gave many of them the training and skills employers wanted. Moreover, the expansion of the public sector was a major source of job opportunities for women because so many of them were in the area of care-giving and social services long associated in popular discourse with 'feminine' talents.

The scope of the welfare state, of course, varied a great deal among countries. It was most widely and systematically developed in those countries with a strong social democratic movement. But even where social democracy was weaker, and Keynesianism was founded less on a commitment to extending equality with universalistic social programs, there were similar effects on women's situation. The similarity is no doubt due to the fact that the growth of the public sector was part of a more general expansion of the service sector. From 1960 until the mid-1980s the service sector outstripped the manufacturing sector in size and economic importance.[8]

By the 1980s, services, including the state sector, accounted for more than half of total production in all seven countries considered in this book. To a certain extent the private and public sectors are interchangeable in this regard. They provide similar services and thus offer similar jobs. For example, no matter whether hospitals are publicly or privately owned they will employ nurses, technicians and social workers. Whether private or public institutions, schools and universities require teachers and other support staff. Private health insurance programs employ clerical and administrative staff, just as publicly organized ones do. Therefore, the consequences of the expanding service sectors have been similar in such diverse states as Sweden, which has a relatively small private sector but a large public one, and the USA, which has the largest service sector overall of the seven cases but whose level of state employment is relatively low.

Despite the rising rates of female employment, for all of the reasons just discussed, participation in the paid labor force was not a complete success for women. The then-dominant Fordist system of production was oriented towards the male, industrial worker. It was *his* job description and *his* wages which were at the center of the bargaining process between employers and unions and which provided the focus of state policies. The jobs that were available to women, even the newly-created ones of the expanding service sector, were generally the worst. Women started at the bottom of the occupational hierarchy, in low-paid, low-skilled jobs; often they were jobs which came into being as a result of deskilling reorganizations of the labor process in workplaces. Previously skilled and better-paid workers were replaced as automated assembly-lines organized the production of goods, and their replacements were often the underqualified women workers who could not command the high wages of skilled men.[9] Moreover, the fact that there was an increase in female employment did not mean that all jobs were available to women. The labor market remained highly segregated, with women workers concentrated in occupations which seemed to replicate, in one way or another, the sexual division of labor. Thus, women were confined to work ghettos which involved serving or caring, or which required patience and dexterity. The stereotypes, based on the deeply-rooted assumptions about proper gender roles and gender relations, shaped labor markets no less in 'progressive' and egalitarian countries like Sweden than elsewhere (chapter 10; Beck-Gernsheim, 1981).

Fundamental economic restructuring during the 1970s turned an already ambiguous situation into a rather precarious one. A succession of economic downturns, lower growth rates, rising rates of unemployment, greatly fluctuating prices and exchange rates all indicated that the period of economic growth and stability had come to an end. In the 1980s, as some of the dust cleared, it became clear that the advanced industrialized countries had not just undergone a temporary recession but that they had experienced a fundamental change in their economic structures. The link between mass production and stable demand collapsed in the face of a process of increasing internationalization of capitalism and inter-penetration of domestic economies by one another. Competition from the newly industrializing countries threatened production – and jobs in industry – in Western Europe and North America. Domestic markets fragmented as consumers sought greater diversification and specialization rather than the homogeniety of mass consumption (OECD, 1983).

Business's response was to cut production, to undertake major rationalizations of operations, which often included substantial reductions in the number of employees or at least the wage bill, through a shift to part-time employees, and introduction of new technologies.[10] At the same time, in part as a result of these very decisions, unemployment rose to levels which would have been unthinkable only a few years earlier. In 1975 there were 15 million people out of work in all of the OECD countries; by the early 1980s the figure had risen to 30 million and remained there throughout the decade (OECD, 1982; 1986).

Under these very different circumstances, the Keynesian policies which had seemed to produce a 'virtuous circle' after 1945 proved less effective. The inability of governments to manage demand, stave off unemployment and prevent inflation made them an easy target for neo-liberal ideologies that blamed the recession on state interference with market forces. Such new politics were on the rise everywhere, be it through a change in electoral majorities – as in the USA, Britain and Germany – or just as a change in the political climate, which occurred in all seven countries. Economic crisis and the political turnaround took, of course, different forms in the several countries, depending upon their respective economic structure, their political system and the balance of political forces as well as the ability of institutions to adjust to the new situation.[11] Not all countries immediately abandoned the goal of achieving full employment and some were quite successful in defending it, as the examples of Sweden and to a lesser extent Germany show (Scharpf, 1987).

Yet, common to all countries were attempts to restructure both business and the state. The response of the state remained confused and contradictory, being a mix of *laissez-faire* rhetoric and new forms of intervention into the structure of the economy, although rarely in the form of new social policies.

Business seemed to react more promptly and somewhat more coherently to the new situation. Business strategies for restructuring have involved cost-cutting, shortening product-cycles and increasing flexibility in the production process to be better able to respond to unstable market conditions. This search for flexibility involves a demand for a new type of labor. Women have emerged as very desirable employees in these circumstances because their relationship to the labor market has traditionally displayed the characteristics of flexibility so much wanted in the current conjuncture. Individual women have had a less continuous relationship to the labor market, moving in and out of employment in response to demand for their labor and their personal possibilities. Similarly, women have been willing to work part-time and to take jobs which lack the full social protections, like health coverage or access to complete unemployment benefits. This weaker relationship to the institutions of the welfare state has made women 'cheaper' to employ. Finally, because women have traditionally had lower rates of unionization than men, employers have seen them as more docile employees, less likely to take militant action in the workplace.

It is not without irony that women, who have always been at the margin of the labor force, now might even replace men as the 'model worker', in a situation where employers frequently seek to base their employment strategies precisely in such marginal categories. The fact that women, as a group, have not been pushed out of the labor market during the years of crisis and restructuring and that their employment, albeit often part-time, has expanded, are all indications of the new importance of female workers.

WOMEN'S POLITICS AND THE FUTURE

There is not, then, much to cheer about in this achievement of record levels of female participation in the paid labor force. This book provides ample examples of the worsening conditions of women's work situation as well as of their private lives. Nevertheless, there is also no 'golden past' to turn back to. The old system of labor relations under Fordism did not provide equality, advancement and greater freedom to women either. Rather, it is important to recognize that the contemporary situation, while currently bleak, also contains possibilities for the improvement of women's situation.

Whether these improvements come will depend in large part on the political actions of those most involved. There is nothing deterministic about the new technologies or the current situation of restructuring The final outcome will be the product of choices made by all the actors involved, including women themselves and the institutions within which they act and which help to structure their everyday lives. First among these institutions are those which represent women in the workplace and politics – the trade unions and political parties – and the state which has the authority to organize the conclusion of struggles among political forces.

The story which this book tells about the politics of these institutions is one of competition, not only over policy itself but also over the very meaning of the conditions which women and men faced in the past three decades of rapid economic and social change. As politics has evolved, different ways of understanding the situation and needs of women in advanced industrial societies have emerged. These differences all revolve around two fundamental notions, however. The first notion is that women's situation is fundamentally different from men's, and it ought to be. The second represents a commitment to the fundamental equality of women and men, even if biological and social differences do exist.

A discourse of difference often informs the neo-liberal ideologies which would cut back the state's role in social policy and return responsibility for many care-giving activities to the family. When such ideologies name the 'family', however, they really mean women; the presumption is that women should be available to perform such roles in the home. The result of acting on such a discourse of difference would, of course, not only force women to take up huge new responsibilities at home but it would also deprive other women who already provide such services for pay in the private or public sector of their means of livelihood. Thus, as several authors in this book point out, the attack on the welfare state mounted by neo-liberalism involves both the reinforcement of this discourse of difference and an immediate deterioration of women's conditions of paid and domestic labor.[12] To the extent that political movements organize to end the use of the state to achieve economic and social equality, they are movements which have a greater impact on women.

An egalitarian discourse has also prompted a great deal of political action, whether in the form of classic assumptions about the goals of labor market policies or women's own actions in favour of affirmative action programs.[13] Affirmative action efforts in several countries (especially the USA) and anti-discrimination policies make use of this discourse. To the extent that they are implemented, they represent a political victory over the operation of segmented labor markets and popular assumptions about the gender division of labor and women's skills and talents. As all these experiences so amply demonstrate, the ability to change the operation of labor markets is very much the result of union, party and state actions.

If politics is so central to the future forms of the feminized labor force, it is important to pay attention to the ways women perceive themselves and the situations in which they live. The process by which women take up gendered identities as well as the content of those identities are crucial factors in accounting for the form of political action which women choose. Women may identify themselves as the equal of men and strive for egalitarian solutions; in doing so they reject biological difference as a determining influence on social relations. Women may also choose to identify a primary line of difference, based on biology but also the product of social action, which causes them, as feminists, to celebrate the special and particular characteristics of their sex. In doing so they hold out to the world an alternative way of living, with greater stress on peace, on nurturing and on communitarian values.[14]

But as in the development of labor market and social policies, the process of identity formation does not 'fall from the sky'. It is a consequence of struggle, often very intense, among individual women and men and within organizations. The organization of women in the workplace, in unions or in separate women's groups, provides one of the major locales for the formation of new identities. Through such organization women have acquired new class and gender identities. This process was never without conflict within the labor movement, since women posed a serious challenge to traditional strategies and mobilizational practices. Unions had to learn how to mobilize and organize a new constituency, one which often expressed different demands than men did, and women had to learn how to organize themselves in effective ways.

The lesson to be learned from all of this – both the overview provided in this Introduction and the individual chapters which follow – is that the current period is one of great flux. States are vacillating over a complete abandonment of the ideals of the social democratic dream, in the face of their need to adapt to new domestic and international conditions. Employers are experimenting with new strategies for the organization of production; no definite course of action is yet firmly established. Therefore, the struggles of women and men to have an influence over such decisions hold out the chance that a more egalitarian system may be put into place, one which would expand rather than diminish the areas of workers' autonomy and control over their working lives and thus provide a progressive influence from the workplace on the rest of their lives.

In this book, for example, we see how there are very different ways of introducing new technologies; flexibility may be achieved in more than one fashion. The decision which, depending on the political strength of workers may be made in consultation or by employers alone, has considerable consequences for the conditions of work.[15] If workers, both female and male, formulate their demands and take charge, they will be able to contribute to a restructuring process which – at worst – does not increase their exploitation and – at best – achieves an organization of work that gives them more freedom to arrange their own lives as they choose.

It is not difficult to imagine the directions which these demands must take. There must be equal protection of part-time work, so that employers are less tempted to substitute part-time for full-time workers. Labor contracts as well as social legislation must provide these protections. There must be real and meaningful participation by workers in the introduction of new technologies, so that the jobs of not only the already-employed but also the non-employed and future generations will be considered. Reskilling and retraining must go hand-in-hand with technological restructuring. Included in it must be a recognition that much that women do has previously not been recognized as skilled, whereas it in fact involves the same type of work as that which men do, and is called skilled by them and their employers. Most important too is the rejection of an ideology which would undermine the limited gains which have been made by forcing women and men to return to a traditional gendered division of labor in which men are the 'model workers', out in the world to support their dependant families left at home.

Throughout this book the message conveyed is that women's situations are neither eternal facts of nature nor social constructs given once and for all. Rather, there is a state of flux. Whether the current open-ended situation will move towards one which gives women both more equality and more freedom is, as we have argued, never determined by technological change or economic conditions alone. It will depend upon the political decisions and actions of women themselves and in alliance with men, in the institutions which organize the world within which they live. These decisions and actions in turn depend upon the social construction of women's identities.

The openness of this situation can only lead to the more general conclusion that there is no single 'woman', no single 'female condition' either equal or different, nor any single theoretical concept which can capture this variety. Even more broadly, our examination of the characteristics of and responses to the feminized labor force shows there is no single construct 'work', no single 'labor force', and certainly no possibility of speaking simply of 'the' workers.

NOTES

1   The extent to which this model was accepted by trade unions, for example, is seen in the popularity of the strategy of the 'family wage'. Unions in many countries sought wages which would be high enough to support not a single person but a man with a wife and several children. Where unions did not pursue this strategy – as in France, for example, where the high rates of female participation were accompanied by a greater recognition of the importance of female labor – unionists organized in opposition to lower wages for women and the notion that women worked for little more than a *salaire d'appoint* (pin money, or a supplementary salary). See Barrett and McIntosh (1980) on the family wage; and Jenson (1984; 1986) on France.

2   On the unions' policies see Bakker, chapter 2.

3   Bakker also documents some of the details of important social policies, including childcare. Britain, France, Italy and the FRG, because they are members of the European Community, have made a series of efforts, each providing some improvement on earlier ones, to organize and implement programs of 'equal pay for work of equal value' (what in North America is often termed 'comparable worth'). Community-wide legislation has been supplemented in each country by national legislation. See Steinberg and Cook (1986) and Remick (1984) for some cross-national overviews. Sweden and Canada also have legislation covering this issue. See Ruggie, chapter 10, and Armstrong and Armstrong, chapter 4. The USA remains the laggard in the formal implementation of policies in this domain.

4   These contradictory effects are described, in more detail, for our seven countries in Bakker, chapter 2.

5   For a description and criticism of this tendency, see Feldberg and Glenn (1979) and Cockburn (1983). See also Daune-Richard, chapter 15.

6   This notion that the workplace is an important locale for the social construction of gender is crucial to the analyses of Cockburn (1983) and Maruani and Nicole (1987). A more general case for investigating the gendering effects of all social activities is made in Higonnet, Jenson, Michel and Weitz (1987).

7   The description of these two regimes is inspired by analyses of the new regimes of accumulation and regulation in the work of Piore and Sabel (1984), Boyer (1986), Lipietz (1987). For an overview of the theory, see Mahon (1987).

8 Canada and the USA were an exception to this pattern, only because their sectors already occupied first place before 1960. See Gershuny and Miles (1983) and Bhagwati (1986).

9 For a more detailed discussion of women as secondary workers see Beechey, chapter 3.

10 The technology most pervasive in new production techniques is microelectronics. Its major advantage is to make automated production equipment cheaper and more flexible. See OECD: ICCP5, (1981).

11 In Canada, for example, whose economic base depends much more on production of primary products, especially oil, the mid-1970s was actually a moment of partial economic upswing, whereas the more industrialized countries experienced the classic downturn described here. Similarly, political conflict in Canada centered more on the adaptive possibilities of the institutions of federalism than in other countries where the issues of industrial expansion and unemployment due to restructuring dominated the political agenda. Another difference, between the USA and the other six countries, was that the economic strength of the USA in the international economy meant that for a time it could 'export' its problems with balance of payments, budget deficits, and capital shortages elsewhere. For a general discussion see OECD (1981).

12 See Humphries and Rubery, chapter 5, Brackman, Erie and Rein, chapter 12, and Armstrong and Armstrong, chapter 4.

13 Sweden provides the best example of a labor market policy premised on a discourse of equality (Ruggie, chapter 10).

14 In this book, Erler (chapter 13) and Sichtermann (chapter 16) best represent this position.

15 For a detailed example see Albin and Appelbaum (chapter 8). For another discussion of the importance of workplace organization for the outcomes of such decisions, see Mahon (1987).

REFERENCES

Barrett, M. and M. McIntosh (1980) 'The Family Wage', *Capital and Class*, no. 11.
Beck-Gernshein, E. (1981) *Der Geschlechtsspezifische Arbeitmarkt* (Frankfurt: Campus).
Bhagwati, J. (1986) *The Emerging Service Economy* (Oxford: Pergamon).
Boyer, R. (1986) *La Théorie de la régulation: une approche critique* (Paris: La Découverte).
Cockburn, C. (1983) *Brothers: Male Dominance and Technological Change* (London: Pluto).
Feldberg, R. and G. N. Glenn (1979) 'Male and Female: Job versus Gender Models in the Sociology of Work', *Social Problems*, vol. 26, no. 5.
Gershuny, J. I. and I. D. Miles (1983) *The New Service Economy: The Transformation of Employment in Industrial Societies* (London: Pinter).
Higonnet, M., J. Jenson, S. Michel and M. Weitz (1987) *Behind the Lines: Gender and the Two World Wars* (New Haven: Yale University Press).
Jenson, J. (1984) 'The "Problem" of Women', in M. Kesselman and G. Groux

(eds.), *The French Workers' Movement* (London: Allen and Unwin).

Jenson, J. (1986) 'Gender and Reproduction: or Babies and the State', *Studies in Political Economy*, no. 20.

Lipietz, A. (1987) *Mirages and Miracles: The Crisis of Global Fordism* (London: Verso).

Mahon, R. (1987) 'From Fordism to?: New Technology, Labour Markets and Unions', *Economic and Industrial Democracy*, vol. 8.

Maruani, M. and C. Nicole (1987) 'Du Travail à l'emploi: l'enjeu de la mixité', *Sociologie du Travail*, no. 2.

OECD (1981) *The Welfare State in Crisis* (Paris: OECD).

OECD (1982) *The Challenge of Unemployment* (Paris: OECD).

OECD (1983) *Industry in Transition* (Paris: OECD).

OECD (1986) *Main Economic Indicators* (Paris: OECD).

OECD: ICCP5 (1981) *Microelectronics: Productivity and Employment* (Paris: OECD).

Piore, M. and C. Sabel (1984) *The Second Industrial Divide: Possibilities for Prosperity* (New York: Basic Books).

Remick, H. (1984) *Comparable Worth and Wage Discrimination: Technical Possibilities and Political Realities* (Philadephia, PA: Temple).

Scharpf, F. (1987) *Sozialdemokratische Krisenpolik in Europa* (Frankfurt: Campus).

Steinberg, R. and A. Cook (1986) 'Policies Affecting Women's Work in Other Industrial Countries', in A. Stromberg and S. Harkness, *Women Working* (CA: Mayfield, 2nd edn).

2

Women's Employment in Comparative Perspective

Isabella Bakker

INTRODUCTION

The typical 'new' female worker is a self-assured, attractive, middle-level manager, with two happy children (in school or daycare), a smooth-functioning household (thanks to all the new labor-saving household technology), and blessed with a supportive husband. So goes the mainstream media portrayal of the 'feminization' of the labor force. Thanks to the new feminist scholarship of the last two decades, however, this stereotype has been debunked and the realities of women's economic position and political power have come into somewhat clearer focus.

Women, of course, have always worked both in the domestic sphere, where initially all family members contributed to necessary subsistence work, and then with the advent of industrialization, for wages in exchange for their labor power. Research is gradually exposing the difficult conditions under which women labor; the introduction of women's work into standard economic analysis has revealed problems related to the definition and measurement of this work and demonstrated the shortcomings of market analysis. Some production does take place in the household and without an examination of the social relations of domestic labor it is not possible to understand fully the nature of women's participation in the labor force. Moreover, inadequacies also directly result from current definitions and measurements of work. A United Nations review of social indicators highlights the limits of the present statistics' ability to describe accurately the situation of women. First, conventional statistics often fail to capture differentials in the socio-economic situation of men and women or to indicate the extent of inequality in a given society. Second, the statistics do not reflect the real productive roles of women in the economy, the significance of those roles, and the interaction between changing family situations and economic responsibilities. The use of familiar indicators leads to frequent under-reporting of women's economic participation, particularly because of their involvement in the informal sector and as unpaid family workers. More adequate indicators, as well as differentiating among groups of women, would also allow comparison of women and men's situation over time [UN, 1984].

Despite growing popular recognition that women are a vital part of the labor force, underestimation of women's work and the inability to quantify fully the economic position of women makes it difficult to say with certainty why women's formal economic participation in the labor force so dramatically changed after World War II. With these restrictions in mind, however, a consideration of women's formal economic participation and the impact that this intensification of women's participation has had on the labor market and political policy debates, is an important first step in a very complicated topic.

THE FEMINIZATION OF THE LABOR FORCE –
SEVERAL INDICATORS

Participation rates (defined here as the number of people in the total labor force divided by the size of the working-age population) are a helpful first indicator of women's economic activities. Their rising rate of participation in the labor force is most commonly referred to as a prime measure of women's altered economic status after World War II. This change is especially evident when looking at the female share of the labor force (table 2.1). Increases have been especially dramatic for married women,

TABLE 2.1   *Female Share of the Labor Force*
(percentages of population aged 15–64)

	1950	1977	1982
Canada	21.3	37.8	40.9
France	35.9	37.6	38.6
Germany	35.1	37.6	38.2
Italy	25.4	31.9	33.8
Sweden	26.3	43.7	46.2
United Kingdom	30.7	38.2	39.1
United States	28.9	40.3	42.8

Source: OECD [1985b: 14].

with or without dependants. Over the last decade, the rate of increase in female participation has levelled off somewhat, although it is still on the rise in all countries.

While the male participation rate in the OECD area as a whole declined from 87.4 to 84.3 per cent from 1950 to 1984, the female participation rate rose steadily from 38.2 to 55.9 per cent (table 2.2). In other words, a decline in male rates has occurred in most OECD countries while, as noted, the female participation rate has been on the increase everywhere and has, in some countries, more than doubled.

TABLE 2.2 Male and Female Participation Rates[a]
(percentages)

					Female					
	1950	1970	1975	1979	1980	1981	1982	1983	1984	1985
Canada	26.2	43.2	50.0	55.5	57.2	58.8	58.9	60.1	61.2	62.4
France	49.5	48.3	49.9	52.5	52.5	52.5	52.9	54.3	54.7	55.0
Germany	44.3	48.1	49.6	49.6	50.0	50.1	49.8	49.6	49.4	50.4
Italy	32.0	33.5	34.6	38.8	39.8	40.5	40.3	40.5	41.1	41.3
Sweden	35.1	59.4	67.6	72.8	74.1	75.3	76.0	76.6	77.4	78.0
UK	40.7	50.7	55.3	58.2	58.5	56.9	56.2	57.8	59.0	59.8
US	37.2	48.9	53.2	58.9	59.7	60.7	61.4	61.8	62.8	64.0
N. America	31.7	46.1	51.6	57.2	58.5	59.8	60.2	61.0	62.7	63.8
OECD Eur.[b]	41.4	48.1	51.7	54.9	56.4	55.8	56.3	57.1	49.6	n/a
Total OECD	38.2	45.6	48.1	51.1	52.2	52.5	52.8	53.6	55.9	n/a

					Male					
	1950	1970	1975	1979	1980	1981	1982	1983	1984	1985
Canada	94.2	85.7	86.2	86.2	86.3	86.4	84.9	85.0	84.5	84.8
France	93.0	87.0	84.4	83.2	82.5	81.2	80.4	79.4	77.4	76.3
Germany	98.0	92.5	87.0	84.5	83.4	82.3	81.2	80.0	79.3	79.8
Italy	99.0	86.8	84.2	82.7	82.9	82.8	81.8	81.0	79.7	79.2
Sweden	98.6	88.8	89.2	87.9	87.8	86.5	86.2	85.9	85.5	85.7
UK	97.2	94.1	92.2	90.6	90.5	89.8	89.1	87.9	87.6	87.7
US	92.5	87.1	84.7	85.1	84.7	84.5	84.3	84.7	84.9	84.9
N. America	93.4	86.4	85.5	85.7	85.5	85.5	84.6	84.9	85.0	84.9
OECD Eur.[b]	98.4	90.4	87.6	86.0	85.8	85.2	84.4	84.0	80.7	n/a
Total OECD	97.2	90.9	87.4	85.8	85.6	85.3	84.4	84.3	83.8	n/a

[a] Defined as labor force of all ages divided by population aged 15–64.
[b] OECD Europe: Austria, Denmark, Finland, France, Germany, Italy, Norway, Spain, Sweden, Switzerland, United Kingdom.
Source: OECD [1984: 106]; OECD [1985: 40]; OECD [1986: 140].

Participation rates also reveal differences across age groups. Since 1975, the participation rates of both female and male older workers (age 55 and over) have fallen steadily, although the rate of decline slowed after 1979 in many countries. Labor force participation rates for youth, especially teenagers, have also declined, with the rate for young women usually being substantially less than the rate for young men [OECD, 1983: chapter VI].

In order to understand the behavior of participation rates, it is necessary to examine structural changes both in countries' economies and in their social and political activities. Thus, rises or declines in participation rates can be linked to rates of unemployment, levels of job vacancies, discouraged and added worker effects, as well as long-term factors such as changes in demography, marriage and divorce patterns, inflationary pressures, and institutional interventions in the labor market such as state equal-opportunity policies.[1] Structural changes in the OECD economies have had a particularly significant impact on women workers' participation in the labor market. In the period 1975–9, the service sector was the major source of net job creation, and this trend has been even more pronounced since 1979 [OECD, 1983: 21]. By 1980, between 60 and 85 per cent of working women in each OECD country were concentrated in the service sector, with the exception of the southern European region where the agricultural sector still accounted for a large share of the female labor force [Paukert, 1982].

While the private sector has expanded female employment opportunities, albeit in a small range of occupations within the service sector, public-sector employment growth has also had a significant effect. A 1982 OECD report mapped several trends in female public-sector employment, showing a clear tendency for the public sector to become more female-intensive over time. Moreover, there is a positive correlation between higher rates of feminization of public-sector employment and the size of the public sector. In other words, the more public employment, the more likely public employees are to be women [OECD, 1982: 29]. This trend has had an impact on the occupations taken up by women, although the future looks less promising, given the budgetary restraints in many of the OECD countries which have slowed down hiring.

An additional significant structural shift over the past two decades has been the decline in the average hours worked per person each year, which is associated with a pronounced growth of part-time employment since 1973 [OECD, 1983: 43]. The average length of the work week has dropped, but rather than all workers reducing their hours, there has been an increasing segmentation of the labor force into full-time and part-time workers. This segmentation has very great implications for women; the number of jobs held by women on a part-time basis has been on the increase in every OECD country. In several countries – namely Sweden, UK and Canada – part-time employment accounts for more than 30 per cent of the jobs held by women (table 2.3), and in the US and Germany almost one-quarter of women workers have part-time jobs. Moreover, in *all* countries, part-time workers are overwhelmingly female. It is safe to say that the part-time labor force is a feminized one.

There are also crucial differences between male and female part-time workers. In Europe, the men who work part-time are older workers. In North America, there is a concentration of male part-time workers among the young, while female part-time workers, on the other hand, are concentrated in the prime age group (25–34 years of age). Moreover, young women (under 25) also constitute between 20 and 35 per cent of total female part-time employment in Canada and the United States [OECD, 1983: 50].

The OECD *Employment Outlook* found that part-time employment tends to be more stable in the aggregate than full-time employment, 'in the sense that the overall number of part-time jobs has proved less responsive to cyclical fluctuations than the overall number of full-time jobs' [1983: 45]. However, this finding need not imply that any individual part-time worker has more stable employment prospects than any full-time worker. The distinction and complexity are clear if part-time work is divided into two types: voluntary part-time employment and involuntary part-time employment. Sometimes women's part-time work is explained as the result of women's own preferences, reflecting family responsibilities and choices about how to spend time. This might be called voluntary part-time employment. It is involuntary part-time work which is, however, on the

TABLE 2.3 Part-time Employment

| | Ratio of part-time to full-time work | | | | | | Women's share of part-time employment | |
| | Both sexes | | Men | | Women | | | |
	1973	1981	1973	1981	1973	1981	1973	1981
Canada[a]	10.6	13.5	5.1	6.8	20.3	31.8	69.5	72.0
France	5.1	7.4	1.4	1.9	11.2	15.9	82.1	84.6
Germany	7.7	10.2	1.0	1.0	20.0	25.7	92.4	93.8
Italy	3.9	2.7	2.3	1.4	8.5	5.8	55.4	64.1
Sweden	18.0	25.2	3.7	7.2	38.8	46.4	88.0	84.5
UK	15.3	15.4	1.8	1.4	38.3	37.1	92.1	94.3
US	13.9	14.4	7.2	7.5	24.8	23.7	68.4	70.3

[a] 1975 and 1981
Source: OECD [1983: 44].

rise in many countries. According to the OECD, 'involuntary part-time working occurs when a worker is forced to take a part-time job instead of a full-time job because of the difficulty in finding the latter (this definition thus excludes short-time working)' (ibid.). Given this definition, the OECD has concluded that involuntary part-time work has risen in Canada and the United States since the mid-1970s.[2] An American study indicates that in 1982, 7.7 per cent of the female labor force was engaged in involuntary part-time work [Stone and Rix, 1983]. In 1975 in Canada only one woman in nine worked on a part-time basis because she could not find a full-time position. This situation changed dramatically during the 1981–2 recession, however, when one quarter of the women working part-time would have preferred to be in a full-time job [ECC, 1983: 81].

PARADOXES OF FEMINIZATION OF THE LABOR FORCE

There is real danger, then, that part-time employment in the OECD area will develop as another form of labor market segregation and inequality if part-time jobs come to be considered a 'niche' for women workers. Part-time work is often beneficial to employers because in a time of economic retrenchment part-time employment can keep labor costs down and can act as a buffer to business-cycle fluctuations. Since part-time workers are excluded from pension schemes and other social programs in some countries, they are cheaper to employ and they frequently have less job security, often being the first to be laid off and easier to lay off [OECD, 1983: 17]. Part-time work also has had the effect of limiting options. For example, the Canadian Commission of Inquiry into Part-Time Work (1983) concluded that

> . . . what the distribution of part-time workers across industries and occupations does show quite categorically is that part-time workers are markedly concentrated within a few industries, and that they have a limited range of occupations in comparison to the range of occupations of full-time workers. [Labour Canada, 1983: 58]

Unless part-time work is presented as a viable option for all workers (not just for women with children) and all workers demand more flexible working hours without loss of job security and benefits, women face the danger of becoming entrenched as a secondary and marginalized part of the labor force.

There is a host of other indicators that highlight women's unequal entry into the labor force and signal their status as 'special workers'. For example, their higher unemployment rates and multiple spells of unemployment relative to male workers are signs that all is not well in the labor

TABLE 2.4   *Contributions of Full- and Part-time Employment to Employment Changes, 1973–81 (000s)*

	Both sexes		Men		Women	
	f-t	*p-t*	*f-t*	*p-t*	*f-t*	*p-t*
Canada[a]	1085	485	447	110	638	375
France	493	540	169	64	324	476
Germany	−270	685	−158	1	−112	684
Italy	2120	−154	747	−111	1373	−43
Sweden	−18	364	−90	81	72	283
UK	−626	−86	−918	−67	292	−19
US	10274	2158	3553	437	6720	1720

Change in employment over the period

[a] 1975–81.
Source: OECD [1983: 45].

market. Differential unemployment rates between women and men may lead to some insights about the strength of the respective group's attachment to the labor force and its ability to hold its ground in periods of recession.[3] The 1960s and 1970s witnessed generally higher female than male unemployment, both in absolute terms and in the rate of increase. Since 1980, the rate of increase in female unemployment for the entire OECD area has been slightly below that of the male rate but the absolute unemployment rate is still higher than that of males. In the countries focused on in this book, there is a substantial variance in the unemployment statistics available for 1985 (table 2.5). In Canada, the female

TABLE 2.5   *Unemployment Rates by Sex, 1973–84*

	1973		1975		1979		1981		1982		1983		1984		1985	
	M	F	M	F	M	F	M	F	M	F	M	F	M	F	M	F
Canada	4.9	6.7	6.1	8.1	6.6	8.7	7.0	8.3	11.0	10.8	12.0	11.6	11.1	11.4	10.2	10.7
France	1.5	4.6	2.8	6.3	4.0	8.9	5.0	10.9	5.6	11.5	6.3	11.1	7.7	12.6	8.2	12.7
Germany	0.9	1.2	3.7	4.5	2.5	4.5	3.8	5.9	6.0	7.7	7.5	9.3	7.6	9.4	7.6	9.4
Italy	4.1	11.4	3.7	10.5	4.8	13.1	5.3	14.2	6.0	14.7	6.5	16.0	6.6	17.0	6.9	17.2
Sweden	2.3	2.8	1.3	2.0	1.9	2.3	2.3	2.7	3.0	3.4	3.4	3.5	3.0	3.3	2.8	2.7
UK	2.9	0.9	4.3	1.4	5.5	3.3	10.9	6.0	12.6	7.1	13.3	7.9	13.1	8.4	13.4	8.8
US	4.0	6.0	7.7	9.3	5.0	6.8	7.2	7.9	9.7	9.4	9.6	9.2	7.2	7.6	6.8	7.4

Source: OECD [1984: 104]; OECD [1985: 126]; OECD [1986: 141].

rate is 0.5 per cent above the male rate; in France, the female rate is 4.7 per cent above that of men; in Germany, women's unemployment rate is 1.8 per cent higher; in Italy, there is the greatest disparity, with female unemployment rates 10.3 per cent higher than the male rate; in the UK, women's unemployment rate is below that of men by 4.6 per cent, probably because of women's high participation in part-time employment; and in the US, women's unemployment rate is 0.2 per cent higher than that of men.

Despite these differences, there has been a tendency for the two rates to converge. Conventional explanations for the narrowing gap point to the decline in the goods-producing sector (where many male workers are concentrated) and the expansion of the service sector (where many women work) along with a slowdown in the rate of growth of the female labor force since 1979. But women's withdrawal from the labor force or a delay in re-entering the workforce because of lack of available work may be an alternative explanation of the narrowing of the unemployment rate differential. In both Sweden and the US during the 1970s, for example, the probability of employed women leaving the labor force altogether – and thus disappearing from the unemployment statistics – was about twice as high as that of men [Bjorklund, 1984: 29].

This point is particularly important because official definitions of unemployment include only those workers actively seeking employment and exclude discouraged workers. When they are counted, the picture changes markedly. Calculations of Canadian unemployment rates, for example, which take into account the discouraged workers who stop looking for work because they believe no work is available in the market, have found that from 1976 to 1982, the discouraged worker effect was greater for women than it was for men [Agarwal, 1985: 412–13]. Moreover, in some countries (for example, the United Kingdom) married women do not register as unemployed because coverage of unemployment and related benefits is restricted according to marital status. Such programmatic details increase the tendency for unemployed women, but not men, to be excluded from the unemployment statistics [Glucklich, 1984]. Women predominate among the unregistered unemployed and 'this under-registration of women makes them less accessible as a target for employment policies, and could serve to perpetuate the view that male unemployment is somehow a more serious problem' [MacLennan and Weitzel, 1984: 240]. There has, in addition, been a tendency since 1973 for the proportion of women in long-term unemployment (12 months or more) to rise, and this can only partly be attributed to the rise in female participation rates [OECD, 1985a: 102]. From all these perspectives, then, the narrowing of female–male unemployment differentials may be more of a statistical than a real phenomenon.

The fact that the burden of unemployment does not fall equally upon women and men has been well documented. Less well known, but equally relevant, is the fact that

the incidence of unemployment tends to vary also by income groups and by type of family. Unemployment rates are higher among single-parent, female-headed households, and divorced, separated or widowed women have higher unemployment rates than married or single adult women. In addition, in countries for which data are available, relatives living in single-parent families have higher unemployment rates than those living in two-parent families. [OECD, 1985b: 23]

The 'unemployment rate of minority women in the US has averaged about 80 per cent above that of white women over the last quarter of a century' [Amsden, 1980: 23]. Thus, women not only run a higher risk in many countries of being unemployed or forced into part-time work than men, but also suffer from a set of social conditions which are highly associated with poverty and joblessness.

Gender-differentiated earnings contribute to this set of social conditions; they are a very real manifestation of the discriminatory and structural barriers that women face in the labor market. For working women, their vulnerability to unemployment and their wage rates are intimately linked. One study concludes that women's concentration in low-wage occupations is the primary factor that explains their low wages. The study found that women earn, on average, about 20–40 per cent less than men, despite a slight narrowing of the earnings gap over the last decade [OECD, 1985b: 69; chapter III].

The rate of change in the earnings gap between women and men as well as its size varies across countries (table 2.6). Despite difficulties in making cross-national comparisons, table 2.6 is useful in pointing out the direction and level of overall change *within* each country.[4] In France, women workers' average hourly earnings as a percentage of men's have increased only slightly (under 2 per cent) over the period. In Germany, the increase has also been very small, only 3.4 per cent in 1970–82. Italy reveals a more substantial increase at 9.7 per cent. Sweden has experienced the largest increase (9.9 per cent) and has the smallest earning gap, with women's average hourly earnings at 89.9 per cent of men's. In Sweden, the remaining difference is amost entirely accounted for by worker characteristics such as age and length of experience. The UK shows an increase in women's average hourly earnings of 9.4 per cent but this case is characterized by the largest earnings gap between women and men of the six countries (30.5 per cent). The US is not included in Table 2.6 but an earlier OECD report (1980) reveals that average female earnings as a percentage of males were 66 per cent in 1973 and remained at the same level in 1977, thereby indicating that no relative improvement for women occurred in that period.

TABLE 2.6   *Average Hourly Earnings in Non-agricultural Activities of Women Workers, as Percentage of Those of Men, 1970–81*

	1970	1973	1975	1979	1980	1981
Canada	n/a	n/a	n/a	n/a	74.7	–
France	–	78.8	78.7	79.2	79.2	80.4
Germany	69.2	70.3	72.3	72.6	72.4	72.5
Italy	74.2	78.3	78.7	83.2	83.2	83.9
Sweden	80.0	–	84.8	89.1	89.8	89.9
United Kingdom	60.1	62.5	67.6	70.7	69.7	69.5

Notes

Canada:	Estimate based on full-year earnings of all workers, and the number of male and female full-time and part-time workers and their average weekly hours.
France:	Wage-earners aged 18 and over. Excluding mining, quarrying, public utilities, the public sector and private domestic service. October.
Germany:	Wage-earners, including foremen, but excluding apprentices. Based on payroll data for January, April, July and October. Including family allowances paid directly by employer. Excluding services.
Italy:	Wage-earners in industry. October.
Sweden:	Adult wage-earners in mining and manufacturing.
UK:	Adult wage-earners. Excluding coal mining, commerce and ISIC major division 8. October.

Source: OECD [1985b: 70].

There are also important differences between women's and men's wages across different sectors of the economy. For the countries of concern to this book, Table 2.7 illustrates a considerable variation, with relative female earnings ranging from the mid-40 per cent point to the mid-90 per cent point. For all OECD countries, women's highest relative earnings appear to be in government service and their lowest in manufacturing and wholesale trade.[5] The extent to which the situation for women is better in the public sector may well be due to the stricter application of equal pay legislation by public rather than private employers. Nevertheless, women's status in the public sector still varies according to the economic resources of a country, the size of the public sector, the rate of unionization of female workers, and the level of political organization of groups demanding equality. Women's low economic status in the manufacturing sector of all OECD countries seems related to the fact that women in manufacturing tend to be found in the lower-paying industrial sub-sectors [OECD, 1985b: 83].

Leaving aside institutional factors, several general conclusions emerge

TABLE 2.7   Earnings of Full-time Female Employees as Percentage of Male Employees, in Six Sectors

	Pay period	Year	Manu-facturing	Whole-sale trade	Retail trade	Banking	Insur-ance	Govt service
	1	2	3	4	5	6	7	8
France	Month	1974	58.0	66.6	66.1	71.8	67.6	–
		1978	61.7	69.7	67.5	74.5	66.1	83.9
Germany	Month	1971	63.5	67.0	60.1	71.6	73.9	–
		1981	66.4	68.3	64.9	77.4	76.5	–
Italy	Month	1974	61.9	79.0	85.8	79.5	71.1	–
Sweden	Month	1970	58.6	60.9	80.3	84.6	82.4	–
		1981	72.1	72.3	92.2	92.5	86.1	88.3
UK	Week	1971	44.3	44.2	47.1	46.0	56.7	–
		1980	53.2	54.1	56.1	49.9	60.9	–
US	Year	1970	59.4	51.0	52.5	50.5	64.8	–
		1980	61.4	56.1	60.0	45.5	65.4	–

Notes

France: Column 3: Total Industry, in 1972 and 1978. Column 8: 'salaires des agents de l'Etat' (annual).

Germany: Column 3: Industry.

Italy: Column 3: Industry, 1972.

Sweden: Columns 4 and 5: clerical employees and shop personnel respectively in the entire trade sector. Column 6: intermediate staff in Savings Banks. Column 7: 'staff with responsibilities' in Insurance Companies. Column 8: State employees in 1980.

UK: Adult non-manual workers. Columns 6 7: Insurance, Banking, Finance and Business services.

US: Average money earnings of all year-round full-time workers. Column 3: clerical and sales workers in manufacturing. Columns 6–7: Finance, Insurance and Real Estate.

Source: OECD [1985b: 84].

from the examination of pay differentials. The OECD *Employment Outlook* concludes '. . . that the hourly earnings of part-time workers are on average lower than those of full-time workers' [1983: 51]. This finding is hardly surprising, given that more women than men are employed on a part-time basis and that male workers may have greater access to overtime work than women.[6] It has also been observed that while pay tends to increase with age, women's pay tends to increase much less than that of men [OECD, 1985b: chapter III].

Studies that have assessed returns on experience have also found these to be lower for women than for men [Treimann and Hartmann, 1981:

chapter 3]. This finding has led to a more intense examination, on the part of researchers, of occupational and industrial sector segregation as significant institutional features which maintain a gender-based division of the labor force. In 1980, the OECD in *Women and Employment* attempted for the first time to measure international differences in gender-based segregation by category of activity, branch of manufacturing, and occupation. Segregation was defined 'as a difference between the female share of a category and the female share of total employment, or, equivalently, as a difference between the percentages of male and female labor forces in any category' [OECD, 1980: 39]. In order to make comparisons between

TABLE 2.8   *Indexes of Sex Segregation for Selected OECD Countries and Years*[a]

	Year	Index	Year	Index
By Occupations[b]				
Canada	1971	63.5	1978	52.9
France	1968	50.9	1975	48.3
Germany	1970	44.6	1978	45.7
Sweden	1970	51.6	1977	50.4
US	1970	51.4	1977	51.1
By Industries				
Canada	1967	49.7	1977	39.0
Germany	1967	35.1	1977	35.5
Sweden	1970	50.5	1977	45.1
UK	1967	39.6	1977	40.9
US	1973	34.6	1977	33.1
In Subdivision of Manufacturing				
Canada	1975	41.8	1978	42.8
Germany	1973	32.5	1977	33.0
Sweden	1973	43.0	1977	33.8
UK	1973	35.2	1977	36.5
US	1973	35.1	1978	32.7

[a]   Indexes 1st year: sum of absolute differences from one of the coefficients of female representation in each category (in the 1st year) weighted by the percentages of total employment in the second year in the corresponding categories.

   Indexes 2nd year: sum of absolute differences from one of the coefficients of female representation in each category (in the second year) weighted by the percentages of total employment in the corresponding categories.

[b]   For occupations, the X category ('workers not classifiable by occupation') is excluded from the calculation of the index.

Source: OECD [1980: 45].

countries or between different years for one country, the OECD developed an 'index of segregation', that is 'a measure of the extent to which the female share of an "average" occupation or industry differs from the actual female share of the total labor force'.[7] The value of the index is 0 with no segregation and 100 if there is a situation of total segregation. Table 2.8 shows the OECD index calculated for all of the three categories – by industry, manufacturing branch, and occupation. Because women tend to be concentrated in a small range of occupations within different industries, the index of occupational segregation is higher than the index of industrial segregation for all of the countries surveyed.

An OECD update of this study in *The Integration of Women in the Economy* (1985b) comes to several descriptive conclusions, after observing that the data continue to reveal much occupational and industrial segregation along gender lines in all countries. First, a high degree of occupational and industrial segregation by sex remains the reality in most countries, even at the aggregate level. Second, the degree of segregation tends to vary a great deal between countries. In general, the countries with the highest levels of participation also have greater measured occupational segregation. This leads to a tentative conclusion that increased female labor force participation rates may intensify the 'overcrowding' process whereby the concentration of women workers in certain sectors and occupations results in increased competition and a decline in women's relative pay [OECD, 1985b: chart 1, H4]. A third conclusion is that the degree of segregation by *industrial sector* is less than by broad *occupational grouping*. It is noted that, 'this is clearly because women tend to be concentrated in a small range of occupations within different industries' (ibid.).

Finally, concern with change over time leads to a consideration of the economic restructuring process and its effect on segregation.

TABLE 2.9 Concentration of Women Workers by Occupation
(percentage of female labor force)

	Clerical	Sales	Occupation Professional and technical	Administrative and managerial	Service workers
Canada	34.0	10.5	19.3	4.8	18.0
France	26.9	10.4	19.7	1.5	15.3
Germany	31.0	13.2	13.8	1.5	16.9
Italy	14.4	12.4	13.1	0.2	13.5
UK	30.8	12.2	12.2	0.9	23.3
US	34.3	6.8	15.2	5.9	21.0

Source: OECD [1985b: 19].

A priori it might be expected that the major structural changes in employment have been working towards greater segregation, these changes being the major structural change towards a greater and greater tertiary sector and a smaller manufacturing sector coupled with a corresponding change towards more tertiary white-collar jobs. Women have shared in this movement to a greater extent than men, and might have been expected to become more heavily concentrated into the tertiary sector, increasing measured segregation as a result . . . for the industrial data there is a clear tendency for the structural effect to increase overall segregation by industrial sector. (Ibid.: 47)

EXPLANATION OF PATTERNS FOUND IN THE FEMINIZED LABOR FORCE

It is necessary at this point to move beyond a description of patterns to a consideration of the reasons for their existence. A variety of arguments can be drawn upon. One set of explanations relates women's segregation in part-time work and the tertiary sector to their primary responsibilities for childcare and domestic labor. Starting from the labor supply side and focusing on the division of labor in the home, people argue that a specialization among family members results in a difference in women's and men's supply of labor to the market and in their investment in education and training. There is an assumption that women form their labor force 'choices' on the basis of an expected period of absence from the labor market. Hence, they select occupations that make it possible to combine domestic and waged work. Women as economic agents with a free choice (according to this theory) will enter different segments of the labor market from men and these will be characterized by greater mobility (in terms of re-entry) and less monetary reward due to a reduced human capital investment.

This theory of the sexual division of labor has been criticized extensively and will be only briefly dealt with here [Bakker, 1984a; Dex, 1985: chapter 3]. At best, it can be only a partial explanation and, to the extent it is useful, it is probably as description. Generally, the approach can be criticized for its middle-class bias and for its characterization of the home as a 'little firm', with economic actors having equal power and being engaged in a process of rational decision-making. Furthermore, this approach sheds no light on the difficult conditions under which women perform both domestic labor and wage labor [Folbre, 1986].

An alternative explanation might be that the very conditions which have fostered structural changes in the economy have also nurtured increased segregation. It is notable that over the last two decades, at the same time that economic crisis has led to restructuring of national and international economies, it has intensified the division of labor into 'women's' and 'men's' work. In part, both the industrial and the occupational structure reflect women's response to labor force demands [Armstrong and Armstrong, 1984: 41]. The intensified segmentation of labor markets within many firms has helped to reinforce women's secondary economic status [Edwards, 1979; Wilkinson and Rubery, 1980; Gordon et al., 1982]. This has led to the paradox of, on the one hand, an enormous growth in female labor force activity and, on the other hand, an intensified segregation of women into secondary, low-wage jobs. Women as a group have more work but it is often poorly paid, unprotected and part-time, because restructuring has brought fewer 'good jobs' in its wake.

This observation leads to a related consideration: are women workers more dispensable than their male counterparts, from the employer's point of view? In part, these concerns have already been addressed in the earlier examination of occupational segregation and earnings differentials. But there is also a developing body of literature, within both conventional economics and political economy, that links unemployment rates and cycles in an attempt to explain the nature of women's labor force participation. There are indicators from this literature that the factors that look like a worsening of working women's condition are also a sign of the rising attachment of women to the labor force.

From a political economy perspective, several studies have taken up Marx's concept of the reserve army of labor. In this view, women's position in the labor force is related to their role as a buffer supply which is drawn upon when there is a high demand for labor, and expelled in times of economic downturn. The reserve army concept has been used to explain married women's increasing participation in the labor force and to gauge the state of women's employment relative to other groups over cyclical fluctuations in the economy. The concept does have explanatory utility when it is applied empirically to women's experience in their society at any historical moment and it therefore draws attention to the efficacy of case studies in explaining the specific conditions surrounding women's employment [Power, 1983].

But Marx did not focus on the reserve army of labor as a separate, discrete group; rather, he noted that its existence and reconstitution was a general law of capitalist accumulation [Marx, 1977: 781]. Therefore, efforts, using the reserve army concept, to link women's and men's positions in the home and the labor market provide an interesting extension of Marx's analysis. Yet, when it is used alone to explain, in a general way, a complicated set of institutional, social, economic, political and ideological relations, it falls short, offering instead a functionalist analysis of what is best seen as an historically-specific process. Hence, the concept can be analytically useful in describing the specific role that women play as a reserve army at any given historical point in a particular country, but this cannot be considered an adequate general explanation of women's subordinate status in the labor force or of the dynamics of the division of labor by gender. For example, women's segregation in sectors and industries with few men in them makes the threat of men entering those jobs more distant, while women still remain in a more vulnerable position in the wage sphere. But a more telling weakness of the argument is that female participation rates continue to rise. This signals women's permanent attachment to the labor market rather than their reserve army status [Yanz and Smith, 1983].

Interestingly, some (but not all) of the more conventional studies considered below also describe female labor force participation as a reflection of cyclical conditions. However, it must be remembered that fluctuations in women's employment do not necessarily confirm the marginal nature of their labor force status because it is quite certain that women's employment will fluctuate if the *aggregate* employment figures of which they are a part also fluctuate [Dex, 1985: 199]. Again, a cautionary note needs to be struck about making conclusions based on aggregate trends and the less than satisfactory nature of unemployment rates as an indicator of true employment.

A comprehensive long-term study by Jain and Sloane (1981) compares the relationship between changes in employment and unemployment for racial minorities and women to that for 'majority employees' in Canada, the United States and UK, over most of the postwar years. They conclude:

> . . . changes in both employment and unemployment are more volatile for men than for women and there is no significant time trend. In summary, it appears that both in the U.S. and Britain non-white workers may suffer disproportionately to white workers in terms of employment experience when economic conditions worsen, but there is no clear evidence that this is also true for women in any of the three countries examined. In addition, in each of the three countries female labor force participation rates have held up better than for men. [Jain and Sloane, 1981: 10–11)

Despite the favorable conclusion about women's resilience to cyclical fluctuations, Jain and Sloane do point to rising absolute levels of unemployment (as opposed to changes in the rates) for women and minority workers as an indicator of a clear disadvantage relative to males. Indeed, the picture is incomplete without a more thorough consideration of women's employment, taking into account factors such as full-time versus part-time employment, earnings differentials, sectoral concentration, and significant demographic shifts.

The findings of other empirical studies also cast light on the characteristics of women's attachment to the labor force. An OECD study found that in the 1975 recession, women workers were affected differently from male workers:

> Women, because of their disproportionate concentration in the service sector were insulated from the harshest effects of the recession which had its greatest impact on the industrial sector. However, those women who did hold industrial jobs experienced greater employment losses than men. The effect of the recession on the employment of women has therefore been to slow down the growth of their employment in those industries in which they have been traditionally under-represented. [OECD, 1976: 30–1]

An American study suggests that women have been worse off relative to men in periods of low unemployment than in periods of high unemployment, when they fare better [Dex, 1985: 199–204]. The heterogeneity of women's relationship to the labor force, moreover, is indicated by studies which demonstrate cyclical sensitivity declines as more comprehensive measures of labor supply (e.g. age groups, number of children) are used. Hence, perceiving all women as marginal or secondary workers is a mistake. Rather, the experience of women workers differed in response not only to their *own* training, age and family status, but also to the conditions of the labor market. The labor market itself changes in response to both the economic cycles and pressures for restructuring. These labor market changes are also affected by the location of each national economy in the international system as well as by its domestic structure. Therefore, the consideration of the aggregate data about women's employment teaches caution in the face of generalizations about 'women' in all national settings, as well as about all 'women'. More specificity in analysis is absolutely essential.

RESPONSE OF THE STATE AND UNIONS TO FEMINIZATION OF THE LABOR FORCE

The increasing visibility of women's formal economic participation and their varying political mobilization across countries has placed increased pressure on the institutions of the state and the labor movement to remove existing inequities. The central social, political and economic role of trade unions in the industrial countries with market economies has meant that these institutions have had an important influence on the nature of female employment. In a recent collection of studies of eleven industrialized countries, Alice Cook notes that the perceived response of unions to women's special needs and demands within the union structure may be more a result of women's expanded participation and autonomous political organization than due to spontaneous drives toward greater social equity and justice [Cook, 1984: 17]. The overall stable or growing level of union membership in the 1970s was almost entirely the result of female participation, since male membership declined in many cases. For all of these reasons, women's status within the unions is an important element to consider in any discussion of the feminization of the labor force. Consideration of women's participation in collective labor institutions adds an important dimension to the already intricate portrait elaborated over the preceding pages.

One of the crucial questions posed by women's position in the labor movement is whether or not the increase in women's membership in labor unions has resulted in a re-evaluation of their status and influence within these organizations. Cook points out – and the point is made often in the literature – that

> when a woman tries to better her lot through collective action, she faces a second issue: union participation becomes a burden to be added to family and paid work. Even women who can overcome such barriers find that union activity is neither immediately accessible to them nor easy to manage. Moreover, the few women who are able to carry this triple burden very rarely rise to positions of power, even in those unions where women make up a substantial part of the membership. [Cook, 1984: 313]

The countries which are the main focus of this book deviate very little from the general patterns of female participation in unions. Again, as with earnings, the most significant comparison is in terms of a country's overall rate of unionization and how women's participation compares to this. This indicator provides a benchmark measure of the strength of unions within a particular society as well as an assessment of women's participation. However, rates of unionization alone are not always a sufficient measure of the collective power of organized women workers, because other factors intervene, such as 'the extent to which unions are free to express workers' interests, equality policies are promoted by the leadership, and labor legislation allows the collective bargaining process free rein and promotes equality' [ILO, 1985: 51].

With this caveat, however, table 2.10 provides a measure of the relationship between women's participation in the unions and their representation in the labor force, for several countries. In Canada, the vast majority of women are not unionized, with only 27 per cent of women workers in unions in 1980 as compared to 43 per cent of male workers [White, 1980: 21]. While women remain under-represented on union executive boards, the situation has improved. Women's participation and influence also varied according to the types of unions (international,

public-sector or other Canadian unions), the level of public-sector employment for women (since the public sector is more highly unionized) and the
size of the workplace. In the United States, women's participation in
unions must be examined in the context of a shrinking number of organized
workers in the labor force and with the number of union members among
wage and salaried workers remaining virtually the same as two decades
ago. While more women are found in unions than before, 'the clustering of
women in sex-stereotyped jobs is paralleled by the concentration of two of
every five women union members into just seven unions and major
associations' [Wertheimer, 1984: 297]. The increase in the number of
women in unions from 2.9 million to 6.9 million between 1954 and 1978
was largely due to the rapid growth of public-sector unions in the 1970s and
the large number of women in those unions. Low participation rates among
women union members are the reality as in the other countries.

TABLE 2.10   Percentage of Women in Unions and in the Labor Force
(various years after 1975)

	Percentage in unions	Percentage in labor force
Canada	27	37
France[a]	n/a	37
Germany	20	37
Italy[b]	29 (CGIL)	30
	62 (FLM)	
Sweden[c]	36 (LO)	44
	50 (TCO)	
UK	33	38
US	20	43

[a] France has poor or no statistical information on union members since membership is
neither well defined nor sustained.
[b] CGIL: General Confederation of Italian Labor; FLM: Federation of Metal Workers and
Machinists.
[c] LO: Confederation of Labor; TCO: Central Organization of Salaried Employees. These
categories reflect the existence of two federations: LO – blue-collar; TCO – white-collar.
Source: Cook [1984: 18]; for Canada, White [1980: 22]; and for Italy, Beccalli [1984: 99].

French trade union figures are uncertain and characterized by sharp
fluctuations, partly corresponding to political developments. Maruani
states that in 1975, 'when women were 38 per cent of the labour force, they
accounted for a more or less comparable percentage of union membership'
[1984: 125]. Similarly, women have been very involved in the Italian trade
union movement and yet remain somewhat marginal to it. Their membership in unions is approximately in proportion to their labor force participa-

tion but despite this relatively high degree of unionization, 'female representation in the union hierarchy goes down as one goes up the bureaucratic ladder' [Beccalli, 1984: 198–9].

In the UK, there is a great deal of disparity amongst individual unions concerning attitudes, practices, policies and structures, despite a general policy for women workers developed by the Trades Union Congress (TUC). In 1980, women made up 28 per cent of the affiliated membership of the TUC and women had found a more favorable, left-wing audience in the large unions and the TUC General Council. This trend has apparently been reversed since the early 1980s. Women are also vastly under-represented in terms of their positions in individual unions and in the TUC [Lorwin and Boston, 1984: 140, 156]. Anger against this under-representation manifested itself in the drawing-up of a ten-point charter in 1980 demanding 'Equality for Women Within Trade Unions'. In the FRG, women's membership in the unions has increased steadily since a major drive was initiated in the Year of Working Women (1972); the main increase has taken place in white-collar unions. There has been a slow improvement in women's participation in union office, but again this varies among unions, regions and according to the level of representation [Cook, 1984: 63–70]. Of our cases, Sweden represents the country with the highest proportion of working women organized, at approximately 70 per cent. In terms of women's role in the unions, several studies have indicated that women's participation, although increasing in recent years, still remains low, especially in terms of participation in decision-making bodies.

The inability of the unions and policy-makers to address effectively the inequitable sexual division of labor has manifested itself to some extent in women's disproportionate concentration in part-time jobs and their inten-sified double burden of work in the labor force and at home. Social and economic infrastructures to meet the needs of childbearing and childrear-ing vary between countries, representing a continuum from those countries with social policy programs directed towards an alternative and equal management of family and work roles, to those countries that have done virtually nothing in this area [Kamerman and Kahn, 1983]. Certainly the countries that have witnessed increased unionization of women and their rising political participation, be it through the formal legislative process or in the women's movement, appear to have responded more to the need for policies and infrastructures to meet the needs of working parents.

A recent six-country study focuses on differing policy responses to the situation of working parents. Compensation for income loss and employ-ment protection due to childbirth has become an urgent consideration in many countries. Maternity leave with protection of employment exists as an entrenched right in all of the European OECD member countries [Paoli, 1982]. In most OECD countries, the duration of compensated leave is between 12 and 18 weeks; in Sweden it is 360 days.

Parental leave, involving a recognition that fathers should be involved in childcare as well as mothers, exists in fewer countries. The countries in which social democracy is very influential tend to be at the forefront of these efforts. The Swedish law on parental leave makes a distinction between four different rights to childcare leave:

1 leave to care for the newborn
2 occasional care for sick children
3 special childcare to be used with great flexibility
4 the right to reduced working hours [Gustafsson, 1984: 136].

Nevertheless, the way in which the regulations of the Swedish maternity and parental leave are enforced makes it very important to be already established in the labor force before having a child because benefits are paid as a compensation for loss of income. Acknowledgement of parental leave, although the provisions are not as extensive as in Sweden, also exists in the Federal Republic of Germany and unpaid parental leave has existed in France since 1977.

The state of institutional childcare varies a great deal across countries and the provision of public daycare is not very well documented. Table 2.11 highlights patterns in provision although it does not necessarily reveal the actual relief for parents with small children. The FRG provides very limited organized childcare for children under three years of age. Instead, a 'mother's wage' encourages women to remain at home to care for children. Not only does this reinforce women's primary role in childrear-

TABLE 2.11   *Percentage of Children in Public Daycare Centers*
(by age group)

	0–2		3–6		7–12	
	1965	1979	1965	1979	1965	1979
Germany	0.6	1.6	33.2[a]	77.8[a]	1.2	2.1
Sweden	n/a	n/a	9.6[b]	27.2[c]	n/a	13.0
UK	n/a	n/a	n/a	4.0[d]	n/a	n/a
US	n/a	5.0	n/a	20.0[e]	n/a	4.0[f]

[a]   Including part-time places.
[b]   1971.
[c]   Age group 0–6; including 10.9 per cent places with publicly subsidized daycare mothers (i.e. parents pay the same fee as at the daycare center); 1981 the figure was 33.9.
[d]   Age group 0–5.
[e]   Age group 2–5.
[f]   Age group 6–11.
n/a = not available.

Source: Schmid and Weitzel [1984: 284].

ing, it also weakens their market position, because they lose seniority and work experience. France represents a mixed picture, with official policy supporting the right of women either to stay in the labor force or to remain home, with a minimum of economic hardship. The focus is on giving low-income mothers the same options as middle-income mothers, and France has, in fact, the greatest number of very young children of any western country in subsidized, low-cost, licensed family or center-based care [Paoli, 1982]. Moreover, children may enter the public school system at the age of three.

Sweden has focused on the expansion of daycare centers as a means to maximize women's equality and is engaged in a policy to facilitate increased care of children by both parents through such proposals as a shortening of the workday to six hours for the parents of young children. In Sweden, the 1970s witnessed a rapid increase in the number of places for children in daycare centers and only a small proportion (8.8 per cent) of total costs is paid through parental fees [Gustafsson, 1984: 140]. An interesting calculation of the social costs and benefits of daycare for 1979 'shows that women with children at pre-school age who entered the labour market during the past ten years and working at least half time have increased GNP by an amount twice as big as the costs of the places at day care centers for the children of these women' [ibid.: 141].

The United States, despite its increasing rates of female labor force participation and growing incidence of single-parent, female-headed families, has no explicit childcare policy even for families with young children [Kamerman and Kahn, 1983: 27]. There is also no family income supplement, with the exception of the minor provisions of food subsidies and an earned income tax credit. As Kamerman and Kahn note, 'there is no acknowledgement in the U.S. policy of childrearing and contributing to the continuity and betterment of society generally, and therefore, no interest in subsidizing in any way the cost of childrearing' [1983: 70].

Canada's involvement in this area, through the Canada Assistance Plan, is based on a 1966 definition of user need. With large increases in labor force participation for all women, and a particularly dramatic rise in participation for women with dependants, current provisions are inadequate and are in the process of being reviewed. In 1981, for example, women in the labor force had 963,000 pre-school age children but there were only 123,962 childcare spaces in Canada in 1982. By 1983, the number of women in the labor force with children under three years of age had reached 460,000 but the increase in childcare facilities had not kept pace [Canada, 1984: 183]. Recently, a Child Care Tax Credit has been proposed that will amount to 30 per cent of expenses or 30 per cent of $3000, whichever is the smaller. However, parents must be able to produce receipts and this would exclude most parents, since only 8.8 per cent of Canadian children are in licensed childcare services. For those unable to obtain a receipt or for a parent at home, tax credits of a few hundred dollars per year have been recommended.

An interesting issue that has been considered a 'hard' fiscal issue but that has been appropriated by feminists is the issue of the appropriate income unit for taxation and transfers. The fact that many of the main features of the social security and taxation systems were developed in the postwar period, when different social and economic circumstances prevailed, implies that different objectives now need to be met. For example, much of social security and tax policy is based on the notion of a one-earner family, with the husband responsible for the economic well-being of his wife (who is assumed to have no attachment to the labor force) and family. There is also an implicit assumption that a husband and wife will pool their income and share the benefits of that income. The appropriate income unit for social policy is a critical issue, as there may be an inadequate redistribution of income in some families. If the starting point for policy in this area were that financial resources are not necessarily pooled or shared in all households, new policy implications would ensue [Land, 1977]. For example, estimates based on the family as the income unit can lead to an underestimation of the figures describing the number of people living in poverty [Edwards, 1979: 14].

Within Europe in recent years there has been a growing concern about the social security and income taxation systems' possible biases, both overt and discreet, against women. Part and parcel of such concern was the realization that, although certain policies might appear to be neutral in principle, in reality they involve certain disadvantages for women. The recognition that income transfer and taxation measures might play a significant role at certain points over an individual's life-cycle and strongly influence their behavior in other areas – for example, labor force participation – has led to an increasingly intense re-evaluation of these systems [EEC, 1979].

Three main factors can be isolated that may contribute to women's disadvantageous position *vis-à-vis* the social security system: interruption of employment; change in marital status; and inequality of employment and earnings differentials between women and men [OECD, 1985b: 166]. All of these factors contribute to problems when the social security system is based on earnings, given women's lower wages and lower life-time earnings, as well as the career interruptions they make due to the unequal family division of labor. A more equitable tax and social security benefit system would make it more viable for spouses to divide their work between them and to participate equally in the labor force.

At the present time, social security and taxation systems are in a state of transition, with some policies based on equal roles for women and men, while others reinforce notions of female dependency. OECD member countries have in recent years drifted away from compulsory joint taxation for married couples. A 1977 report indicates that a desire to encourage married women to participate in the labor force was a major objective of this trend [OECD, 1977]. It appears that the long-range policy goals in this area should be clearly based on notions of equality of opportunity. However, very few countries as yet have concentrated on improving existing measures based on such long-term objectives.

CONCLUSIONS

This consideration of trends in the feminization of the labor force and policy responses to such trends has revealed many differences among countries, but some general conclusions do emerge. In terms of participation, the rates for women have continued to increase or remain stable whereas male rates have slowly declined over the last decades. Women overwhelmingly work in the service sector and they also comprise an important part of a growing part-time workforce. While there has been a narrowing of the unemployment rate differential between women and men, the unemployment rate for women is still higher in many cases. Women's concentration in low-wage occupations is the primary factor contributing to the wage gap between women and men. Women still earn, on average, about 20–40 per cent less than men and the narrowing of the earnings gap over the last decade has been slow and minimal. Protection and improved economic returns through union representation and collective bargaining is offered to women in increasing numbers (except in the US where the number of unionized workers is declining) but has not reached the same level as that for men in any of our seven countries. Social and economic supports to meet the needs of childrearing vary a great deal across the countries considered and in the manner in which they are provided (public, private, mixed), but remain for the most part inadequate. Finally, re-evaluation of taxation from a household to an individual-based system has had a positive impact on labor force participation, although more remains to be done.

All of these patterns (and many others) point to the need to place the issue of the gender division of labor and its consequences at the center of policy demands and initiatives. Such agenda-setting becomes increasingly difficult, however, with the move towards neo-liberalism now being acted out by many governments. A reformulation of problems and political strategies on the part of policy makers *and* feminists is needed in order to insert them into the heart of current economic debates. This involves the restructuring of issues often considered beyond the purview of women-centered discussion – trade, for example – to include a consideration of their impact on women.[8]

Given uneven patterns of economic development, the impact of any macro-policy linked to a specific economic strategy must be assessed separately for population groups in observably different conditions [Bakker, 1984b]. For example, models of the economy used to justify policy shifts away from the political and economic consensus of Keynesianism, with its commitment to full employment, will hurt women more than men because so many women are at the margin of the labor force. Secondly, policy likely to be effective in changing women's conditions is different in times of economic duress as opposed to times of economic expansion.

Policies are selected for both political and economic reasons and their double genesis must be recognized. Moreover, choice of one policy sets limits on all others linked to it. Thus, a policy goal of containing wage growth as a way to encourage investment and profits represents a clear pre-selection of policy directions and sets up the parameters to which other policies must accommodate themselves. Hence, any discussion of policy options and political strategy for women must recognize the constraints and biases of the state and the capital accumulation process at every moment in time. Any analysis of the feminization of the labor force must consider these differences and must be conducted both at the level of the labor market and at the level of the economy as a whole.

NOTES

I would like to thank Jane Jenson for her skilful editing and insights, and Riel Miller for his comments.

1 'Discouraged workers' is a term that applies to workers who have left the labor force and are no longer actively seeking work. The 'added worker effect' refers to a situation when some people who would not normally be in the labor force enter it in order to maintain household incomes. Married women are usually referred to in the mainstream literature as a primary example of added workers, Neither of these effects is a sufficient explanation of the long-term growth trend in women's labor force participation.

2 OECD information about the extent of involuntary part-time employment, by gender, is only available for Australia, Canada, Finland and the United States [OECD, 1983: 46].

3 The measurement problems involved in attempting an international comparison of unemployment need to be emphasized because the latter is an imprecise concept and it can be measured in various ways. For a discussion, see Bjorkland [1984: 20–43].

4 Table 2.6 shows trends in the relationship between women's and men's average earnings. However, as the OECD report warns, these ratios should not be used to make inter-country comparisons, given the different statistical bases used in each country to evaluate earnings. Statistics vary according to periods of wage payment, full- or part-time status, occupation, and other 'human capital' variables. For a discussion of the resulting methodological and technical problems of attempting such an international comparison, see the

OECD study itself [1985b: chapter III].

5 Reasons offered for this variation by sector may be related 'to factors other than sectoral characteristics, for the ranking of sectors with respect to relative female pay levels differs widely across countries and no sector emerges as having systematically narrower differentials of male and female earnings except the public sector' [OECD, 1985b: 82].

6 Such a conclusion needs, however, to be evaluated on a sector-by-sector basis; in retail trade, for example, part-time female workers often outearn their male counterparts.

7 This measure differs from the more commonly used dissimilarity index (DI index), which relates women's share of each employment category to the share of men in that category as opposed to the total numbers employed in that category.

8 For example, the US Department of Labor commissioned a report in 1980 that examined the links between trade-sensitive industries and the demographic and occupational characteristics of workers. The report found that the industrial sectors which experienced the largest negative impact on job opportunities employed more women. [See Aho and Orr, 1980.] This type of study is also currently being undertaken by the federal government in Canada in an effort to gauge the impact of trade negotiations on regions and different groups of workers.

REFERENCES

Agarwal, N. (1985) 'Economic costs of discrimination in Canada', in *Research Studies of the Commission on Equality in Employment (Abella Commission)* (Ottawa: Commission on Equality in Employment).

Aho, C. and J. Orr (1980) *Demographic Occupational Characteristics of Workers in Trade-Sensitive Industries*, Economic Discussion Paper 2 (Washington, DC: US Department of Labor, Bureau of International Labor Affairs).

Amsden, A. (1980) *The Economics of Women and Work* (New York: Penguin Books).

Armstrong, P. and H. Armstrong (1984) *The Double Ghetto: Canadian Women and their Segregated Work* (Toronto: McClelland and Stewart).

Bakker, I. (1984a) *Feminist Materialism and Economic Activity*, Paper prepared for the Conference on Women and the Invisible Economy, Concordia University, Montreal.

Bakker, I. (1984b) *Women and Economic Development in Canada: Some Methodological Approaches for Assessing the Impact of Economic Policies on Women*, Paper presented to Working Party No. 6 on the Role of Women in the Economy (OECD, Paris, January 1986).

Beccalli, B. (1984) 'Italy', in A. Cook (ed.), *Women and Trade Unions in Eleven Industrialized Countries* (Philadelphia: Temple University Press).

Bjorkland, A. (1984) 'A look at the male–female employment differentials in the Federal Republic of Germany, Sweden, United Kingdom, and the United States of America', in G. Schmid and R. Weitzel (eds), *Sex Discrimination and Equal Opportunity* (Aldershot, England: Gower Publishing).

Canada (1984) *Equality in Employment: A Royal Commission Report* (Ottawa: Supply and Services Canada).

Cook, A. (1984) *Women and Trade Unions in Eleven Industrialized Countries* (Philadelphia: Temple University Press).

Dex, S. (1985) *The Sexual Division of Work: Conceptual Revolutions in the Social Sciences* (Sussex: Harvester Press).

Economic Council of Canada (ECC) (1983) *On the Mend: Twentieth Annual Review 1983* (Ottawa: Economic Council of Canada).

Edwards, R. (1979) *Contested Terrain* (New York: Basic Books).

EEC (1979) *Directive on the Progressive Implementation of the Principle of Equal Treatment for Men and Women in Matters of Social Security* (Brussels: EEC).

Folbre, N. (1986) 'Cleaning house: New perspectives on households and economic development', *Journal of Development Economics* (22).

Glucklich, P. (1984) 'The effects of statutory employment policies on women in the United Kingdom labour market' in G. Schmid and R. Weitzel (eds), *Sex Discrimination and Equal Opportunity* (Aldershot, England: Gower Publishing).

Gordon, D., R. Edwards and M. Reich (1982) *Segmented Work, Divided Workers: The Historical Transformation of Labor in the United States* (New York: Cambridge University Press).

Gustafsson, S. (1984) 'Equal opportunity policies in Sweden', in G. Schmid and R. Weitzel (eds), *Sex Discrimination and Equal Opportunity* (Aldershot, England: Gower Publishing).

ILO (1985) *Equal Opportunities and Equal Treatment for Men and Women in Employment, Report VII* (Geneva: ILO).

Jain, H. C. and P. J. Sloane (1981) *Equal Employment Issues: Race and Sex Discrimination in the United States, Canada and Britain* (New York: Praeger).

Kahn, H. (1987) *Reconceiving Part-Time Work: New Perspectives for Older Workers* (Totowa, New Jersey: Rowman and Littlefield).

Kamerman, S. B. and A.J. Kahn (1983) *Child Care, Family Benefits and Working Parents – A Study in Comparative Policy* (New York: Columbia University Press).

Labour Canada (1983) *Part time Work in Canada, Report of the Commission of Inquiry into Part-time Work* (Ottawa: Labour Canada).

Land, Hilary (1977) 'Social security and the division of unpaid work in the home and paid employment in the labour market', in *UK Department of Health and Social Security, Social Security Research* (London: HMSO).

Lorwin, V. and S. Boston (1984) 'Great Britain', in A. Cook (ed.), *Women and Trade Unions in Eleven Industrialized Countries* (Philadelphia: Temple University Press).

MacLennan, E. and R. Weitzel (1984), 'Labour market policy in four countries: are women adequately represented?', in G. Schmid and R. Weitzel (eds), *Sex Discrimination and Equal Opportunity* (Aldershot, England: Gower Publishing).

Maruani, M. (1984) 'France', in Alice Cook (ed.), *Women and Trade Unions in Eleven Industrialized Countries* (Philadelphia: Temple University Press).

Marx, K. (1977) *Capital* (New York: Vintage Books).

OECD (1976) *The 1974–1975 Recession and the Employment of Women* (Paris: OECD).

OECD (1977) *Like Treatment of Family Units in OECD Member Countries under*

Tax and Transfer Systems (Paris: OECD).

OECD (1980) *Women and Employment* (Paris: OECD).

OECD (1982) *Employment in the Public Sector* (Paris: OECD).

OECD (1983) *Employment Outlook* (Paris: OECD).

OECD (1985a) *Employment Outlook* (Paris: OECD).

OECD (1985b) *The Integration of Women in the Economy* (Paris: OECD).

OECD (1986) *Employment Outlook* (Paris: OECD).

Paoli, C. (1982) 'Women workers and maternity: some examples from Western Europe', *International Labour Review*, vol. 121, no. 1.

Paukert, L. (1982) 'Personal preference, social change or economic necessity? Why women work', *Labour and Society* (October – December).

Power, M. (1983) 'From home production to wage labor: women as a reserve army of labor', *Review of Radical Political Economics* (Spring).

Ovist, G., J. Acker and V. Lorwin (1984) 'Sweden', in A. Cook (ed.), *Women and Trade Unions in Eleven Industrialized Countries* (Philadelphia: Temple University Press).

Schnid and Weizel (1984) *Sex Discrimination and Equal Opportunity* (Hants: Gower; New York: St Martin's Press).

Stone, A. and S. Rix (1983) *Employment and Unemployment: Issues for Women* (Washington, DC: Women's Research and Education Institute).

Treimann, D.J. and H.I. Hartmann (1981) *Women, Work, and Wages: Equal Pay for Jobs of Equal Value* (Washington, DC: National Academy).

United Nations (1984) *Compiling Social Indicators on the Situation of Women*, Series F, no. 32 (New York: United Nations).

Wertheimer, B. (1984) 'The United States of America', in A. Cook (ed.), *Women and Trade Unions in Eleven Industrialized Countries* (Philadelphia: Temple University Press).

White, J. (1980) *Women and Unions* (Ottawa: Supply and Services Canada for the Canadian Advisory Council on the Status of Women).

Wilkinson, F. and J. Rubery (1980) 'Outlook and Segmented Labour Markets', in F. Wilkinson (ed.), *The Dynamics of Labour Market Segmentation* (New York: Academic Press).

Yanz, L. and D. Smith (1983) 'Women as a reserve army of labor: a critique', in *Review of Radical Political Economics*, vol. 15, no. 1.

3

Rethinking the Definition of Work
Gender and Work

Veronica Beechey

Recent years have seen enormous changes in the structure of the labor force and the organization of paid work in modern capitalist countries. The forms of restructuring have varied from country to country, but overall the division of labor has become increasingly internationalized, new technologies have been introduced on a large scale, the economies of many advanced capitalist countries have experienced considerable deindustrialization, and there has been a massive growth in service work. In Europe in particular these changes have been associated with very high levels of unemployment and a halting economic recovery. Paradoxically, despite high levels of unemployment, the size of the labor force has increased and its structure has been changing in fundamental ways. A very important structural change has been the feminization of the labor force. In some cases the labor force has also become more ethnically diverse as the indigenous black working population has grown, while in others the indigenous labor force has been augmented by migrant workers. 'Nonstandard' forms of work have also been increasing,[1] with a huge expansion of part-time work in a number of countries and a growth in more casual forms of work and self-employment. These changes are having far-reaching consequences. At the broadest level they are affecting relations between different areas of the world in the international economy while at the local level relations between women and men, parents and children within individual households are being transformed. And between the grand sweep of international relations and the intimacy of family life lies a whole range of other transformations – in regional and local economies, in class and sexual relations, in relations between dominant populations and ethnic minorities, and in the nature of cities, suburbs, and rural life.

The aim of this chapter is to discuss an aspect of this complex set of changes. I want to consider some of the questions which arise when one attempts to analyse gender at work and to look at the processes of restructuring in gendered terms. My discussion falls into three parts. In the first I discuss two approaches to the analysis of production which have been widely used to analyse gender divisions – Marxist analyses of deskilling, and dual and segmented labor market theories. I argue that these are more useful for analysing work in manufacturing industries than work in the service sector, but even for industrial work they have been very limited by their use of sex-blind categories which cannot adequately grasp the ways in which gender relations are embodied in the organization of production. The theories are also limited, I suggest, by their acceptance of the division between public and private spheres. Next, I briefly discuss recent attempts to revise these theories by developing more fully a theory of social reproduction. These, I argue, have been important in shifting the focus of analysis beyond conventional definitions of 'the economy', but they run the risk of providing a reductionist and functionalist form of explanation. Moreover, the search for explanation of labor force cleavages within the sphere of social reproduction leaves the analysis of production untouched by feminist analysis. Production is still too often analysed in terms of sex-blind categories and the theories are therefore unable to account adequately for the construction of gender divisions within production. In the final part, I tackle the much more difficult question of how to theorize gender in the sphere of work. Although feminists have been arguing for some years that it is important to analyse gender and work, and questions relating to gender have been foregrounded in many empirical studies of work, the task of developing a theory of gender has scarcely begun. My discussion is therefore a fairly exploratory one, based on some of the findings of recent empirical studies of work (mainly studies of Britain), and it tries to specify some of the questions which a theory of gender will have to address. I conclude with a brief discussion of some attempts to develop a theory of gender in other areas of feminist scholarship, attempts which may prove fruitful for the analysis of work.

THE NEW POLITICAL ECONOMY

The late 1960s and the early 1970s saw the growth of new social movements which drew popular attention to the fact that there were substantial inequalities among different social groups (blacks and whites, women and men) in the heartlands of advanced capitalist societies. There was also the development of theoretical frameworks within the social sciences which attempted to understand, or at least take account of, these inequalities. Two such frameworks which sought to understand divisions within the workforce were Marxist labor process theories and dual and segmented labor market theories. Neither of these took the analysis of women's employment or gender divisions as its central focus of analysis. However, both have been influential as frameworks for analysing women's employment – although, as will become clear below, the attempts to fit women into a basically economistic framework of analysis has proved to be extremely problematic.

Both Marxist labor process and dual and segmented labor market theories, especially in their early formations, developed rather general analyses of how production is organized in capitalist societies. Braverman (1974), for instance, discussed the degradation of labor in terms of Marx's deskilling theory, and through this linked an analysis of changes in the composition of the working class to an analysis of alterations in the occupational structure and changing capitalist strategies. The increase in women's employment (and the decrease in men's) was for Braverman part and parcel of the general process of the degradation of work which had been taking place throughout advanced capitalist countries – in both manufacturing and service sectors and among 'new middle' as well as working-class occupations.

Like Braverman, dual labor market theories (as they were called at first) approached the labor market from the 'demand' side. Early formulations (e.g. by Doeringer and Piore, 1971) argued that firms develop internal labor markets in order to hold on to workers who have specific knowledge and skills, and suggested that the distinction between primary and secondary sector workers arises from, and corresponds to, these labor market strategies. According to the basic model it is work behavior which determines which workers fill which jobs. Thus, the growth in women's employment is linked to the propensity of employers to hire secondary sector workers for certain jobs, and the fact that it is women who fill these jobs is explained in terms of attributes (for example, dispensability, lack of interest in acquiring training) which women are assumed to possess.[2]

In recent years Marxist and dual labor market theories have moved in a variety of different ways. Marxist theory has been used to analyse the casualization of the labor force while dual labor market theory has been used to analyse part-time work. Dual labor market theory has also been used to analyse the new forms of flexibility which employers have recently been striving to attain. Here the emphasis is on core and peripheral groups rather than primary and secondary workers. Thus, it is argued (e.g. by Atkinson, 1984) that firms are developing new forms of flexibility in order to reduce their labor costs, and are increasingly dividing their workforces into core and peripheral groups. Studies of flexibility have often noted that women are usually employed as peripheral workers rather than core ones, but, like other versions of dual labor market theory, they have tended to ignore the ways in which gender enters into the definition of jobs.

Both Marxist and dual labor market theories have generated a good deal of critical comment over the past decade, and both have been substantially revised by subsequent writers and researchers. It is beyond the scope of this chapter to offer a detailed account of these criticisms and refinements, although it is perhaps worth pointing out that the key concepts have been critically interrogated, and many refinements have been made to the theories through empirical analyses of workplace organization.[3] Among the most important of these have been a refinement of the analysis of employers' strategies and an elaboration of the forms of control used by employers, and an analysis of trade union strategies for controlling labor supply and resisting restructuring.

The theories have also been subjected to some fairly powerful critiques by feminist writers and researchers. Feminist studies have called into question the notions of skill and deskilling which are central to Marxist analyses of restructuring. A number of studies have shown how definitions of skill can have more to do with men's attempts, through trade unions, to retain some control over the labor process and keep skill designations for their own work by excluding women from better-paying jobs, than with actual technical competencies which are possessed by men and not by women (although these clearly do play a part, given the relative absence of young women from training schemes and apprenticeships in traditionally masculine areas of work). These studies have thus called into question the view that deskilling can be seen as a neutral process, an attribute of capitalist economic strategies in organizing the labor process, and have argued that deskilling has a gendered dimension to it.[4] Studies have also called into question the notion that control over the labor process is a phenomenon which operates independently of the gender of the workers who are being controlled. Game and Pringle (1983), for instance, have argued that the forms of control operating in the industries they studied in Australia (the white goods industry, banking, retailing, computing, nursing and housework) had as much to do with gender as with straightforward capitalist economic strategies of control. Whether the control was direct and personal, technical or bureaucratic, they argue management used different forms of control when men were employed from those they used when women were employed.

Feminist writers have also criticized dual and segmented labor market theories, and have argued that the image of women as secondary workers is contradicted by empirical evidence. It has been shown that many of the jobs which women do – nursing and teaching, for instance – have career ladders, and that in particular sectors of the labor market women have lower levels of job change than men and comparable levels of career commitment. Furthermore, studies show that many women would like further training, a finding which suggests that dual labor market theory is mistaken in its assumption that women have a low interest in acquiring training. As Heidi Hartmann (1987) has suggested, the parallel between economic segments (core and periphery), labor market segments, and worker outcomes postulated by dual and segmented labor market theory does not hold because the relevant dimensions of employment do not clump together in easily identifiable segments.

Basically, feminist research has highlighted some fairly fundamental problems with labor process and labor market theories, all of which revolve around the ways in which production has been conceptualized and gender ignored. First, both theories have been formulated, implicitly, from the standpoint of the skilled male working class in manufacturing indus-try.[5] They are thus better able to analyse production work in the manufacturing sector than work in the service sectors. Public-sector employment where workers enjoy relative security of employment, pensions, etc. but are low-paid and where jobs often involve complex competencies and responsibilities but are not defined as skilled – as is the case of many caring occupations – is particularly difficult to conceptualize as part of a secondary workforce. The theories are thus better able to analyse men's work than women's.

A second and related point is that the concepts of skill and the primary–secondary worker distinction are problematic. Skilled workers and primary workers form the focal point of the analyses, and these concepts are fleshed out more fully than their opposites. The concept of secondary sector worker is particularly poorly delineated, being characterized negatively in terms of its difference from primary sector workers who are defined by reference to a white male norm (Kenrick, 1981; Beechey and Perkins, 1987). Many critics have pointed out that Braverman ignored the fact that skills have at least as much to do with ideological and social constructions as with complex, technical competencies and have suggested that the processes whereby skills are constructed and certain groups of workers (women especially) have become associated with unskilled work need to be investigated (Beechey, 1980; Phillips and Taylor, 1980). A similar point can be made about the primary secondary worker distinction. The notions of skill and training are absolutely central to the ways in which primary sector workers are defined (and, by implication therefore, to the way in which secondary workers are defined) and it is generally assumed that these can be treated as objective phenomena. It is quite clear, however, that gender enters into the definition of skilled work and also plays a part in defining what counts (and does not count) as training. This suggests that the principal defining characteristics of primary sector workers, like skilled workers, may have as much to do with ideological constructions and bargaining strength as with objective skills and knowledge.[6]

A third point is that it has become increasingly clear from recent studies that the labor market is not a sexually-neutral entity and that gender relations are embodied in the very organization of production. The research into part-time work which Tessa Perkins and I recently carried out provides a very clear example of this. We had expected to find that part-time employment could be explained in purely economic terms. However, we discovered that employers' practices had a gendered component: they only created part-time jobs when they hired women. It was certainly possible to specify a number of features of the labor process which had led employers to create part-time jobs, among them the need to extend the length of the working day and week, and the need to gain the maximum flexibility in the use of labor. But the single most striking finding to emerge from our research was that employers only used such strategies when they employed women. Where men were employed, other strategies (for example, use of overtime and short-time working and employment on temporary contracts) were used (see Beechey and Perkins, 1987).

The argument that the labor market is not a sexually-neutral entity is a contentious argument which has far-reaching implications. Some of these are spelt out in a paper by Alison Scott (1985), who suggests that 'pure economic forces' are modified by political and ideological forces in two ways. First, economic institutions are articulated with other institutions that sustain gender inequalities in modern capitalist societies, for example, the family, the education system and the state. Secondly, gender relations are interwoven with production relations at the level of the labor process. Thus, the division of labor itself embodies gender relations which are manifested in the system of occupational segregation.

Scott grounded her argument in an historical and cross-cultural analysis. In UK, she argues, the kinship system with its emphasis on monogamy, the indissolubility of marriage, patrilineal property and inheritance rights, its nuclearized household structure and its dual sexual morality and authoritarian power relations within the family gave women a secondary and dependent status within the family at the same time as it allocated them primary responsibility for day-to-day and generational reproduction. This, she argues, was carried over into the organization of production. In the early industrial period the ideology of domesticity provided a moral justification for the forms of segregation which emerged in the labor market. An idealized form of the family which enshrined women's dependency also underpinned, and was incorporated into, a whole range of state policies – protective legislation, Poor Law reform and the developing system of state education in the nineteenth century. Central to Scott's argument is the claim that 'the economy' has been shaped by wider social forces in the course of its development. Among these are domestic ideology and the division of labor by gender. These originally existed before the development of industrial capitalism and were incorporated into the form of labor market and system of job segregation which emerged in industrial capitalist societies.

The analysis proposed by Scott is important for a number of reasons. It provides a more historical approach to the analysis of labor markets than dual and segmented labor market theories do, and it underlines the importance of analysing the historical interconnections between the family, the state and the labor market. It thus succeeds in getting away from the static forms of analysis and the functionalism which have pervaded so many previous analyses of the relationships between production and reproduction. Secondly, it emphasizes the role of ideological and political processes as well as economic ones in constructing women as a distinctive kind of labor force. Finally, it suggests that the labor market is not only linked to other institutions which sustain gender inequalities, but is itself gendered. This is the most contentious aspect of the argument, and one on which Scott is not always consistent. At times she writes as if it were possible to isolate 'the economy' and to identify 'pure economic forces', suggesting that these are affected in their development by wider social forces. At other times she advances the stronger argument that economic institutions like the labor market cannot be separated from wider social and ideological relations which have an important role in constructing them. Despite these inconsistencies, Scott's article raises the important theoretical question of what is the precise form of relationship between gender and labor markets. Are they interconnected as a matter of historical contingency? Or have labor markets developed in such a way that gender relations are part of their very fabric?

The final problem highlighted by feminist critics is that both Marxist and dual segmented labor market theories endeavor to analyse divisions within the workforce in internal terms, and they share a common delineation of 'the economy'. 'Production' and 'the economy' are treated as synonymous. Thus, domestic labor is excluded from the framework of analysis – a serious omission so far as an analysis of women's work is concerned (Baxandall, Ewen and Gordon, 1976; Beechey, 1980; Game and Pringle, 1983). Furthermore, although external factors are sometimes mentioned (for instance, in discussions of where women's secondary worker characteristics emanate from) these are not generally granted any explanatory power (Beechey, 1978). Feminist critics of both Marxist and segmented labor market theories have argued that it is impossible to explain the basis of gender divisions within the labor force solely in terms of an analysis of production, and have also argued that the concept of 'the economy' should be extended so that it covers the domestic sphere. Feminist theories have thus tried to transcend the division between public and private spheres which is incorporated into the framework of both classical political economy and much of the new political economy, and to provide an analysis which can incorporate these different spheres.

A good example of a study which shows the ways in which gender enters into the structuring of work relations can be found in Rosemary Crompton and Gareth Jones' analysis of the service class (1984). They point out that the so-called service class of managers, professional and administrative levels of white-collar workers are mainly to be found in routine clerical and administrative jobs. There thus exists a clear form of occupational segregation by sex between the different levels of white-collar work. However, Crompton and Jones argue, women have contributed to the creation of the service class and to its maintenance in two different ways, which are not generally recognized in theoretical analyses. They contribute to it through their domestic labor in the household. This affects the conditions under which men can embark on service-class careers and sometimes contributes directly to the men's work. Women also make a direct contribution to the position of men in the service class by supplying backup services for sevice-class occupations in their paid work – as typists, secretaries, punch card operators, etc. Without this work done by women, men could not perform their service-class functions. The authors suggest that analyses which focus solely on occupational positions cannot account for these phenomena because they ignore the ways in which men rely on women's work. And, in accepting the division between public and private spheres and focusing solely on the public sphere, they also ignore the contribution of women in the home.

SOCIAL REPRODUCTION

It has been fairly widely recognized by people concerned with gender divisions that these cannot be adequately explained in terms which are 'internal' to the organization of production. Both feminist writers and a number of labor market segmentation theorists (e.g. the Cambridge Group) have argued that the framework for analysing labor markets needs to be broadened in order to account for the links between production and other institutions and to theorize the relationship between production and reproduction. In this part of the chapter I want to focus on an important attempt to develop this line of argument, by Jane Humphries and Jill Rubery (1984). In this paper Humphries and Rubery make the important point that the sphere of social reproduction should be seen as an integral part of the economy, and they attempt to develop a framework for analysing social reproduction (which they treat as coterminous with the family) as relatively autonomous. They argue that neoclassical economists, dual labor market theories and Marxist and feminist theories have all fallen into the trap of seeing social reproduction either as absolutely autonomous from production or as related to it in reductionist/functionalist terms. Both formulations are problematic, according to Humphries and Rubery, because they provide one-sided analyses of women's oppression, seeing it as rooted either in the family or in the organization of production. The consequence of this is that it becomes impossible to analyse the interaction between the two spheres.

In developing an alternative to the absolute autonomy and reductionist/ functionalist frameworks Humphries and Rubery argue that social reproduction is articulated to the sphere of production but is relatively autonomous from it.[7] They suggest that both the demand- and supply-side structures exist independently and can adapt to each other – thus the supply-side structures can shape and limit the scope for capital to mold the labor market to fit its current requirements. They conclude, therefore, that there is no *a priori* connection between the spheres of production and reproduction, but rather a series of connections which need to be analysed historically.

Humphries and Rubery are quite correct to broaden the framework for analysing the economy, and their point that the structures of production and social reproduction should be seen as relatively independent and mutually interacting is a very important one. However, there are a number of problems with their mode of analysis which render it less useful than it might be. The first problem is that the analysis is highly economistic and, despite all their theoretical strictures, Humphries and Rubery's own analysis of the relationship between the family and female labor supply in the postwar world has rather functionalist overtones. Their analysis focuses too closely on a set of predominantly economic linkages between the family and capital's strategies, and it does not take sufficient account of a whole range of other factors which have a role in determining female labor supply and which are much more loosely connected to the organization of production at any particular point in time.

A second point is that Humphries and Rubery do not see the family as embodying conflicting interests between women and men. They write, for instance, of decisions made by 'the family' about the extent to which waged work should be substituted for non-waged. This not only implies that economic calculation is the only basis of decision making about the balance between waged and non-waged work. It also suggests that families make decisions based on rational calculation *for the unit as a whole*. Such an analysis ignores the extent to which women and men may have different economic interests, and also ignores the fact that women do paid work for non-financial as well as financial reasons, as a number of empirical studies have shown.

A third point concerns Humphries and Rubery's decision to restrict the analysis of social reproduction to an analysis of the family. This is now fairly commonplace in studies of women's employment, but such a conceptualization is too narrow. Jane Kenrick (1981) has argued that the construction of women as second-class workers largely takes place within a wider set of social relations and points to the role which family law, craft organization and national economic regulation have played historically in constructing women in this way. She thus broadens the analysis of social reproduction beyond the boundaries of Humphries and Rubery's analysis. Kenrick suggests that the concept of patriarchy should be redefined to describe the control of men over all the processes of social reproduction – economic, political and ideological, and concludes that 'patriarchal forces have had a major impact on the conditions on which women have supplied their labor from the origins of the labor market onwards' (1981: 182).

It is important to extend the framework for analysing labor markets beyond an analysis of production, as Humphries and Rubery do. It is important, too, that analysis of reproduction give due weight to political and ideological processes, as Kenrick argues. The point I want to emphasize here, however, is that even when the analysis is broadened in this way it will remain problematic unless the analysis of production is itself transformed. Analysts of labor markets and labor processes need to get away from the view that production can be analysed in sex-blind terms, and to build an analysis of gender into their conceptual frameworks.

THEORIZING GENDER

It is now widely recognized by feminist sociologists doing empirical research (though not, I think, by many economists) that gender operates within the sphere of production. In the first part of this chapter I discussed some of the findings from recent workplace studies which document some of the ways in which gender affects the definitions of skill and the distinction between skilled/non-skilled work. Workplace studies have suggested that gender also plays a role in defining jobs as either 'women's' or 'men's' jobs – i.e. in the sex-typing of occupations (Beechey, 1983; Scott, 1985) – and in the construction of the division between full-time and part-time work (Beechey and Perkins, 1987). Gender has also been found to affect the forms of authority and supervision within the workplace (Game and Pringle, 1983; Lown, 1983), to have an impact on women's and men's experiences of work and their orientation to work (Pollert, 1981; Cavendish, 1982; Cockburn, 1983; Westwood, 1984), to influence women's and men's hours of work and their views about the future organization of working time (Shimmin, McNally and Liff, 1981; Rimmer and Popay, 1982; Beechey, 1985), to affect the extent to which women and men benefit from the unpaid work of their spouses (Finch, 1983), to have an impact on women's and men's capacities to participate actively in trade unions (Ellis, 1981; Coote and Campbell, 1982) and to affect their experiences of redundancy and unemployment (Martin and Wallace, 1984; Coyle, 1984). There is considerable evidence, therefore, that 'gender matters', to purloin a phrase of Alison Scott's.

It is far from clear precisely how gender matters, however, and we should beware of exaggerating the role of gender without reference to more systematic empirical research on women and men's experience. As a number of critics have pointed out, there is a danger of too cavalierly adopting a 'gender model' to analyse women's employment and a 'job model' to analyse men's (Feldberg and Glenn, 1979; Beechey, 1983; Siltanen and Stanworth, 1984). This is problematic because it stresses the differences between women and men and may well understate the similarities. Moreover, it all too easily confines women, within theory, to the private sphere (Siltanen and Stanworth, 1984).

Let us assume for a moment, however, that further research does show that gender is important - there are certainly strong grounds for thinking that it has an important role in the construction of both women's *and* men's jobs. The question then arises as to *how* gender is to be analysed. At the moment the analysis of gender within the sphere of work is still rudimentary, despite a growing body of extremely good empirical studies. Often the category of gender is used to signify differences between women and men and to suggest that these are socially constructed rather than biologically based, as well as to indicate the limitations of an economic analysis, but the category rarely forms part of a well-developed theory. How, then, can we begin to develop a more theoretically adequate analysis of gender?

One way of approaching this question is by identifying the key questions with which a theory of gender would have to deal. Recent studies suggest that the following are particularly important:

- What is the basis of the separation of public and private spheres and what are the consequences of this for both women and men?
- What are the reasons for the existence of job segregation, and for its persistence across many different kinds of society?
- How do workplace cultures operate, and how do they contribute to maintaining inequalities between women and men?
- How are people's identities bound up with the public–private split and with gender relations at work? How are subjectivities constructed at work?
- How are changes in the organization of work and in the sexual definition of jobs linked to changing representations of work?
- How are gender divisions linked to other divisions – e.g. divisions of race, ethnicity and class?

This list of questions might seem rather broad to people who are accustomed to thinking about work in predominantly economic terms. However, recent studies have demonstrated fairly conclusively the need for a broader approach. In addition to documenting occupational segregation and inequality within the workforce, they have shown how social interactions (between management and workers, women and men) play an important part in the processes by which the boundaries between women's and men's jobs are maintained. They have also shown how people's identities are constructed at work. Recent discussions about unemployment and the future of work also suggest to me that analyses need to take account of changing representations of work as well as changes in the organization of work (Beechey, 1987).

Attempts to theorize gender in the area of work have tended to be based on specific case studies. Thus researchers like Cynthia Cockburn (in England) and Anne Game and Rosemary Pringle (in Australia) have developed analyses of gender on the basis of quite specific analyses: a study of male compositors in the print industry, in the case of Cockburn, and a study of a number of industries in Australia, in the case of Game and Pringle. Both Cockburn and Game and Pringle argue that gender is a relational category, in the sense that it refers to relationships between women and men, and is asymmetrical in that women and men have differential relations to gender. Both studies stress the importance of the cultural aspects of gender relations, and both show that gender is a part of people's lived experience in the workplace and is involved in the construction of subjectivities.

Their specific analyses vary somewhat, however. Game and Pringle define gender as the social meaning of being 'a woman' or 'a man'. This is involved in the definition of women's jobs and men's jobs and is also bound up with questions of identity and sexuality. Gender for them is fundamentally about difference. What is striking about Game and Pringle's research is not the consistent content to the identification of women's and men's jobs but the consistency of difference between them. Game and Pringle argue that gender is also about power; the domination by men and subordination of women which is reproduced in the labor process as well as other sites in capitalist societies. Gender, they argue, is one of the defining characteristics of capitalism. It is constitutive of it rather than being simply functional to it. Game and Pringle analyse two elements of gender. They investigate the particular division of labor existing in each workplace, looking at the ways in which it is constructed, and how it is related to the private sphere. They also pay considerable attention to the level of the symbolic in constructing both women's and men's experience of work.

Cynthia Cockburn too combines an analysis of workplace cultures and of women's and men's experiences of work in her study of compositors. Cockburn argues against a formulation of gender in terms of the structures of patriarchy and capitalism. This is too general, historical and abstract for her and she favors instead an analysis which sees the two structures as 'constitutive processes'. She also argues against the distinction between 'economic' and 'ideological' levels with which Marxist feminists have traditionally worked. For Cockburn the proper complement of 'the ideological' is 'the material', which she defines as being broader than 'the economic' since it also includes the socio-political and the physical. An analysis of the socio-political, Cockburn argues, opens up questions about male organization and solidarity, and about the part played by institutions like churches, unions and clubs in reproducing gender relations. The concept of 'the physical' is also analysed in social terms. 'The physical' refers to the meanings ascribed to physical difference and to the ways in which they are inscribed in social relations. In Cockburn's study of compositors, 'the socio-political' emerges in the shape of the printing unions and their interests and strategies. 'The physical', on the other hand, finds its expression in the compositors' capability, dexterity and strength, and also in their mastery of tools and technology. Cockburn explicitly rejects the view that sexual relations in the workplaces of modern capitalist societies can be accounted for by the sexual division of labor in the family. Like other researchers who have analysed particular workplaces in detail, she argues that gender difference and hierarchy are created at work as well as at home. Instead she argues for the concept of a sex-gender system in which men dominate women 'inside and outside family relations, inside and outside economic production, by means which are both material and ideological, exercising their authority through both individual and organizational development' (Cockburn, 1981: 55).

I do not find either of these formulations entirely satisfactory. Game and Pringle's is more precise than Cockburn's, but they do not get very far in constructing a theory of gender, as distinct from outlining some of the mechanisms by which gender works. Cockburn's book is wonderfully insightful, but her categories – 'the material' and 'the physical', for instance – are rather all-embracing, and her analysis of patriarchy and capitalism is problematic because it is dualistic.[8] It may be useful, therefore, to look beyond studies of work in order to develop a theory of gender which can be used in the analysis of work.

Two recent analyses seem to me to provide a way forward in theorizing gender. The first is Joan Scott's recent article 'Gender: A Useful Category for Historical Analysis' (Scott, 1986), which provides an interesting and erudite analysis of some of the problems involved in recent attempts to analyse gender: attempts to explain the origins of patriarchy, Marxist-feminist approaches which have attempted to provide a 'materialist' analysis of gender, and psychoanalysis which explains the production and reproduction of gendered identities in terms of sexual difference. Scott argues that all of these approaches are problematic in different ways, and that unlike these different approaches the analysis of gender needs to be historical. It also needs to be deconstructionist in the sense of not searching for a single cause of gender. Scott defines gender as a constitutive element of social relations which is based on perceived differences between the sexes. It is also, she argues, a primary way of signifying relations of power.

Gender, for Scott, has four interrelated elements:

1 culturally available symbols that evoke multiple and often contradictory representations;
2 normative concepts that set forth interpretations of the meaning of
   these symbols and which typically take the form of binary oppositions;
3 kinship systems, labor markets, the education systems and the polity;
4 subjective identities.   (

Sandra Harding provides an analysis of gender which is remarkably
similar to Scott's in her recent book, *The Science Question in Feminism*
(1986). Harding's book has a very different aim from Scott's article in that
what she wants to do is to provide a feminist analysis of, and epistemology
for, science. However, her analysis also has a number of similarities with
Scott's. Harding, like Scott, argues that gender is multifaceted, and her
approach to the analysis of gender is, like Scott's a deconstructionist one.
Gender, for Harding, consists of three levels: (1) gender symbolism, (2)
the division of labor, and (3) gendered identities and desires. Gender, for
her, is individual, structural and symbolic, and it is always asymmetrical.

These kinds of formulations are clearly a far cry from earlier feminist
and Marxist-feminist frameworks for thinking about work, but there is a
sense in which I think they provide a way forward. They move beyond the
interminable questions which have not proved very fruitful for feminist
analysis about the relative primacy of 'the economic' and 'the ideological'
and they have a much more complex view of what constitutes gender which
can embrace the kinds of question which feminist empirical studies of work
have identified as being important – questions to do with the experience of
work as well as its structural organization, questions of culture and
subjectivity as well as questions of job segregation and pay. As a program
for research they suggest the importance of investigating a number of
different strands when analysing work, and they underline the importance
of not reducing them to each other. It is important to emphasize, however,
that these more deconstructionist approaches to the analysis of work will
only be useful if the different levels of analysis identified by Scott and
Harding are kept in play at the same time. Only then will we avoid the
problems associated with the kinds of deconstructionism which are currently fashionable, which lose sight of material reality and reduce everything to an analysis of discourses and texts.

CONCLUSION

I have suggested in this chapter that gender operates within both the
sphere of production and the sphere of reproduction and not, as feminists
have often assumed, solely within the domestic sphere. One implication of
this paper is that the family is not a privileged site of women's oppression,

but is rather one site among others. Another is that analyses of work need to identify the different levels at which gender operates in both spheres, and to analyse the connection between these different levels, both historically and contemporarily. It seems important in this context to point out that the sphere of social reproduction is not only a place where labor powers are produced but is also a place where consumption and other kinds of work – domestic and voluntary work, for instance – take place. We need to analyse the processes by which different kinds of work have been constructed in the different spheres, and also to trace the ways in which they have shifted between public and private spheres. In addition to the trend documented by Braverman, for goods and services to shift from domestic to capitalistic production, are other important changes. Of particular importance in the postwar world have been the shifting, in both directions, of service work between the domestic and welfare spheres and the massive growth in consumption work. In this context we need to understand how the allocation of different kinds of work to public and private spheres is linked to gender relations, since it seems to be predominantly women's work which has shifted about. We also need to understand the processes by which some kinds of work have been paid while others have not, and to see how these are linked to gender relations. Finally, we need to analyse changing representations of work. For in a period in which work in every sphere is being massively restructured it has become increasingly evident that analyses of work cannot be divorced from analyses of its representations.

NOTES

Many thanks to the editors, to Hal Benenson and Jill Rubery for comments on earlier versions of this paper, and to Erik Olin Wright and graduate students in the class analysis program at the University of Wisconsin for stimulating discussions of many of the ideas in this paper.

1 This term is used by Goldthorpe (1985).
2 Barron and Norris (1976) list the following characteristics of a secondary workforce – dispensability, clearly visible social difference, low interest in acquiring training, low economism and lack of solidarity.
3 See e.g. Edwards, Gordon and Reich (1975); Edwards (1979); Rubery (1980); Wood (1980); Rubery, Tarling and Wilkinson (1984); Labor Studies Group (1985).
4 See e.g. Coyle (1982); Cockburn (1983); Game and Pringle (1983).
5 This point has been made in various ways by Beechey (1978); Kenrick (1981); Game and Pringle (1983); Benenson (1984); Beechey and Perkins (1987).
6 These arguments are developed at greater length in Beechey and Perkins (1987).
7 Rubery and Humphries' empirical work, like much of the Cambridge Group's,

does analyse the concrete relationships between the family and production, but their analysis in the 1984 paper is rather more functionalist than their more empirical writings.

8   I have criticized this formulation elsewhere. See my *Unequal Work*, especially the Introduction and the essay 'On Patriarchy'.

REFERENCES

Amsden, A. H. (1980) *The Economics of Women and Work*, Harmondsworth, Penguin Books.

Atkinson, J. (1984) *Manning for uncertainty – some emerging UK work patterns*, Institute of Manpower Studies, University of Sussex.

Barker, D. and Allen, S. (eds) (1976) *Dependence and Exploitation in Work and Marriage*, London, Longman.

Barron, R. D. and Norris, E. M. (1976) 'Sexual divisions and the dual labour market', in Barker and Allen (1976).

Baxandall, R., Ewen, E. and Gordon, L. (1976) 'The working class has two sexes', in *Technology, the Labour Process and the Working Class*, Special issue of *Monthly Review* (Vol. 28, No. 3).

Beechey, V. (1978) 'Women and production: a critical analysis of some sociological theories of women's work', in A. Kuhn and A. Wolpe (1978).

Beechey, V. (1980) 'The sexual division of labour and the labour process, a critical assessment of Braverman', in S. Wood (1980).

Beechey, V. (1983) 'What's so special about women's employment?', *Feminist Review*, No. 15.

Beechey, V. (1985) 'The shape of the workforce to come', *Marxism Today*, Vol. 29, No. 8, August.

Beechey, V. (1987a) 'It's off to work we go!', *Marxism Today*, May.

Beechey, V. (1987b) *Unequal Work*, London, Verso.

Beechey, V. and Perkins, T. (1985) 'Conceptualizing part-time work', in B. Roberts, R. Finnegan and D. Gallie.

Beechey, V. and Perkins, T. (1987) *A Matter of Hours: women, part-time work and the labour market*, Cambridge, Polity Press.

Benenson, H. (1984) 'Victorian sexual ideology and Marx's theory of the working class', in *International Labour and Working-class History*, No. 25, Spring.

Blaxall, M. and Reagan, B. (eds) (1976) *Women and the Workplace*, Chicago, University of Chicago Press.

Braverman, H. (1974) *Labor and Monopoly Capital*, New York, Monthly Review Press.

Brown, C. and J. A. Pechman (eds), (1987) *Gender in the Workplace*, Washington DC, The Brookings Institute.

Cavendish, R. (1982) *On the Line*, London, Routledge and Kegan Paul.

Cockburn, C. (1981) 'The material of male power', in *Feminist Review*, No. 9, Autumn.

Cockburn, C. (1983) *Brothers*, London, Pluto Press.

Coote, A. and Campbell, B. (1982) *Sweet Freedom*, London, Picador.

Coyle, A. (1982) 'Sex and skill in the organization of clothing industry', in West

(1982).

Coyle, A. (1984) *Redundant Women*, London, The Women's Press.

Crompton, R. and Jones, G. (1984) *White-collar Proletariat: Deskilling and gender in clerical work*. London, Macmillan.

Crompton, R. and Mann, R. (eds) (1985) *Gender and Stratification*, Cambridge, Polity Press.

Doeringer, P. B. and Piore, M. J. (1971) *Internal Labor Market and Manpower Analysis*, Lexington, D. C. Heath.

Edwards, R. (1979) *Contested Terrain: the transformation of the workplace in the twentieth century.*, New York, Basic Books.

Edwards, R., Gordon, D. and Reich, M. (eds) (1985) *Labor Market Segmentation*, Lexington, D. C. Heath.

Ellis, V. (1981) *The Role of Trade Unions in the Promotion of Equal Opportunities*, ECC. SSRC Joint Panel Report.

Feldberg, R. and Glenn, G. N. (1979) 'Male and female: job versus gender models in the sociology of work', *Social Problems*, Vol. 26, No. 5, June.

Finch, J. (1983) *Married to the Job: women's incorporation in men's work*, London, George Allen and Unwin.

Game, A. and Pringle, R. (1983) *Gender at Work*, Sydney, George Allen and Unwin.

Goldthorpe, J. (1985) 'The end of convergence: corporatist and dualist tendencies in modern western societies', in Roberts, Finnegan and Gallie (eds) (1985).

Harding, S. (1986) *The Science Question in Feminism*, Milton Keynes, Open University Press.

Hartmann, H. (1976) 'Capitalism, patriarchy and job segregation by sex', in Blaxall and Reagan (1976).

Hartmann, H. (1987) 'Internal labor markets and gender: a case study of promotion', in Brown and Palmer (1987).

Humphries, J. and Rubery, J. (1984) 'The reconstruction of the supply side of the labour market: the relative autonomy of social reproduction', *Cambridge Journal of Economics*, No. 8.

Kendrick, J. (1981) 'Politics and the construction of women as second-class workers', in Wilkinson (1981).

Kuhn, A. and Wolpe, A. (eds) (1978) *Feminism and Materialism*, London, Routledge and Kegan Paul.

Labour Studies Group (1985) 'Economic and social and political factors in the operation of the labour market', in Roberts, Finnegan and Gallie (1985).

Lown, J. (1983) 'Not so much a factory, more a form of patriarchy: gender and class during industrialization', in Gamarnikow, Morgan, Purvis and Taylorson.

Martin, J. and Roberts, C. (1984) *Women and Employment, a lifetime perspective*, London, HMSO.

Martin, R. M. and Wallace, J. G. (1984) *Working Women in Recession: employment, redundancy and unemployment*. Oxford, Oxford University Press.

Phillips, A. and Taylor, B. (1980) 'Sex and skill: Notes towards a feminist economics', *Feminist Review*, No. 6.

Pollert, A. (1981) *Girls, Wives, Factory Lives*, London, Macmillan.

Rimmer, L. and Popay, J. (1982) 'The family at work', *Employment Gazette*, June.

Roberts, B., Finnegan, R. and Gallie, D. (1985) *New Approaches to Economic*

Life, Manchester, Manchester University Press.

Rubery, J., (1980) 'Structured labour markets, worker organization and low pay', in Amsden (1980).

Rubery, J. Tarling, R. and Wilkinson, F. (1984) 'Labour market segmentation theory: an alternative framework for the analysis of the employment system'. Paper delivered at the BSA conference on 'Work, Employment and Unemployment'.

Scott, A. M. (1985) 'Industrialization, gender and segregation and stratification theory', in Crompton and Mann.

Scott, J. W. (1986) 'Gender: a useful category of historical analysis,' *The American Historical Review*, Vol. 91, No. 5, December.

Shimmin, S., McNally, J. and Liff, S. (1981) 'Pressures on women engaged in factory work', *Employment Gazette*, August.

Siltanen, J. and Stanworth, M. (eds) (1984) *Women and the Public Sphere*, London, Hutchinson.

West, J. (ed.) (1982) *Work, Women and the Labour Market*, London, Routledge and Kegan Paul.

Westwood, S. (1984) *All Day Every Day*, London, Pluto Press.

Wilkinson, F. (ed.) (1981) *The Dynamics of Labor Market Segmentation*, New York, Academic Press.

Wood, S. (ed.) (1980) *The Degradation of Work?* London, Hutchinson.

PART II

A Changing Labor Force: Paradoxes of Feminization

4

Taking Women into Account
Redefining and Intensifying Employment in Canada

Pat Armstrong and
Hugh Armstrong

INTRODUCTION

Guided by Keynesian theory, pushed by workers whose organizational
strength had grown with labor shortages as well as with heavy capital
investments, and sustained by the economic boom, state intervention grew
enormously in the postwar years. Because in Canada this intervention
resulted at least as much from the pressure of collective demands as it did
from a commitment to Keynesian principles, state policies were not evenly
or consistently developed. Nevertheless, until the mid-1960s, state regulations, investments, and both employment-related and universal programs
all contributed to the maintenance of relatively full male employment, to
the extension of the economic boom and to the smoothing out of
capitalism's worst consequences and uncertainties. Such programs were
common not only in Canada but in almost all advanced industrial societies
where fears of a return to the economic hardships and political uncertainties of the 1930s turned policy-makers in new directions at the end of
World War II.
   Although seldom explicitly sex-biased, these policies reflected and
reinforced the primacy of the male wage, the ghettoization of female labor
and the segregation of women in the home, directing consumption. At the
same time, however, labor shortages accompanying the boom, growth of
the tertiary sector and state expansion of services eventually drew many
women into the labor force. With the expansion of state programs came
higher taxes and mortgage costs. Combined with mounting economic
pressure to purchase consumer goods rather than produce them in the
household, taxes and mortgages pushed up household cash requirements

beyond levels that could be satisfied even by growing real male wages. More and more women entered the market in search of a wage, although they were often proletarianized in the process (Cuneo, 1985).

Because Keynesian strategies were never designed to alter fundamentally the basis of capitalist society, they could only delay, not prevent, future economic crises. This was particularly the case in countries such as Canada where no consistent postwar economic plan was developed. As signs of economic decay began to appear in the 1960s, so too did indications of disenchantment with Keynesian approaches. With profits beginning to fall, corporations searched abroad for cheaper sources of labor and resources. In the domestic economy they sought to intensify labor, primarily through the reorganization of the labor process, as well as through the introduction of new technology and hiring more part-time workers. As the organizational strength of workers declined, corporations went on the offensive against state programs and intervention. One result was that unemployment and underemployment began to rise and real wages to fall.

While the Canadian state professed its commitment to full employment, it consistently redefined 'full' employment to accommodate higher and higher levels of unemployment. This redefinition was mainly based on the argument that much of the rising unemployment was caused by, or at least was experienced by, secondary workers, a category dominated by female workers. Then, as unemployment and female employment grew simultaneously throughout the 1970s, full employment disappeared from the political agenda, to be replaced by the concept of 'normal unemployment'. The state based its acceptance of higher levels of unemployment on the assumption that rising female employment created unemployment for 'prime age males' at the same time that it made such unemployment easier to bear, because these men had employed wives. Labor surpluses weakened the collective power of workers, making it easier for the state to respond to employers' demands and to place accumulation at the top of the agenda.

This chapter outlines the postwar reconstruction of domestic and wage labor, a reconstruction which has altered the employment possibilities for men as well as for women. In tracing the growth and decline of the Canadian welfare state, along with the embracing and then the abandonment of Keynesian economic theory, the chapter argues that the consequences have always been different for women and men. In the main, economic theory and policy assumed and reinforced women's attachment to the home and men's to the labor force, even if the policies reflected more a shared and unquestioned view of women's place than they did a conscious conspiracy to subordinate or exclude women. But the policies often had a contradictory effect; they drew women into the labor force, making it impossible for them to stay in or return to the home. While relying heavily on classical economic theorists, and largely rejecting Keynesian methods, contemporary decision-makers have expanded their approach to take women's domestic and wage labor, their volunteer and homework into account. Women are still being blamed for current economic difficulties, their unemployment is dismissed as unproblematic and their domestic responsibilities enforced.

POSTWAR BOOM, FULL EMPLOYMENT AND THE WELFARE STATE

The Great Depression challenged the analysis of unemployment put forward by classical economic theorists and put into question strategies based on this analysis. Massive unemployment could not be blamed primarily on recalcitrant workers; too many men, too many families, had no alternative but government relief programs. At the same time, market forces were taking much too long to produce a recovery in profits. During World War II, states started to intervene more in the economy. The state financed this intervention in part by going much further into debt to pay for military goods and services. This was a strategy that, by the conventional wisdom of the day, dangerously depleted the public coffers; yet profits soared and unemployment virtually disappeared. The lesson policy-makers learned from the wartime experience was that continued state intervention could, while stimulating profits, prevent high unemployment. It could thus limit the risk of a return to the unrest that, a quarter-century earlier, had characterized the period just after World War I in almost all of Western Europe and North America.

If the fear of postwar unrest provided a motivation for continued state intervention to prevent high unemployment, the theory advanced by John Maynard Keynes provided a justification. Developed in the Depression crucible, his concept of and arguments for full employment marked the end of classical economic theory's hegemony and the beginnings of a new direction. In *The General Theory of Employment, Interest, and Money*, he argued that for classical theorists the 'two categories of "frictional" unemployment and "voluntary" unemployment are comprehensive. The classical postulates do not admit of the possibility of a third category', a category Keynes termed involuntary unemployment (Keynes, 1936: 6). The classical theorists' categorization rested, in turn, on the assumption 'that the wage bargains between the entrepreneurs and the workers determined the real wage' (ibid.: 11), and gave rise to the conclusion that apparent unemployment 'must be due at bottom to a refusal by the unemployed factors to accept a reward which corresponds to their marginal productivity' (ibid.: 16). From this classical perspective, unemployment then results either from a short-term mismatch in skills, in jobs, in the location of work, or it results from 'legislation, social practices, collective bargaining or slow responses to change or human obstinacy' (ibid.: 6).

For Keynes, the reality of unemployment during the Depression clearly refuted this classical analysis. Labor had not been 'more truculent in the depression than in the boom – far from it. Nor is its physical productivity less' (ibid.: 9). In any case, the general level of real wages was not in the main determined by collective bargaining. Nor did lower wages and weaker unions automatically or necessarily create full employment, by which Keynes meant the absence of involuntary unemployment. The problem was a lack of jobs, not people who were unwilling to work, lacked the appropriate skills, or belonged to strong unions.

Lord Keynes argued that the volume of employment was determined, not by the level of wages but by the 'propensity to consume and the rate of investment' (ibid.: 30). Neither could it be guaranteed by unrestrained market forces. It follows from his argument that the state has a responsibility to maintain appropriate levels of investment and consumption in order to sustain full employment, and to provide jobs which pay enough for the 'satisfaction of the immediate primary needs of a man and his family' (ibid.: 97). State intervention is necessary to ensure that all men have access to jobs providing a decent family wage.

It should be noted here that Keynes defined full employment in terms of the absence of involuntary unemployment *for men*. A Canadian contemporary pointed out that to 'the woman with no other resources than her job – unemployment is an even more serious problem of dependency than to a man. She is very far from having the freedom of movement that is open to a man' (Marsh, 1939: 255). It may have been that such women were relatively few in number, but it is certainly the case that, in his concern for the problems faced by male breadwinners, Keynes ignored the needs of women. Moreover, when making his argument about the impact of workers' struggles on the redistribution of wages, Keynes never considered any effects on the redistribution of jobs between women and men.

Keynes' theory provided a coherent justification of and guide for a Canadian government already deeply involved in shaping the economy and concerned about the possibility of future depression and social unrest. In its 1945 *White Paper on Employment and Income*, the federal government announced its intention to manipulate aggregate demand as a means of maintaining 'a high and stable level of employment and income' (Canada, Minister of Reconstruction, 1945: 1). Public investment, especially in infrastructure, conservation projects and training programs, was intended to stimulate rather than supplant private investment. At the same time, these public projects would be used to help sustain employment in periods when private-sector demand for workers slackened.

Consumer demand for goods and services would be maintained in two ways. First, employment-related schemes such as unemployment insurance would 'maintain consumption expenditures and maintain employment in the industries producing consumption goods' (ibid.: 13) as well as keep a reserve of labor available for employers. According to a member of the Royal Commission recommending this strategy,

> The current singling out of unemployment insurance for governmental attention in many countries is dictated by the appalling costs of direct relief and hope that unemployment insurance benefits will give some protection to public treasuries in future depressions and will, by sustaining purchasing power, tend to mitigate these depressions. (quoted by Finkel, 1979: 83)

Such schemes had two additional advantages. They would place a large part of the financial burden of unemployment on those currently employed. They would also create, the promoters argued, 'a more contented and better citizen' (quoted in Cuneo, 1979: 153). Given that the overwhelming majority of paid workers were male, employment-related schemes were primarily for men and the Canadian state seemed to follow Keynes in defining full employment mainly in terms of a family wage for men.

The second strategy for maintaining demand – the introduction of universal programs unrelated to paid work – was designed, however, to have an impact on women's employment. The state and employers had instituted programs during the war to draw large numbers of women into the labor force. The new universal programs would help maintain demand while encouraging women to drop out of the labor force, leaving the places for men demobilized from the armed forces. Family allowances, paid to all mothers, would not only 'augment the income of families in the lower income groups' but would also 'provide a means for maintaining or increasing the consumption of these groups. . . . The supplementary effect which they have in increasing or maintaining employment will be evidence that what is in the first instance a transfer of income will be ultimately paid for, in substantial part, out of an increase in income' (Canada, Minister of Reconstruction, 1945: 13). Like unemployment insurance programs for men, family allowances paid to women would also make them more contented citizens. It was a very small wage for housework which would be, as a federal subcommittee formed to advise on 'post-war problems of women' explained, 'an alleviating factor in the mental attitude which may result from surrender of the double income'. The subcommittee made its assumptions about women quite clear:

> We believe that at the present time the normal urge towards marriage, and home, and family life is strong, and that this is a factor which can be relied upon to reduce largely the number of women now listed as gainfully employed, provided there is sufficient well-paid employment for men. (Canada, Advisory Committee on Reconstruction, 1944: 16)

The subcommittee was not, however, entirely confident that this normal urge would be strong enough. It thus recommended various programs in addition to family allowances designed to entice or push women into the home and which would, as a consequence, contribute to the goal of creating full employment for men. Better housing would 'materially lessen the time-consuming drudgery of housework'; special courses would make 'the vocation of household work . . . sufficiently attractive to well-trained intelligent girls and women' (ibid.: 14, 11); and part-time nurseries would replace the full-time ones established during the war, allowing women to exchange information on childrearing, to leave their children for short periods and to undertake part-time or voluntary work.

Although primarily concerned with returning or confining women to the home, the subcommittee did not ignore the possibility of some women's continuing labor force involvement. Recognizing that many single women, widows, women displaced from the farm and women married to men without sufficient incomes would require paid work and that many women entering the labor force during the war might 'feel a sense of frustration if they have not the opportunity to exercise these abilities', the subcommittee conceded women's right to paid work and recommended that

> To women in each group, the right to choose what occupation she will follow must be conceded as a right to which every citizen is entitled. She must also have the right to equality of remuneration, working conditions and opportunity for advancement. (ibid.: 10, 9)

Nevertheless, in recommending equal treatment, the subcommittee was not prepared, as it was in the case of housework, to support this recommendation with proposals for state action. It recommended only a change in attitudes, not a change in programs or legislation. And the list of employment possibilites mentioned – household work, distributive trades, new government services, the manufacture of plastics and household gadgets, with professional work restricted to household science, music, libraries and extension courses – clearly indicated that these representatives of the state did not think that women should compete for traditional male work and thus interfere with full male employment. Instead, women would confine themselves to traditional female areas or newly-emerging jobs in some sectors of the manufacturing and service industries. The state moved to ensure these notions were translated into practice, by restricting the employment of married women in federal civil service jobs (Archibald, 1970: 17).

During the long boom which, with brief interruptions, characterized the first two postwar decades, the strategies based on Keynesian theories and outlined in these documents seemed to work. Immediately after the war, most married women who had been employed returned to the home. The expansion of employment-related programs such as pensions, workers' compensation for injury, and unemployment insurance for the still primarily male employees did serve to sustain demand and limit opposition. New universal programs were introduced and old ones extended. Such programs affected more women than men, given that women constituted the majority of the aged, of those on welfare, of those paid family allowances and of those seeking medical service. These strategies, too, helped to maintain purchasing power, while simultaneously supporting women's dependency and discouraging their full participation in the labor market.

Between 1951, when the lingering effects of the war effort had worn off, and 1971, total state spending by all levels of government in Canada grew from the equivalent of 24.2 to 33.2 per cent of Gross National Product, while 'exhaustive' state spending on goods and services grew from 15.9 to 23.6 per cent of GNP (calculated from Canadian Tax Foundation, 1972). This is spending that results in goods and services being used up, as distinct from non-exhaustive spending that simply reallocates funds from one level of government to another or from governments to individuals or corporations. As John Calvert points out in his historical study of the public sector, 'in the context of a growing economy, it was possible to increase services without incurring major government deficits' because growth 'generated sufficient additional tax revenues to pay for more public services' (1984: 75).

Perhaps more importantly, the motivation for state spending was there. Male-dominated unions made significant wage gains as their often transnational employers were willing to buy labor peace out of rising profits. Facing demands from strong unions for more security, services and fringe benefits, many corporate owners were susceptible to proposals for more regulation of labor relations, for more employment-related and universal schemes. Such programs shifted the pressure for protection from the employer to the state and some of the costs from employers to employees for, as Calvert has shown, 'social programs have not been financed through redistributive taxation but by increasing taxes on ordinary Canadians' (1984: 88).

Not all employers were equally enthusiastic, however. Employers who could draw on a large reserve of labor, especially female labor, did not often face strong unions and did not pay high wages. They, therefore, had little economic interest in passing costs or power on to the state. But the boom contributed to their profits too, and, in the face of demands on the state from many workers, from organized political groups, and support from other employers, their opposition was weak. Many of the smaller employers were, however, successful in obtaining exemptions from or avoiding state intervention.

As services and social programs expanded, the state became a major employer. Indeed, it was mainly state employment which prevented rising levels of unemployment; the state became the employer of last resort. By conservative estimates, between 1946 and 1971, 40 per cent of new Canadian jobs went directly to state workers (Armstrong, 1977). Untold more new jobs went to workers employed indirectly by the state through its purchases from the private sector of goods and services, ranging from paper clips to medical examinations, highway construction to garbage collection.

Nevertheless, while the rapid growth in state employment both prevented male unemployment from soaring and drew many women into the labor force, women and men were hired to fill different jobs. Between 1941 and 1961, in public administration and defense, and in senior administrative posts elsewhere in the state bureaucracy, 80 per cent of the new jobs went to men (Canada, Dominion Bureau of Statistics, 1966). In general, however, the state did not compete for men in the tight market and did not push up wages; it hired women instead. Two-thirds of the workers added in education, health and welfare were drawn from the large reserve of women not previously in the paid labor force (ibid.).

Although women were hired both because their wages were lower and because they were considered to possess appropriate attitudes as well as skills, they did not long remain docile. Women encountered political, economic and working conditions that encouraged them to fight for improvements. The rapid expansion of state education and health and welfare services had widespread political support among the general population. The government itself, unlike private employers, was not generally able to threaten to relocate in low-wage areas when costs mounted. Therefore, especially in the rapidly growing occupations where certification was required, such as teaching and nursing, public-sector workers were able to unionize and win considerable improvements in their low wages and poor working conditions. The many other women who did clerical and service work for the state had varying degrees of success in organizing for and winning contracts. While their skills were less scarce, in other respects they shared with teachers and nurses the propitious conditions for unionization of the state sector. By the end of the 1960s, more than half of all unionized women in Canada worked in the public sector (White, 1980: 27).

It was not only in the state sector that clerical and service work was expanding. But unlike women working for the state, women in the private sector faced employers who could and did move their enterprises when protest and/or organization threatened. Many of these employers operated on a seasonal basis as well. Few of the jobs required recognized skills, further limiting workers' power. Moreover, women were often forced to choose among the few jobs within commuting distance of their husbands' higher-paying work. Taken together, all these aspects of paid employment kept turnover rates high and opportunities for unionization and decent wages low.

Integral to the postwar economic boom, then, was not only an interventionist state inspired, or at least legitimated, by Keynesian economic theory, but also a restructuring of the labor force. The male-dominated agricultural sector declined, while service, finance and trade industries, where women were much more likely to find work, expanded. The demand for workers in traditionally female, non-unionized, low-wage industries began to grow initially during a period of relatively full male employment, but jobs in areas where men usually found work grew more slowly or even decreased in later years (Armstrong, 1984: 54-5).

Women were not only drawn into the labor force by the availability of work; they were also pushed into the market by their growing economic need and the changing structure of domestic work (see Nakamura et al., 1979; MacLeod and Horner, 1980; Armstrong and Armstrong, 1984: chapter 6; Pryor, 1984). Households required more and more money to meet the rapidly rising costs of mortgages, taxes, heating and transportation. The new products, appliances and services that appeared in the postwar years made it both possible and necessary to combine domestic and wage labor. Some labor-saving devices actually reduced domestic work, and the prices of products such as prepared foods and ready-made clothes meant they were often cheaper to purchase than to make at home. Yet, commodification also meant that the household required more money to buy what were rapidly becoming necessities, as alternative, non-market ways of producing these necessities at home became relatively more costly, and some of the skills and facilities needed to do so disappeared. At the same time, the design of many new commodities locked some domestic work more securely into the private household, maintaining many of women's traditional responsibilities and limiting their full participation in the market. Washing machines, for example, ensured that most clothes would be cleaned at home.

Even in these years of postwar boom, however, there were signs of future economic difficulties. Gradual, if uneven, increases in unemployment, periods of rising prices and falling profits, and continued inequality between women and men all indicated that the simple application of Keynesian theory was not sufficient to guarantee sustained and equitable economic growth. In addition to the commodification process just noted, widening income disparities put pressure on women married to low-income husbands to enter the labor force (Armstrong, 1984: chapter 6). From the early 1970s on, with the end of the boom, slight declines in some real male wages and increases in male unemployment prompted many more married women to seek paid employment. As their participation rates rose, so too did the official unemployment rates of women in all the OECD countries (chapter 2, table 2.5, p.23). In Canada, by 1969, women's unemployment surpassed the rising rates experienced by men.

In a classic case of blaming the victim, employers and state officials have argued that high and rising female unemployment was a cause for concern, not because it meant hardship for women and not because it signalled the failure of full employment policies, but because the rising labor force participation of women was partly responsible for the failure to achieve full employment for men (Ryan, 1971). According to a Canadian federal government Task Force on Labour Market Development, commonly referred to as the Dodge Report,

> Although there is little direct evidence, it is reasonable to infer that the rising relative unemployment rates of youth and adult women in the past fifteen years have been related to the ability of the economy to absorb the extraordinarily large numbers of new entrants and reentrants to the labor market with limited experience and, in many cases, with limited training. Moreover, hiring practices and procedures may have further restricted job opportunities to a narrow range of occupations. (Employment and Immigration Canada, 1981: 11).

From this perspective, too many women with too few skills – and perhaps some employers who discriminated against them – provided most of the explanation of women's employment situation. In other words, the problem was defined in terms of people, not jobs. As the Economic Council of Canada, a federal government agency, puts it, 'the work attitudes, wage aspirations, and participation patterns of the most rapidly expanding age-sex groups in the labour force differ sufficiently from those of prime-age males to produce labour market friction' (1976: 212). The causes, according to government analysts, were primarily women's low investment in their own human capital, women's decisions to seek paid work, and the cultural values of both employers and women. Changing economic conditions in the household and in the labor force attracted little, if any, attention. All these ideas represented a post-Keynesian return to the old classical recipes of frictional and voluntary unemployment applied now to women, with dollops of human capital theory and false ideas added for good measure.

Held largely responsible for the long-term rise in unemployment and for their own employment problems in particular, women's situation also provided a convenient excuse for redefining the standard for full employ-ment and for underplaying the consequences of a deteriorating economy. As recently as 1964, the Economic Council of Canada (ECC) suggested 3 per cent unemployment as a realistic target for achieving full employment. The subsequent upward drift in unemployment was accompanied by the blurring of a receding target, much as was the case in the United States too (Duboff, 1977). By 1976, the ECC argued that

> basic changes in the labour market have rendered the message of the unemployment rate today rather different than that of a decade ago

. . . the increasing participation of secondary workers in the recent past makes the unemployment of family heads a more meaningful measure than the convenient one in which primary breadwinners and supplementary earners seeking part-time work are weighted equally . . . The aggregate unemployment rate,

the Council concluded, needed to 'be augmented by a number of other measures in order to achieve a balanced interpretation for purposes of government policy-making' (Economic Council of Canada, 1976: 211-12). Some unemployment – principally experienced by women – had to be weighted downward if policies were to be 'realistic'.

Soon, the seriousness of 'family head's' or 'primary breadwinner's' unemployment also began to be challenged. The 1976 Economic Council skepticism about the financial burden of male unemployment was picked up in the 1981 Dodge Report, which asserted that 'the hardship associated with unemployment today is much less than it was 15 years ago' (Employment and Immigration Canada, 1981: 15). The *Canadian Statistical Review* brought these themes together:

Unemployment clearly affects the economic well-being of many families. However, from the data presented here, it appears that this impact may be less serious now than 10 years ago, for the following reasons: first, an even larger majority of the unemployed are no longer the traditional sole breadwinners of families; second, there has been a substantial increase in the number of families with two or more earners; and third, government transfer programs such as unemployment insurance provide a large measure of protection against loss of income in case of unemployment. (Statistics Canada, 1983: vi).

The suggestion being made none too subtly here is that we should not worry so much about current, double-digit unemployment levels. Many of those without paid work are, after all, women rather than male 'traditional sole breadwinners' (the term 'family heads' having fallen into disrepute). Yet even when these male breadwinners are out of work, their unemployment does not leave their families in dire straits precisely because their wives, and possibly their children, are earning incomes. No longer does every man need a job in order to provide for 'the satisfaction of the immediate primary needs' of himself and his family, as Keynes had put it. We are being counselled to accept, without protest, higher and higher levels of unemployment, especially for women but also for men, largely on the basis of rising rates of female labor force participation. Full employment targets recede as unemployment is discounted, no matter which sex the unemployment strikes, because multi-earner families and state income support are assumed to cushion the impact of job loss.

Evidence to contradict this line of argument abounds, of course. First, there is no direct relationship in Canada between rising female labor force participation rates and unemployment rates for either women or men. Since 1966, the female participation rate has increased every year save one, while the female and male unemployment rates have each declined on seven annual occasions, although not always during the same years. In 1982, when the female participation rate held steady, unemployment increased sharply, and for men especially. The movement of the female and male unemployment rates in different directions on four separate occasions was an indication of the continuing segregation of the labor force, a situation revealed in particularly dramatic fashion during 1982–3 when the male unemployment rate exceeded the female rate (see chapter 2, table 2.5, p.23).

Second, while the skills women possess are frequently unrecognized or undervalued, their educational attainment compares favorably with that of men. Women are more likely to reach and to graduate from secondary school. Although men are more likely to have attended and graduated from university, it is the other post-secondary institutions, where women are over-represented, that most directly prepare students for the labor force. Moreover, women's rapidly growing university training has not been equally reflected in labor market gains. Women cannot be accused, then, of having neglected to make human capital investments in their own education relative to men.

Third, neither women's low wages nor unemployment insurance benefits provide much of a cushion against the long-term unemployment that is becoming more and more common. The feminization of poverty and the growing number of husband-and-wife families living below the poverty line (National Council of Welfare, 1985) testify to their limited effectiveness. Economic crisis, the failure of state policies, and a restructured market have more to do with rising unemployment rates for women and men than do women's desire for paid employment or their lack of skills.

Finally, the evidence suggests that unemployment is frequently a family problem. In nearly one quarter of all families experiencing some unemployment, there was no other employed family member, and in '33.3% of all families with at least one unemployed member, the husband or lone parent was unemployed' (Rashid, 1986: 93). Such unemployment necessarily means hardship, however it is measured.

Although the state has defined higher rates of both male and female unemployment as normal or acceptable, it continues to recognize some involuntary unemployment and undertakes efforts to alleviate it. Based on the assumption that it is primarily male unemployment that is serious, crisis-related and involuntary, the state directs job creation schemes toward male-dominated industries. Like the programs recommended after the war, these job creation schemes are officially committed to women's equal right to paid employment, but do little to guarantee it. As the Department responsible explained, 'the objective of the program is to deal with cyclical unemployment, *not* to deal with or redress imbalances suffered by females' (Employment and Immigration Canada, n.d. [1983]; emphasis in the original). Some programs explicitly directed to women and 'other minorities' have been included under the job creation program, but with an emphasis on skills and training. Once again, women's unemployment is viewed as being their own fault, for not investing enough in themselves. Training programs meanwhile not only blame the victim, they also fail to address the massive scope of unemployment. Instead of creating jobs, they simply intensify the competition for the scarce existing ones. Similarly, the limited numbers and restricted scope of affirmative action programs can be seen as another means of legitimating higher levels of unemployment without disrupting significantly the male job classification.

RETREAT FROM KEYNESIANISM AND THE WELFARE STATE – THE INTENSIFICATION OF WORK

Along with the redefinition of 'full employment' has come a rethinking of the state's responsibility for maintaining demand and the next generation of workers. Conditions in the 1980s are quite different from those of the immediate postwar period. No longer enjoying steadily growing profits, facing male-dominated unions weakened by massive layoffs in their industries as well as by generally rising unemployment levels, and contemplating removal to low-wage zones, especially as their capital equipment deteriorates, employers in the primary and secondary sectors have been withdrawing their support for state intervention in the form it has taken since the war. Never enthusiastic about that kind of state intervention and seldom faced with strong unions in their female-dominated workforce, employers in the service sector have become increasingly vociferous in their demands for cutbacks in state services as a means of reducing the deficit and disciplining workers. The growing strength of public-sector unions and the organizing efforts amongst women now working permanently in the private sector have posed an increasing threat. Like classical theorists, both groups of employers have argued (despite little evidence, as Keynes had pointed out) that legislation, social practice and collective bargaining limit market forces and create unemployment. In addition, state support for demand through both job-related and universal programs has, they have claimed, made workers too lazy to work at wages reflecting their worth. And high levels of unemployment and the sex segregation of the labor market have inhibited worker resistance to these claims.

Employers' calls for privatization, deregulation and for cutbacks not only in state services but also in state bureaucracies were responded to

sympathetically. The state as employer was now in a very different position
from that of the immediate postwar period. While it still could not run
away, it could now draw on a large reserve of well-educated women seeking
employment and competing more and more directly with men for scarce
jobs. Ironically, women's wage victories in some areas made traditional
women's jobs increasingly attractive to men, especially as work disappeared
from traditional male sectors. With growing demands placed on state
coffers by the increasing numbers of unemployed, and with mounting
pressure from employers, the state was prompted to use its not inconsidera-
ble power to discipline workers, lower wages, reduce union strength, cut
costs and increase the labor reserve.

The continuing crisis allowed and encouraged the state to argue that
reduction of the public debt and increase in profits were the sole legitimate
priorities for the state in these trying times. As labor's sole representative
on the 1985 (Macdonald) Royal Commission on the Economic Union and
Development Prospects for Canada explained, the Report is 'obsessed with
Canada's competitiveness', rather than concerned with 'full employment or
social justice' (quoted in Drache and Cameron, 1985: x). Sustaining
demand and contenting workers are no longer major concerns.

At the same time, state workers have been 'maligned for alleged
featherbedding, earning excessive incomes, engaging in irresponsible strike
activities and, in general, being a burden and parasite on society' (Canadian
Union of Public Employees, 1985: 42). It is easier to adopt such tactics
because a high proportion of workers are women and because, unlike
private-sector employers, the state does not face huge losses from strikes.
Indeed, money is saved when employees do not work since there is no loss
in sales and essential services can be maintained by government decree.
Moreover, strikes are often a means of building support for restrictions on
state-sector workers. Such processes have severely limited the strength of,
and are now reducing membership in, unions crucial for women.

The other half of the disciplining of state workers is the cutback in
social services as well as in employment-related and universal programs.
State programs are defined as too expensive and as a major cause of rising
unemployment. Green and Cousineau (1976: 112), for example, argue in
their state-sponsored study that 'where there is more than one earner in a
family some of what appears to be unemployment is really enjoyment of
leisure or the participation in non-labor market work activities' because one
member – clearly a woman – stays home to collect unemployment
insurance. But even with a very broad definition of such voluntary
unemployment, Green and Cousineau (1976: 110) were able to attribute
only a maximum of 1.1 percentage points of unemployment to these
work-related schemes. Nor is there much evidence that the universal
schemes paid to women in the form of welfare or family allowance deter
people from taking available jobs.

With these cutbacks women are not only losing some of their best-paid jobs but they are also pushed to take on these jobs as unpaid workers in the home or as volunteers in the market (Armstrong, 1984: chapter 6). Just as the wartime subcommittee understood that reducing daycare services after the war would limit women's possibilities for fully participating in the labor force, so too do contemporary policy-makers understand that restricting funding for lunch hour and after-school programs, for services to the elderly and the sick, will limit women's alternatives in the labor market and perhaps send some of them home.

And just as the subcommittee acknowledged women's right to paid employment but offered little means of ensuring this, so too with today's state commitment to equality through affirmative action. Like training programs, even strict affirmative action programs address the terms of competition for what are now scarce jobs rather than the creation of new jobs. The Canadian state seems unwilling, however, to order compliance, preferring instead merely to threaten the embarrassment of disclosure for employers who fail to comply. Such weak policies were supported by the Macdonald Royal Commission, which bowed to pressure from employers and rejected more effective equal pay for work of equal value legislation. The Royal Commission argued that introducing the means for equal pay would reduce jobs. Moreover, 'employers may react by raising job requirements and working conditions may deteriorate since higher wages add to production costs' (quoted in Slotnick, 1985: 9). The emphasis is placed on individual responsibility and skills rather than on collective strategies or on segregation, even though the primacy of such segregation for an understanding of sex inequality has been demonstrated in research reports (Ornstein, 1983). In times of high unemployment, such programs may serve to suggest that women, not jobs, are the problem, pitting women against men without significantly improving the conditions faced by most women who work for pay.

While the state is reducing services and jobs for women and offering a weak form of affirmative action in exchange, it is also moving toward deregulation and privatization. Both strategies are likely to create worse conditions for women. Women constitute the majority of those who work at, and therefore mainly benefit from, minimum wages and standards (Armstrong and Armstrong, 1983: 76–103). If such standards are removed or reduced through deregulation, it is primarily women who will suffer. Privatization may also have a detrimental impact on women. Research by Denton and Hunter (1984) clearly demonstrates that pay differentials between women and men are higher in the private than in the public sector. If state enterprises are privatized, the women who work in them are likely to see their pay reduced.

INTENSIFICATION OF LABOR

During these years, employers' strategies to increase profits have not, however, been limited to calling for state cutbacks, deregulation, privatization and the disciplining of workers. In addition to relocating abroad in order to gain access to cheaper labor and natural resources, they have also been constantly seeking to intensify labor by introducing new technology, by reorganizing the labor process, and by hiring more workers part-time.

Partly in response to women's earlier resistance and the growing inflexibility of their labor force attachment, employers have developed new strategies to intensify labor. The most visible one is the introduction of new technology. Microelectronic technology allows the extension of scientific management techniques to the office, where work and unions have been growing but productivity has not, where mental rather than manual work has been a large component of the labor done, and where skills as well as the difficulty of measuring tasks have given the workers some degree of control over their work. The new technology allows the separation of many office operations into repetitive, easy-to-learn tasks, taking much of the decision-making and skill out of workers' hands. At the same time, it facilitates the quantification of work, making it easy for the employers to measure performance and to control the speed of the work (Armstrong, 1984: chapter 7). Because supervision is done by machines and because jobs are deskilled, employers may even transfer much of the work to private homes or into low-wage zones in other areas and countries (see chapter 8). These strategies, or even the threat of employing them, also increase employers' control by reducing the possibilities for organized resistance.

Less visible than new technology but no less effective in strengthening employers' hands, and perhaps more effective in creating a labor reserve, is the use of part-time employees. Part-time work has become an important vehicle for intensification and the principal means for ensuring that some women, at least, remain available for work at peak periods of demand during the day, week or year. Like women's work in general, part-time work in particular has allowed for a redefinition of full employment. As Maryanne Webber (1985: 85) points out in her Statistics Canada study of hours worked, 'an additional person working part-time is counted on exactly the same basis as an additional full-time worker in spite of the fact that, on average, those employed full-time work more than twice as many hours as part-time workers'. When the state counts job creation, it typically fails to distinguish full-year or full-week jobs from short-term or part-time ones. State statistics on the percentages of women participating in the labor force, or employed, rarely indicate in published analyses the percentage – less than 36 per cent for 1985 – employed full-time (calculated from Statistics Canada, *The Labour Force*, December 1985).

This erosion, and the redefinition of full employment to include any work for pay, no matter how brief, were made possible by the movement of women into the market and the accompanying shift of employment to the tertiary sector. Much of the work in the service and trade industries is easily fragmented by tasks and divided into short-time slots. Periods of high demand vary over the day or year. And many jobs require little formal on-the-job training, especially when performed by women who have often acquired the necessary skills early in life (see Bellew, 1982/83). Employed for only short periods of time, women can work at speeds or under conditions which would otherwise be intolerable. Not surprisingly, part-time workers are also more productive, primarily because high output with few errors is more possible for limited stretches of time (see Weeks, 1977; Bayefsky, 1985). And they are cheaper and getting even cheaper relative to other workers, because they are paid only while they work, because the state and collective agreements require that only a few receive fringe benefits or promotion, because equal pay legislation has little effect, and because fewer of them are unionized and they are seldom paid overtime (see Canadian Advisory Council on the Status of Women, 1982; National Union of Provincial Government Employees, 1982; Tremblay, 1985). Moreover, computers which are within the price-range of most employers can dramatically reduce the costs of hiring part-time employees, since computers can be used to organize and simplify pay, hiring and scheduling.

CONCLUSION

The rising labor force participation rates of women that have accompanied the restructuring of domestic and wage labor have provided a basis for redefining full employment and redirecting policy initiatives. At the same time, the restructuring of the labor force and rising unemployment have limited resistance. Although most households in Canada now have at least two members in the labor force (Statistics Canada, 1984: 8), primarily because they need the income (Armstrong and Armstrong, 1984: 168-78), women's paid work has been used as a justification for reducing both employment-related and universal state programs. As well, rising unemployment levels have been blamed on women and used to define as acceptable higher and higher levels of unemployment, both in the aggregate and for women. While a limited amount of male unemployment is still considered involuntary and therefore requiring state intervention, women's unemployment is recognized as involuntary mainly on the basis of their lack of skill, their failure to invest in their own human capital. Formally committed to the equal access of women to limited jobs, the state has nevertheless been introducing programs to send women and their work into the home or into volunteer jobs uneasily connected to the labor force. Meanwhile, women's labor has provided a major means of intensifying labor, especially through their employment as part-time workers. But the state has defined this work, too, as mainly voluntary. As a result of all such changes, women's work has been integrated into standard economic theory, but used to provide a justification of and a means for increasing the labor reserve and making profits the priority.

NOTES

We would like to thank Carl Cuneo and Elisabeth Hagen for their careful and helpful comments, some of which we acted upon. Once again, our thanks go to Irene Christie for her patience and skill at transforming a confusing mess into a clean typescript. This research was supported in part by the Social Sciences and Humanities Research Council of Canada under grant no. 482-83-0002.

REFERENCES

Archibald, K. (1970) *Sex and the Public Sector* (Ottawa: Queen's Printer).

Armstrong, H. (1977) 'The labour force and state workers in Canada', in L.V. Panitch (ed.), *The Canadian State: Political Economy and Political Power* (Toronto: University of Toronto Press).

Armstrong, H. (1979) 'Job creation and unemployment in post-war Canada', in R. M. Novick (ed.), *Full Employment: Social Questions for Public Policy* (Toronto: Social Planning Council of Metropolitan Toronto).

Armstrong, P. (1979) 'Women and unemployment', in R. M. Novick (ed.), *Full Employment: Social Questions for Public Policy* (Toronto: Social Planning Council of Metropolitan Toronto).

Armstrong, P. (1980) 'UIC: Reform or revolution', *Perception* 3, 4 (March/April).

Armstrong, P. (1984) *Labour Pains: Women's Work in Crisis* (Toronto: The Women's Press).

Armstrong, P. and H. Armstrong (1983) *A Working Majority: What Women Must Do For Pay* (Ottawa: Supply and Services Canada for the Canadian Advisory Council on the Status of Women).

Armstrong, P. and H. Armstrong (1984) *The Double Ghetto: Canadian Women and Their Segregated Work*, revised edition (Toronto: McClelland and Stewart).

Bayefsky, E. (1985) 'Part-time work: Patterns of implementation', in E. D. Pask, K. E. Mahoney and C. A. Brown (eds), *Women, the Law and the Economy* (Toronto: Butterworths).

Bellew, M. (1982/83) 'A study into part-time work in the Maritimes', *Communiqué*, The Institute for the Study of Women, Mount St Vincent University (Winter).

Calvert, J. (1984) *Government, Limited: The Corporate Takeover of the Public Sector in Canada* (Ottawa: Canadian Centre for Policy Alternatives).

Canada, Advisory Committee on Reconstruction (1944) *Post-War Problems of*

Women: Final Report of the Subcommittee (Ottawa: King's Printer).

Canada, Dominion Bureau of Statistics (1966) *Census of Canada. Labour Force. Occupation and Industry Trends*, Cat. no. 18–3 – 1966 (Ottawa: Trade and Commerce).

Canada, Minister of Reconstruction (1945) *White Paper on Employment and Income* (Ottawa: King's Printer).

Canadian Advisory Council on the Status of Women (1982) 'Part-Time Work. Part-Time Rights. A Brief Presented to the Commission of Inquiry into Part-Time Work' (Ottawa: Author).

Canadian Tax Foundation (1972) *The National Finances, 1972–73* (Toronto: Author).

Canadian Union of Public Employees (1985) 'Scapegoating the public sector', in D. Drache and D. Cameron (eds), *The Other Macdonald Report* (Toronto: Lorimer).

Cuneo, C. J. (1979) 'State, class and reserve labour: The case of the 1941 Canadian Unemployment Insurance Act', *The Canadian Review of Sociology and Anthropology*, 16 (2).

Cuneo, C. J. (1985) 'Have women become more proletarianized than men?', *The Canadian Review of Sociology and Anthropology*, 22 (4).

Denton, M. A. and A. A. Hunter (1984) 'Equality in the workplace. Economic sectors and gender discrimination in Canada: A critique and test of Black and Walker . . . and some new evidence' (Ottawa: Supply and Services Canada for Women's Bureau, Labour Canada).

Drache, D. and D. Cameron (eds) (1985) *The Other Macdonald Report* (Toronto: Lorimer).

Duboff, W. (1977) 'Full employment: The history of a receding target', *Politics and Society*, 7(1).

Dulude, L. (1985) 'Fringe benefits and the female workforce', in Economic Council of Canada, *Towards Equity*, Proceedings of a Colloquium on the Economic Status of Women in the Labour Force, November 1984 (Ottawa: Supply and Services Canada).

Economic Council of Canada (1964) *Economic Goals for Canada to 1970: First Annual Review* (Ottawa: Queen's Printer).

Economic Council of Canada (1976) *People and Jobs: A Study of the Canadian Labour Market* (Ottawa: Information Canada)

Employment and Immigration Canada (1981) *Labour Market Development in the 1980s* (Ottawa: Supply and Services Canada).

Employment and Immigration Canada (n.d. [1983]) 'Notes prepared in response to a newsletter from the National Action Committee [on the Status of Women]'.

Finkel, A. (1979) *Business and Social Reform in the Thirties* (Toronto: Lorimer).

Fox, B. J. and J. Fox (1983) 'Effects of women's employment on wages', *The Canadian Journal of Sociology*, 8, 3 (Summer).

Green, C. and J. M. Cousineau (1976) *Unemployment in Canada* (Ottawa: Supply and Services Canada).

Keynes, J. M. (1936) *The General Theory of Employment, Interest, and Money* (New York: Harcourt, Brace).

Labour Canada (1983) *Part-Time Work in Canada*, Report of the Commission of Inquiry into Part-Time Work, Wallace Commission (Ottawa: Supply and

Services Canada).

Labour Canada (1986) *Women in the Labour Force, 1985–1986 Edition* (Ottawa: Supply and Services Canada).

MacLeod, N. and K. Horner (1980) 'Analyzing post-war changes in Canadian income distribution', in *Reflections on Canadian Income*, Economic Council of Canada (Ottawa: Supply and Services Canada).

Marsh, L. (1939) 'The mobility of labour in relation to unemployment', Offprint of Papers and Proceedings of the Canadian Political Science Association.

Marsh, L. (1975) *Report on Social Security for Canada*, first published 1943 (Toronto: University of Toronto Press).

Nakamura, A., M. Makamura and D. Cullen in collaboration with D. Grant and H. Orcutt (1979) *Employment and Earnings of Married Females* (Ottawa: Statistics Canada).

National Council of Welfare (1985) *Poverty Profile 1985* (Ottawa: Author).

Ornstein, M. (1983) 'Equality in the workplace. Accounting for gender differentials in job income in Canada: Results from a 1981 Survey' (Ottawa: Supply and Services Canada for the Women's Bureau, Labour Canada).

Pryor, E. (1984) *Canadian Husband–Wife Families: Labour Force Participation and Income Trends* (Ottawa: Supply and Services Canada).

Rashid, A. (1986) 'Labour market activities of high income families', *The Labour Force*, July, cat. no. 71–001 (Ottawa: Supply and Services Canada).

Ryan, W. (1971) *Blaming the Victim* (Toronto: Random House).

Slotnick, L. (1985) 'Steps toward equal pay raise fears of job loss', *The Globe and Mail* (9 September).

Statistics Canada, *The Labour Force*, various issues, cat. no. 71–001 (Ottawa: Supply and Services Canada).

Statistics Canada (1984) *Canadian Statistical Review, October,* cat. no. 11–003E (Ottawa: Supply and Services Canada).

Statistics Canada (1984) *Canadian Husband–Wife Families: Labour Force Participation and Income Trends*, cat. no. 8–3100–543 (Ottawa: Supply and Services Canada).

Statistics Canada (1984) *Labour Force Annual Averages*, cat. no. 71–529 (Ottawa: Supply and Services Canada).

Statistics Canada (1985) *Women in Canada: A Statistical Profile*, cat. no. 9–0503E (Ottawa: Supply and Services Canada).

Tremblay, F. (1985) 'La politique du salaire minimum: que se passe-t-il?', *Bulletin de l'Association d'Economie Politique* 6 (2 December).

Webber, M. (1985) 'Total hours worked in Canada: 1976 to 1984', in *The Labour Force*, March, cat. no. 71–001, (Ottawa: Supply and Services Canada).

Weeks, W. (1977) *Part-Time Work in Canada: A Study of Ideology and the Implications for Women*, MA Thesis (Sociology), McMaster University, Hamilton.

White, J. (1980) *Women and Unions* (Ottawa: Supply and Services Canada for the Canadian Advisory Council on the Status of Women).

White, J. (1983) *Women and Part-Time Work* (Ottawa: Supply and Services Canada for the Canadian Advisory Council of the Status of Women).

White, J. (1985) 'Part-time work: Ideal or no deal?', in E. D. Pask, K. E. Mahoney and A. Brown (eds) *Women, the Law and the Economy* (Toronto: Butterworths).

5

Recession and Exploitation

British Women in a Changing Workplace, 1979–85

Jane Humphries and Jill Rubery

Women's domestic circumstances influence the terms and conditions under which they are able and willing to offer themselves for paid work, and simultaneously impact directly, although not always rationally, on employers' demand. Not surprisingly therefore women constitute a distinct segment of the labor force. Analysts frequently hypothesize that women act as a labor reserve, mobilized according to employers' need. According to this *buffer hypothesis*, relative female employment varies with pressures in the labor market associated with cyclical and secular economic trends. Studies abound which identify channels in addition to the market mechanism of rising wages, whereby labor shortages characteristic of booms and wartime are accommodated by variation in female participation. Crucial here are *enabling measures* taken by both employers and the state which help women to integrate their domestic responsibilities with wage labor, either by a reorganization of employment or by a substitution of market goods or state services for unpaid work in the home. Maneuvers of this kind do not necessarily involve conscious intent on the part of employers or the state. The former may simply respond to recruitment difficulties by offering part-time work and on finding this a successful ploy, decide to pursue it more aggressively. Policy-makers may be subject to political pressures not intended to facilitate increased female participation though this may be their consequence: rising public-sector revenues during booms, for example, might allow demands for the extension of nursery education prompted by educational or egalitarian motives to be met.

It also follows from the buffer hypothesis that female participation can be dampened down in periods of surplus labor not only via declining wages or job opportunities but also by *disabling measures*: changes in firms' and the state's behavior which make it more difficult for women to combine paid work and domestic family responsibilities. Again historical analyses of recessions and postwar demobilizations document typical disabling maneuvers.

If female labor is accurately conceptualized as a flexible reserve, then analysis of historical trends would show procyclical variation in participation rates and wages, as well as swings between enabling and disabling policies. But there are two complications. First, the family circumstances of women, and therefore the effects which enabling measures have to overcome, are not fixed. They change both exogenously and as a result of enabling measures. Once under way changes may not readily be reversed (Humphries and Rubery, 1984; Humphries, 1988).

Second, women do not constitute only a flexible labor reserve. Additional, if not necessarily competing, models of women's labor market experience exist (Rubery, 1988). The *segmentation hypothesis* proposes that supply-side characteristics of women workers interact with the different needs of employers to produce a distribution of women workers across industries and occupations which differs from that of men. In addition, female-intensive jobs have been remarkably resilient in the face of the economic restructuring in many advanced industrial economies in recent years. This pattern seems to suggest that the volatility of female employment and the impact of swings in enabling and disabling measures are both reduced by the segmentation of female employment.

A third conceptualization, the *substitution hypothesis*, suggests that the relative cheapness of female labor under certain circumstances promotes the replacement of men by women. In the British case, as we shall see, women's availability to work less than full-time hours, and thus earn lower weekly wages, also proves attractive to employers. However, the circumstances under which such substitution is likely are controversial (Rubery and Tarling, 1982): some authors argue that it will be more common in the downswing, when employers are pressed to cut costs (Humphries, 1983), while others claim that, to the extent that substitution requires a restructuring of the labor process and facilitating investment, it is more likely to occur in the upswing (Dex and Perry, 1984). If substitution takes place in recession the resulting intensified use of female labor occurs without the mediation of substantive enabling measures. Indeed, it frequently occurs in the context of both disabling changes by firms and the state and stagnant or even falling family income. Under these circumstances substitution must involve an increase in the expenditure of women's total labor time relative to their standard of living. Though it is impossible to measure this precisely it can be described as an increase in exploitation.

The fundamental supply-side characteristic that distinguishes women workers – namely their primary responsibility for social reproduction – changes only slowly if at all. However, the burden of this responsibility is affected by changes in family structure such as fewer children, more marital breakup and therefore more single parents, and more elderly dependents due to an aging population. In the 1960s and 1970s, reduced fertility and greater public responsibility for both children and the elderly, relieved some of the pressures of their caring roles for many women. But simultaneously a subgroup with relatively unrelieved caring responsibilities – that is, single parents with dependent children – increased disproportionately, from 2 per cent of all families in the early 1960s to 4 per cent by the late 1970s. Some eight-ninths of single parents in Britain are women (Hansard, 23 July 1981). But important though these changes are, they have only gradual effects on women's labor market behavior. A more dramatic short-run influence is the impact of general economic conditions and intertwined with this, state social policy.

In what follows we apply these concepts to the British economy in the 1979–85 period: years of disastrous economic decline, when a simplistic interpretation would predict disabling measures, falling relative wages and a decline in relative employment. Disabling measures are readily identified. But this is not the whole story. As we shall see, each of the hypotheses presented above accurately describes the recent experience of some *subgroup* of British women. In the particular context of the 1980s, the disabling measures have impacted on the terms and conditions of women's work rather than on the female participation rate.

THE BRITISH CONTEXT

Unemployment has more than doubled since 1979. Most of those who join the ranks of the unemployed experience a sharp drop in their living standards, and for the long-term unemployed, the hardship is intense. By the mid-1980s, over one million people had been unemployed for over a year.

The recession has also affected the labor market in other ways. Pay differentials have widened markedly. Low-paid manual workers fortunate enough to remain in employment have suffered a deterioration in their relative pay: in 1979 the lowest-paid 10 per cent of male earners earned 66.8 per cent of the national average, but by 1982 their earnings had fallen to 64.1 per cent. At the same time, the highest-paid 10 per cent saw their earnings rise from 157.9 per cent of the average to 169.7 per cent. 'It is the poor who have borne the brunt of the recession' (Mack and Lansley, 1985: 5).

The government has done little to obviate these trends. Indeed, when Mrs Thatcher came to power in May 1979, she was committed to a radical change in the role of government. All previous postwar governments had tried, more or less, to use taxes and benefits to offset increases in inequality in income distribution originating in the labor market. In contrast, the Thatcher administration was committed to 'rolling back' the frontiers of the state. Although the consequent changes have been less radical than heralded, they have nevertheless fuelled the trend toward a more unequal society. In the latest official statistics on the distribution of income, the mark of the Conservative government is clear: the share of after-tax income received by the bottom 20 per cent declined from 7.4 per cent in 1976 to 6.9 per cent in 1983, while the share of the top 20 per cent increased from 37.9 per cent to 39.3 per cent (Central Statistical Office, 1986; for other evidence on increasing inequality, see Mack and Lansley, 1985).

Changes in taxation and social security programs have contributed to these trends. Since 1979, the average level of taxes (income tax and national insurance) on income has increased, with the incremental burden falling disproportionately on the poor. According to Mack and Lansley, between 1979 and 1984, the well-off and the rich gained about £2600 millions. At the same time, there have been changes in income maintenance programs which have made those dependent on benefits poorer. In 1980, the individual unemployment benefit was cut; in 1982 it was taxed. Earnings-related supplements for all short-term benefits – unemployment and sickness benefits, maternity and widow's allowance – were abolished as of April 1981. In addition, the statutory link between increases in long-term benefits, such as pensions, and the rate of growth in earnings were abolished; henceforth, the former were increased in line with price inflation only. Over the same period inflation has been allowed to erode the real value of child benefit.

The coverage of social security benefits has also been restricted. For example, people who quit jobs have to wait longer before they can claim unemployment benefits, and mothers cannot register as unemployed, and therefore collect benefits, unless they can demonstrate that they have childcare arrangements in hand. Access to housing benefits has also been reduced. Families on unemployment benefits lost about £4.65 per week in real terms between 1979 and 1984.

Despite the cuts in levels and coverage of benefits, as unemployment continued to rise and governmental provision of subsidized housing and accommodation for the elderly continued to decline, the number of people dependent on social security – and particularly on means-tested benefits – continued to increase (Walker, 1988). Government expenditure rose in its wake. Consequently, as announced in the 1985 White Paper, *Reform of Social Security, Programme for Action* (Cmnd 9691, 1985), and published in the Social Security Bill (1986), further changes were advertised. The intent continued to be to economize while simultaneously changing Britain 'from a dependent to a self-reliant society'.[1] While collective responsibility and mutual aid have been denigrated as dependence, survival strategies based on the family, the marketplace and the individual have been elevated as self-reliance (Erskine, 1986).

According to economic theory, this (unequally experienced) squeeze on the living standards of British families could have two opposing effects on the labor market behavior of the women in those families. On the one hand, rising unemployment signals to women that labor market conditions are tight and therefore 'discourages' them from looking for work or trying to convert part-time jobs into full-time ones. This reasoning is implicit in the buffer hypothesis. On the other hand, falling real incomes raises the marginal value of income and stimulates women to seek jobs and work longer hours. This is the response predicted by the substitution hypothesis.[2]

The British experience from 1979 to 1985 does not suggest that women have been disproportionately shed either from employment or from the labor force; there is evidence in aggregate statistics that substitution of female labor has been occurring. But caution has to be taken in interpreting these findings. As we shall see, this increase in the female share of employment has involved a growth in part-time relative to full-time work and is not associated with greater homogeneity between the male and female labor forces. Further, because this relative expansion of women's paid work has been accompanied by a swing to a disabling stance on the part of the state, it involves increased exploitation as described above. Indeed, we shall argue that the form that disabling measures have taken has had a major, if unintended, impact on the responses of both employers and women to the recession and, therefore, to the pattern of use and terms and conditions of women's work. The next section looks generally at the experience of women workers in the recession. The superficially optimistic evidence that more women are working is countered in the following sections, which look in more detail at the disabling measures of the state, the relative expansion of part-time work, and the growth of homeworking.

WOMEN'S LABOR MARKET EXPERIENCE

As can be seen from table 5.1, while male employees in employment have declined more or less continuously since 1973, and quite dramatically after 1979 (column I), the number of female employees in employment increased from 1972–9, with a small interruption in 1976, declined from 1979–83, though much less dramatically than male employees, and then increased again from 1983 (column II). In terms of trends, then, the series for women looks relatively robust. The same conclusion can be drawn from column III. Women's employment as a share of total employment climbs continuously from 1971, including the recession years, 1979–85. Thus, in the aggregate, at least, it looks like women, rather than bearing the brunt of the recession, were disproportionately retained and hired.[3]

The relative impact of unemployment on men and women is difficult to

TABLE 5.1 *Trends in men and women's employment and unemployment 1971–1984 (Great Britain)*

	Employees in employment (June)						Unemployment[a] (annual averages)	
	Males	All females	Females as % of total	Female full-time employees	Female part-time employees	% share of part-timers in all female employees	Percentage of male labour force unemployed	Percentage of female labour force unemployed
	1971=100	1971=100		1971=100	1971=100			
1971	100	100	38.0	100	100	33.5	4.5	1.2
1972	99.2	101.3	38.5	99.7	104.4	34.5	5.0	1.5
1973	100.4	105.8	39.2	101.4	114.7	36.3	3.5	1.0
1974	99.6	108.6	40.1	100.8	124.1	38.3	3.6	1.0
1975	98.6	109.1	40.4	99.2	128.8	39.6	5.4	1.9
1976	97.6	108.9	40.6	98.2	130.1	40.1	7.0	3.1
1977	97.4	110.6	40.9	99.4	131.2	40.0	7.3	3.7
1978	97.6	111.5	41.2	100.3	133.8	40.2	7.0	3.8
1979	98.2	115.0	41.8	102.2	140.4	40.9	6.5	3.7
1980	97.0	114.8	42.0	100.6	142.9	41.7	8.1	4.7
1981	91.5	110.7	42.6	96.7	138.4	41.9	12.7	6.7
1982	88.9	109.0	42.9	95.1	136.6	42.0	14.8	7.8
1983	87.0	108.0	43.2	93.7	136.4	42.3	15.5	8.8
1984	86.5	110.7	43.9	95.7	140.4	42.5	15.5	9.3
1985	87.0	113.0	44.3	97.9	143.0	42.4	15.9	9.9
1986	86.5	114.8	44.8	99.3	145.5	42.5		

Source: Department of Employment Gazette, January 1987; Census of Employment, and historical Supplement 1 & 2, August 84, April 85 (Rubery, 1988:101).

[a] Series based on new basis for unemployment figures introduced in 1982, that is benefit claimants, not those registered for work. Figures prior to 1982 have been adjusted on the basis of estimates to provide a continuous series, and should be treated with caution. The 1983 and 1984 figures for men have been further affected by the change in regulations which did not require men over 60 to register at an unemployment benefit office.

assess because of changes in the definition of unemployment related to eligibility conditions for unemployment benefit. These eligibility conditions are probably primarily responsible for women's historically low unemployment rates *and* for the relative rise in female unemployment since the mid-1970s. There is, moreover, little evidence that women have formed a flexible labor reserve, even within individual industries. Although studies have found women's employment significantly more volatile than total employment within some parts of manufacturing, analysis at a more disaggregated level suggests that even this limited evidence of a flexible reserve mechanism arises more from the concentration of women in cyclically volatile industries than from a tendency to displace women within individual firms (Rubery and Tarling, 1988). On the other hand, there is also no evidence that women are particularly sheltered from the recession because of their concentration in jobs which are treated as fixed overheads, independent of the level of output. There were even fewer industries where the rate of change of women's employment was significantly less than that of total employment (even after taking account of trend changes in the female employment share).

The apparent robustness of the trends in women's employment seems matched by gains in relative pay secured by women in the mid-1970s under the impact of the Equal Pay Act and the periodic application of income policies which tended to narrow pay differentials (Zabalza and Tzannatos, 1985). This finding is all the more remarkable because, as suggested above, restructuring of the earnings distribution has led to a widening of differentials for other disadvantaged groups.

However, further analysis shows that evidence of resilience in women's employment and pay must be qualified. Women's employment growth has been very uneven, with shares of employment in manufacturing declining over a long period. More importantly, if we break down women's employment into part- and full-time, the conclusion that women have fared relatively well in the recession is further eroded. As table 5.1 shows, although full-time employment remained fairly constant between 1971 and 1979, it declined significantly in the early 1980s, and only regained its previous level in 1986 (column IV). It is the growth in female part-time work (column V) which has driven up the aggregate series (column III). This growth in part-time work has repercussions on women's relative earnings. While the ratio of female to male full-time earnings has remained stable, the share of women in part-time jobs, which are lower-paid than full-time jobs on both an hourly and a weekly basis, has increased and the overall effect is a continued wage gap (chapter 2: table 2.6, p.26).

We shall show in the next section that the relative expansion of female part-time work is not only related to the particular form that disabling changes in social service provision have taken, but is also indirectly promoted by other aspects of recent government policy.

THE DISABLING STANCE OF THE STATE

The disabling stance of the state has involved both a direct attack on women's right to paid work and an indirect, perhaps more damaging, assault on their ability to perform wage labor through the selective withdrawal of services which have hitherto supported wage-earning wives and mothers. Both attacks are consistent with the government's aim to reduce the role of the state and make individuals and families more self-reliant, and with the practical corollaries of this grand design: privatization, cuts in government spending and the liberalization of the market, including the labor market.

The direct attack on women's right to paid work has been rationalized and legitimated by the idealization and reification of the family and women's domestic role which is at the heart of the Conservative government's emphasis 'on replacing state provision with greater personal responsibility and independence' (*Sunday Times*, 20 February 1983). Only if the family is an organic and essential human structure, as certain Conservative ideologues have contended, can it more naturally, efficiently and humanely assume the responsibilities shed by a retreating state (Humphries, 1983). On the other hand if, for example, substantial numbers of women are unable, because of marriage breakdown or male unemployment, to rely on male wages for the support of themselves and their children, social policy designed to promote the male breadwinner family is likely to be ineffective or worse.

Although much of Tory family policy has remained rhetorical, where it has merged with labor market policy, jibes such as that by the then-Minister of Social Services, that 'I don't think mothers have the same right to work as fathers. If the Good Lord had intended us to have equal rights to go out to work, He wouldn't have created men and women' have accompanied legislative changes which directly discourage married women from working. The right to take maternity leave was eroded by the 1980 Employment Protection Act, a serious loss given the role that re-entry plays in the downgrading of women's employment (see below). Unemployment benefit is only paid to people who are 'available for work', and since 1982 part of the availability test has included proof that arrangements have been made for the care of children and dependents. This is another serious blow to women, in view of the very limited non-familial childcare available, let alone affordable, in Britain (see Walker, 1988; Greater London Council, 1985).

Apart from the Equal Value Amendment which was adopted in January 1984 at the insistence of the European Parliament, Mrs Thatcher has also declined to strengthen the anti-sex discrimination laws, contending that she is 'absolutely satisfied that there is nothing more you can do by changing the law to do away with discrimination. After all, I don't think there's been a great deal of discrimination against women for years' (Thames Television, 1 January, 1981).

Moreover, the government's moves to liberalize the labor market have selective implications for women workers. The exclusion of workers under 21 years of age from the purview of Wages Councils, which have historically regulated the wages and conditions in certain low-paid industries, while ostensibly aimed at expanding employment by preventing workers from pricing themselves out of jobs, has potentially serious consequences for the pay, conditions, and security of older women workers. The latter remain protected by Wages Council legislation and are bound to appear more costly to employers compared with the under-21s.

Important though such measures have been, however, they have not had such widespread or serious effects on women's ability to go out to work as have the cutbacks in government spending that are, as explained above, a keystone of government policy. As Walker has shown, cuts in government expenditure 'have not been evenly applied across the whole spectrum of government expenditure . . . [but] . . . have fallen primarily in the areas of social consumption, that is those areas concerned with the reproduction of labour power, to which women in their role as primary domestic labour, have a specific relation' (Walker, 1988: 231). Expenditure on housing and education, including school meals and nursery provision, has been cut while expenditure on health and personal social services has failed to keep pace with the rapidly growing demands on them.

THE RISE AND RISE OF PART-TIME WORK

Part-time work has been increasing throughout the postwar period. The majority of part-timers are women (Robinson and Wallace, 1984). The feminization of part-time work results from both supply- and demand-side pressures, although the way in which these forces interact and their implications have differed over time.

Prior to the mid-1970s, the growth in part-time employment related to shortages of full-time workers, particularly in periods of boom and in expanding sectors (Mallier and Rosser, 1979). Part-time employees provided managers with ways of adjusting their labor forces to the short-run variations in demand (daily or weekly) characteristic of the growing service sector, and of coping flexibly with business cycle upswings in manufacturing (Robertson and Briggs, 1979; Dex and Perry, 1984). Simultaneously tight labor markets required recruitment of women, if vacancies were to be filled. In addition, many of the expanding services already had a tradition of employing women. Also in keeping with the buffer hypothesis, part-time jobs were used in these relatively prosperous years as a supplement to scarce full-time labor, and moved in the same rhythm as the latter (Rubery and Tarling, 1988).

On the supply side, although by 1980, as the *Women and Employment* survey revealed, most women had a positive attitude to paid work, they rarely saw it as a central life interest. Rather, they balanced work with domestic demands and it took a secondary role in most women's lives (Martin and Roberts, 1984). Part-time work reflected these attitudes. Thus, while marital status had no effect on whether or not a woman worked, it was an important determinant of whether a woman worked full-time or part-time. Married women, with or without children, were significantly more likely to work part-time than non-married women, with or without children, when other factors are held constant (Martin and Roberts, 1984: 208; Ballard, 1984).

But, even though part-time work may appear to result from women's *choice*, we must also emphasize the constraints involved. While the correlation between marital status and hours of work reflected the attitudes of married women to work, as the *Women and Employment* survey and other sources showed, the hours and scheduling of work was crucial in enabling women to combine paid employment with their domestic responsibilities. Few working women with young children worked full-time, and patterns of work varied systematically with the ages of dependent children. Night and evening work was most common among women with children under five, whereas once the youngest child was at school, patterns which fit in with school hours became much more common, particularly mornings, short days (a.m.) and midday working, which all finished before the end of the school day.

Significantly fewer women working part-time had to make childcare arrangements than full-timers, being able, for the shorter periods involved, to rely on fathers, grandmothers and friends (Ballard, 1984: 412). The expense and paucity of institutional childcare in Britain makes its use a major disincentive to women seeking paid employment, and for this reason alone, the availability of part-time work has been crucial in facilitating British women's increased lifetime work experience by enabling them to combine caring for young children with paid employment (Walker, 1988).

Although part-time work could more readily be organized around domestic responsibilites, a close look at the typical part-timer's schedule suggests that this accommodation was not easy. In 1980, the majority of part-time workers worked more than 16 hours a week while only 10 per cent (4 per cent of all women workers) worked less than eight hours a week. For the great majority, too, a five-day working week was the norm. So, part-timers spend the same amount of time as full-time workers getting to and from work, as there is not evidence that part-timers systematically work closer to home. They also have to get ready for work just as often.

Part-time work is also financially disadvantageous. The *Women and Employment* survey confirmed existing evidence from the Department of

Employment's *New Earnings* survey demonstrating that part-timers had lower *hourly* earnings than full-time workers. Fifty-four per cent earned less than £1.50 an hour in 1980, compared with 30 per cent of full-time workers, a differential largely due to the concentration of part-timers in relatively poorly-paid occupational groups (Martin and Roberts, 1984: 205).

In addition, although all employees have a number of statutory rights which are not dependent on the number of hours worked per week, much employment protection legislation applies only to employees working 16 hours a week or more, and is conditional on employees having worked for their employer for a qualifying period of two years. Currently these provisions also apply to people working less than 16 but more than eight hours per week who have worked for their employer for five years or more. Evidence of the usual number of hours and length of service from the *Women and Employment* survey suggests that 67 per cent of full-time employees have protection compared to 60 per cent of part-timers. Only 10 per cent of part-timers were not covered because they worked less than eight hours a week, but 19 per cent were not covered because they did not have five years' continuous service with the same employer. Unless replaced by effective trade union organization, this diminished protection means that many part-timers are vulnerable to unfair dismissal and cannot qualify for many basic statutory rights.

There is also an important financial incentive for employers to make wider use of part-time workers on low weekly hours. Currently, if wages can be kept below £38 per week, employers stand to gain on labor costs because they do not have to pay any national insurance contribution on the wage. If earnings are higher than £38 weekly, then national insurance must be paid.

These factors are crucial in understanding the continued upward trend in part-time employment in Britain in the 1980s. The upsurge starting in 1983 is patently *not* an exigency in the face of shortages of full-time workers; nor have part-time workers been a source of supplementary labor to cope with strengthening demand. In the early 1970s there was evidence within manufacturing of increasing use of part-time female labor in the face of declining female and male full-time employment. However, since then, and including the most recent period, part-time employment has tended to rise or fall along with full-time female and full-time male employment in the same industry, so that at most, substitution has occurred through a relatively faster rate of increase or slower rate of decrease and not through labor displacement (Rubery and Tarling, 1988). Some evidence supporting the hypothesis that part-time work is being substituted for full-time does exist at the micro-level: for example, in Robinson and Wallace's study in which managers were shown to be expanding part-time work in the face of lists of women seeking full-time employment and part-time employees wishing to transfer to permanent full-time work (1984: 397).

However, whether or not part-time work involves direct substitution for full-time work, it is clear that the continued expansion of part-time working is based on employer preference for it as an organizational form, and not because it facilitates the utilization of female labor supplies. As Robinson and Wallace put it, 'employers' preferences for part-time rather than full-time labour were essential to the adoption of cost-effective employment policies dictated by pressures to improve efficiency in highly competitive conditions' (1984: 396). The contribution of part-time work to such policies varies by sector; in manufacturing it allows the employer to maximize the utilization of capital equipment without incurring premium rates for overtime or shift working; in services it gives greater freedom to managers to fine-tune manpower to patterns in operational or customer requirement, even if this means using labor intensively for very short periods of time.

The savings in terms of the avoidance of national insurance payments are relevant in all sectors. Their pursuit is perhaps most graphically illustrated by developments in the public sector. The cost-cutting privatization of ancillary services, such as cleaning, laundry and catering, has been accompanied by a substitution of part-time private contract workers for full-time (or fuller time) public-sector employees. It is accepted that one source of the economies generated by privatization is that the reduced hours of contract as compared with in-house workers enable the contractor to avoid national insurance payments (Coyle, 1985; Greater London Council, 1985; Walker, 1988). As the Civil Servants Union put it:

> It is not hard for contract cleaning companies to keep wages below this level . . . (viz. £38 per week) . . . the method is simple and involves manipulating the hours of individual cleaners to keep the cleaners' wages down. This can be done by halving the hours worked by each cleaner, for example, by splitting shifts and using two separate groups of workers to do each part of the work, with a separate morning and evening shift. It can also be done by halving the cleaners' hours and doubling the workload or 'shift'. Done this way the method is perfectly legal. (quoted in Greater London Council, 1985: 449)

The substitution hypothesis acquires a new dimension in this context, for in Britain it is not that the employers have tried to cut wage costs by the substitution of women for men directly, but that lacunae in the coverage of protective employment legislation, uneven patterns of demand, favorable fiscal arrangements, and encouraging developments in technology have attached significant economies to the use of part-time work. In practice, therefore, the expansion in the number of females employed has been brought about not only by substituting female for male labor-hours at the aggregate level, but by the sharing out of female labor-hours over an increasing number of women. This process is exacerbated not only by the increasing share of female part-timers but also by the trend decline in hours worked by part-timers (Rubery and Tarling, 1988). Remember that in Britain student labor is only seasonally available and male part-timers uncommon compared with women whose domestic circumstances make them captives in this segment of the labor market.

As the medium of substitution, the relative expansion of part-time work has another source. Simultaneously, technological change is very much in its favor (Blandy, 1984). In contrast, hitherto it has been argued that the expensive restructuring of the labor process associated with the substitution of women for men inhibited the pursuit of this strategy in the downswing (Blandy, 1984: 3).

Nor has the recession left the supply conditions of women workers untouched. The additional domestic labor imposed upon women by the alterations in government policies in conjunction with the greater importance of women's earnings, must have left many women increasingly desperate for some earnings while simultaneously increasingly unable to work full-time.

HOMEWORKING

Another significant, though quantitatively less important, trend is the increased number of women working at home. Table 5.2 provides estimates of numbers of homeworkers between the late 1960s and the early 1970s. The last two surveys were prompted by concern in political circles that homeworking was increasing.[4]

Although comparisons between surveys carried out at different times

TABLE 5.2 *Numbers of homeworkers*

Author	Date	Area	Estimates	
			Broad	*Narrow*
Poverty Survey (Townsend, 1979)	1968–9	UK	1,100,000	430,000
DOE[a] (Hakim, 1980)	1980	UK		200–400,000
WIRS [b] (Hakim and Field, 1984)	1980	GB	111,000 outworkers +281,000 freelance	
Homeworkers Survey (Hakim, 1984)	1981	England & Wales	1,680,000	660,000

[a] Department of Employment.
[b] Workplace Industrial Relations Survey.
Source: Hakim, 1984.

and for different purposes, using different definitions and geographic bases, are problematic (Cragg and Dawson, 1981; Rubery and Wilkinson, 1981; Hakim and Dennis, 1982; Leighton, 1983; Low Pay Unit, 1984), Hakim's evaluation is convincing: 'There is clear evidence here of an increase in home-based work over the last 12 years' (Hakim, 1984: 9). On the broadest definition, Townsend (1979) found 1.1 million home-based workers in 1968–9 in the United Kingdom. The 1971 Population Census identified 1.5 million home-based workers in Great Britain, about 6 per cent of the labor force. The upper bound of 1.68 million home-based workers derived from the homeworking survey, obtained from supplementary interviews to the Spring 1981 Labor Force Survey, is for England and Wales only, and it represents just over 7 per cent of the labor force (ibid.). Unfortunately, it is not possible to isolate the particular group of home-based workers who are our concern – that is, women working at home usually for a single employer – from either the Townsend study or the 1981 homeworkers survey. However, the evidence that the numbers of homeworkers have increased suggests that an increase has also been occurring in our particular narrowly-defined category.

The 1981 survey also covered the industrial distribution of home-based workers. The most startling results here concerned the proportion of homeworkers engaged in manufacturing activities. The survey indicated that only 72,300 people were engaged in manufacturing homework; if the focus is restricted to people working at home, manufacturing homeworkers comprise 29 per cent of all such workers. Even if attention is further restricted to *women* working at home, the relevant percentage is still only about a third. The broader the definition of homeworking, the smaller the proportion concerned with manufacturing; only 7 or 8 per cent of all home-based workers are engaged in manufacturing (Hakim, 1984).

While even the latter is not so small that manufacturing homeworkers can be called a 'tiny minority' (ibid.: 10), these findings do undermine the stereotype of the homeworker as engaged in long-established manufacturing tasks. White-collar and service work, both traditional and modern, appear to have made substantial progress in homeworking even before the new information technology exerted its full influence on work arrangements.

As always, however, aggregate estimates can obscure important regional variation. In some parts of Britain, and especially inner-city areas and Greater London, there is evidence that traditional manufacturing homework remains important and has been waxing rather than waning in the last five years. London not only has a larger homeworking population relative to its labor force (because of the concentration of minority groups who, in turn, are more likely to be homeworkers), but also it has a relatively large home-based manufacturing sector because the industries associated with such off-site work (for example, clothing, toys, novelties and paper products, as well as electronics and information technology) are well-represented in the metropolitan area (Greater London Council, 1985).

Another stereotype which fares better according to the 1981 survey is that of the homeworker as a married woman with young children who is tied to the home. Roughly equal numbers of men and women are found among homeworkers, and within both groups, the same proportion (84 per cent) is married. However, men predominate among those who work *from* home, while women are the great majority of those who work *at* home. 'This is the most significant difference between male and female home-based workers with implications for the jobs done, and their freedom to manoeuvre, or freedom to negotiate with employers' (Hakim, 1984: 11).

Our predisposition to correlate the feminization of this kind of homeworking with women's domestic commitments is further supported by comparisons between homeworkers and the aggregate labor force. Although similar in many respects, a higher proportion of home-based workers are married – 84 per cent compared with 68 per cent for the labor force as a whole. The link between marriage and home-based working is greater for women than for men, as 38 per cent of homeworkers are married women as compared with 26 per cent of the whole labor force; 'stronger support . . . for the view that family responsibilities act as a constraint on women, leading disproportionate numbers to work at home' (ibid.).

What factors lie behind the expansion in homeworking, and particularly working at home by women who are not genuinely self-employed? On the demand side, the Workplace Industrial Relations Survey (WIRS) provides some insight through the investigation of establishments' use of off-site labor, which although not identical to home-based work is sufficiently close to allow results on motivation to be generalized. The WIRS study confirmed that the use of outworkers is widespread. All industries make some use of off-site labor and all types of areas have establishments which use this type of labor. However, a minority of establishments in any industry use outworkers, and those that do typically use very few (ibid.).

Use of outworkers is not always, or even normally, associated with seasonal or other variations in demand which might prompt changes in an establishment's labor force by way of the intermittant use of non-permanent labor. One-fifth of the establishments surveyed used the same number of outworkers year-round. Three-fifths reported some minor variation in the numbers employed. Only for the final one-fifth was there substantial variation (40–100 per cent changes, for example) in manpower. Only in a minority of cases, then, does the obvious explanation seem to hold.

The key point is that not only do outworkers provide firms with flexibility in the organization of employment, but they are also often cheaper. Again, the evidence is fragmentary. Information on pay is based on isolated samples and surveys, and there is the additional problem that as homeworking is normally done on piece rates, many homeworkers do not have an accurate idea of their hourly wages. The Low Pay Unit's sample, collected for its 1984 report *Sweated Labor*, had national coverage but does not claim to be necessarily representative. The hourly rates calculated ranged from 7p to £4 per hour; a third of the traditional homeworkers earned 50p an hour or less, and just over three-quarters earned £1 or less. A Department of Employment survey carried out in 1979–80 found that 30 per cent of a sample of 50 homeworkers earned 50p an hour or less, and 54 per cent earned £1 or less. The House of Commons Select Committee on Employment recorded in 1981 rates of pay as low as 10p an hour. Many other examples of very low hourly pay are provided in *The London Industrial Strategy* (Greater London Council, 1985). Approximately 10 per cent of homeworkers are, in principle, covered by Wages Councils, but even for these workers, the regulations are not widely enforced. Moreover, the powers of the Councils and the size of the Wages Inspectorate have recently been significantly reduced.

Of course, these data do not adequately convey either the poor remuneration of homeworkers, or the savings in labor costs that can be made by their employment. In addition, homeworkers have to meet their own overhead costs. They are also excluded from certain protective labor legislation; for instance, attempts to extend the Equal Pay Act to cover their case have not been successful. Further, when employers do not give homeworkers employee status, they can also evade the responsibility of paying national insurance or providing benefits such as sickness and maternity pay. 'Self-employed' homeworkers have no security of employment and no entitlement to redundancy pay.

Thus, although in 75 per cent of establishments in the WIRS survey managers said that outworkers had the same rates of pay as inhouse workers doing similar work, in reality this means that no allowance is being made for the outworker's overheads. In those cases where outworkers' pay was different, it was typically lower for the same or similar work.[5]

Nor are these differences in the terms and conditions of employment confined to traditional homeworking. The Low Pay Unit's 1984 report *Sweated Labour* compared the findings of a survey of 'new' homeworkers carried out in 1982 with the conditions of a group of traditional homeworkers surveyed in 1983. Although the former were well-paid compared with other homeworkers, the report found many similarities between the two groups. In particular, the position of the 'new' homeworkers was worse than that of comparably skilled employees working in offices: hourly wage levels, for example, were £2 lower for homeworkers than they were for office workers. The report concludes that 'when such new technology homeworking extends to more humble office jobs, as it is likely to do with the advent of cheap cable networks, then large new categories of low-paid workers could be created' (quoted in Greater London Council, 1985: 423; see also Huws, 1984).

An ominous suggestion from the WIRS survey is that establishments using outworkers and/or freelancers are doing better on balance than establishments not using these types of labor. Hakim argues that, 'this suggests that the flexibility afforded by these types of labour can of itself be a significant factor in a firm's expansion or in its ability to ride through the recession' (Hakim, 1984: 148). It should be remembered, however, that this survey did not include firms with less than 25 employees.

Interestingly, in Mitter's study of the clothing industry she argues that the recorded increase in productivity, which has allegedly been achieved in response to declining profits and competition from the Third World, is actually partly accounted for by a decline in officially registered employees in the industry, accompanied by an increase in the number of 'invisible' workers in undeclared workplaces, particularly the home (Mitter, 1985; Greater London Council, 1985). She supports her argument by reference to the rather slow rate of technical change in the clothing industry and the buoyant market in second-hand sewing machines.

But homework is not a strategy pursued only by firms in declining industries. It is also exploited by expanding new small firms (Rubery and Wilkinson, 1981; Hakim, 1984; Hakim and Dennis, 1985). This suggests that outworking might become increasingly important in the next few years despite the contraction in industries traditionally associated with this kind of labor. The latter may well be offset by the increasing use of outworkers in the growing information technology industry (Huws, 1984), a development not unconnected to the fact that the pay and conditions of these 'new' homeworkers are rather traditionally affected by their off-site status as discussed above.

Perhaps a key attraction of homeworking in the uncertain conditions of contemporary Britain is that it allows the employer to displace the risks of business more successfully than is possible with a conventional workforce (Rubery and Wilkinson, 1981). Failure to recognize and compensate outworkers for their greater insecurity makes them a genuinely lower-cost source of labor independently of any differentials in pay. With developments in the information technology industry, wage-cutting by risk displacement threatens to spread to other white-collar and management jobs. Employers' retreat from previously accepted responsibilities parallels the state's privatization of many of the costs of social reproduction which it had hitherto shouldered. Not surprisingly, given the implications of outworking for the terms and conditions of labor, it is concentrated in the least unionized establishments in both manufacturing and services.

The incentives to use homeworkers are relatively universal and cannot, therefore, explain its increase through the recession. However, concurrent changes have facilitated such an employment strategy. The increased risks of operation in Britain make risk displacement onto workers more attractive, while the development of information technology and the decline in unionization have probably allowed homeworking into hitherto untouched establishments. Simultaneously, in the bleak conditions of 1979–85, many firms have been pushed to the extremities of cost-cutting. Finally, the government's express intent to liberalize the labor market, manifest in anti-union legislation and the threatened abolition of Wages Councils, and most directly, pertinently here the decision in 1981 *not* to investigate homeworking further with a view to its regulation, has undoubtedly encouraged employers to pursue such employment practices.

On the supply side, the demonstrated link between women's homeworking and domestic responsibilities suggests that in the same way that the recession and the government's policies have indirectly and perhaps unintentionally promoted part-time work, so homeworking has been stimulated. The relationship between the rise in homeworking and the economic squeeze on many poor families is captured in Mitter's description of the effects of the closure of the clothing factories and sweatshops in the East Asian community around London's Brick Lane. While the unemployment rate among Bangladeshi men rose to 60–70 per cent, the women experienced a rise in the supply of machine work coming into their homes (Mitter, 1985).

Declining availability of local authority and voluntary childcare, the substitution of labor time in the home for services hitherto provided by the state, or purchased with a higher family income, and a more rigid imposition of immigration rules, must all have extended existing incentives to work at home. In many places these forces have been compounded by a deterioration in public transport associated with local authority spending cuts, which make travelling to work more difficult and expensive. Under these circumstances, it is perhaps easy to echo the Greater London Council's judgement (1985) that homeworking is not a relic of the past, but the recreation of a harsh present.

CONCLUSION

Contrary to a superficial reading of labor market indicators, the evidence presented here suggests that the adverse economic circumstances and closely related government policies since 1979 have impacted with particular severity on British women, and particularly on unskilled and minority women and single mothers. If there is a bright side to this generally depressing story, it must be the determined effort by women to preserve their stake in the labor market, as evidenced in their reduced turnover rate (Rubery and Tarling, 1988) and increased acquisition of credentials •(Crompton and Sanderson, 1986). The well-documented increase in families' dependence on women's earnings (Walker, 1988) clearly dictates women's behavior; their wages are keeping the wolves from the doors of many UK homes. Simultaneously, behind those doors, longer hours must be spent – and primarily still by women – in essential caring and domestic work. And these increased hours of work buy only a stagnant or even falling standard of living. Although we cannot measure this in any precise way, the conclusion is inescapable: many British women have suffered an increase in exploitation.

NOTES

1 See Prime Minister Thatcher's speech to the Small Business Bureau, 2 August, 1984. In reality, the economies demonstrably impact on the less well-off (Byrne and Pond, 1985; Lonsdale and Byrne, 1986; Lynes, 1986).
2 We cannot say *a priori* which response will predominate, although historical studies and classical econometric analyses favor discouraged worker effects. See Joseph (1984: 41ff) for a summary of the former and Bowen and Finegan (1969) for an example of the latter. In the United States, at least, women's labor market response appears to be decreasingly cyclically sensitive (Humphries, 1988).
3 Eligibility for benefits has always strongly affected British unemployment figures, from which were derived the registered unemployed. An important incentive to register was that it was a prerequisite to obtain benefits. Women were less likely to have established the right to collect benefits and were thus much less likely to register as unemployed, even when they were looking for jobs. This policy differential explains why women's unemployment rate has historically been lower than men's. Moreover, since 1982, unemployment figures have been based *entirely* on benefit claimants; people who are looking for work but not claiming benefits are excluded from measured unemployment, whether or not they register.
  Such changes in measurement have influenced the statistics in the last four years, and make interpretation difficult. Superficially, it looks as if women experienced increased unemployment relative to men because, although the rates for both sexes have increased, women's have risen relative to men's. However, the rise in the ratio of female:male unemployment dates from the mid-1970s. It has continued to increase in the last four years because the female rate has risen while the male rate has stabilized. The latter is, however, a statistical illusion caused by the exclusion of men over 60 from the male unemployment register after 1982. Any suggestion that the unemployment figures mean that women have suffered relative to men has to be regarded with caution.
4 For a discussion of the course of the political concern, see Greater London Council (1985: 129–30).
5 The exception, according to this study, was the Wages Council sector, where outworkers' pay is either greater than or equal to that for equivalent work

done on the premises, as outworkers in this sector were receiving mark-ups for overheads, pay in lieu of holidays, and so on.

REFERENCES

Ballard, B. (1984) 'Women part-time workers: Evidence from the 1980 Women and Employment Survey', *Employment Gazette*, September.

Blandy, A. (1984) 'New technology and flexible patterns of working time', *Employment Gazette*, October.

Bowen, W. G. and T. A. Finegan (1969) *The Economics of Labor Force Participation* (Princeton, NJ: Princeton University Press).

Byrne, D. and C. Pond (1985) 'A (dis)credit to the family: Government plans for a new Family Credit Scheme', *Low Pay Review*, Autumn.

Central Statistical Office (1986) *Social Trends* (London: Her Majesty's Stationery Office).

Coyle, A. (1985) 'Going private: The implications of privatization for women's work', *Feminist Review,* Winter.

Cragg, A. and T. Dawson (1981) 'Qualitative research among homeworkers', Research Paper No. 21 (London: Department of Employment).

Crompton, R. and K. Sanderson (1986) 'Credentials and careers: some implications of the increase in professional qualifications among women', *Sociology*, vol. 20, no. 1.

Dex, S. and S. M. Perry (1984) 'Women's employment changes in the 1970s', *Employment Gazette*, April.

Erskine, A. (1986) 'Fowler's foul plans: Social Security reforms', *Capital and Class*, Spring.

Greater London Council (1985) *The London Industrial Strategy* (London: Garden House Press).

Hakim, C. (1980) 'Homeworking: some new evidence', *Employment Gazette*, October.

Hakim, C. (1984) 'Homework and outwork: national estimates from two surveys', *Employment Gazette*, January.

Hakim, C. and R. Dennis (1982) 'Homeworking in Wages Council industries', Research Paper No. 37 (London: Department of Employment).

Humphries, J. (1983) 'The emancipation of women in the 1970s and 1980s: from the latent to the floating', *Capital and Class*, Summer.

Humphries, J. (1988) 'Women's Employment in restructuring America: the changing experience of women in three recessions ', in Jill Rubery (ed.) *Women and Recession* (London: Routledge).

Humphries, J. and J. Rubery (1984) 'The reconstitution of the supply side of the labour market: the relative autonomy of social reproduction', *Cambridge Journal of Economics*, December.

Huws, I. (1984) 'New technology homeworkers', *Employment Gazette*, January.

Joseph, G. (1983) *Women at Work* (Oxford: Phillip Allan).

Leighton, P. (1983) 'Contractual arrangements in selected industries', Research Paper No. 34 (London: Department of Employment).

Lonsdale, S. and D. Byrne (1986) 'A poor deal for mothers – The new statutory

Maternity Pay', *Low Pay Review*, Summer.

Lynes, T. (1986) 'How Fowler's benefits work', *New Society*, August.

Mack, J. and S. Lansley (1985) *Poor Britain* (London: George Allen and Unwin).

Mallier, T. and M. Rosser (1979) 'The changing role of women in the British economy', *National Westminster Bank Quarterly Review*, November.

Martin, J. and C. Roberts (1984) 'Women's employment in the 1980s: evidence from the Women and Employment Survey', *Employment Gazette*, May.

Mitter, S. (1986) 'Industrial restructuring and manufacturing homework: immigrant women in the UK clothing industry', *Capital and Class*, Winter.

New Earning Survey, HMSO, selected years.

'Reform of Social Security, programme for action' (1985) White Paper, Cmnd. 9691.

Robertson, J. and J. Briggs (1979) 'Part-time working in Great Britain', *Employment Gazette*, July.

Robinson, J. and J. Wallace (1984) 'Growth and utilization of part-time labour in Great Britain', *Employment Gazette*, September.

Rubery, J. (ed.) (1988) *Women and Recession* (London: Routledge).

Rubery, J. and R. Tarling (1982) 'Women in the recession', *Socialist Economic Review* (London: Merlin).

Rubery, J. and R. Tarling (1988) 'Women's employment in declining Britain', in Jill Rubery (ed.) *Women and Recession* (London: Routledge).

Rubery, J. and F. Wilkinson (1981) 'Outwork and segmented labour markets', in F. Wilkinson (ed.), *The Dynamics of Labour Market Segmentation* (London: Academic Press).

Townsend, P. (1979) *Poverty in the United Kingdom: A Survey of Household Resources and Standards of Living* (London: Allen Lane).

Walker, J. (1988) 'Women, the state, and the family: the case of the U.K.', in Jill Rubery (ed.), *Women and Recession* (London: Routledge).

Women and Employment Survey (1984) prepared by J. Martin and C. Roberts (London: HMSO).

Zabalza, A. and Z. Tzannatos (1985) 'The effects of Britain's anti-discriminatory legislation on relative pay and employment', *Economic Journal*, September.

6

Women in a Changing Workplace
The Case of the Federal Republic
of Germany

Elisabeth Vogelheim

DETERMINED TO WORK – SOME FINDINGS ON WOMEN'S PARTICIPATION IN THE LABOR FORCE

In their important book on women and work published in the 1950s, Alva Myrdal and Viola Klein (1956) described the three stages of women's working biographies. After a period of paid employment immediately after leaving school, women returned to the family and housework after marriage or the birth of a child. They then entered the paid labor force when the children were older and family duties had lightened. This three-phase pattern of interruptions and discontinuity no longer describes the reality of German women today. In 1985 40 per cent of all employees contributing to the social security system in the FRG were women.[1] This statistic reflected a major increase in numbers; while in 1972 there were 9,806,000 women in the labor force, in 1984 there were 10,171,000 (see table 6.1).

The percentage of employed women in the entire female population rose from 46.2 per cent in 1970 to 51.7 per cent in 1984; at the same time male participation rates declined from 88.2 per cent to 81.4 per cent. Such a statistical combination occurred because the separate phases described by Myrdal and Klein had collapsed. The larger number of working women represents an increase in the employment of married women and mothers. The participation rate of women with children under the age of six rose from 24.1 per cent in 1972 to 36.4 per cent in 1982, while that of mothers of children under 15 rose from 26.4 per cent to 42.6 per cent in the same years.

From these statistics we can conclude that women are more committed to working than ever and are searching for ways to reconcile both work and family. Yet in part, this effort to reconcile two social roles creates differences between women's and men's employment biographies. Men's concept of their working lives remains based on the notion that they will have and retain full-time, socially-secured employment from the time they leave school or training programs, until they retire. Men do not expect their working lives to be interrupted, nor do they expect to have different relationships to the labor market at different times in their lives. For women, however, the situation is very different. The work day of women who are married or have children does not begin when they arrive at the office or when the factory whistle starts the shift. Nor does it end when they leave. Women are still the only ones responsible for household and childcare. They are not only doubly burdened but are doubly responsible to their employer on the one hand, to their family on the other. This dual responsibility is one of the differences between male and female bio-graphies.

TABLE 6.1   Development of Female Employment (000s)

	Thousands of people				
	1972	1976	1980	1983	1984
Employed[a]	9,806	9,580	11,092	10,126	10,171
Wage-workers	8,021	8,074	8,813	8,810	8,853
40 hours/week and more	5,673	5,658	6,218	5,866	6,052
21–39 hours/week	1,456	1,294	1,243	1,299	1,318
up to 20 hours/week	892	1,122	1,352	1,645	1,483
Registered unemployed[b]	106	494	462	985	989
Silent reserve[c]	50	314	326	708	809

Sources:
[a]   Stat. Bundesamt, fachserie 1, Reihe 4.11, jeweils Erhebung April ab Juni 1984.
[b]   Bundesanstalt für Arbeit, Amtl. Nachrichtenm, Jahresdurchschnitt.
[c]   H. Thon, Neuberechnung des Erwerbspersonenpotentials 1970–1982 in Mitt. AB 4/84, 1983 u. 1984, vorläufige Schätzung Brinkmann Reyher: Erwerbspersonenpotential und Stille Reserve.

An important consequence of this dual responsibility is that women are much less likely than men to work full-time. Part-time work is increasing in the FRG, but only 1 per cent of this group are men. Therefore, part-time work is overwhelmingly 'women's work'. The percentage of women working part-time rose from 14 per cent in 1960 to fully 33 per cent in 1984. Even among metalworkers, where only about 21 per cent of the workers are women, every fifth woman works part-time. Finally, while part-time workers who are employed at least 15 hours a week are covered by social security protection, this is not the case for people working less than 15 hours a week, the overwhelming number of whom are women.

A second important difference between women's and men's relationship to the labor market is that women are disproportionately affected by unemployment. In 1985 the overall unemployment rate was 9.3 per cent but only 8.6 per cent of men were unemployed while 10.7 per cent of women were. Table 6.1 shows the huge increase in registered unemployment among women from 1972 to 1984. This trend continued so that by December 1985 more than one million women were registered as unemployed.

These figures, dramatic as they are, do not include the 'silent reserve', which increased almost twice as fast as the registered unemployed from 1972 until 1984, as table 6.1 shows. In the 1980s, there were almost as many women in the 'silent reserve' as there were registered unemployed, which means that there were more than 800,000 women who had given up registering for state unemployment benefits because they had either lost their rights to benefits or did not think the effort worthwhile, since the chance of finding work was so remote. Under different economic circumstances these same women would either be employed or at least registering as active jobseekers.

Of course, the importance of this hidden form of unemployment is usually denied by politicians – especially conservative ones – and labelled a 'fake problem'. They tend to lump the issue of the silent reserve together with the fact that about 20 per cent of the unregistered female unemployed are looking for part-time employment and they use these statistics to claim that women are 'not really interested' in working or put their families before their commitment to the labor market. The politicians then conclude that women's unemployment is not a real social problem. Other evidence, however, points to the increasing determination of German women to enter and remain in the labor force, to the extent that economic conditions will permit.

MANAGEMENT STRATEGIES BETWEEN BOOM AND CRISIS: FROM WOMEN AS 'UNDER-UTILIZED POTENTIAL' TO WOMEN AS A 'PROBLEM GROUP'

There has been a remarkable shift in the way that managers and businessmen interpret the changing statistics about women's employment. In the early 1970s – before the economic crisis shook postwar German prosperity and challenged several of its organizing principles – industrialists and other businessmen looked with enthusiasm on the potential for their firms which more female workers seemed to represent. In 1970 the Federal Institute of Industry (*Deutsches Industrieinstitut*) published a paper entitled 'Women's Employment: An International Comparison'. The paper began with the assumption that in 'all current debates on labor market policies there is a general agreement on the fact that women represent a remarkably under-utilized source of potential domestic labor' [Buttler, 1970: 8]. Of course 1970 was a year of full employment: the unemployment rate stood at 1 per cent and foreign workers were being hired to fill jobs for which no German workers could be found. The economy was short of labor and therefore women represented a huge untapped potential or at least under-used supply.

The Federal Institute of Industry recognized that this was not an unproblematic source of new workers, however.

In light of women's contribution to economic life, their fundamental right to work can hardly be denied. Nevertheless, a question does arise whether – in some phases of a woman's life – her family responsibilities are not of prime importance and that employment must be reconciled with her family duties. These questions aside, however, the chronic shortage of labor in all highly industrialized economies requires that women increasingly take up paid employment. [Buttler, 1970: 10]

Therefore, the articles catalogued all possible arguments against women's employment, discussed them and *refuted* them all.

As part of this detailed consideration, the author of the report gave particular attention to the situation of women with children. He argued that housewives' unhappiness and vulnerability would in fact be reduced if they were employed.

The expectation that mothers will be devoted primarily to their families should never be seen as without consequences for women themselves. Irrespective of training, skills or work performed before their children were born, mothers' entire possibilities are confined within the household. Full-time housewives lose their former financial independence when they have to depend on the money given to them by their husbands. They lose the variety of social contacts when they are limited to contacts with the family or those mediated by family members. Many housewives report that they suffer from boring monotony and feelings of isolation. [Buttler, 1970: 12–13]

Children's lives would also improve if their mothers worked outside the home. The reduced influence of the mother would be replaced by stronger ties to professional educators, teachers, other family members and relatives. This shift 'could even make the children more independent and performance-oriented' [Buttler, 1970: 14].

Since it seemed women's participation in the paid labor force would benefit so many – women themselves, their children, their employers, the whole economy – the article made a number of recommendations which were designed to facilitate women's entry into the labor market. Read today the recommendations represent a first-rate catalogue of demands for policy to improve women's situation.

1   A society profiting from women's employment must provide all the necessary facilities – crèches, nurseries, kindergartens – to guarantee adequate childcare.
2   The reintegration of older women into the labor force requires attention. Women who wish to return to the labor force need special training programs to update their skills or to prepare them for new kinds of work.
3   Working conditions should be changed to reflect the needs of women with families. For example, part-time employment might provide the opportunity to stay in the labor force or to return to a previous occupation. However, part-time workers are often the first fired when the labor market loosens up and therefore care must be taken to reduce part-time workers' vulnerability.
4   Coordination of work and school schedules would help mothers.
5   Housework should become less labor- and time-intensive with reliance on things like meals at the workplace or school or on the service sector more generally.
6   Men's attitudes must be changed so that they learn to appreciate women's double burden and men must become willing to participate in domestic labor. This is, however, a change which is unlikely to happen from one day to the next and the learning process must be initiated among school-age children.

This study, presented in 1970, reflects companies' needs and experience at that time. Management took such recommendations to heart and offered company daycare facilities, additional transportation and some measures for reintegration of women who had interrupted their work lives to undertake family responsibilities.

New attention to a whole category of potential labor supply is very visible in *Der Arbeitgeber*, the magazine of the Federal Employers' Association. Throughout the early 1970s the magazine promoted non-employed women as a good source of workers in the tight labor market situation. Thus the magazine encouraged its readers to innovate in their personnel policies. Failing to involve female employees who were suited and motivated for further training was criticized as poor personnel management. 'Human capital' was ignored at any firm's peril and in particular when reliable and qualified workers were so in demand.[2] This enthusiasm for making full use of women's labor force potential reached its peak in 1973 when *Der Arbeitgeber* pressed the demand, 'Women instead of Turks'.[3] For employers, German women represented an alternative labor supply, a substitute for foreign workers who were attracted to

Germany by the tight labor market conditions. Since managers thought there were problems involved in hiring foreign workers, they proposed to fill the gap with Germans – first women and then pensioners and others willing to work part-time.

The magazine gave frequent attention to the complexities of a labor force made up of married women with children. It advised firms to demonstrate clearly to the many women who mistakenly believed that they had to choose between family and work that such a choice was unnecessary. In addition, it advised firms to keep in touch with former female employees at home with their families by providing regular information on company changes, events and developments. Such networks would maintain the bond with the firm and encourage women to think about returning to work as soon as possible.[4]

Employers also recognized that women workers faced a double burden, that 'the dual role of a woman in the family and at work remains a dual burden compared to the traditional male role as supporter of the family'.[5] Therefore, its publicists recommended family-oriented policies. In 1975, on the occasion of the International Women's Year, the Federal Employers' Association put out 'The Woman in the Economy and Society' ('Die Frau in Wirtschaft und Gesellschaft'), which began with the assumption that the problem of women's employment could only be addressed by taking into account the interests of the entire family. The report recommended that firms develop personnel policies which recognized women's double burden and which took action to relieve it. It also stressed that girls needed encouragement to take up their educational opportunities and that these opportunities needed to be extended. Firms themselves were advised to develop special promotion and training programs for young, unskilled female workers within the company and for older women seeking reintegration into the labor force. According to the report, companies had the basic responsibility of facilitating women's reintegration into the labor force with vocational training measures, long-term job-planning and career opportunities.[6]

Then in 1977 the Federal Employers' Association published a note entitled 'Women in the Workplace' ('Die Mitarbeiterin im Betrieb') which reads like a manifesto against discrimination on the basis of gender. It stressed the importance of changing popular attitudes, to make them consistent with the realities of the times. Working women were described as a heterogeneous group and the idea that they were all the same or had the same responsibilities was rejected as totally outdated. Rather, the note stressed that 'the variations in motives and work expectations that women have must be emphasized more in the future if any company wishes to avoid loss of efficiency and disappointment of women's expectations about work'.[7] There was, of course, nothing in this document which really dealt with the issue of (women's) reproductive work. That gap represented a deficiency, which in times of economic boom could be ignored as long as the job market needed women workers.

Throughout the 1970s, at least until 1977, employers did not see women's family responsibilities or lack of training as fundamental handicaps. Quite the opposite, in fact. Management sought ways to alter working hours and conditions which would relieve or at least recognize the double burden of employment and family. Personnel policy, especially with regard to training and promotion, could be adapted to the particular needs of undertrained or out-of-practice women. Part-time work, in the eyes of management, was not an inferior form of employment but a magic trick to allow women to reconcile both paid work and family, and thus to offer themselves in the labor market.

All of this enthusiasm for hiring women and making adjustment to their special needs depended, of course, on the economic conditions of the time. Economic prosperity and a shortage of labor meant that special measures were both feasible and desirable. All this was soon to change. As the economic crisis of the 1970s fianlly threatened Germany too and 'Modell Deutschland' began to lose its glow under new pressures, unemployment rose. Foreign workers were encouraged to return home, the labor market contracted and unemployment statistics failed to respond to the usual policy interventions. Suddenly, female employment became a serious problem for employers.

The new thinking was most visible in the way that unemployment rates were analyzed and their intractability explained. *Der Arbeitgeber* published its revisionism in 'Women's Employment Realistically Assessed' ('Frauenarbeitslosigkeit nüchtern gesehen') in January 1979. According to the new analysis, women's failure to find work was due to their unwillingness to take full-time work; of unemployed women, well over one-third sought 'only' part-time work. This unwillingness to work as men do, which was interpreted as a lack of commitment to the labor force, was explained, according to *Der Arbeitgeber*, by the very structure of women's relationship to the labor market.[8]

Women's employment was hindered in ways that men's was not. Women behaved differently in the labor market because of their narrow training and lack of skills, their limited professional and regional mobility, family commitments, and their disproportionately high demand for part-time work and adjusted schedules. Since women did not offer themselves on the labor market in the ways that men did, they could be labelled inferior, second-class employees; this designation rationalized both discrimination against women workers and their ouster from the labor force into unemployment. Male employees served as the model for working life. They were largely free from reproductive work, easily available in terms of time and location. They were considered first-class employees for any employer. This approval did not extend to women – especially not to the ones who had a family to care for. Management strategies and state policies began to highlight the supposed deficiencies of female life patterns, particularly in times of economic downturn, and then to blame women themselves for all their disadvantages.

The terms of discussion had clearly changed. From 'unrealized potential' women had become a 'problem group', but the problems were now of their own making. Women's increased motivation for work, reflected in their insistence on registering as unemployed or looking for work, was what was causing the unemployment rate to rise. But this motivation, according to the new analysis, was not as 'real' as men's, because it was 'only' for part-time work or work which they could adjust to their family schedules.

Employers also changed their position on helping women overcome their double burden. Whereas earlier their spokesmen had stressed the advantages to families of women working and the need for husbands and men in general to adjust their attitudes to women's labor force participation, by the 1980s the family – indeed, the whole German society – was threatened by women's work. According to Otto Esser, President of the Federal Employer's Association, the country needed to integrate family policy and policies towards women. His starting point was the decline in the birthrate, and the necessity of designing family policy to halt the fall. For Esser,

> any considerations of female employment, particularly those aimed at relieving women of their double burden, must be seen in the light of family policy. The crucial importance of the family for the state, economy and society requires the attention of management. The current drastic decrease in birth rates and the corresponding change in the age structure of our population creates problems not only for the provision of old-age security but also for economic growth, employment, standards of living and the entire field of education. In the face of this development, we must stress the importance of family policy much more than in the past.[9]

Once women acquired a new label, as inferior and second-class participants in the labor force – a 'problem group' – it then became possible to develop a special solution just for them. By the 1980s, a new buzz word had appeared in the lexicon – 'flexibility'. To be a flexible worker was to be an ideal worker. Being flexible meant offering one's labor everywhere, anywhere, anytime. Obviously, only men could reach this ideal flexibility; women could not because of their family responsibilities. Therefore, a special concept of flexible work was needed for women. This concept, specifically for women, was unveiled in 1984 under the promise 'More Employment Through Flexible Part-Time Work'. By flexible part-time work, employers meant 'regulation of work time which deviates from the

strict requirements of agreed working hours' [BDA, 1984: 8]. This notion
was strongly opposed by the trade unions but intensely pressed by
management.

Behind these new concepts promoted by German employers lay technological changes. New high-technology systems are only fully efficient when
in continuous use. Therefore, they need workers who are willing to work
anytime and to adjust to the unevenness and unpredictability of the
systems so that at times of pressure or when other workers are not
available, the system can still operate. From management's point of view:

> the increasing international segregation of work as well as inter-
> national competition means that we need to use more flexible and
> cost-saving production systems. Quick adaption to changing market
> needs requires flexible employment. Furthermore, high and ever-
> rising labor costs require the best possible coordination of worktime
> with workloads. And last but not least, expansion of telecommun-
> ication systems, the so-called information and communication techno-
> logies, and relocation of work all make possible electronic workplaces
> at home. [BDA, 1984: 8]

In this way, paid work would again be home-based. Women workers would
no longer have to go to the factory, the office or shop in order to work. Nor
would they come into contact with fellow workers and the unions which
protect them. Instead, they could stay in the home, combining childcare
and wage-earning. This solution is praised by employers and their associations as the new, 'modern' solution to meet the needs of the 'problem
group'.[10] According to them, women no longer need job training and
promotion, which will move them up the career ladder in the firm. Instead,
their 'special' needs are met by relocation of work, exclusion and flexibility.

TWO EXAMPLES OF STATE POLICY: EMPLOYMENT POLICY AND
THE LAW ON PARENTAL ALLOWANCES

The state has also moved to supplement these new management strategies.
In October 1982 the conservative coalition made up of the Christian
Democrats (CDU), the Christian Socialists (CSU) and the Free Democrats
(FDP) came to power in the FRG. This move from the coalition led by the
Social Democrats (SPD) has been labelled a 'U-turn in government and
policy'. It has meant a new political direction for the country, based on
drastic social, financial and legal changes. The major reversals of previous
policies have involved cuts in spending on social programs, lower taxes for
high-income groups, reductions in employees' rights to protection in the

workplace, and even limitations on trade unions' right to strike.

These moves towards a German version of the neo-liberalism which several European governments have embraced touch women in particular. The severe reductions in educational opportunities and the loss of social benefits following cuts in social spending have reinforced the effects of an already tight labor market to create a new form of feminized poverty.[11] Two policies presented by the government after 1982 are good examples of this U-turn in policy and its special impact on women. On 1 May 1985, a new employment policy came into effect. The labor law changed in ways which were supposed to expand employment by opening up several new kinds of work contracts and relaxing restrictions on employers' contracts with their employees. Some people have described this change as the 'Americanization of the labor market and workers' rights'.

Until 1985 German labor law had provided a standard work contract based on a permanent contract, which was protected by law and by collective agreement. The new policy permits temporary contracts between employers and employees, which are not subject to the usual restraints which govern permanent contracts. This provision can be used, for example, to circumvent the existing protection against dismissal for pregnancy. Young women can be hired under temporary contracts and then, if they become pregnant, employers are not subject to the provisions of the Maternity Protection Law, which applies only to permanent employees. Moreover, previously negotiated labor-management agreements for workers' equality have become ineffective because temporary staff do not have the same rights in the workplace and for access to social benefits that permanent employees have. The law also promotes part-time work. According to the Minister of Labor, 'work on call' (in which workers are called up to work only when work is available) and job-sharing should be 'socially acceptable'.[12] Of course, part-time work is not only less protected and less well-paid but it is also 'women's work'. In these ways the law both encourages and legitimates the development of a two-tiered labor force, with a core of permanent, protected employees surrounded by a periphery of part-time or temporary unprotected ones. This law to permit greater 'flexibility' in management's relations with its workforce represents the German state's contribution to the demand for a more flexible labor force. It is also likely to be a law which will push women into unprotected and marginalized relationships to the labor market.

The second example of the policy U-turn is provided by the Parental Allowances Law, which is celebrated by conservative politicians as a great achievement in family policy. The parent of any child born after 1 January 1988 receives a monthly allowance of DM 600 for up to twelve months (after the seventh month the allowance is based on family income). A parent can claim leave from her (or his) job for ten months but the allowance will be paid only if the parent has no income, or works less than

20 hours a week.[13] In effect, the law differentially affects women and men, and discriminates against mothers who work full-time.

Since in any family it is likely that the man will earn more than the woman (given current social norms and the structure of the labor markets for female and male workers), it can be assumed that only women will take advantage of the allowance. The family would lose more income if the father gave up his job or reduced his hours to 20 or less. Therefore, the law tends to encourage the present gender division of labor within the family. In addition, the pool of female part-time workers expands, as all recipients of the family allowance search for part-time jobs, which are, again, likely to be poorly paid and unprotected.

Heide Pfarr of the University of Hamburg has shown the ways in which the two laws just considered are intimately linked. Since full-time workers have maternity protection, employers are more likely to engage women only on a temporary basis, thus eliminating the risk that women will claim maternity benefits, including keeping their post open for ten months. All young women are affected, whether they as individuals intend to have children or not, because employers see them as potential threats to the prerogatives of personnel management.[14]

Statements by employers and their spokesmen make it clear that these criticisms of the two laws are a correct reading of the intent which lay behind them. Much evidence clearly reveals that the Parental Allowances Law is less a policy to improve women's or families' situations and more a population policy and an effort to sanitize labor market statistics at women's expense. For example, in an article titled 'Fewer Chances for Young Women', the President of the Employer's Association wrote that the law increased the handicaps young women faced in searching for employment and was a means of reducing their job opportunities.[15] The magazine *Der Arbeitgeber* claims that young women's chances in the labor market are substantially reduced by the legal requirement that a job be kept for them during maternity leave. The editor-in-chief of the managers' magazine predicted in March 1985 that 'many small firms will be more reluctant to employ young women than they were before [the law was passed]'.[16]

Both these laws and other decisions of the post-1982 government contribute to the social segregation of the labor force. Hand-in-glove with employers, the state is involved in worsening women's opportunities in the labor force and restructuring their location within it. These legal changes, like the employers' move towards relocation of work, exclusion and flexibility, all push women toward the margin of the labor force and leave them farther behind the male workforce. The 1970s interest in women workers and the moves toward equality have been completely eclipsed by new management strategies and state actions.

WHO IS GOING TO CHANGE ALL THIS? FUTURE GOALS FOR UNION
STRATEGIES

The German labor movement has been very concerned about mounting
unemployment. It has adopted as its counter-strategy an across-the-board
reduction in working hours. The goal is a 35-hour week for everyone,
without loss of pay. In 1984, after a seven-week strike, the Metal Workers'
Union (IG Metall – IGM) won a reduction to 38.5 hours from the previous
40-hour week. This movement for reduced working time is not only a
strategy to tackle unemployment by opening up more positions as the
average time worked is reduced. It is also a strategy pushed for by the
women of IG Metall as part of their concern for improving the working
conditions of women. They hope that a reduction in the work week, via a
reduction in the work day to seven hours, will reduce some of the pressure
on families and encourage a better and more equitable distribution of
domestic labor and family responsibilities between women and men.
Union members have clearly expressed their ideas on these matters and
have put them on the table in union negotiations with employers.[17]

The success in 1984 was not a complete victory, however. For the first
time in negotiations about the length of the work week, the agreement did
not apply to individual employees' hours. Rather it was an agreement
about company averages. Thus, although an average of 38.5 was agreed on
overall, individual employees' hours could range from 37 to 40 hours. This
was a first step by management toward differentiated and flexible working
hours. Works councils in some firms resisted the establishment of an
unequal working week in their own workplaces, but management pressed
hard for such variability and future negotiation is bound to see more
pressure for similar agreements.

In the face of such pressures unions are faced with challenges which go
beyond what can be gained by an overall reduction of working time. They
must also develop a response which can effectively counter management's
efforts and still respect women's real needs for adjustments in working
conditions and schedules. Women in unions know from first-hand experience that people – particularly those with children – want to be able to
adjust their work time to meet their different needs at particular phases in
their lives. Because of these ambitions people are receptive to management's efforts to make 'flexibility' palatable to them.

Recognizing these interests, the women in IG Metall have drawn up
their own proposals, which both respect the desire to reduce working time,
especially for employees with heavy family responsibilities, and protect
workers from management's efforts to make special arrangements a basis
for weakening workers' social and collective rights. Thus, at the Twelfth
Women's Conference of IG Metall, held in November 1985, the following

statement was made:

> In addition to the reduction of the work week across the board, we
> must consider whether and to what extent particular life situations
> require additional collectively negotiated or legally guaranteed reduc-
> tions. The union's policies on working hours must focus on individuals'
> needs, with the goal of establishing a collectively and legally binding
> framework. We need to develop special strategies to permit the
> reconciliation of family and work.[18]

The Chairman of the IGM has outlined this position further:

> We advocate not only a general reduction to a 35 hour week, with 30
> hours the ultimate goal, but also a reduced work week for particular
> categories. Important among such categories would be those whose
> situation at the moment requires it, such as parents with children
> under three, or under six, or shift workers . . . this type of flexible
> adjustment, however, can never be a substitute for a more general
> reduction; it is only an important supplement.[19]

These policy statements are novel because the time and effort involved in
raising children has finally been made an issue in collective bargaining. It is
something new for trade unions and a success for those demanding
attention for women within the union!

Beyond these proposals about adjustments in working hours, women in
IG Metall are also pressing for affirmative action programs. At this point
affirmative action is not required in Germany, even within state-owned
companies. Therefore, union women are trying to initiate such programs
and are pressing for them in collective bargaining. Of course, whether they
are successful or not depends not only on management's responses. The
union itself must be willing to take up the issue and promote women's
interests and individual women within IGM. Since women are under-
represented in IG Metall – as they are in other German unions and political
parties – real changes in women's working lives, and social situation more
generally, depend upon greater visibility within the union and on its
negotiation agendas. Working women in Germany are involved in debates
and struggles to make this change happen. They know that the union's very
credibility and realization of its goals depend to a large extent on their
participation in it.

NOTES

1 In FRG statistics, 'employee' refers to all individuals either earning wages, carrying out a trade, self-employed or working in agriculture.
2 *Der Arbeitgeber*, no. 18, 1971.
3 *Der Arbeitgeber*, no. 10, 1973.
4 *Der Arbeitgeber*, no. 4, 1972.
5 *Der Arbeitgeber*, no. 18, 1974.
6 For details see BDA (1975: 87-8).
7 *Der Arbeitgeber*, no. 12, 1977.
8 *Der Arbeitgeber*, no. 1, 1979.
9 *Der Arbeitgeber*, no. 10, 1980.
10 *Der Arbeitgeber*, no. 6, 1984. See also Chapter 5.
11 For a discussion see Geschaeftsbericht zur 12. Frauenkonferenz der IG Metall, Frankfurt 1985, 90.
12 Arbeitsrecht im Betrieb 5/85.
13 Das Mitbestimmungsgespraech 12/1985.
14 Mitteilungen für Frauen 2/1985.
15 *Quick*, 25 July 1985.
16 *Manager Magazine*, no. 6, 1985.
17 See, for example, Protokoll der 11. Frauenkonferenz der IG Metall 1982, Frankfurt and Protokoll des 14. ordentl. Gewerkschaftstages in München 1983.
18 Protokoll der 12. Frauenkonferenz der IG Metall, Frankfurt 1985.
19 Lecture at the 'Analytik', Düsseldorf, December 1985.

REFERENCES

BDA (1975) Geschaftsbericht der Bundesvereinigung der Deutschen Arbeitgeberverbande (Cologne: author).

BDA (1984) 'Mehr Beschaeftigung durch Flexible Teilzeitarbeit', Bundesvereinigung Deutscher Arbeitgeberverbaende (Cologne: author).

Buttler, Gunther (1970), 'Frauenerwerbsarbeit im internationalen Vergleich', *Beitrage des Deutschen Industrieinstituts* (Cologne: author) Heft 8/9.

Myrdal, A. and V. Klein (1956) *Women's Two Roles: Home and Work* (London: Routledge).

7

Women in a Changing Workplace
The Case of Italy

Daniela Del Boca

Any individual woman can make choices about whether to participate in the labor market, the extent to which she will participate (number of hours), the wage she will accept, and the type of job and career to seek. The expected value associated with the choices available to individual women is, however, importantly influenced and often constrained by the actions of firms, unions and the government. Changes in the labor market experiences of women over long periods of time result from changes in the options available to women, and the 'objective' values attached to these options – for example, the wage rates available to women in different occupations, or the costs associated with various forms of training. Changes also result from the subjective valuation of these options on the part of women. These two factors, in broad outline, are changes in demand conditions and shifts in supply.

In assessing the role of demand factors in determining the labor market experiences of women, it is important to specify the attitudes each of the institutional agents have toward female workers. For example, the attitudes of firms will depend largely on the presence or absence of discriminatory behavior, women's level of productivity, the level of remuneration of female workers, and the 'overhead' costs associated with employing women (due to turnover rates, the possibility of maternity leave, etc.). Unions, largely comprised of male workers, sometimes overtly or subtly resist the entrance of women into the labor market on grounds of narrow economic self-interest. On the other hand, unions often support women's employment on ideological grounds and thus take actions which improve labor market opportunities for women. Governments have traditionally viewed women not only as a labor resource but also as a source of population growth and the instruction of youth. To the extent that labor market participation diminishes the value of women in these roles, governments may have an incentive to create policies which either effectively preclude the participation of women in the labor market or insure that their role is such that conflicts with other, more traditional roles, are minimized. Provision of maternity leave and 'protective' legislation are often designed to reconcile this conflict.

In this chapter I trace the evolution of women's role in the Italian labor market from the 1950s to the present, and explain how the choices of these three actors all influenced women's labor market experience. The analysis is carried out within an institutional framework, since I believe that government actions and external economic factors largely account for the observed changes in the labor market attachment of women in Italy.

The first part of the chapter discusses factors affecting the demand for female workers in Italy. Even though female employment behavior follows the overall trend of other advanced industrialized countries, Italy is in many ways a special case. First, participation rates did not, as in the other countries discussed in this book, rise continuously during the postwar period. Instead, female labor force participation went through a period of decline during the 1960s before rising again in the 1970s. And it is still lower than in most other advanced industrialized countries. Second, Italy has a large sector of small firms, many of them in the unofficial (or black) economy, which is a major source of female employment. Third, there is considerably less part-time work than in most other countries. The origin of these peculiarities and their influence on the labor market experience of women are discussed. The second part of the chapter deals with the factors that influence female labor supply. Several studies on household work are taken as a point of departure to demonstrate how little women's position in the reproductive sphere has changed and how this position still dominates decisions about whether to offer oneself for paid work. In the third part of the chapter a short summary of legislation concerning women is given. It shows that even relatively progressive legislation may not substantially change women's condition if there are many social and economic factors working against it.

CHANGES IN THE ECONOMIC STRUCTURE: THE DEMAND SIDE

The redistribution of female employment across sectors

The postwar Italian economy, like the economies of other advanced industrialized countries, underwent a structural change caused by the decline of agriculture and the rise of the industrial and service sectors. It was the female labor force that experienced the most pronounced adjustment problems during the process of urbanization which accompanied these shifts. Since the Italian agricultural sector was larger and had a higher proportion of female workers than in most other European countries, many more women were affected by its contraction. In addition, women found it difficult to find work in the industrial sector.

During the 1950s and 1960s, millions of people left their farms in the south, attracted to the factories in the urban areas of the north. In the first decade of this migration process, it was mostly men who went north, leaving women and the rest of the extended family on the farm in the south. The percentage of female workers in agriculture even increased during these years, predominantly in the category of 'family workers'. By staying on the farms, women played a very important, though largely unrecognized, role in the process of structural adjustment in the Italian economy. The income from agriculture remained important to many families because industrial wages were low; with only the wages of men working in the factories in the north, families could not sustain a decent standard of living.

The low wages of the 1950s reflected excess supply in the labor market and the weakness of the unions, and these two factors clearly favored the process of industrialization. Beginning in the latter part of the decade, increased demand for Italian products and changing production processes resulted in a growth in demand for relatively unskilled labor in manufacturing and the service sector. That meant there was also an increased demand for female labor, and female employment began to expand into other sectors of the economy. From 1958 to 1963 the percentage of female employment decreased from 35.6 to 27.9 per cent in the agricultural sector, but it increased from 29.3 to 39.3 per cent in the industrial, and from 33.1 to 41.3 per cent in the service sectors.

Economic growth during that period led to the achievement of virtually full employment and then increasing pressures of excess demand. Unions gained strength and successfully bargained for large wage concessions, and a single wage could now support a whole family. That in turn resulted in domestic inflation and a sharp loss in international competitiveness. In order to regain their market position, businesses began to restructure. They became more selective in their hiring choices, preferring higher-skilled, prime-age men to the low-skilled women. Moreover, at the beginning of the 1960s, the principle of equal pay for equal work was introduced through a collective bargaining agreement and women were therefore no longer much cheaper to employ than men. As a result, between 1963 and 1970, only male employment increased, while female employment decreased sharply.

In those years more than one million women left the labor force, many of them from the agricultural sector. Continued urbanization and higher industrial wages encouraged women to leave the farms to join their husbands in the north. Once there, however, women could not find jobs in industry because they were untrained. Leaving agriculture, therefore, meant leaving the labor force for many women. Female labor force participation rates declined for the rest of the 1960s and reached their lowest point in 1972 at 32.4 per cent (see table 7.1).[1]

TABLE 7.1   *Female Labor Force Participation Rates in Italy, 1955–85*

Year	%
1955	30.0
1958	33.3
1960	33.3
1963	36.5
1965	34.6
1968	32.9
1970	32.8
1972	32.4
1975	34.6
1978	37.1
1980	39.8
1982	40.3
1985	41.3

Source: OECD (1980, 1983, 1986).

The trend began to reverse in 1973. Of the 1.5 million people newly employed between 1972 and 1980, only 253,000 were men and 1,247,000 were women. This change during the 1970s was paralleled by remarkable changes in women's education and in demographic patterns. Women accounted for 50 per cent of high school and university students by the end of the 1970s, as compared to no more than 35 per cent in the 1950s. The fertility rate during the same period declined from 68 per thousand women to 48 in 1980. Industrial employment patterns of Italian women also changed markedly. Industries in which women had traditionally been employed (such as tobacco and textiles) contracted, and large numbers of jobs held by women were lost, while the level of female employment in such industries as food and leather stayed constant. But women's employment grew rapidly in the expanding industries – precision machinery, shoes, wearing apparel, electric machinery and chemicals. In these industries, the labor process did not require high levels of training; more relevant were dexterity, precision and patience. Nevertheless, while the demand for female labor increased after 1973, the supply grew even more, as reflected in a steady rise of the female unemployment rate from 11.4 per cent in 1973 to 17 per cent in 1984.

The small firm sector and the underground economy

A phenomenon that was in many ways unique to Italian industry during the 1970s was the growth in the number of small firms and the development of a large unofficial economy. The growth of these sectors can to a large extent be explained by changes that took place in the climate of industrial relations during the 1970s. Business strategies to regain international competitiveness were directed toward halting further wage increases, rationalizing production, and raising the utilization of capital equipment that had been installed earlier. The resulting deterioration of working conditions and redistribution of income from labor to capital led to intense strike waves. While the strikes were initially successful, they had far-reaching consequences for firms as well as for the whole economy and these affected the larger employment picture.

The unions won large wage increases, reductions in the working week, and a new labor law (*Statuto del Lavoratori*). That law drastically limited the ability of employers to lay off workers in medium and large firms, but did not apply to small firms. Employers responded by resorting to the 'unprotected' sector of the labor market. They started subcontracting to small firms that could evade union control or payment of social security contributions. Employers also began again to put out work, virtually returning to a cottage industry system. They constructed new, small plants which employed mostly women and where unions had very little influence (Flanagan, Soskice and Ulman, 1982). Table 7.2 demonstrates the growth of small firms during the 1970s. Associated with this development was the rise of the unofficial sector. It is estimated that at the end of the 1970s there were about 3,745,000 workers in underground manufacturing, 60 per cent of whom were women. The increasing use of home work is part of the whole phenomenon.[2]

TABLE 7.2   *Per Cent Increase in Employment in Manufacturing Firms Between 1971 and 1981*

Number of employees	% Increase
2–5	37.7
6–9	44.8
10–49	43.4
50–99	4.5
100–499	5.0
500–999	−1.4
1000 or more	−5.2

Source: Censimenti dell'Industria (1971, 1981).

The vitality of small firms and the unofficial sector is based upon the subordinate role of the Italian economy in the international division of labor. Italy does not have a leading position in many areas of advanced technology and has to adjust to the fluctuation of international markets. Small firms are better suited to provide the flexibility necessary for this adjustment. They can keep down labor costs by relying heavily on apprenticeship and unreported activities and they can bypass the ceilings on overtime or wage differentials and the high cost of firing imposed by collective bargaining agreements. On the other hand, not all small firms merely function as a buffer for structural adjustment processes. The success of the small firms, especially in central Italy, might also be considered a reemergence of the traditional pattern of Italian economic development during the 1950s, based upon labor-intensive products. During the 1970s and 1980s, then, small firms and self-employment have become much more widespread, beyond the traditional sectors in manufacturing, and extending even to the trade and service sectors.

Female employment increased most markedly during the last decade in small firms and the underground economy. All of the usual characteristics of women's labor force participation – high turnover, willingness to work fewer hours, a discontinuous work life – which made women less sought-after in the larger industrial sector, turned out to be advantageous for the small firm sector. In fact, employers have incentives to hire women. Since demand variability is rather high, high female turnover rates sustain flexibility, allowing employers to avoid costly lay-off procedures. Furthermore, in firms with less than 15 employees, the lack of unionization permits the employer not only to dismiss workers at will, but also to avoid social security payments and maintain a high sex-linked wage differential (table 7.3). Moreover,

TABLE 7.3   *Dismissals by Firm Size, 1977*

Number of employees per firm	Dismissals per 100 workers
10–49	23.73
50–99	18.24
100–199	18.18
200–499	6.71
500–999	3.14
1000 or more	1.96

Source: Confindustria (1977).

absenteeism is lower in small firms, as is the gap between female and male absenteeism, and this pattern further reduces the disadvantage of female workers that employers always claimed existed (see table 7.4). This latter fact may again be due to less union protection in small firms, but it may also be the result of the more flexible working schedules which allow women to combine their paid employment with their household duties. All of these factors have contributed to a more rapid increase of female employment in the small-firm sector than elsewhere.

TABLE 7.4　*Hours Lost Per Worker by Firm Size, 1978*

Size of firm	Production workers	
	(M)	*(F)*
more than 1000	262.8	513.1
501–1000	233.3	414.7
51–500	232.2	388.6
1–50	152.2	259.1

Source: Ministry of Labor (1980).

The rise of this sector also reflects family needs to allocate work time. It is often the family itself that is the productive unit in these firms. This is especially the case among those which come out of an artisan tradition but are now performing in an industrial setting. The percentage of self-employment has risen perceptibly since the end of the 1970s, not only in the industrial sector but also in the tertiary sector, especially in the textile and apparel industries and in retail trade, where there are many family-owned micro-businesses.

Limited options of work time

In most advanced industrialized countries, part-time work or various forms of flexible time schedules are widespread and are especially taken up by women. Not so in Italy, where there is very little part-time work. In 1981, the percentage of part-time workers among all employees was 14.4 per cent in the US, 25.2 per cent in Sweden, but only 2.7 per cent in Italy. From 1973 to 1981, the ratio of part-time work even fell, and especially for women, declining from 8.5 per cent of female employment (1973) to 5.8 per cent (1981) (see chapter, 2, table 2.3, p. 21).

There are several reasons for the low level of part-time work. One is the relatively small service sector in the Italian economy. This sector has been one of the main sources of part-time work in other countries. Another reason is the character of Italian labor legislation. Part-time work is subject to the same regulations as full-time work; it is protected by the same employment legislation and is entitled to the same insurance benefits, maternity leave and severance pay. A third factor is the absence of a wage differential between part- and full-timers, when hours worked are taken into account (Del Boca and Forte, 1982). A final consideration is union strategy on part-time work. As we shall discuss later, unions have traditionally defended the position of workers already employed and opposed part-time work, demanding instead equal treatment of all workers. Only in 1984 were labor contracts altered to allow for a more liberal application of labor-time arrangements. Consequently, part-time work in Italy has not given employers in firms covered by labor legislation as much flexibility as it has in other countries.

For all of these reasons, part-time workers could not be used as a source of cheap and more flexible labor or to save on overhead costs associated with full-time contracts. In other European countries, part-time workers, in particular female part-time workers, were substituted for full-time workers during the recent economic downturn.[3] In Italy, it was the small firms and the unofficial sector that took on the function of adjusting to demand fluctuations.

Yet in both the small firms and the unofficial economy, the impact on women's working conditions is negative. Women are paid less than men and less than official workers; they have fewer benefits, work in low-skilled jobs, and have very few career opportunities. Thus, the Italian example shows that the provision of more part-time work in the official sector in the context of industrial restructuring may be the lesser evil; forcing employers to set up small firms and resort to underground employment will have worse effects for women.

As we shall discuss in the next section of the chapter, there is an immediate demand among women for more part-time jobs. If women are driven into the underground economy to find the work arrangements they need, they may be even less protected and have fewer opportunities to return to full-time work in the official labor market. In that respect, the limited availability of part-time jobs serves as a barrier to entry into the labor market. The low participation rate and high unemployment rate of Italian women are evidence of the problem.

THE GROWTH OF THE SERVICE SECTOR AND THE WEAK INFLUENCE OF THE PUBLIC SECTOR ON FEMALE EMPLOYMENT

There is a close relationship between the growth of the service sector and female employment in all advanced industrialized countries; Italy is no exception. The relationship works in two ways. First, the expansion of social services such as welfare, childcare and social work indirectly increases the ability of women to join the labor force by relieving them of work previously done in the household. Second, the service sector directly raises the demand for female labor because so many jobs are seen as 'women's work'. During the 1970s and 1980s, the service sector provided almost all of the new jobs in the Italian economy while industrial employment remained relatively stable. General services (+54 per cent), transporation (+26 per cent) and trade (+23 per cent) have expanded most rapidly. In turn, female employment figures witnessed stable growth during the last decade. Yet the level of female employment in the service sector is still considerably lower in Italy than in other countries. There are two reasons for this phenomenon. First, overall employment in the service sector is relatively low, i.e. it is lower than in all the other countries discussed in this book. Second, the public sector provided fewer jobs to women than it did in other countries.

There is a paradox to the minor role of the public sector in job provision for women. Looking at sheer numbers, the public sector is a large part of the Italian economy. Total government expenditures in the 1980s, as a percentage of GDP, are higher in Italy than in all other countries examined except Sweden (OECD, 1985). Nevertheless, government expenditures do not go to administrative purposes to the same extent that they do elsewhere. The number of government employees is half that of Britain and one third that of Sweden. There are many fewer social services provided directly by the government and therefore fewer job opportunities for women. Thus it is not the scope of the public sector that is important for female employment but its particular structure and the kind of services it provides.

There were, of course, welfare policies in Italy, especially during the 1950s and 1960s, but they took the form of transfer payments rather than the provision of social services. The government preferred to transfer money directly to families and firms, because that strategy appeared to be easier in the short run (Turvani, 1986). It did not involve any structural changes of social organization and therefore met with less resistance from conservatives while it still brought the political support of those who received the benefits. Women became responsible for organizing the social services for the family and utilizing the cash benefits made available by the state. In this way, the transfer payments system had the effect of keeping intact the traditional female role in the gender division of the labor force and made the choice between labor force and domestic activities even more difficult for women, especially those with children.

LABOR SUPPLY AND INSTITUTIONAL FACTORS

Household production

In this section, we turn to an analysis of women's decisions about labor force participation. On the supply side, there are several relevant trends: the increase in women's education, the decline in the birthrate, and the increase in women's relative wages.

While these phenomena certainly had a positive effect on the female labor force participation rate, other phenomena have reduced women's probability of working. The lack of an efficient social service system, the limited number of part-time or flexible-time opportunities and an excessively protective legislation, which has discouraged employers from hiring women in some official sectors, have contributed to a reduction of labor market opportunities for women in the official sector.

Lack of social services has meant that Italian women have needed to dedicate time and energies to domestic activities. This has created incentives to maintain traditional economic relationships among family members. Surveys of residents of two urban areas, Turin (1980) and Milan (1981), indicate that, in many cases, other family members (mothers, fathers, etc.) live with the nuclear family. When women work, as they did in 55 per cent of the families, other members of the family do the housework, and especially take responsibility for childcare, even if they do not live together. This pattern of intra-family labor represents an extension of the family which, although it often does not coincide with living arrangements, is compensation for the inefficiency of the social service system (Del Boca and Forte, 1982).[4]

In most Italian families, the household division of labor has remained substantially unequal. The surveys of families in Turin and Milan reveal that women spent on average 45 hours a week in work 'for the family'. In this work, 75 per cent reported receiving no help from their partners (Del Boca and Forte, 1982; Zanuso, 1982).

In the same surveys, of those women who were interviewed and were out of the labor force, 65 per cent reported that they would accept work only if it were part-time. Among women already employed, 40 per cent reported that they would like to work fewer hours a day and fewer weeks a year (Del Boca and Forte, 1982). The demands of housework were a major reason for preferring part time work or more flexible working schedules. More than half of the women interviewed reported that, in the last five years, housework had become more onerous, especially 'investment' activities – those aimed at increasing individual and family production, such as education of children, training, job-seeking, searching for a good school, seeking out goods and services of better quality (due to higher income and educational levels) and more 'personalized' services. The difficulty of obtaining them, because of cost and/or inadequate quality, encouraged greater reliance on the family organization for the production of goods and services. The introduction of technological change in housework has increased productivity in the activities devoted to 'maintenance', but not in 'investment' activities.

The study found that total time dedicated to non-market activity has not declined in the last twenty years. Higher consumption standards have been created, but the quality of consumer goods has decreased. Therefore, more time is spent on repairing, choosing and replacing goods, and in compensating for the lower quality of goods and services purchased in the market. The complexity of such activities (which, unlike maintenance activities, cannot easily be delegated to those outside the family) increases the marginal value of extra-market time for the individual engaged in them, while reducing her availability for labor force participation. Therefore, women engaged in family production (especially in the most intensive stages of the family life-cycle) have a higher marginal value of time than do other members of the family. For women, the supply of underground or semi-underground activities seems to depend on the limitations of prevailing working schedules and the growing complexity of extra-market activity which make it difficult to organize their time according to the prevailing work schedules.

The supply of underground activities also seems to depend on higher expectations of a more educated workforce, no longer willing to accept work under any conditions. A well-educated workforce is now confronted with limited job opportunities in the tertiary sector because of its small size, and even less attractive possibilities in the industrial sector, where the routinization of work frustrates the desire for autonomy and the development of one's skills. Faced with these undesirable choices, people seem to prefer various forms of self employment. This explains why, in urban areas, there is a large supply of labor, especially by women, for the unofficial sector. In sum, opportunities for making use of time are not sufficiently flexible, nor do individuals face a range of alternatives sufficient to allow them to achieve the best possible distribution of their time between the labor market and other activities.

In the last few years, economists have stressed the importance of adopting policies aimed at making work time more flexible and consequently offering more choices in time allocation. While the existence of an unofficial sector of the economy is often taken to reflect only widespread tax avoidance, that sector may also exist as a result of extremely limited ranges of choices (to workers and firms) in the official labor market. As long as these restrictions remain, the existence of a large unofficial sector in Italy is assured, regardless of tax policy.

Italian legislation concerning working women

State legislation regarding women's work has been fairly progressive, and union-backed policies have been directly and indirectly favorable to women. But neither the state nor the unions have developed specific labor market policies on behalf of women. The history of Italian legislation relating to women workers can be divided into two periods. The first was characterized by protective standards for women that dealt with working hours and conditions of mothers. Protective policies were reinforced under the Fascist regime and carried over into the postwar period, when the principle of equal pay and equal rights for women and men workers was introduced. The second period began with the Equal Treatment Act of 9 December 1977, based on anti-discrimination legislation in other countries (Ballestrero, 1980).

Besides laying down the principle of general equality, Article 37 of the 1948 Constitution reads: 'The working woman has the same right and, for equal work, the same remuneration due to the man. Working conditions should permit the fulfilment of her essential family function and ensure adequate protection to the mother and her child'. In accordance with the ideas of the time, the Constitution focused on women's family role. Only in 1960 did a collective agreement enforce the principle of equal pay for equal work. During the 1960s, great disparities between the wages of women and men persisted, owing to the lower skills of women and to the lower value given to stereotypically female jobs. In 1971, motherhood became an object of legislative attention. During pregnancy and for seven months after childbirth, women could not be assigned to heavy, dangerous or unhealthy work. The length of maternity leave was fixed as two months prior to the estimated date of delivery and three months after. The prohibition of dismissal covers the whole period of pregnancy and confinement, until the child reaches the age of one year. Maternity leave pay was introduced at the equivalent of 80 per cent of usual remuneration. With special regard for childcare, the 1971 Act entitled women workers to protracted maternity leave for a further term of just under six months. Working mothers may also be absent from work owing to illness of any of their children up to three years of age.

This example shows that Italian women enjoy ample maternity protection – more than in many other countries. Whereas in the US, three-fifths of women have no right even to unpaid leave, and no right to return to their former jobs, Italian women have 20 weeks of paid leave plus the right to return to their old jobs. In France, women are entitled to only 16 weeks, in UK 6 and in FRG 14 weeks [for a detailed comparison see chapter 2].

Undeniably, legal job restrictions and protective legislation also have a price. They make female labor more rigid and more costly and reduce employers' interest in hiring female workers (Padoa Schioppa, 1977; Del Boca and Turvani, 1979). It has been argued, however, that legislation has not, in itself, constituted discrimination. Other forms of differential treatment are regarded as more relevant: social security legislation, drafted on the assumption that the primary breadwinner is always male; a lower retirement age for women; unfavorable standards relating to women's old age pensions, survivors' pensions and family allowances (Ballestrero, 1980).

The Equal Treatment Act 1977 prohibits any discrimination on the basis of sex. The prohibition covers direct and indirect discrimination (as in such apparently neutral criteria as height, weight, experience and education). The 1977 Act introduced special measures aimed at reducing the negative consequences of assuming dual responsibility for family and employment. The most important measure extends to the father, as an alternative to the working mother, the right to be absent from work for childcare and assistance. But he can exercise this right only if the mother expressly waives hers; and the right to be absent from work does not apply to the father when the mother is self-employed or employed in the unofficial sector. This provision is, however, rarely taken up; deeply-rooted social conventions and lack of information keep fathers from taking up childcare leave.

Some of the changes in the new law were intended to correct the previous protective measures but the definition of norms and the lack of resources to enforce equal treatment or restrain discriminatory policies remain weak points in the 1977 law. The woman alone has responsibility for proving the existence of discrimination. The sanctions are very weak: only the retraction of the discriminatory act is guaranteed, once the existence of discrimination is established.[5] Although the Italian law of 1977 opened up to women some of the previous segregated jobs, it lacks clear rules for monitoring and enforcement (Beccalli, 1985).

Italian unions have been traditionally oriented toward the defense of class interests wider than those of their members. Especially since the beginning of the 1970s, the trade unions are committed to equality in general, but not to specific policies to help disadvantaged groups. The guarantee of an acceptable standard of living for the majority of workers, rather than the defense of the more advantaged segments of the working class, has characterized trade union policies up to now. This strategy was regarded as the one drawing the most support, particularly among the large number of workers recruited in the postwar period. The egalitarian orientation of trade union policies resulted in across-the-board increases in basic wages, simplification of the job classification ladder based on skill differentials, and flat-rate indexing agreements to protect against inflation. These policies favor the earnings of women. In manufacturing the average hourly earnings of women were 70 per cent of those of men in 1970, but were 84 per cent in 1981.

As table 2.6 and 2.7 (p. 26 and p. 27) show, sex-linked wage differentials decreased faster in Italy than in any of the countries considered in this book. Yet the unions have not pushed for more job opportunities, nor questioned segregation by sex, nor urged more flexible work schedules which would allow women to increase their labor supply. Job segregation by sex has not remained unchanged in the last twenty years: a recent study of the evolution of sex segregation in manual and non-manual occupations found a slight increase in such segregation (Barile and Zanuso, 1984).

In the recent union debate about the need for overcoming excessive protection of female workers, ideological solutions rather than realistic and effective ones have been proposed. One example is the position of the trade unions on part-time work. The unions have traditionally objected to the introduction of large numbers of part-time jobs for women, arguing that such work would contribute to job segregation, and have asked instead for a reduction in the working week for all workers. Another example is the debate over the possibility of women working night shifts. The unions' argument is that such a change would only be acceptable if the entire organization of labor were altered (Beccalli, 1985). The openness of trade union policies toward women workers has resulted mainly from the general orientation of Italian trade unions rather than from a specific concern for women. Legislation concerning women's work and trade union policies toward women have been relatively better than in other industrialized countries, but labor market policies affecting women have been extremely deficient.

CONCLUSION

In this chapter, an attempt has been made to explain intertemporal movements in the female labor market participation rate in Italy from the 1950s until the 1980s, through a detailed consideration of factors affecting the demand and supply for heterogeneous labor over this period. I have argued that the status of women in the Italian labor market with regard to participation and unemployment rates, earnings, etc. reflects the policies of the employers, government and trade unions, as well as the opportunity costs attached to the participation of women in the labor market.

In terms of supply of labor by women over this period, two trends are particularly relevant. First, the decline in the birthrate implies that less time will be spent in the house on childcare activities. Second, rising average levels of education in the female population increase the market wages women are offered for their services. Both trends would lead, other things being equal, to a greater propensity of Italian women to seek employment. Of course, changes in fertility and schooling patterns are unlikely to be 'exogenous' with respect to the labor market participation process. In general, women have changed their attitudes toward and ability for performing labor market activities in response to institutional, demographic and societal changes which have directly affected the demand for female labor. For this reason, in this chapter, I have been primarily concerned with the manner in which institutional changes have impacted on the labor market status of women in Italy over this period.

I have been more successful in explaining changes in the female participation rate in Italy over the 1950s and 1960s than after that, in part because the institutional environment has become increasingly complex since the late 1960s. In the earlier period, female labor was in highest demand when male labor was scarce; such was the case in all industries during and immediately following World War II, and most importantly, in the agricultural sector over the entire period of the 1950s and 1960s. Most southern women remained on the farms to raise their children, and as a result were not able to acquire labor market skills. In this period, women were 'marginal' workers, who could find employment only when the supply of male workers relative to the demand was sufficiently low. When employed, women tended to occupy jobs requiring little training and providing little opportunity for investment in human capital.

During the 1970s and 1980s, the effects of various institutional changes on the market participation rates of women are more difficult to disentangle. Over the 1970s, some enabling measures (in the sense of Humphries and Rubery) have been taken by the government and employers to facilitate the combination of market and home work for women. First, change in the relative wages of females to males has resulted in the substitution of some male time spent in domestic work for the time of women. Second, the growth of the public sector in Italy has served both to increase somewhat the number of employment opportunities for women and to provide services which substitute for women's domestic work. These factors, in concert with the secular growth of the Italian economy, have acted to increase both the demand for and supply of female labor.

It seems clear, however, that other enabling measures have actually tended to retard the growth of female labor market participation in Italy. Highly protective legislation (stipulating the types of jobs in which women can be engaged and allowing for liberal maternity leaves) has effectively increased the price of female labor, particularly in high-paying, stable jobs. These 'constraints' on the behavior of employers are not legally binding on small firms, which explains the fact that women tend to be employed in small firms rather than large ones. The price differential between male and female labor and the resultant diminution of the demand for female labor, also is largely responsible for the substantial presence of women in the underground economy and the relatively low participation rate in the official economy.

The effects of institutional changes on the economic welfare of women in Italy are difficult to assess. On the one hand, recent legislation has acted to decrease wage discrepancies between female and male workers and has facilitated the combining of familial and labor market activities. On the other hand, by increasing the relative costliness of employing female labor, demand in the official market sector has probably decreased. This has probably resulted in substantial increases in the female participation rate in the underground economy, the welfare consequences of which are not clear. While women employed in this sector are less protected and probably remunerated at a lower rate, they do have the advantage of more flexibility in their employment relationship.

The trade-off between improving the situation of the employed at the expense of those not fortunate enough to find employment in the official sector is a common policy question faced in all advanced economies. The Italian situation is particularly difficult to analyse in that such radical changes in social policies have occurred over the matter of a few decades. It is probably premature to speculate on how these institutional changes will affect the welfare of Italian women in the long run.

NOTES

1 In comparison, in 1972, participation rates were 49.9 per cent in the US, 51.4 per cent in the UK and 61.9 per cent in Sweden (OECD, 1980).
2 The greater magnitude and importance of homework in Italy can be compared to the much smaller home-working sector discussed by Humphries and Rubery (chapter 5).
3 See Humphries and Rubery's report for the UK (chapter 5) and Jenson's for France (chapter 9), Armstrong and Armstrong (chapter 4).
4 For a similar inter-generational pattern of shared housework, despite a more service-based set of social programs, see Daune-Richard (chapter 15).
5 In contrast, in the US the vulnerability of the individual who reports discrimination is recognized: if the discrimination is established, all groups in the same condition (in the same productive unit) obtain the same compensation. This is also reinforced by the US Equal Employment Opportunity Commission, which has the human and financial resources necessary to promote claims and to coordinate antidiscriminatory policies. For a discussion of French procedures after 1981 see Jenson (chapter 9).

REFERENCES

Ballestrero, M. V. (1980) *Della Tutela alla Parita: la legislazione Italiana sul lavoro delle donne* (Bologna: Il Mulino).

Barile, P. and L. Zanuso (1984) *La Segregazione occupazionale in Italia* (Milan: Franco Angeli).

Beccalli, B. (1985) 'Women and Trade Unions in Italy', in A. N. Cook, V. R. Lorwin and A. K. Daniels (eds), *Women and Trade Unions in Eleven Industrialized Countries* (Philadelphia: Temple University Press).

Del Boca, D. and M. Turvani (1979) *Famiglia e Mercato del Lavoro* (Bologna: Il Mulino).

Del Boca, D. and F. Forte (1983) 'Empirical Survey and Theoretical Interpretation of the Parallel Economy in Italy', in V. Tanzi (ed.), *The Underground Economy in the U.S. and Abroad* (Boston, MA: D. C. Heath).

Flanagan, R. J., D. Soskie and L. Ulman (1982) *Unionism, Economic Stabilization and Income Policies* (Washington, DC: The Brookings Institution).

OECD (1985) *Economic Outlook* (Paris: OECD).

OECD (1972, 1980, 1986) *Labor Force Statistics* (Paris: OECD).

Padoa Schioppa, F. (1977) *La Forza lavoro femminile* (Bologna: Il Mulino).

Turvani, M. (1986) *Occupazione femminile e welfare*, Biblioteca della Liberta, no. 2.

Zanuso, L. *La Qualita della vita a Milano: un'indagine sulle famiglie milanesi*, Research report, City of Milan.

8

The Computer Rationalization of Work

Implications for Women Workers

Peter S. Albin and
Eileen Appelbaum

The organization of work in the US and other advanced industrial economies is in flux. Not only is the introduction of computer technology into a wide variety of production environments changing the nature of the output of firms, it is also altering the relationship between firms and the end-users of their products, the relationship of workers to the production process and, most importantly, the organization of the labor process itself. It is the scope of the new and emerging computation and information technologies that establishes their revolutionary character. Market forces mediate the transformation of production and work organization, but outcomes are not uniquely determined by the search for efficiency within an impersonal price mechanism. Instead, as with the nineteenth-century managerial responses to industrialization and market extension, this latest transformation is strongly influenced by extra-economic motives in planning, strategic, entrepreneurial and adaptive processes undertaken by firms. However, in comparison with earlier technologies, the flexibility of computer-based production processes and their associated systems architectures has increased the discretionary range of managerial (and social) choices with respect to job design and organizational form.

The development of computer technology and solid-state circuitry in the 1960s advanced the technology for controlling machinery far beyond what could be accomplished by earlier electromechanical devices. Computerized devices for controlling machinery greatly increase the speed with which information can be cycled from sensors through machine or human decision-makers to production equipment and take account of previous measurements stored in long-term memory. The flexibility gain over earlier automated production processes follows. We have termed automated production systems integrally based on computerized control technology, whether in industry or services, *computer-rationalized production*.

GOVERNANCE OF COMPUTER-RATIONALIZED SYSTEMS

The introduction of computer-rationalized production systems, like the development of mass production technologies a century earlier, created a crisis in the control of the overall production process by firms. Dynamic models of large-scale production systems have proven to be too complex to be effectively constructable. In an integrated production system, in which a high degree of interdependence exists among the various subsystems, the lack of such models to coordinate, integrate and predict the combined effects of the separate automatic controls means that the technology alone cannot solve the problem of effective governance. Indeed, failures of process control technology have sometimes been spectacular.

Two distinct responses of firms to this crisis of governance over computer-rationalized production processes have emerged. In the early developmental stages, systems analysts and planners were confident that they could design computer-controlled processes to operate optimally without intervention of skilled operators to make adjustments and corrections. Many firms remain committed to this approach today and continue to design the production process to approximate a situation in which the information system that controls the production equipment or process anticipates all possible inputs or environmental changes and, using algorithmic decision rules, makes all decisions. The guiding principle of such a design approach, which we have termed the algorithmic organization of production and work, is to limit the need for workers' skills and to reduce the role of human knowledge and judgement in the production process by designing ever more perfect, self-regulating production systems. To do so, however, in light of the difficulties discussed above, requires a simple (or contrivedly simplified) environment and information preprocessed and *reduced* to the limited number of inputs anticipated by the information system controlling the production process. However, this design approach sharply curtails the potential of a computer-controlled production system for flexibility – for responding quickly and easily to changes in the design of products and parts, in market conditions, or in the volume of output. Such a system is well *adapted* for the circumstances which it was designed to anticipate, but it is *not adaptive*. It lacks the ability to respond easily and flexibly to changes in ambient conditions and may prove less than optimal in future circumstances – that is, it lacks a property that in other contexts has been termed 'system robustness'.

Robust computer-rationalization

The availability of relatively inexpensive microprocessors has opened up a second, alternative path of development. The low cost of microprocessors makes it possible to use them to increase the knowledge and enhance the capabilities of a wide range of workers, increasing both the skill levels of workers and the flexibility of work organizations in allocating labor. Computer-rationalization of production proceeds in this case by substantially *increasing* the amount of information that can be stored and processed, enchancing the decision-making capacities of clerks, operators, engineers and design personnel alike. It differs fundamentally from computer-rationalization based on standardizing and reducing information inputs and applying algorithmic decision rules to fully anticipated situations.

A microprocessor used to monitor and control one part of a production process can also store, process and transmit large amounts of data on its operation and performance characteristics. The data are available to operators and clerks, as well as technical and managerial personnel; all can intervene manually to make adjustments and corrections or to correct programming errors. Thus, the microprocessor enables access to a detailed knowledge base and, as the data are used and analyzed, a more complete understanding of the dynamics of the production system can be developed.

The decision by firms to employ forms of work organization designed to promote learning, flexibility and adaptive behavior on the part of workers – what we have termed the robust organization of production and work – is a relatively new development. It remains a relatively uncommon form of work organization, but one which is exceptionally well suited to the requirements of integrated and flexible production systems in industry or services.

Robust organizations are frequently associated with sociotechnical work settings. The computer is used to provide information on operating characteristics and do technical calculations, create illustrations, rotate designs, calculate building costs, analyse cross-sections of tissue and, generally, to provide answers to questions posed by operating and production personnel as well as by technical staff and managers. The system is designed to inform decision-making at every level. This includes the shop or office floor where operators or secretaries may have a better 'feel' for a poorly understood process than do engineers or analysts. Computerized controls are designed to facilitate learning and to inform rather than pre-empt decision-making by workers. Over the long run, the goal is better results than might be obtained were the production process simplified or standardized so it can be governed completely by the computer.

Robustness, however, cannot be characterized simply in terms of the work setting. Robustness refers to the organizational adaptiveness of the firm and, as such, is properly a systems property describing how the firm, or a significant subset of its activities, functions. The distinction is important because it is not unusual for certain activities – for example, software development or design of new products – to be carried out in socio-technical work settings in even the most algorithmic firms. The critical organizational characteristics of robust forms have to do with the relationships among employees at different levels within the firm. Workers at higher levels are familiar with the work done at lower levels as well as with the people doing it. Confidence in workers at lower levels allows managers to hand over problems with current products or services to lower levels for solutions while freeing those at the upper levels to develop new products and markets. Workers at each level have some knowledge of the whole production system, though the extent of this knowledge and the level of abstraction in understanding the system increases at higher levels. Workers at any level in such firms are familiar to a significant degree with work at the next higher level, and communication among peers at the same level and between workers at one level and those just above or below them is extensive.[1] There are many cross-links between the levels in such an organization. The organization is still hierarchical, although there are often fewer levels of hierarchy than in more algorithmic firms and, unlike the algorithmic firms, communication is not intended or formally structured to be primarily one-dimensional and top-down; two-way communication is both encouraged and facilitated.

Algorithmic computer-rationalization

In contrast to the robust organization of production associated with computer-rationalization based on the exploitation of the computer's enormous memory and information-processing capacities and on the enhancement of worker capabilities, the more common, algorithmic form of computer-rationalization accepts only pre-selected information and reduces worker initiative and knowledge of the production process. The computer is used to limit decision-making and creativity in the jobs of operators, clerks, technicians and service workers and to centralize and control these functions higher up in the bureaucracy. Centralization and control over the work done are pushed as far as the technology will allow, while further development of the technology is motivated by the desire to push such control even farther. Knowledge of the nuances of the product or the production process by workers is redundant, since only knowledge already embedded in the information system controlling the production process has any effect on the product or service produced. Since the system cannot use the knowledge of workers, firm-specific skills are devalued and companies following this path of development are reluctant to invest in training their workers. Internal labor markets are weakened as the importance to employers of developing a trained and loyal workforce declines. Skills are lost or not developed, jobs are simplified and workers become extensions of the machines with which they work.

Despite the fact that computerization automates the most routine tasks, product knowledge decreases, job complexity is reduced and the production, clerical and service jobs not eliminated by automation are, in algorithmically organized firms, deskilled. The job skills that remain depend on the relationship of the job to the computer technology and to the extent of software development. Thus, data entry, machine tending, dial watching, data processing, even programming in this context, require little knowledge of the company's product or service. The degree of computer sophistication in these jobs varies from almost none to extensive, with most workers in jobs that require very little computer literacy. It is ironic, however, that while tasks are simplified and craft skills decreased, the system's dependence on workers' responsibility increases. A momentary lapse in watching the dials, a clerical error in entering data, or a bug in a computer program, may prove to be extremely expensive and, because of the interconnectedness of computer-based systems, may lead to unexpected errors elsewhere in the operation. An algorithmic computer-rationalized system can be ludicrously ineffective in its attempts to diagnose or correct interconnected errors. This increase in system sensitivity is especially stressful to workers who lack the knowledge and training to respond to unexpected errors or incomprehensible failures. In its effect on worker skills, initiative and decision-making, algorithmic computer rationalization can be seen as an extension of Taylorist principles and a continuation of the older, bureaucratic forms of control over workers and the amount of output they produce.

Productivity implications of organizational design choices

Thus, in many production and service activities, information technology allows either more 'algorithmic' or more 'robust' solutions to questions of organization and structure, and the outcome depends on high-level decisions made by managers, engineers and systems planners. Such decisions involve the evaluation of the terms of many trade-offs – including that between short-run cost savings and the potential for long-term productivity growth, both of which may be difficult to specify in advance. In evaluating strategies for change, the immediate cost factors – especially the costs of training or retraining workers, rearranging the work floor, developing new management techniques and involving workers in decision-making – must be weighed against the potential long-run productivity gains associated with learning-by-doing, flexibility in production, responsiveness to changes in tastes, design or market conditions and effective management of unexpected failures. There is, thus, a large volitional element in such trade-off decisions, conditioned by the objectives and sophistication of managers, the strength of workers and their unions, and important cues communicated by policy makers. The positions along the continuum from more algorithmic to more robust forms of computer rationalization and work organization selected by firms represent the different conclusions which these firms have drawn about the terms of these trade-offs.

There are significant costs associated with implementing robust forms of organization. Training costs for workers at lower levels tend to be higher in robust than in algorithmic organizations. Moreover, robust organizations pay an overhead for all the internal communication. In small firms, or in firms in which technology, products or markets are not likely to change very quickly, these higher costs may not be justified. Robust firms achieve efficiency in the long run, rather than in shorter time-periods, because the primary advantage of robust firms is a built-in capability for reorganization that is lacking in algorithmic firms. The robustness of such firms is demonstrated when they adapt easily and flexibly to changing conditions; and it can be seen over time in such things as the speed with which internal failures are noticed and corrected and the timeliness of the development of new products and services. Higher initial costs are less important to the profitability of firms facing a changing environment than the ability to adapt to new conditions.

The robust/algorithmic distinction is sharpest in a comparison between firms facing a fairly stable environment with a technology that is changing slowly at best and those in an environment characterized by fairly rapid changes in supply or demand conditions. Firms in a stable environment will want to be as fully *adapted* as possible for the conditions in which they are currently functioning. In these instances, algorithmic forms of organization may be not be inappropriate. Firms in a rapidly changing environment, however, require flexibility and adaptiveness. Algorithmic computer-rationalization in such firms limits worker skills and thereby sharply constrains the capability of the technology to respond flexibly to changing or unpredictable conditions. Where flexibility cannot be achieved through optimal use of the technology, firms turn, instead, to labor practices that replace full-time workers by part-time or temporary workers to achieve this goal.

Thus, decisions made at the micro-level by firms implementing computer-rationalization of production have implications for a diverse set of economic outcomes. These include the long-term growth path of the economy, the skill content of jobs, the dynamic comparative advantage of firms in international trade and the availability of full-time work. The remainder of this chapter considers those implications which are of particular importance to women workers.

COMPUTER-RATIONALIZATION AND CLERICAL WORK

Microprocessor-based technologies currently have a determining cost impact on the input and processing of data. As a result, they are transforming the nature of clerical work – and clerical workers are, almost everywhere in advanced industrial economies, disproportionately female (table 2.9, p. 29). The number of workers potentially affected by these changes is very great in the US, where administrative support personnel, including clerical workers, numbered 18.1 million in January 1987 (16.6 per cent of the labor force) and are projected to increase to 23.7 million by 1995 (again, approximately 20 per cent of the labor force). Of these, 14.4 million are women (US Bureau of Labor Statistics, *Employment and Earnings*, February 1987, Table A–22, p. 29). Of course, the US is not alone in the gender of its clerical workforce. In Sweden too, 89 per cent of the occupational group is female (chapter 10: table 10.2, p. 182).

The distribution of occupations within computer-rationalized firms is closely related to whether the firm has adopted an algorithmic or robust form of organization. More algorithmic forms of organization associate with a preponderance of routine jobs complemented by a small staff of professionals. More robust organizations, on the other hand, require large numbers of workers in middle-range technical jobs responsible for diagnosis, evaluation, operation and system maintenance and in paraprofessional jobs responsible for customer, client and intrafirm services. In comparison with the occupational distribution in firms that are not computer-rationalized, algorithmic rationalization represents a general deskilling of the workforce, although an increase in high-level jobs and a bimodal split in the distribution of occupations can be observed. Robust organization, in contrast, represents a general upskilling of the work force and an increase in both middle- and upper-level jobs.

In evaluating the effects of the implementation of computer and communication technologies on clerical work, three broad issues can be identified: fragmentation vs integration of tasks, extent of contextual knowledge requirements, and entry and mobility characteristics of jobs. With the possible exception of the mobility issue, algorithmic and robust forms of organization differ along each of these dimensions.

When computerization was first introduced into the office environment, managers generally adopted the same principles that had guided the older factory pattern of automation associated with Taylorism and scientific management; accordingly, the labor process fragmented further. The logic of scientific management in a factory setting meant that work was rationalized and disaggregated as it was automated. Productivity increased, but in the process worker skills were devalued, tasks became repetitive, and workers' sense of responsibility for the company's product diminished. In large office settings, such as those in the insurance business, work had long been fragmented. As companies introduced computers, they applied the technology to tasks that were already discrete. Computer-rationalization proceeded along algorithmic lines, extending the specialization and fragmentation of work. Skill levels tended to decline, and the newly automated tasks were routine and repetitive.

As microprocessor-based technologies developed and experience with office automation increased, technology's capability for integrating work processes began to be recognized. At least a few managers saw that computer and communication technologies are most effective in reducing costs when control, communication and decision-making are decentralized and when hierarchic organization and the functional specialization of tasks are reduced. Applying the technologies to take advantage of these properties and achieve the inherent productivity gains, some companies have eliminated both less-skilled clerical jobs and routine technical and professional jobs, creating instead multi-activity, skilled clerical positions to handle these functions. In robust organizations, this use of technology results in what we have termed the para-professionalization of clerical work.

Despite the possibilities of the technology, however, many companies still follow Taylorist principles when automating their offices. They use recent advances in computers and telecommunications to fragment work even further by uncoupling the work process and geographically dispersing the various stages of production. Not uncommon are huge clerical processing centers, located in economically depressed small cities or in suburban areas where women who seek jobs have few alternatives. Most of the women employed at these locations are clerical workers performing routine data-entry functions; a few have risen to fill the limited number of positions available as clerical supervisors.

This uncoupling of the work process, with different stages carried out at separate locations and then reintegrated via telecommunications to form the finished product, has been carried even further by some companies who have turned to the use of homework or have moved routine data entry jobs offshore (Appelbaum, 1984; Appelbaum, 1985: 21-6; Baran, 1987). There are no avenues for upward mobility for clerical workers at these remote locations both because there are no opportunities for workers to acquire additional skills and because the workers are geographically removed from any higher-level jobs within the firm. Labor cost savings are achieved not through making the most productive use of the technology but by the use of low-wage and/or part-time or temporary workers who are denied fringe benefits and by closely monitoring clerical workers and setting standards such as those for keystrokes per minute.

The role of contextual knowledge (by which we mean knowledge of the firm's products, production processes, procedures or regulatory environment) in the design of jobs is a second important dividing-line between algorithmic and robust forms of work organization. Many jobs in computer-rationalized firms organized along algorithmic lines are low in contextual knowledge requirements. Job skills in these firms are related to the development of software and not to the historical roots of the industry. Valued skills are not firm-specific but relate instead to the technology. These include skills ranging from data entry and word processing to graphics design and programming of numerical production controls.

Of particular importance in clerical work is the way contextual knowledge distinguishes between routine and paraprofessional jobs in the expanding areas of customer service and intrafirm communications. Routine jobs require little contextual knowledge. Data gatekeeper jobs (such as directory assistance operator, classified ad-taker, or airline ticket reservations clerk) are important because they are on the boundary between the firm and its customers or suppliers, but they can be performed by workers without much knowledge of the industry or the firm. In contrast, other intrafirm or customer service jobs – such as personal loan officer, travel agent, insurance claims examiner, administrative assistant or secretary – require moderate to extensive contextual knowledge and can be characterized as para-professional jobs.

The distinction between the routine and para-professional job is generally not technologically-determined, but results from strategic job design decisions made by firms. Algorithmic firms give great weight in job-design decisions to the immediate cost savings realizable if these positions can be filled with less-skilled workers rather than by para-professional employees. They tend to ignore worker satisfaction, human resource development and long-run productivity and cost-containment issues. Robust organizations, in contrast, design multi-activity customer service jobs to be filled by workers with substantial training and knowledge of the firm's products, processes and procedures and with the authority to make decisions and resolve customer problems. Increased communication requirements among groups working at the same level within robustly organized firms or between levels of the hierarchy also imply a need for highly skilled clerical employees knowledgeable about the firm's operations. Initial costs, especially those associated with training, are higher in more robust firms, but the flexibility and adaptability of such firms often gives them a competitive advantage (Albin, 1984; Koppel, et al., 1987).

While computer and information technologies are transforming clerical work, the long-standing reluctance of employers to provide costly training for female clerical workers has contributed to the managerial bias in favor of more algorithmic forms of computer rationalization. These micro-level decisions by firms regarding job design and training requirements in female occupations have profound negative implications for women, who find themselves disproportionately represented in more algorithmic work processes. There are implications for the growth of American productivity as well. It is possible that, distorted by the desire to organize clerical work so that firm-specific training costs are low, these decisions are not even locally efficient but undermine the firm's competitiveness. This is an analytical argument developed more fully elsewhere (Albin, 1985: 703-30).

Entry-level jobs and career paths

The job design decisions of firms have a third set of implications. In particular, they affect the nature of entry-level clerical jobs. Computer-rationalization, whatever form it takes, eliminates the most routine clerical jobs – mail handling, coupon sorting and filing, for example. In robustly organized firms, routine keyboarding jobs are eliminated as well, by incorporating data entry and word processing into the multi-dimensional jobs held by skilled clerical or, as we prefer to term them, para-professional workers. Community college graduates or women with some college education are preferred for these positions. The jobs do not require specific skills learned in college; even computer skills required in these jobs are easily learned without formal programming experience. The requirements for skilled clerical work are high general literacy skills, good verbal and written communication skills, and aptitude for arithmetic and problem-solving tasks. Employers use college credentials to screen for these abilities.

More algorithmic forms of computer rationalization in office settings have led to a proliferation of routine keyboarding jobs (text or data entry, accessing programs and retrieving information) and routine gatekeeper jobs, often relocated at remote sites, away from large central cities. These routine keyboarding jobs and data gatekeeper jobs, however, face the greatest immediate risk of technological displacement. Computer terminals and screens already have an instantaneous response rate, and the speed of throughput in these jobs is limited only by the speed of human response or human speech. Current technology already allows data to be entered on-line at the point of sale or when a service is rendered. When fully implemented, these practices will eliminate many routinized data-entry jobs. The development of cheaper and more effective optical scanners will destroy many more. Moreover, the move to self-service threatens other data gatekeeper jobs. These activities can be turned over directly to the consumers of a company's services, as when catalogue sales or inquiries about the status of one's bank account are conducted via personal computer and without assistance. Only the speed of diffusion of routine computer skills slows the elimination of many of these jobs. As a result, self-service operations will probably increase more rapidly for transactions among firms, where these skills are more prevalent, than for the delivery of services to consumers. The combined effect of automation and the location decisions of firms thus limit entry-level job opportunities for inner-city black women and for less-educated, urban, white, working-class women.

The computer rationalization of work curtails opportunities for upward mobility for clerical workers whether in algorithmic or robust organizations. This effect is obvious in algorithmically-organized firms where clerical workers are given little training in firm-specific skills or where technology has been utilized to locate data entry, text entry, computerized billing and similar processing activities away from the central headquarters or field offices where the firm's main business is carried out. In more robustly organized companies, where the productive capabilities of office auto-mation technologies are more fully utilized, skilled clerical work continues to increase as the more routine aspects of professional work are automated and become part of the clerical function. The remaining professional jobs require years of formal training at the university or postgraduate level. In other words, automation of lower-level professional jobs has interrupted the traditional learning sequence by which skilled clerical workers could acquire professional skills through on-the-job experience, and has elimi-nated the jobs which formerly served as the rungs of a career ladder from clerical to professional work. Thus, the gap between the skills of clerical workers and those of professionals has widened despite the reduction in less-skilled clerical work. Skill requirements for clerical workers have increased at the same time that the jobs have become overwhelmingly dead-end.

One further point can be made about job mobility for clerical workers. It is clearly the case that jobs in algorithmically-organized firms have low contextual knowledge requirements and provide little firm-specific training; there is little upward mobility within the firm. However, the clerical occupations that we have identified as data gatekeeper jobs have very similar skill requirements. They require telephone communications skills, the ability to interact with the public, and the ability to use a computer to access, store and retrieve information. The extensive overlap in job skills in seemingly different industries suggests the possibility that lateral mobility through the external labor market may increase as vertical mobility within firms decreases. Such mobility requires labor market institutions to facilitate the process and temporary help service firms have begun to fill this role. They institutionalize the movement of labor resources across indus-tries and meet some needs of algorithmically-organized firms.

Algorithmic organization and casual labor

The explosive growth of temporary work and the increase in involuntary part-time employment in advanced industrial economies have been widely noted (see table 2.4, p. 23).[2] In the US, monthly employment data show a slight decline in the proportion of women employed part-time between May 1979 and May 1986, from 29.9 to 28.3 per cent of wage and salary workers (Bureau of Labor Statistics, *Employment and Earnings*, January 1980, table A–9). Retrospective data, which are available for the years from 1975 to 1983, show the proportion of women with some part-time employment constant at about 32.7 per cent of the total number of women with work experience (Bureau of Labor Statistics, 1976; unpublished data for 1983). Nevertheless, the proportion of women employed part-time in retail trade and personal services (the sectors which account for most of the part-time jobs) increased from 47.7 per cent to 50.9 per cent in retail trade and from 40.4 per cent to 41.8 per cent in personal services between 1970 and 1984.

Significantly, despite the fact that the proportion of women who work part-time has been constant since the late 1970s, the part-time employment of women is increasingly involuntary. The proportion of the female workforce employed part-time for economic reasons, despite a desire for full-time work, increased from 3.6 per cent of the total in 1970 to 6.1 per cent in 1984 and 6.2 per cent in 1986. Involuntary part-time employment of women, which accounted for 12 per cent of part-time women workers in 1970, now accounts for 22 per cent.[3] Finally, the hours of women working part-time have declined. The proportion working only 15–29 hours a week increased from 15.9 per cent in 1970 to 17.1 per cent by 1980, where it remained in 1984. The proportion working nearly full-time (30 to 34 hours a week) declined from 11.8 per cent to 9.9 per cent over the same period (Bureau of Labor Statistics, unpublished data; for a fuller discussion, see Appelbaum, 1987: 276–96).

While part-time employment has paralleled the expansion of traditional service industries, the growth of temporary employment has outpaced the American economy as a whole. Following the recession of 1981–2, annual average employment in temporary help services was 17.5 per cent higher in 1983 than the previous year. By comparison, annual average employment in non-agricultural establishments increased by less than one per cent between those two years. The increase in the number of temporary jobs between 1982 and 1983 equalled 12.6 per cent of the number of non-agricultural jobs added that year, despite the fact that temporary help services accounted for less than one-half of one per cent of total non-agricultural employment in 1982. In 1983, temporary help service firms filled an average of 472,000 jobs a day with temporary workers. By 1986, they placed an average of 750,000 workers a day, more than 460,000 of them women, in temporary positions.[4] More than five million American workers were placed in jobs through temporary help agencies at some time last year, but these figures do not include the more than 240,000 temporary jobs filled by the federal government, or the uncounted numbers of workers hired directly on a temporary basis by private employers.[5]

Underlying employment patterns

Our earlier analysis suggests several important links between computer-rationalization of work and these recent increases in casual and reduced-time employment. We have found it useful to distinguish between information-knowledge services (S1), in which computer-rationalization is proceeding, and the older services jobs (S2), which continue to be organized along traditional lines. Technological change and falling unit labor requirements in the S1 sector of the US economy, occurring over the last decade in the context of high interest rates, unfavorable exchange rates and two severe recessions, have reduced or slowed the growth of employment opportunities in the technologically progressive industries. Excluded from these jobs, workers have accepted employment in the S2 sector where high employment levels and rapid job growth are predicated on low wages, short hours and few fringe benefits. Expansion of this sector, particularly retail trade and personal services, accounts for the steady expansion in the number (though not the proportion) of part-time workers, and may connote disguised unemployment resulting from prolonged macroeconomic slack. This interpretation is supported by the increase in involuntary part-time employment to 5.5 million workers, 2.9 million of them women, and by the increase in the proportion of part-time workers employed 15–29 hours a week, most without fringe benefits or other protections afforded full-time workers.

But this is not the only factor leading to an increase in temporary and part-time work. The explosive growth in temporary employment also results from attempts by algorithmically-organized firms to contain costs and respond flexibly to increased international competition, deregulation and changes in federal payment procedures. While robustly-organized firms can adapt continuously to changing competitive conditions and can reduce labor costs by increasing productivity, these options are sharply curtailed for more algorithmic firms. In this context, the use of workers only casually attached to the firm, who are not entitled to fringe benefits and are easily let go, is an attractive option for managers. Moreover, short of reorganizing the work process, it may appear the only option available for controlling costs and improving the competitive position of the company. For this reason, many companies have begun organizing on a core and ring basis, holding the number of permanent, full-time workers to a minimum and supplementing this staff with temporary workers. The temporary workers function as an employment buffer – available to meet surges in the demand for goods and services and easily dispensed with when demand declines.

In the US, the constraints on employers with respect to job assignment, layoffs, firing and promotion policies, and benefit packages that exist as a result of both explicit and implicit contracts between companies and their full-time employees are largely nonexistent in the case of temporary workers.[6] Flexibility in meeting staffing needs and the ability to retrench quickly are beginning to take precedence over the desire for a loyal, well-trained workforce and low turnover rates. The process is facilitated by the declining importance of internal labor markets in algorithmically-organized firms, and by the increase in clerical and professional jobs in which contextual knowledge is unimportant and in which the relevant skills relate to the technology and are largely the same across industries.

Temporary employment is even more important in the S1 sector of the economy than in the S2 sector since firms in the traditional service industries typically employ part-time workers and meet surges in demand by increasing the hours of work of these employees. Temporary employment is an important strategy for addressing workload fluctuations in firms in banking, insurance, business services and in the public sector (Mayall and Nelson, 1982: 68, 74, 79, 83). According to one estimate, 49 per cent of the 1984 receipts of temporary help firms came from clerical work and 34.9 per cent from technical employment, with medical and industrial employment accounting for the remaining 16 per cent (Wasser, cited in Pfeffer and Baron, 1985). Temporary help services are concentrated in large cities and place workers in large firms. Aggregate data show that the ten largest Standard Metropolitan Statistical Areas (SMSAs) account for 40 per cent of the jobs in the industry and the 40 largest for 80 per cent (Mayall and Nelson, 1982: iii). Data from a major study of the use of temporary help services by 900 California firms indicate that only 12.7 per cent of firms with 1–4 employees and 25.7 per cent of those with 5–19 employees made use of these agencies. However, the proportions rose to 68.9 per cent for firms with 250–999 employees and 74.7 per cent for firms with more than 1000 employees (Mayall and Nelson, 1982: 38).

Survey responses reported by Mayall and Nelson lend support to our argument that temporary help service agencies are used to fill positions with low contextual knowledge requirements in which skills are transferable across firms and industries, and that many temporary occupations are growing as the result of the spread of algorithmic computer-rationalization of work. Employers distinguish between 'standardized' positions with transferable skills, including some professional or technical occupations, which they fill through temporary help agencies, and 'specialized' positions which require substantial contextual knowledge and firm-specific skills. Employers generally do not find temporary workers capable of filling these positions, and develop internal mechanisms for covering employee absences or meeting temporary overload situations.

CONCLUSION

The computer-rationalization of production and the reorganization of work are proceeding in all of the advanced industrial economies. Computer and information technologies are much more flexible than earlier automation technologies. As a result, organizational form and job design are subject to managerial discretion and social influence to an extent not previously possible. A key trade-off involves choice between more robust and more algorithmic forms of organization. In the US, the decision has characteristically been made by managers who often appear more concerned about immediate cost savings than about long-term productivity growth. As a consequence, implementation of computer rationalization in the US has tended to follow the more algorithmic path.

Algorithmic computer-rationalization has negative implications for productivity growth, dynamic as opposed to instantaneous cost containment, and international competitiveness. These prospects translate into mediocre income and career paths for all US workers, women among them. However, algorithmic computer-rationalization has particular pernicious effects that fall most heavily on women – particularly ethnic minority and inner-city women. These effects include the routinization and deskilling of clerical work, creation of casual jobs, and extension of the secondary labor market.

We have examined these effects at length and we can only reiterate our view that the negative impacts are not inevitable. The technology offers a wide range of choice over work and organizational designs. Favorable productivity and human resource outcomes appear to be feasible, but the social and political forces needed to effect such change have not yet been mobilized.

NOTES

This research was supported in part by funds from the Congress of the United States, Office of Technology Assessment, Washington, DC. The authors wish to thank their colleague, Ross Koppel, for his many helpful comments.

1 These concepts are developed at length by Joel Moses (1985).
2 There are two main sources of data on part-time employment in the US – monthly employment data which report the number of part-time jobs in the economy, and retrospective data which report the number of people who held a part-time job at some time during the year.
3 These statistics are derived from the Bureau of Labor Statistics, *Employment and Earnings*, various issues, Tables A–7, A–8 or A–9.
4 See Bureau of Labor Statistics, *Employment and Earnings*, 1984 and 1987, Tables B–2 and B–3; *Supplement to Employment and Earnings, Revised*

Establishment Data, 1984 and 1987, for SIC 7362, Temporary Help Supply Services.

5 Data provided by Sam Sacco, National Association of Temporary Services, Alexandria, VA; and Mary Ann Madison, Office of Technology Assessment, US Congress.

6 Even in Western Europe, where part-time and temporary workers have won some protection through collective bargaining and state actions, they are not as protected as full-time workers (see chapters 2, 9 and 10).

REFERENCES

Albin, P. S. (1984) 'Job design within changing patterns of technical development', in E. L. Collins and L. D. Tanner (eds), *American Jobs and the Changing Industrial Base* (Cambridge, MA: Ballinger Publishing Co.).

Albin, P. S. (1985) 'Job design, control technology, and technical change', *Journal of Economic Issues*, XIX (3).

Appelbaum, E. (1984) 'The impact of technology on skill requirements and occupational structure in the insurance industry, 1960–1990', mimeo (Temple University).

Appelbaum, E. (1985) 'Technology and work organization in the insurance industry', *ILR Report*, XXIII.

Appelbaum, E. (1987) 'Restructuring work: temporary, part-time, and at-home employment', in H. Hartmann (ed.), *Computer Chips and Paper Clips: Technology and Women's Employment*, vol. 2 (Washington, DC: National Academy Press).

Baran, B. (1987) 'The technological transformation of white-collar work: a case study of the insurance industry', in H. Hartmann (ed.), *Computer Chips and Paper Clips: Technology and Women's Employment*, vol. 2 (Washington, DC: National Academy Press).

Koppel, R., E. Appelbaum and P. S. Albin (1987) 'Implications of workplace technology: control, organization of work and the occupational structure', in I. H. Simpson and R. L. Simpson (eds.) *Research in the Sociology of Work*, vol. 4 (Greenwich, CT: JAI Press), forthcoming.

Mayall, D. and K. Nelson (1982) *The Temporary Help Supply Service and the Temporary Labor Market*, Report submitted to the US Department of Labor.

Moses, J. (1985) 'Reductionism and holism: approaches to the organization of robust systems', unpublished paper (Computer Science Department, Massachusetts Institute of Technology).

Pfeffer, J. and J. Baron (1985) 'Taking the worker back out: recent trends in labor contracting', unpublished paper (Department of Economics, Stanford University).

US Department of Labor, Bureau of Labor Statistics (1976) *Work Experience of the Population in 1975* (Washington, DC).

US Department of Labor, Bureau of Labor Statistics (1984 and 1987) *Supplement to Employment and Earnings, Revised Established Data* (Washington, DC).

US Department of Labor, unpublished data from the Current Population Survey, March 1971, 1976, 1981, 1984 and 1985; unpublished data on work experience of the population in 1979 and 1983.

PART III

The Policy Process: Promises Broken
or Rencwed?

9

The Limits of 'and the' Discourse
French Women as Marginal Workers

Jane Jenson

It may be a truism but it is worth repeating: it is impossible to understand the French state's responses to an increasingly feminized labor force in isolation from state employment and industrial policies as a whole, because the state itself makes no such clear distinction. As a result, the gendering effects (that is, the differential consequences for women and men) of all policies often remain invisible because policy strategies and instruments do not acknowledge that the labor force is differentiated by sex. A second consequence is that policy initiatives from those branches of the state which do recognize that the labor force comes in two genders must be made compatible with employment policy as a whole. This means that programs directed at women are inevitably and profoundly limited by the policy environment in which they must be promoted.

None of this is meant to imply, however, that the best way to understand state responses to the feminization of the labor force is to search for a coherent and unified policy analysis and set of programs which organize employment policy. Rather, I shall assume that policy initiatives are developed in a context of competition, in which actors struggle to impose their own understandings and preferences on others. In many situations there is profound disagreement about causes and consequences of labor market structures. These differences may arise from theoretical and political divergences over the nature of capitalist society or out of more narrow differences over policy instruments. But no matter the profundity of the differences, competition exists.

It is useful to characterize this competition as being at least in part over meaning systems or discourses (Jenson, 1986: 25–7). All policy-makers utilize assumptions about the set of actors who are legitimate participants in the political process, about the range of issues included within the realm of political debate, and about the alliance strategies which will make change feasible. Policy-makers' assumptions – along with those of other significant political actors – set limits on the alternatives considered feasible for policy implementation. These assumptions, taken together, compose the universe of political discourse, which can be defined as a universe of meanings constituted out of political struggle.

One implication of this notion of the universe of political discourse is that, while competition over policy initiatives exists and is, in part, a result of competition over meaning, not all possible positions are represented in every dispute. Systems of closure based on economic and political power exist and these may block the full expression of some discourses. Therefore, while these discourses are a crucial level of analysis for understanding state policies, they can never be seen as completely autonomous of the unequal power relations which inevitably exist in any capitalist society. Material conditions – and especially the labor process of capitalism – unequally structure the universe of political discourse because they differentially allocate positions of potential power. This said, however, it is also important to recognize that the particular consequences of this unequal structure cannot be known or predicted in advance; they result from concrete historical struggles.

Moreover, because the universe of political discourse includes the definition of actors and strategies, it is primarily within this universe that the multitude of possible relations of difference within any social formation are given meaning. All societies are divided by a plethora of relationships of difference and in many cases the recognition of difference is accompanied by inequality of power. For example, the recognition of childhood usually means the subordination of children to adults. Recognition of racial difference has in the past led to all the familiar evils of racism. Despite this, however, it is obvious that mere existence of a difference does not lead to its congealment as a system of unequal power; such a system is socially constructed and as such can be resisted. It is within the universe of political discourse that competition over the meaning and consequences of relations of difference occurs.

In France, attention to the rising rates of female employment (observed at each census since 1968) has occurred concurrently with a redefinition of the employment policies of the state at a moment of dramatic change in conditions of capital accumulation and class relations. The redefinition has responded to recognition of two conditions: that a fundamental restructuring of the labor force is under way and that economic crisis both drives and must be accommodated within any policy response to restructuring. Moreover, in the minds of many policy-makers the problem of 'unemployment' is in part linked to the increased participation of women in the paid labor force.[1]

Nevertheless, whether the state's response to the problem of 'unemployment' requires gender-specific policy actions or not, and if so, what they should be, has been disputed by the different branches of the state. Therefore, it has involved conflict among competing discourses, all of which articulate a place for women in the workplace and society. Since the conflict could only be resolved by political struggle, part of the competition for political power involved the discursive construction of women as workers and citizens. In any full rendering of the French state's response to the feminized labor force, then, we must appreciate *this* construction as well as the objective conditions in which women found themselves and the balance of political forces within which policy was made.

WOMEN'S LOCATION IN THE POSTWAR FRENCH ECONOMY

After 1945 it appeared that the employment rate of French women – always high in comparative terms – was in decline.[2] At each census, the percentage of women in the paid labor force was slightly lower than before. Then some important indicators began to change. Between the 1962 and 1968 censuses (and at each subsequent one) participation rates rose rapidly. Thus, when the economic crisis arrived in the early 1970s, it became clear that its effects were not gender-neutral. While women's unemployment rate was higher than men's, more of the jobs created after 1972 went to women. Beneath such national aggregate statistics there were three patterns shaping women's employment which are worth briefly describing, because they provide the background to recent policy debates.

First, while agriculture always accounted for a very large pecentage of female employment in France, it became less labor-intensive in the postwar years and the number of female agricultural workers declined. Simultaneously, however, the participation rate of women in industrial and service-sector occupations rose (Bouillaguet-Bernard and Germe, 1981: 109). Industry in particular absorbed many women displaced from agriculture. If the patterns observed between 1965 and 1970 are generalized to the whole period, almost one-half of the non salaried agricultural workers who entered the salariat moved into industrial jobs.[3] Therefore, in the early postwar years, the seeming decline in female participation rates actually masked increased industrial and service-sector employment.

Secondly, the feminization rate rose in industries which had previously employed few women. While traditional 'women's jobs' were being lost in some areas (textiles, clothing, shoes and leather goods), new jobs were begin created in more dynamic industries (for example, electrical and electronic, agribusiness and food, smelting, metal-working, chemicals and pharmaceuticals) where the rate of female employment had previously been low (Bouillaguet-Bernard and Germe, 1981: 110–12). Between 1968 and 1975, 53 per cent of the industrial jobs created went to women. Since most of the new industrial jobs were not skilled, so many women were hired as semi-skilled workers (OS) or laborers (*manoeuvres*) that these categories rapidly became feminized. By 1975 83 per cent of the *manoeuvres* and 74 per cent of the OS workers in the private sector were female (Documentation Française, 1982: 33, 36).

The third important pattern was the continuing feminization of the tertiary sector. Women had always constituted a large proportion of the service sector and their numbers increased either as a result of transfers from other types of jobs or when previously non-employed women took up jobs for the first time. As in the industrial sector, women in the service sector were increasingly ghettoized in the least qualified and worst paid categories (Bouillaguet-Bernard and Gauvin, 1979: 79, 81, 83). Automated work became increasingly 'women's work'; in 1978 one-tenth of OS men and one-quarter of OS women had to follow the automatic rhythm of a machine, while the proportion of each group doing repetitive assembly work was one-third versus two-thirds (Documentation Française, 1982: 41). Both of these patterns of industrial and service-sector segmentation reflected that it was women with the least training and education whose rate of employment was rising most quickly (Club Flora Tristan, 1984: 9).

In general, these three patterns cumulate towards the following portrait of women's employment in France after 1945. As agricultural employment declined, women moved into industry and service work – simultaneously becoming waged – but they were disproportionately concentrated in the lowest paid and non-trained categories. These changes can only lead to the conclusion that female employment served as a basic element in the modernization of French mass production industry in the postwar years, which was based upon a new regime of accumulation.

After 1945 the French economy experienced fundamental economic and social changes which put a new regime of accumulation into place.[4] A Fordist wage relation – meaning the ensemble of conditions for use and reproduction of the labor force (the labor process, systemization of qualifications, labor mobility, incomes and salaries) – was solidified. The consolidation of this wage relationship was based upon a set of compromises between labor and capital. Labor accepted modernization, designed to increase productivity, in exchange for higher wages. Capital and labor thus split payoffs from higher productivity, with most attention in union–management relations going to nominal salary growth. Industrial conflict was almost completely reduced to salary settlements, as attention to wage increases, especially for the lowest paid workers (Boyer, 1984: 33-4), replaced issues of workplace control and working conditions. Other aspects of the regime of accumulation involved an increase in the contribution of indirect salary to total income and access to social programs which did not depend on labor market situation. At the same time, salaried work became dominant and, finally, mass consumption life-styles developed (Boyer, 1984: 29ff).

From this brief description of the postwar regime of accumulation and the Fordist wage relation, the specificity of women's employment is obvious.[5] Women were the semi-skilled and unskilled workers on the assembly-lines, the employees in new mass merchandising, the state workers providing social programs and the second family income on which the whole system came to depend. The rising rates of female employment, although ultimately the consequence of individuals deciding when and how to enter the labor force, reflected much more than changing social mores and individual preferences. The modern French economic system had come to rely upon women workers.[6]

ECONOMIC CRISIS AND THE EFFECTS OF POST-FORDISM ON WOMEN'S EMPLOYMENT

The postwar regime of accumulation and Fordist wage relations worked as a 'virtuous circle' until the 1960s. By the middle of that decade, however, contradictions began to appear. Management intensified the pressures of deskilling and made efforts to gain higher productivity by speeding up assembly-line work. Therefore, while the second half of the 1960s was a period of accelerated growth it was also one in which issues which had been dormant since 1945 re-emerged in industrial conflict. Workplace opposition to some forms of work organization intensified in the early 1970s, especially among assembly-line workers and the least skilled of those. In other words, OS militancy increased. Secondly, opposition to plant-level authority hierarchies grew. Later, since restructuring French industry often included geographical relocation, conflicts developed over the loss of jobs and life possibilities in many regions.

These changes in labor–capital relations – beginning about 1965 – were symptoms that the postwar compromise around a productivity/wages trade-off was showing signs of wear; by 1976 there was a clear recognition that the regime of accumulation was in crisis. Programs were instituted by capital and the state to permit and legitimate a 'two-tiered' labor force, in which only a minority of workers could expect a well-paid, permanent job guaranteeing not only work but also the protection of social legislation. By the end of the 1970s notions of a 'dual society' – with a well-paid core of skilled workers and peripheral groups of temporary, part-time, and marginalized workers – began to be discussed by neo-liberal ideologues (Boyer, 1984: 41–2). The labor movement lost ground as the wage relation was restructured around capital's resort to more precarious work, to less-skilled and lower paid workers (Loos, 1984).

In the breakdown of the post-1945 regime of accumulation, women workers emerged on the front line of change. As the postwar economic arrangements became more intractable and as the trade-off of higher wages for capital's control over the organization of work could no longer be sustained, two management strategies were identifiable; both implied that women would emerge as more desirable employees (Bouillaguet-Bernard and Gauvin, 1985: 10, 12). The first was to try to find a more tractable labor force by employing workers whose relationship to the labor market seemed more transient and, therefore, workers who seemed less likely to engage in labor militancy. A second strategy was to break out of the constraints which high wages and protected labor placed on investment decisions, by increasing resort to a more 'flexible' labor force (Boyer, 1984: 36).

The goal of such management strategies was reduction of the firm's commitment to particular workers, so as to minimize costs and maximize response to changing demand for the companies' products. Pursuit of both strategies meant a continuing struggle to reintroduce 'flexibility' into management practices. State-organized constraints on wage-rates and working conditions – often the product of working-class political victories after 1945 – began to be bypassed by a number of management practices. All of them resulted in a work situation which was increasingly precarious, as employers made use of temporary workers, part-time workers and limited contracts.

Women were more likely than men to be found among the workers with limited contracts and only part-time work, which meant that they were increasingly becoming the most marginal part of the labor force (Documentation Française, 1982: 45-9).[7] Women tended to have the least interesting non-salary benefits, as well as the low incomes which follow from being located at the margin of the labor force. Even when they were employed full-time, their jobs were the lowest paid and had the least opportunity for advancement.[8] Therefore, ironically, despite the fact that women *as a category* were becoming more essential to the production process, *individual* women's work situation became increasingly precarious as they were offered temporary or part-time work, less protected by collective agreements and state regulations.

STATE RESPONSES

The French state developed two different policy responses to the feminization of the labor force under these conditions. The first involved policies designed to establish equality between women and men by reducing the effects of both conscious and unconscious discriminatory practices. The second involved policies to encourage, discourage and/or regulate types of labor force activities which are disproportionately feminized but not necessarily labelled or understood as such. Analysing these policies, it is possible to see the ways in which the discourses of different branches of the state as well as other political actors conceptualized the situation of women. The examples demonstrate quite different amounts of attention to the needs of women, different ways of posing the problem of employment, and variable degrees of consciousness that the policies advocated affected women's situation. It is also possible to see how the balance of power within the state shaped the ways that individual branches modified their programs and even altered their discourses.

As did many European countries, France took explicit legislative steps to provide equality of employment. The Constitutions of the Fourth Republic (1946) and the Fifth Republic (1958) both affirmed the principle of workplace equality. France also ratified Convention 100 of the ILO and Article 119 of the Treaty of Rome, both of which dealt with equal pay for women and men. Then, by the 1970s, the prohibitions on gender-based discrimination in wages and in hiring and firing were incorporated into a series of state initiatives directed toward marginal categories of the labor force. A 1971 ordinance against discrimination on the basis of age was followed by one in 1972 prohibiting wage discrimination on the basis of sex. Employers were enjoined to give equal pay for work of equal value, and enforcement procedures were established in 1973. In 1975 discrimination in hiring and firing was similarly prohibited. France also supported the Council of Europe's 1976 affirmation of the need to eliminate both direct and indirect discrimination based on sex or family status.

Despite these legislative efforts and constitutional provisions, however, there was a general recognition that the steps taken were not effective. Segmentation of the labor force continued at an increasing rate, the gaps between the average female and male wage did not narrow in any meaningful way and women's unemployment rate remained substantially higher than men's. Therefore, after the election of the Left government in 1981, further steps against discrimination in the workplace were taken, primarily at the initiative of the Minister of the Rights of Women, Yvette Roudy.

The *loi Roudy* (13 July 1983) was designed to fill the gaps in rights and procedures left by the relatively ineffectual 1970s decrees. It was also intended to provide a format for drawing institutions of workplace representation into greater responsibility for gender equality, thereby creating a more favorable social climate for women's equality. The origin and content of the law reflected the concerns not only of the Ministry and the women's movement, but also the trade unions.

The first and most basic principle of the law was to make it impossible (with rare exceptions) to exclude women from a job solely on the basis of sex and the supposed characteristics of that sex. Instead, all workers were to be treated equally.[9] The legislation also gave trade unions and other associations the right to take complaints to the courts and through grievance procedures. In other words, individual women did not have to make their own case; it would be argued by their representatives, even without their participation.[10] Finally, partly for purposes of education and publicity – to change the social mores – the law created several quite innovative procedures. Among these were the provisions that individual complaints could be settled by requiring an employer to produce a plan to improve gender equality in the whole workplace, that catch-up measures should form part of sectoral collective agreements, especially to deal with training, and that works committees (*comités d'entreprise*) must annually study the situation of women in their own firms and prepare proposals for improving equality.

Another important move toward gender equality came with the reform of the status of spouses of artisans and merchants (Law of 10 July 1982). It was estimated that almost 300,000 people worked with their spouses in a family business, without being paid and without the recognized rights of employees. The new law regularized the position of the spouse by designating the relationship one of either collaboration, salaried work or partnership. This regularization mitigates the employment effects of divorce or death by legally acknowledging the contribution of the spouse. Finally, many of the remaining bans on women's employment in specific civil service categories and jobs were removed by another law promoted by Roudy (7 May 1982).

These legislative changes all reflect the discourse which Roudy's Ministry developed to account for women's inequality. It gave attention to both structural blockages (gender differences in schooling and training) and attitudes. The discourse stressed not only employers' tendencies to discriminate against women or to make assumptions about the 'proper' work for women but also women's attitudes derivative of childhood socialization which create assumptions that employment is only temporary or which produce a fear of non-traditional jobs. The Ministry pointed out the identifiable and measurable consequences of educational choices made by students (often with the encouragement of their teachers) which track them into 'women's jobs' and the gender imbalance in vocational and apprenticeship programs which mean that girls are overwhelmingly prepared only for low paying and/or unskilled work. The Ministry emphasized that women needed not only expanded rights but also real opportunities to overcome the inequalities that follow not simply from discrimination but from structures and ideas.[11] Therefore, accompanying the laws were several major publicity campaigns around themes like '*Allez les femmes!*' ['Let's Go, Women!'] and '*Supprimons les obstacles*' ['Eliminate the Obstacles']. Joint action with the Ministry of Education moved to eliminate sexist imagery from school books and other educational material.

This discourse was further embedded in a particular analysis of history which emphasized the changes in industrial society which now made untenable any distinction between women's and men's employment. Explaining the present discriminatory practices as the inheritance of the past when unsanitary conditions, heavy labor and unsafe working conditions made some protection of women necessary and desirable, the Ministry then pronounced that technological change (including control of fertility) made equality not only desirable but achievable. What was needed was a serious, voluntarist effort to make it happen; and that voluntarist enthusiasm was what the Ministry intended to provide.

Most of the rest of the Left government agreed with the efforts to provide equality of employment for women. The various branches used a similar discourse and were willing to develop programs to extend gender equality. The new system of collective bargaining, established by the Auroux Laws, gave works committees the responsibility for investigating discrimination and establishing programs for gender equality.[12] The Ministry of Education cooperated in a number of programs designed to encourage schoolgirls to strive for more than traditional jobs. For example, educational officials and delegates from the Ministry of the Rights of Women worked together to set up special transfer classes to move girls from traditional literature and humanities programs into science and technical streams, and developed school materials to encourage girls to prepare for non-traditional careers [*Citoyennes à part entière*, no. 38, January 1985: 4; no. 48, December 1985: 5 (hereafter *Citoyennes*)].

The reasoning behind the notion of firm-level and sectoral plans for gender equality was that more than legislation and the declaration of rights was needed if the labor force were to be realigned in the direction of gender equality. These plans could be negotiated at the initiative of the unions or the representatives of the Ministry itself. A network of ministerial delegates in each region of the country provided the institutional basis for pushing employers to develop training programs, re-evaluate the value of work done by women, and establish special programs to promote equality in the workplace.[13]

A major part of the Ministry's early efforts to promote equal opportunities was its encouragement to women to move into high-technology jobs. This effort was coordinated with the state's industrial strategy for reconversion [*Citoyennes*, no. 32, June 1984: 3, 9ff]. There were publicity campaigns and development of training programs for women to adapt their skills and efforts to move them into science and technical courses. For example, the Ministry offered national scholarships for girls entering science and technical programs and convinced several regional governments to do the same at the regional level.[14]

While no doubt the institutions and the energy existed for these initiatives in the infrastructure of the ministerial delegates, the actual success rate is difficult to measure. For example, a plan was negotiated with Moulinex in which the company agreed to select OS women and train them for a certificate in electronics so they could be assigned to skilled jobs, a category almost exclusively filled by men at Moulinex. Eleven went through the program [*Citoyennes*, no. 46, October 1985: 6]. Similar programs were negotiated at SOFINCO (a banking concern) and Aerospatiale. The numbers were small but the results were concrete.

Part of the difficulty in evaluating these programs arises from the fact that their efforts were bucking trends in the labor market itself. The Ministry's discourse was one which set elimination of gender differences as its goal; this is the essence of any discourse of equality. Programs were designed to break down any structure which isolated women in sectors which were highly feminized and usually poorly paid. Therefore, a premium was placed on programs which – while recognizing the need for specific actions to improve women's situation – denied the legitimacy of any policies which permitted labor market segmentation to continue. As French capitalism restructured, however, pressures developed for a new kind of gender-biased division of labor and labor market [Maruani and Nicole, 1987: 234–8].

THE EFFECTS OF EMPLOYMENT POLICIES ON WOMEN

The now general trend toward acceptance of a two-tier labor force made the promotion of a discourse of equality very difficult. The Ministry of the Rights of Women had to operate within a universe of political discourse in which women were defined not as the equals of men but rather as 'different'. Not only capital but also other branches of the state and labor movement were more comfortable with a discourse which treated 'women' as a category of the labor force, different in many ways from the norm. Employers valued women workers for what they thought to be their specific characteristics of not only dexterity but also weaker commitment to the labor force [Bouillaguet-Bernard and Gauvin, 1985: 12]. The state tended to view women's employment as being at the margin of the labor force. While it moved to regularize and humanize conditions at the margin, it did so without attacking the very structures which created the concept of 'margin' in the first place. The consequences of different discourses about women and work are most visible and have most effect in efforts to control unemployment and simultaneously limit the effects of flexibility and precarious work.

From the mid-1970s, efforts to control unemployment – especially among young people and workers in regions where industries were closing down – dominated the French state's labor market agenda. In 1974 unemployment rates shot up, and accompanying this mounting unemployment was the other great change in employment trends – the rising rate of female employment. As more women entered the labor force both women's unemployment rate and the rate at which they took up newly-created jobs rose.

State statisticians, trade unionists and feminists 'discovered' the lack of meaningful opportunities for many women and the segmenting effects of the labor market and quickly produced an analysis in which women were described as being at the margin of the labor force. Marginal workers were never exclusively female, because young people and immigrants were fitted into the same category. Nevertheless, in the discourse of these actors, it was increasingly the case that if not all marginal workers were women, all women were marginal workers. For example, the labor unions' very understanding of women's condition in capitalism was premised on the notion of women as marginal workers. Unions used this discourse to make sense of the consequences of employers' efforts to respond to the crisis and the changing regime of accumulation, and it was from the alternatives available in that discourse that proposed solutions flowed [Jenson, 1984].

Resort to various forms of 'atypical' labor contracts has been described as one of management's major strategies for coping with economic crisis and changes in the regime of accumulation. There are multiple forms of atypical work; part-time work and limited-term contracts are the most common. These kinds of contracts could be used by managers to reduce wage bills and especially to lower payments for social benefits because atypical workers were not protected in the same ways as full-time workers – they could be hired and fired more easily and without incurring costs; they were not enrolled in some social programs to which employers made contributions.[15] Such employment, particularly temporary employment, increased rapidly in the late 1970s [Thélot, 1985: 57]. After 1981, however, the situation changed somewhat. The Left government strictly regulated the conditions under which employers could make use of temporary workers and employees with fixed-term contracts. It also regulated part-time work so as to make it as similar to full-time and protected work as possible.

One essential aspect of the employment policy of the Mitterrand government was the maintenance of existing jobs in existing workplaces.[16] These programs differentially affected women and men [Maruani and Nicole, 1987: 240-2]. For example, the increase in public-sector hiring, which was an important element of the Left's first year in government, created 167,000 jobs, 70 per cent of which went to women. Similarly, the Employment-Investment Contracts negotiated by the state with corporations in certain industries helped women's employment. One of the major contracts was in the textile and clothing sector, where in 1980–1 26,000 jobs were lost whereas in 1982 the comparable statistic was only 4,000 [*Citoyennes*, no. 33, July – August 1983: 11].

As well as generally encouraging firms to hire and not to lay off workers, the government implemented several programs to reduce the work week and increase job-sharing. The retirement age was lowered to 60, various provisions for leave (including parental leave which all employees could claim) were set up, and the work week was officially reduced to 39 hours, with incentives to employers who reduced it even further (the goal being 35 or even 30 hours) [Benoit, 1984: 57-62]. Part-time work was also used as a job maintenance and creation strategy, although it seems not to have created many really new ones because firms which moved to part-time workforces rarely increased the number of employees [Benoit, 1984: 60-1]. Nevertheless, the state gave various kinds of advantages to companies which maintained jobs, even if it meant shifting from full- to part-time.

Part-time work, thus encouraged, has increasingly become a feminized ghetto. Approximately 20 per cent of all women work part-time and over two-thirds of part-time workers are women [Jallade, 1985: 153]. France differed from many European countries until the 1970s because it had very little part-time employment and women workers had been overwhelmingly employed full-time. This began to change in the 1970s and the rate of part-time employment continues to rise rapidly. Part-time work had always been popular in the service sector where so many women were employed, but it is now almost equally prevalent in industry. Between 1984 and 1985 78,000 part-time jobs were taken up by women while full-time ones declined by 32,000 [Heller, 1985: table 3, 24]. In the private sector, 26 per cent of white-collar workers (*employées*) and 18 per cent of blue-collar workers (*ouvrières*) have part-time contracts [Heller, 1985: table 4, 24]. Manufacturers are increasingly turning to part-time workers in order to avoid layoffs.[17]

The state encouraged employers in this move toward part-time work. Once employment protections were extended to part-time workers in 1982, the government tended to look upon part-time jobs as a solution to the problem of unemployment. Aiming at job maintenance (where job-sharing is involved) or even more so at job creation, employers who employed only part-time workers were welcomed with as much enthusiasm as those who created full-time jobs. For example, subsidies were given to regionally-based companies which created part-time or full-time jobs; they were not available if the jobs were temporary, however [*Social and Labour Bulletin*, March 1983: 85].

This enthusiasm for part-time work can only be sustained if the assumption is made that part-time work is 'women's work' and women actively seek such a part-time status [Kergoat, 1984: 11]. While the first half of the assumption is correct – part-time work is almost exclusively done by women – the second is more problematic. Critiques and recent studies argue that taking a part-time job is more likely to result from the lack of alternatives than from preference. A detailed study of individuals' strategies in the face of the choice between part-time and full-time work finds the 'choice' of part-time work associated with a lack of interest in the available work or the continuing need of women to sustain the burden of family responsibilities [Kergoat, 1984: 2].

Despite the lack of any evidence that workers, even women workers, prefer part-time to full-time employment, that presumption often informed the state's arguments. But more overwhelmingly than any claim that part-time was *good* work, was the sense that part-time was *some* work. Thus even Mme Roudy was forced to conclude that she much preferred to see a woman working part-time than unemployed. She could not, under the pressure of the government's general employment policy, totally reject part-time work. All she could do was to insist that it be seen as a temporary solution and not a permanent condition for women [*Citoyennes*, no. 40, March 1985: 10]. It is obvious that her stance was much affected by the government's general position on the priority of the battle against unemployment, even if it meant weakening the discourse of equality.

What are the consequences of this acceptance of part-time work? The first and most obvious is that it depends upon a discourse which is profoundly non-egalitarian. Women workers (as part-time workers) are assumed to be 'different' from others who prefer or must have (because of their burdens as 'breadwinners') full-time work. Thus, women come to be discussed as lesser or minor workers, with smaller needs than others. All of this obviously flies in the face of reality as well as justice, but what is being sketched here are the effects of a discourse of marginality rather than any discussion of its appropriateness.[18] A second consequence is that it becomes much more difficult to address the situation of women who do not fit into this category – those who desire or need a full-time job or who already have one but continue to face difficulties in the labor market. These women remain invisible while their needs seem even less legitimate.

Efforts to overcome problems of youth unemployment have also occupied a huge amount of attention since the middle 1970s [Fontaneau and Muet, 1985: 203ff]. France's youth unemployment rate is substantially higher than any other OECD country and this discrepancy has been a state concern since 1974, when the unemployment rates of the below 25-year-olds shot up rapidly [Thélot, 1985: 39].

What is striking about all the discussion of youth unemployment, however, is that it practically never acknowledged that youth came in two genders or that there were more girls than boys in the most problematic categories. The discussions of programs, of goals or even of needs were never presented in gender-specific terms. Instead, for policy-makers, the French labor force consisted of three categories – men, women and youth. Women and men were older than 25 and youth were the rest. For example, the most recent reports on the Left government's employment policy have long discussions of youth unemployment and state policy but never make a single gender-specific statement [Benoit, 1984; Fontaneau and Muet,

1985]. The only 'women' discussed by them are over 25. Of course, young people do come in two genders and unemployed youth are much more likely to be female than male – at the end of 1984, 24 per cent of males under 25 in the labor force were unemployed and 31 per cent of females [Thélot, 1985: 39-41]. Yet in the discussion of programs there was little evidence of any consciousness of this gender difference.

The obvious exception to this lack of attention to the gender of the young unemployed was the Ministry of the Rights of Women. It pressed to have at least half the places in all youth training programs reserved for young women. It organized its own programs for young women and lobbied the Minister of Labor to take their needs more into account [*Citoyennes*, no. 40, March 1985: 8]. This pressure seemed to bear fruit. The rate of unemployment for young women was stabilized as their number enrolled in training programs or hired as a result of special state-employer pacts and other general job-creation efforts rose.

Nevertheless, it is hard to say whether there were long-term effects from this discourse of equality pressed by the Ministry. Young women tended to have greater difficulty finding a job after their training period and tended to remain unemployed longer. Moreover, when they did find work it was likely to be part-time [Heller, 1985: 24]. Therefore, while the efforts of the Ministry were important, they did not overcome the structural blockages for young women in the labor market, which state policies have as yet made little headway in eliminating. Moreover, the regional delegates and even the Minister worked in an invisibility which is astounding. Only the publications of the Ministry itself gave any acknowledgement that there were both young women and young men in these programs. The other branches of the state remained in a world of genderless youth. Moreover, since the return of the Right to government after 1986, the dismantling of the Ministry of the Rights of Women has meant that even that small voice has disappeared. A language of 'difference' dominates the universe of political discourse.

THE LIMITS OF AN 'AND THE' DISCOURSE

This chapter has demonstrated the impossibility of understanding the response of the French state to the feminization of the labor force as distinct from its response to economic crisis. Equal opportunity efforts have developed in a context in which their effects and often their proponents have been overwhelmed by the state's concern with reducing the unemployment rate and restructuring French industry to make it internationally competitive. Within the general area of employment policy, the overriding concern has been to halt the rise of unemployment – particularly among 'marginal' groups like young workers and workers in traditional sectors – at the same time that French firms were allowed to adapt to the changing conditions of the international economy. Within this double constraint, the discourse of the state has altered over time, as greater emphasis has been placed on increasing the 'flexibility' of capital in its labor market and investment decisions.

Of course, such neo-liberal and/or 'modernizing' discourse resulted in policies and programs which had specific and particular effects on the employment situation of women. Restructured industries which had recourse to 'flexibility' and new forms of labor process could set new barriers to the full integration of women into the labor force. At the same time, greater reliance on a part-time workforce and temporary or fixed length contracts meant that firms turned to women in the expectation that they were more willing or 'able' to accept such forms of employment. Thus, subsumed within employment policy and industrial strategy was a 'response' to the more feminized labor force.

This crisis-focused discourse has most commonly seen women as marginal workers, either requiring special attention and/or constituting a promising source of flexible labor, less tarnished by notions of the desirability of full-time and well-protected work. No matter the specifics of the analysis, women were consistently defined as a category of worker, identifiably separate from the 'real workers' who were without gender. I say 'without gender' because the full-time, protected labor force in France has always contained a high percentage of women and continues to do so; this sexual composition, however, was never much recognized or emphasized in state discourse.

In the 1970s there was a move from an ungendered to a gendered discourse, but one of the ironies of the recognition of the feminization of the labor force was the bifurcation of working women into 'real workers' – without gender – and 'women workers', designated as the marginal, the poorly paid, the part-time. While the earlier ungendered discourse obviously hid the real gender effects of the labor market on women and ignored the situation and needs of women, so the new gendered discourse ignores many of the real demands of women for full and equal integration into the labor force.

Activists for women's rights in France have never succeeded in imposing their own discourse on the discussion. Emphasizing the sex-based parameters of the labor force (as well, obviously, as of other social structures), the women's movement tried to establish a discourse in which there were only two fundamental social categories – women and men. Obviously, socialist feminists added class to that dichotomy, but all feminists eschewed the 'and the' formulation of both the state and most parties and trade unions which, when describing French society, would resort to listing the workers, 'and the' youth, 'and the' women, 'and the' peasants, 'and the', etc.[19] However, it is this 'and the' discourse which predominated in programs to combat unemployment. While a discourse of equality was utilized in the explicit efforts to overcome gender discrimination and to extend rights to workers, once the state turned to the problem of unemployment that discourse of equality was replaced by one of difference in which women were marginalized. And, as the bulk of the state's attention was consumed by the unemployment crisis, 'equality' was swamped by an acceptance of marginality.

Why does this matter? It is my argument – and the example of the enthusiasm for part-time work as a 'solution' to the unemployment problem demonstrates that – so long as women are treated in policy as a marginal category, they will have difficulty escaping that categorization and achieving the labor market equality which has been the demand of all feminists both inside and out of the state. In other words, a gendered discourse is not necessarily one which promotes labor market equality; it may in fact hinder its arrival. Therefore, despite the fact that present policy does explicitly address some of the needs of women, many others remain invisible. Without a firm commitment to equality, a job – any job – becomes the goal, rather than the full-time one which most women want. Without a firm commitment to equality, in the face of biological difference, the young women who are now being channelled into part-time work and/or temporary state jobs (the *travail à utilité collective – TUC*) will face even greater difficulties as they begin to bear children. All of these questions and more remain unsolved by state responses which can see – and accept – women only as *marginal* workers and fail to attack that marginalization at its roots.

NOTES

1   See, for example, an overview of recent economic policy which explicitly links the rise of female employment, the economic crisis and unemployment rates [Fontaneau and Muet, 1985: 231]. For a comparable policy discussion in Canada see Armstrong and Armstrong, chapter 4.
2   For the pre-1945 figures and a cross-national comparison, see Daric [1947].
3   Fully 48 per cent of those moving out of non-salaried agricultural work (almost all being *aides-familles*) went into industrial jobs in that half decade [Bouillaguet-Bernard and Gauvin, 1979: 79].
4   This discussion of the postwar French economy is drawn from Boyer [1984], Coriat [1984], Lipietz [1984], and other sources as listed.
5   For a more detailed consideration of the political effects of such economic and social arrangements, see Ross and Jenson [1986].
6   Bouillaguet-Bernard and Germe liken this postwar reconstruction of the economy and women's employment to the second half of the nineteenth century when women also entered the labor force in huge numbers as fundamental restructuring called them into new factories and offices [1981: 91–100].

7 Club Flora Tristan [1984: 21] gives more details for the increasing precariousness.

8 For a detailed examination of five firms' use of female workers in the new search for flexibility see Maruani and Nicole [1987].

9 An exception is granted for the recognition of pregnancy, childbirth and breast feeding, and the special rights which accompany those sex-specific conditions.

10 Only if a women specifically opposed such action were representatives blocked from taking up the action.

11 For details of the Ministry's analysis, see Documentation Française [1982] and *Citoyennes*, no. 33, July – August 1984, which gives a three-year overview of the major policy positions on equal opportunity and employment.

12 This was incorporated in the Third Auroux Law, 28 October 1982.

13 For details see Jenson [1983: 6-7].

14 In 1985, 66 regional scholarships were established [*Citoyennes*, no. 48, December 1985: 5].

15 For details about the regulations on firing, see Benoit [1984: 55-7].

16 This was one of a three-pronged policy. The other two prongs were job creation and more interventionist labor market policies to restructure employment [Benoit, 1984: part II].

17 For example, BSN Gervais Danone, a food producer, and CIT-Alcatel, a telecommunications company, both concluded agreements to save jobs by instituting a 35-hour week, early retirement, and replacement of full-time with part-time jobs [*Social and Labour Bulletin*, March 1983: 69].

18 This same lack of fit between reality and discourse is seen in the discussions in Britain of the notion of the family wage [Barrett and McIntosh, 1980].

19 My thanks to Michalis Spourdalakis for finally suggesting a label for this notion.

REFERENCES

Barrett, M. and M. McIntosh (1980) 'The "family wage": some problems for socialists and feminists', *Capital and Class*, no. 11 (Summer).

Benoit, A (1984) *La Politique de l'emploi: Organisation et moyens* (Paris: Documentation Française).

Bouillaguet-Bernard, P. and A. Gauvin (1979) 'Le Travail féminin. Famille et système productif', *Consommation*, 26 (2).

Bouillaguet-Bernard, P. and A. Gauvin (1985) 'Fonctionnement du marché de l'emploi et place des catégories dites "spécifiques": Un exemple, les femmes', prepared for *Journées d'études sur les structures du marché du travail et politique de l'emploi, Ministère du Travail*, unpublished.

Bouillaguet-Bernard, P. and J.-F Germe (1981), 'Salarisation et travail féminin en France', *Critique de l'Economie Politique*, nouvelle série, no. 17.

Boyer, R. (1984) 'Wage labor, capital accumulation and the crisis, 1968–72', in Mark Kesselman (ed.), *The French Workers' Movement* (London: Allen and Unwin).

Club Flora Tristan (1984) *Les Modalités actuelles de l'activité féminine: sont-elles irréversibles?* (Paris: Club Flora Tristan).

Coriat, B. (1984) 'Labor and capital in the crisis: France 1966–82', in Mark Kesselman (ed.), *The French Workers' Movement* (London: Allen and Unwin).

Daric, J. (1947) *L'Activité professionnelle des femmes en France – Etude statistique, évolution, comparaisons internationales* (Paris: PUF).

Documentation Française (1982) *Les Femmes en France dans une société d'inégalités* (Paris: Documentation Française).

Fontaneau, A. and P. A. Muet (1985) *La Gauche face à la crise* (Paris: FNSP).

Heller, J.-L (1985) 'Emploi et chomage en mars 1985', *Economie et Statistique*, no. 183.

Jallade, J.-P. (1985) 'Reduction and adjustment of working time: lessons from the French experience', *Labour and Society*, Vol. 10, no. 2.

Jenson, J. (1983) 'The work of the *Ministère des Droits de la Femme*', Newsletter of the Conference Group on French Politics, no. 4 (December), 3-9.

Jenson, J. (1984) 'The "problem" of women', in Mark Kesselman (ed.), *The French Workers' Movement* (London: Allen and Unwin).

Jenson, J. (1986) 'Gender and reproduction, or babies and the state', *Studies in Political Economy*, no. 20.

Kergoat, D. (1984) *Les Femmes et le travail à temps partiel* (Paris: Documentation Française).

Lipietz, A. (1984) *L'Audace et l'enlisement* (Paris: La Découverte).

Loos, J. (1984) 'Le syndicalisme à l'épreuve des expériences d'aménagement du temps du travail', *Revue Française des Affaires Sociales*, no. 2.

Maruani, M. and C. Nicole (1987) 'Du travail à l'emploi: l'enjeu de la mixité', *Sociologie du Travail*, no. 2.

Ross, G. and J. Jenson (1986) 'Post-war class struggle and the crisis of left politics', in Ralph Miliband et al. (eds), *The Socialist Register 1985/86* (London: Merlin).

Thélot, C. (1985) 'Les Traits majeurs du chomage depuis vingt ans', *Economie et Statistique*, no. 183, 37–60.

10

Gender, Work, and Social Progress

Some Consequences of Interest Aggregation in Sweden

Mary Ruggie

INTRODUCTION

Sweden is considered a model of success as a progressive social democracy. Its welfare state is highly developed; its population is well educated, politically involved, and as fully and proficiently employed as can be expected. And, by all standard indicators, the status of women in Swedish society is among the highest in the advanced industrial societies. At present about 80 per cent of all women in Sweden work outside the home; about 70 per cent of women with children do so. Women's pay as a proportion of men's is high. The list of government measures supporting women's employment is impressive, and includes high-quality childcare facilities and generous parental leaves for childbirth and for the care of sick children.

One explanation for such success is the cohesive form of social corporatism in Sweden, in which organized labor plays a central role in articulating social interests within a governing tripartite coalition of the state, labor and capital (Ruggie, 1984). Progress for women has been achieved largely as a by-product of a broader emphasis within social corporatism on improving the conditions of all workers. To date, this strategy has brought significant improvements in women's lives. Yet, it now appears to have reached its limits. There remain underlying inconsistencies in the status of women which have not been – and perhaps cannot be – removed within the mode of social and political action that has dominated progress for Swedish women thus far. The latest indicators show a standstill in the advancement of women, both as workers and as women. It is time, therefore, to step back and take stock.

This chapter examines recent developments in the labor movement and assesses the capacity of organized labor in Sweden to address women's interests that go beyond or are different from the interests of 'workers as a whole'. At the same time, the chapter questions the extent to which the formal equality that women in Sweden have achieved has been translated into more generalized social equality. These two questions are connected, I shall argue, through the labor-centered mode of interest aggregation in Sweden.

I first review the history of the labor movement's involvement in advancing women's interests in Sweden. Organized labor has helped women to enter the labor force but it has been less accommodative of any interests or needs not strictly defined in terms of work, such as gender relations beyond the point of production and psychological distress resulting from social status inconsistencies. Second, I discuss the dominant mode of social action and interest aggregation in Sweden, including the crucial role of labor in the governing coalition and the part that women themselves have played in pressing their cause. The labor movement's actions on behalf of women are a direct result of its political position, but at the same time, because of its important position, organized labor has been cautious about engaging in social change beyond the sphere of work. Finally, I examine signs of persisting problems for Swedish women, both as workers (problems such as occupational segregation and an increase in part-time employment) and as women (problems such as alcoholism and other indicators of psychological distress). These issues arise within Sweden's advanced economy, within which, nevertheless, the particular gender-based interests and needs of Swedish women have not been met by the assumptions of a universal and therefore genderless condition of work.

THE LABOR MOVEMENT AND WOMEN'S INTERESTS

Since the nineteenth century, socialist doctrine in Sweden has held that women's emancipation would be realized through their emancipation from economic dependence. The early articulation of this position was strongly influenced by the German feminist, Clara Zetkin, who was active in the international social democratic movement in the 1880s. Zetkin had advocated women's emancipation as a vital element of socialist politics (Dahlström and Liljeström, 1983: 11). But when this position was imported into Sweden, it acquired the overtone that women's emancipation was premised on emancipation of workers as a whole. Achievement of the goals of socialism would automatically resolve 'the woman question', it was maintained. In other words, from the beginning of the labor movement and of social democratic politics in Sweden, the specificity of women's particular interests has been muted in favor of the universal interests of socialism. This general position has been retained consistently throughout decades of social and economic change in Sweden.

Throughout the first half of the twentieth century, the concerns of workers dominated the socialist agenda in Sweden. Lip-service was paid to issues of particular importance to women, such as equal pay, which the LO (Landsorganisationen), Sweden's first and still dominant central trade union, supported in principle early on (1909), but which languished in practice for decades. Other issues, such as univeral suffrage, were promoted by the Social Democratic Party (SDP) and the unions; yet women achieved the vote later in Sweden than in some other countries – 1919, as compared to 1905 in Finland and 1915 in Norway and Denmark. Without a political voice, women were not a force to be reckoned with. Furthermore, in 1920 women constituted only 30 per cent of the labor force.

With universal suffrage, and with the ascension of the Social Democrats to power in the 1930s, issues of particular interest to women came to be addressed and acted upon. Foremost among these were equal pension rights, paid maternity leave, and protection from being fired for married or pregnant women. Progress was stalled on other issues, however. In particular, equal pay for equal work was thwarted by the use of separate pay scales for men and women, a practice which remained in effect until 1939 in the public sector and 1960 in the private sector. Women workers, both organized (within trade unions and the SDP) and unorganized, continually protested about these disparate pay scales, as well as other inequities, such as a ban on night-shift work for women. Yet, for decades their protests were met with 'traditions, prejudices . . . and organizational lethargy' (Qvist, 1976: 126).

In assessing the experience of Swedish women, it is instructive to examine another area of policy related to women's employment – family policy. The division of labor in the family is one area that from the beginning tested the Social Democratic Party and trade unions' approach to women; the situation of workers who are also overburdened by childcare and other domestic chores required special consideration. LO's involvement in family policy goes back at least to the 1930s, when it began to participate in the first population commissions inquiring into the declining birthrate in Sweden, especially among low-income families.[1] From the start, these commissions linked the conditions of work with the conditions of family life, and focused on the untenable constraints women faced both as mothers and wives, and as workers. A solid foundation for family policy was laid, and the importance of women's role as workers was part of the common understanding. The LO's role in so formulating the issue was critical. However, while the LO was concerned with developing policies that would enable married women to work, many of the requisite supporting measures, such as childcare, were controversial and LO's commitment to them was tepid. Moreover, as far as the LO was concerned, in the years preceding women's massive influx into the work force, 'the needs of the labor market and the family were the primary concerns, not some inalienable women's rights' (Qvist, 1976: 134).

Accordingly, without real support women's labor force participation rates remained stagnant, especially those of married women with children. Nevertheless, after decades of dormancy, attitudes gradually began to change, so that by the time women were entering the labor force in greater numbers in the 1960s, family policy did emphasize the need for more childcare facilities. A vast expansion in this and other supporting measures followed. In the 1970s, with women's labor force participation established, family policy turned to issues of maternity benefits and parental leave, emphasizing the importance of greater equality of responsibility between both parents. The position of the labor movement on various family policies, therefore, did change with the times, but, as I shall note again, the special interests of women have never taken precedence over the broader interests of the family.

Thus, policies supporting working women in Sweden are a recent phenomenon (see also Mayer, 1987). Only beginning in the 1960s have women in Sweden progressed as workers. Since then, the expansionist economic policies of the Social Democrats have drawn women into the labor market, and the LO's policy of 'wage solidarity', aimed at closing the gap between higher- and lower-paid categories of workers, benefited women, most of whom were in low-paid jobs. Without singling out women's wages but treating them instead as an element of the general problem of low wages, a significant reduction of the wage gap occurred (Cook, 1980: 63–4). In the early phases of the policy of wage solidarity, the old socialist doctrine of integrating the particularity of women's interests into the universal interests of workers as a whole was maintained – and to the benefit of women. Eventually though, the unions jumped onto 'the equality bandwagon' (Scott, 1982: 43) and began to recognize women as a special category of worker with systematic problems of their own. This recognition has taken the form of several LO pamphlets and policy statements about the goal of equality for women, as well as support for labor market programs which seek to improve the status of women workers (Rollen, 1980; Ruggie, 1984). However, as I discuss below, certain features of women's inferior work status, occupational segregation above all, seem impervious to change, and it is not at all clear that the efforts of either the LO or the Social Democratic Party are sufficient to the task at hand. For despite their contributions to the achievement of formal equality for women, and despite their formal recognition of women's particularity, the LO's and SPD's endeavors on behalf of women remain confined within traditional socialist doctrine.

INTEREST AGGREGATION: LABOR AND THE WOMEN'S MOVEMENT

Organized Labor   Acceptance by the labor movement of the goal of equality for all workers accounts in part for the progress that has accrued to women workers in Sweden. The same can be said for achievements in any other aspect of Sweden's welfare state, whether in the area of work or of lifestyle. It is impossible to appreciate social and economic policy in Sweden without a good understanding of the centrality of organized labor in the policy process and the symbiotic relationship between organized labor and the Social Democratic Party (Korpi, 1978; Stephens, 1979). Representatives of organized labor (almost always from the LO and usually from one or more of the other major unions) sit on relevant governmental boards and commissions of inquiry. For its part, the LO conducts informal meetings of government personnel as well as labor and political leaders to air views and develop policy positions. Organized labor is an integral partner in the governing coalition.

It is also important to understand certain other characteristics of the political process for a full appreciation of policy formation and implementation in Sweden. Most importantly, interest aggregation in Sweden relies predominantly on cooperation and consensus (Anton, 1969; Meijer, 1969; Wheeler, 1975). It is a process that often entails a slow and tedious procedure for policy development, but it is also one that assures a more certain outcome and more successful implementation. After decades of such practices, confrontation and antagonism have been virtually banished from political and social action. Rarely has any disgruntled group had to resort to hostile tactics. These factors are critical to understanding the experience of the women's movement in Sweden, which has continually been absorbed into the non-confrontational and consensual policy process.

Organized Women   Since it was founded in 1884, the Frederika Bremer Association has been the main women's organization in Sweden. There are other, smaller non-aligned women's groups in Sweden (the best known is the more radical Group 8), but their membership comes nowhere near that of the Frederika Bremer Association, which currently has approximately 8000 members (about three times as many as Group 8). Historically, the activities of the Frederika Bremer Association have been traditional and 'bourgeois'. The primarily middle- and upper-class membership was mainly concerned with issues of the legal, civic, economic and political status of (propertied) women. In the 1970s the organization for the first time became much more activist and explicitly feminist, sparked by the unusual and outspoken leadership style of Birgitta Wistrand. Activities focused on redressing women's lack of power in Swedish society through

increasing the number of women in public office and through con-
sciousness-raising. In retrospect it remains difficult to say whether developments in the Swedish women's movement in the 1970s were due more to
the era and the agenda or to the personage of Wistrand. What is clear is
that once Wistrand resigned her presidency, the organization she led
became less activist, 'bourgeois' once again, and the women's movement in
Sweden arrived at its current impasse. Women's activism, within the
structure of an interest group, has now returned to its 'normal' mode. This
is not to say that women are not organized or active; they are both. But the
arena of their activism has narrowed.

Many women, instead of forming their own groups, participate only in
workplace organizations. Since 95 per cent of employed Swedes belong to
trade unions, it is understandable that once women entered the labor force
they would also become union members. LO represents about 95 per cent
of blue-collar workers and the female membership of LO increased from
17 per cent in 1945 to 30 per cent in 1970. Nevertheless, the kind of work
that women began to do as their labor force participation rates increased in
the 1950s – namely, clerical, professional and other white-collar work –
meant that many also joined unions other than LO. Foremost among these
were TCO (Tjänstemännens Centralorganisation or the Central Organization of Salaried Employees), which represents about 75 per cent of
white-collar workers, and SACO (Sveriges Akademikers Centralorganisation or the Swedish Confederation of Professional Associations), which
represents about 90 per cent of professional groups, including doctors,
teachers and social workers. More women are now organized within these
other two unions than in LO. In fact, women now constitute over half of
TCO's membership, where they are mostly clerical workers.

It would seem, then, that a complete discussion of the labor movement's
policies toward women ought to include more than a brief word about
these other unions. However, despite the larger number of women they
organize, they are not as important in this discussion as the LO. This is so
for three reasons. First, the other unions do not enjoy LO's special
relationship with the SDP, and therefore are not as integral to the
policy-making process. Second, LO is clearly the leader among trade
unions, not only because of its favored position, but also because it is the
most active and progressive of the trade unions. Its authority becomes
more apparent with each step toward greater centralization in the labor
movement; already, LO represents TCO and SACO in some central
bargaining sessions with the employers' federation. Finally, LO has done
more for its women members, and women in general, especially through
the equal pay issue, than the other unions. Since the other unions are not
socialist, they prefer differentiated wage scales based on skills, and have
not pressed for equality. This predisposition has characterized SACO in
particular, and has created occasional tensions between the higher- and

lower-paid professional groups within SACO's own membership (Heiden-heimer, 1976; see also Wheeler, 1975).

Although they are union members, women are not especially active in the unions, however. No woman has ever been in the top levels of the LO's organizational hierarchy. The record for the other unions is only mar-ginally better; women constitute about 15 per cent of TCO's central board. Moreover, women attend fewer union meetings and are involved in fewer union activities than their male counterparts. A recent study of participa-tion in the three main unions showed that a roughly equivalent proportion of men and women attend at least one union meeting per year, but significantly more men attend at least three meetings per year (see table 10.1). Investigating further for its own members only, LO found that the disparity in participation in union activities between men and women was greatest within families with small children (LO, 1985: 139). LO's recent publications stress, more than ever, its concern about the lack of participa-tion by women. In an attempt to act on its concern, the LO has made several suggestions for how the situation might be redressed, such as changing the hours of union courses and meetings to accommodate women with children and housework chores, and reducing the formality of meetings so as not to discourage or intimidate women (LO, 1981: 40–1). The suggestions, while well-intended, reveal as much about the persisting norm as about possible future directions.

TABLE 10.1   *Participation at Union Meetings, 1982/3*
(percentage of members who have attended at least three meetings in last 12 months)

	LO		TCO		SACO/SR	
	men	women	men	women	men	women
State employer	36	32	41	27	38	35
Private employer	27	20	35	26	23	n/a
Municipal employer	30	19	45	25	47	35

Source: LO (1985: 129).

Women's main activity within the unions is in women's caucuses, either at the workplace or within the union structure. In these caucuses women discuss their interests and then select representatives to relay their concerns to higher levels, which are invariably male-dominated. For some time, women's main conduit to the power-holders in LO was the Council of Women, which was transformed into the Family Council in 1967. Since 1980, LO headquarters has maintained an office handling equality matters.

The office and its (female) director have done much to remedy women's direct access to, if not influence on, central decision-making.

Why is this picture of activism by and for women within the labor movement so unimpressive? Part of the answer rests on the dominant mode of interest aggregation in Sweden. It is relatively passive, making few claims on rank-and-file initiatives, and gives much authority to representatives at the top of the organizational hierarchy which remains male-dominated. Part of the answer also rests on the nature of socialism in Sweden and the place of women within its agenda. It has always been part of the labor movement's strategy (LO's in particular) to pre-empt the demands of women's groups and feminists and contain them within the labor market, in the unions, and at the workplace. Therefore, while proposing changes, for example, in the hours of meetings and other workplace conditions, the LO has not directly attacked the problem at its source, in the home and in cultural practices which reinforce the traditional gender division of labor. This strategy reflects the reluctance of the unions to see women as anything except workers, and as such it helps to reproduce the existing patriarchy of Swedish society (Dahlström and Liljeström, 1983). It has also been closely attuned both to socialist politics, integrating women's specific interests to those of labor as a whole, and to the dominant mode of interest aggregation in Sweden, which seeks to find a consensual not a confrontational basis for social-political action.

Brief mention should be made of women's organization and activities within the political parties. Although their numbers are fewer in political parties than in the labor unions, ironically within the structure of political parties women have been both more active on their own behalf and more successful in their achievements. Ironically once again, their greatest achievement occurred when the SDP was out of office and a coalition government was in power (1976–81). Women, particularly in the Women's Councils of both the Liberal Party and the Center Party, pressed for and won the only piece of special legislation for women to have been passed in Sweden – the Act on Equality between Men and Women at Work.[2] It became effective in 1980. The Act also created the office of the Equality Ombudsman, the only special governmental agency for women in Sweden.

In sum, women's activism within the independent women's movement has subsided in Sweden. Their involvement within the labor movement, as well as the initiatives of organized labor on women's behalf, has also waned. All around there is less visibility, less discussion, less energy. Those activities which do occur are more decentralized, and the issues discussed are more narrow and focused on the family. None of this should be surprising. Indeed, it can be said merely to suggest a return to the dominant Swedish pattern. Dahlström and Liljeström's statement about the 1950s seems relevant again – 'the labour movement's organized women primarily backed the policy of levelling class distinctions and avoided putting too much of a profile on the conflicts of interest between women and men. They stressed the need for improvements in the conditions of family formation and home-making' (1983: 18).

We might well ask – So what if activism has slackened? Have not achievements for women gone about as far as they realistically can? Does it matter if progress for women as workers in Sweden has been achieved through a process of integrating women's special interests to the more general interests of workers as a whole? Have not sufficient and positive measures been developed? Does it matter if women have not been aggressive and active on their own behalf? Do the results not justify the means? In turning now to answer these questions I assess new data and new facts about women in Sweden. Some of these are just beginning to come to public attention and are not yet well documented, let alone analysed and discussed. The persisting problems as well as some new ones suggest that a stalemate has been reached in women's condition.

PERSISTING PROBLEMS FOR WOMEN

Occupational segregation The most severe employment problem facing Swedish women today is occupational segregation. According to the 1980 census, the top four of the most common occupations in Sweden are saturated with women – 88.6 per cent of secretaries are women, 93.8 per cent of nursing auxiliaries, 77.9 per cent of shop assistants and 89.5 per cent of cleaners (see table 10.2).

The picture has changed little in the two decades of women's increasing employment, a perplexing fact in light of the efforts that have been made to tackle the problem. The National Labor Market Board (representatives of the trade unions and political parties are members) has devised creative and aggressive measures to steer women out of traditional sex-role-typed occupations. Career guidance and job training programs have encouraged many women at least to consider working in engineering or manufacturing. But the efforts have not resulted in any significant occupational shift. In fact, much to the shock of Swedes, a 1980 study by the OECD found Sweden's labor force to be among the *most* segregated in the advanced industrial countries. Some recent Swedish studies report small improvements in the level of occupational segregation as being counteracted by certain structural changes in the labor force as a whole, in particular the expansion of the public sector (Jonung, 1984).

The most convincing explanations that have been offered thus far for this resistance to change have focused on factors in the labor market and the economy (for elaborations, see Rollen, 1980; Ruggie, 1984). For instance,

TABLE 10.2   *The Most Common Occupations in Sweden*

Occupation	Total	%workforce	%women
Stenographer, typist, etc.	275,745	6.9	88.6
Nursing aide	181,433	4.5	93.8
Shop clerk	153,382	3.8	77.9
Charworker	130,312	3.3	89.5
Farmer, forest, horticultural	129,189	3.2	32.3
Machine fitter, repairer	120,194	3.0	7.9
Motor vehicle, train driver	108,110	2.7	6.1
Buyer, commercial traveller	103,060	2.6	17.6
Machine assembler	100,394	2.5	16.5
Mechanical engineer	77,734	1.9	2.4
Nursemaid	77,048	1.9	96.8
Bookkeeper, office cashier	68,080	1.7	82.4
Primary education teacher	63,765	1.6	78.4
Storeroom, warehouse worker	62,076	1.6	19.0
Building woodworker	59,477	1.5	0.6
Public home helper	58,071	1.5	98.2
Install. elect., elect. fitter	55,639	1.4	6.4
Structural engineer, architect	55,235	1.4	5.0
Professional nurse	55,511	1.4	94.8
Secondary education teacher	50,347	1.3	52.9
Kitchen maid (industrial)	48,749	1.2	91.5
Electrician, electrical engineer	48,419	1.2	3.8

Source: Leiniö (1985: 10).

one of the most important developments that first triggered women's entry into the labor force and that has continued to shape the occupational structure of women's employment is government spending. Increased expenditure created jobs in the social services in the health, education and welfare sectors – fields which women traditionally occupy, whether in or outside the home, professionally or not. Women currently comprise by far the vast majority of public-sector employees.[3] But they are more likely to be nurses than doctors, elementary school teachers than university professors, researchers in the Ministry of Social Affairs than in the Ministry of Foreign Affairs.

LO has always fully supported the efforts of the National Labor Market Board to desegregate the occupational structure, including the use of financial incentives to employers and even hiring quotas where these have proved helpful. In its own publications and policy statements, LO's most favored method of occcupational desegregation has been to encourage more women to enter traditional male jobs in manufacturing. The potential displacement of male workers that might result has not been a worry, because the method has been conceptualized as operating within an expanding economy. That this should be LO's preferred method is not surprising, in that LO organizes primarily blue-collar workers. But it is myopic to assume that women can, with only skill retraining, enter a male world and be both comfortable and accepted there. Moreover, while little emphasis is placed on retraining men to occupy traditional female jobs, when this does occur it is recognized that certain changes in the conditions of employment are necessary. Most importantly, salaries in certain occupations, such as teachers' aides in daycare centers, have been increased to attract more men.[4] LO's position is also shortsighted in view of the overall labor market situation of women and the circumstances of their occupational segregation. That is, LO's efforts have been greatest in the industrial sector even though women workers are more concentrated in the nonindustrial sector where their occupational problems are greatest.

But perhaps the most telling feature of LO's position is its resemblance to the traditional socialist doctrine of integrating the particular interests of women with the universal interests of workers as a whole – the whole being dominated by working-class men. The myopia induced by this strategy hinders any understanding of the structural forces behind occupational segregation, particularly those which have arrived with the current restructuring of advanced industrial economies. Thus, the consequences of occupational segregation are magnified, and women continue to occupy a marginal status. This, in turn, has produced a standstill in progress on equal pay and increasing part-time employment.

Equal pay Early reports that the gap between women and men's wages was closing relied exclusively on data provided by LO on its own membership. The data compared hourly wages only and the figures gave the impression that near equality in pay was being achieved.[5] Now that data are becoming available for pay scales of workers in all unions, it appears that we have been too quick to generalize about the Swedish wage gap on the basis of LO's experience alone. Using samples of full-time, full-year workers in all unions, women's pay as a proportion of men's appears to be lower than previously thought – in 1981 it was 80.5 per cent overall (see tables 10.3, 4 and 5 for details).

Women workers organized by LO still do better than those in TCO, where their numbers are greater (84.1 per cent for LO; 78.7 per cent for TCO; only incomplete data are available for SACO in this sample). The larger wage gap in the TCO is disturbing. Despite their earlier reluctance to agree to equal pay between categories of lower and higher paid workers, both the TCO and SACO eventually conceded and have become increasingly involved in centralized wage agreements. Moreover, TCO has been as vocal as LO in promoting women's issues. But clearly, policy positions have not translated immediately into observable outcomes. The wage disparities that continue within these unions reflect differences in the type of work women do and the consequences of occupational segregation.

TABLE 10.3   *Men's income as a percentage of women's income, 1981*
(full year, full-time employment)

	LO	TCO
Private employer	116 (86.2)	137 (73.0)
Municipal employer	122 (82.0)	129 (77.5)
State employer	–	117 (85.5)

Source: LO (1983: 18).

TABLE 10.4   *Percentage of workers with annual income under 70,000 kronor, 1981*

	LO		TCO	
	M	F	M	F
Private employer	34	70	9	38
Municipal employer	17	54	6	23
State employer	–	–	3	14

Source: LO (1983: 21).

TABLE 10.5   *Percentage of workers with annual income over 70,000 kronor, 1981*
(full year, full-time employed)

	LO		TCO	
	M	F	M	F
Private employer	6	1	48	12
Municipal employer	5	1	26	5
State employer	–	–	54	15

Source: LO (1983: 23).

Part-time employment   The issue of equal pay is exacerbated by one more emerging feature of the labor market situation of women workers.

Gradually over the last decade, women's employment has come to be characterized by a new phenomenon that will potentially become as much of a bane as occupational segregation, namely an increase in part-time employment. Whereas in 1968, 39 per cent of employed women worked part-time, the figure in 1981 was 50 per cent (compared to 3 per cent of working men in 1968 and 7 per cent in 1981).

There is no doubt that the increase in part-time employment is connected at least in part with the renewed emphasis on the family and family policy within the labor movement, especially by LO – and it should be noted that more women in LO work part-time than in the other unions. At present, family policy has reached an impasse over one issue in particular – shortened working hours for parents of school-age children. The impasse involves two points of contention – reimbursement for hours not worked, and equality between mothers and fathers in using the benefit. LO wants parents to receive 90 per cent of pay for hours not worked, but it is only recommending (not requiring) that both parents share the responsibility.

Inevitably, a compromise will be reached, and its potential implications for women are less than favorable. Since women's pay is lower than men's and the work they do is marginal in the economy, women will most likely take the shortened working hours and resume their traditional roles within the household. Indeed, they are already doing so, as the figures on part-time employment imply. This development, curiously, seems to be accepted all around. One might suggest that women themselves want to work part-time so they can be with their children more. And yet, the available data about women and part-time employment raise questions about such interpretations. For example, as many as 25 per cent of those women who work part-time work on weekends, a time when presumably the whole family could be together. Also, the data show that part-time employment increases with women's age, suggesting that their employment may be unrelated to the family situation. Finally, women who work part-time continue to be in lower-level occupations. Their numbers are greatest in commerce, hotels and catering (although a sizeable proportion are also in municipal civil service jobs). It appears, in other words, that the increase in part-time employment among women is signalling an increasing marginality of women workers. They are functioning once again as an industrial reserve army in the labor market. And this fact is being masked by the rhetoric of family values.

Psychological distress Several other areas appear to indicate that women's actual condition in Swedish society perhaps has not matched their improved formal status. The material is still under-researched and the evidence is therefore scarce. But what little evidence there is demands attention. Alcoholism among Swedish women is increasing, despite an overall decrease in alcoholism in Sweden (CAN, 1985: 4). While researchers find the magnitude of the increase difficult to document, they note that it appears to be greatest among women aged 30–5. A little more information about women alcoholics is emerging from an experimental treatment facility for women with alcohol problems at the Karolinska Hospital in Stockholm. Approximately 600 women have been treated thus far. They are primarily gainfully employed women; they tend to be 'in settled social circumstances'; their median age is 40; about half are living with a male partner; about three-quarters have one or more children (Dahlgren, 1985). The director of the program observes further that many of the women undergoing treatment are employed in white-collar, even professional jobs (personal interview, June 1985).

Studies of other dimensions of psychological problems point in a similar direction. For example, depression remains higher among women than men, and its increase among women is also greater than among men (Hagnell et al., 1982: 283-8). And a series of studies at the Karolinska Institute, investigating the relationship between unemployment and depression, finds that women suffer from the effects of unemployment as much as (and in some measures more than) the men in the study (Levi et al., 1984: 30). In addition, one study of gender inequalities in health in a number of Scandinavian countries finds that women have higher rates of illness and anxiety than men (Haavio-Mannila, 1986).[6] While we cannot draw any definitive conclusions from this scant information, it does lead us to be more cautious in our assessments of the status of women in Swedish society.

CONCLUSION

Working women's causes have been more successfully promoted in Sweden than in most other advanced industrial societies because the needs and demands of workers as a whole have had a privileged position on the socialist agenda and in the corporatist governance of Sweden. However, whenever conflicts have arisen between the particular interests of women on the one hand, and the general interests of the labor force or the family on the other, the latter have taken precedence. And whenever women's interests could not be articulated in terms of their roles as workers in general or wives/mothers in general, those interests have remained unexpressed and unrealized. The most telling example is occupational segregation. This chapter has discussed other areas where improvements for women, whether in the labor force or not, have faltered in Sweden. The situation of women in Sweden may not appear serious when compared to women's inferior status in other countries. Yet, we do not know the extent to which the lingering and newly arising problems will grow to become more troublesome. Swedish women themselves are not greatly mobilized for change at present, either in autonomous groups or in workplace organizations. Nor is organized labor pressing for renewed attempts to meet more fully and effectively its long-held goal of equality. This standstill may well be due in part to the current economic restructuring in Sweden. But, as I have suggested here, its roots can also be found in the traditional Swedish approach to social and political action on behalf of women – an approach whose limits we may now be witnessing.

NOTES

Research for this paper was made possible by a grant from the American Scandinavian Foundation.

1 Earlier commissions of inquiry had already begun the development of Swedish family policy by, for example, minimizing the legal and financial consequences of illegitimacy. Also, the Marriage Code of 1920 established women's legal and financial equality within the family. The LO was not directly concerned with these early family commissions.
2 While much preparatory work had been done by the Advisory Committee on Equality under the previous Social Democratic government, it is uncertain whether that government would have actually passed such a law. Among other things, the law gives central authorities a strong role in overseeing labor-related matters.
3 The exact figure is unavailable because personal data on public employees is no longer kept.
4 This is another example of a policy initiative not originally intended to benefit women, but which has done so in the long run.
5 Hourly wages are usually higher than annual income. Based on these figures, women's wages were reported to be approximately 90 per cent of men's, depending on the industry.
6 The study also notes that the rates of illness are higher among full-time housewives than working women, and that the strain of combining family and work among women is more likely to be manifest as anxiety rather than in physical illness (Haavio-Mannila, 1986: 141 and passim).

REFERENCES

Anton, T. J. (1969) 'Policy-making and political culture in Sweden', *Scandinavian Political Studies*, vol. 4.
CAN (The Swedish Council for Information on Alcohol and Other Drugs) (1985) *Report 84 on the Alcohol and Drug Situation in Sweden* (Stockholm: Garnisonstryckeriert).
Cook, A. (1980) 'Collective Bargaining as a Strategy for Achieving Equal Opportunity and Equal Pay: Sweden and West Germany', in R. Steinberg Ratner (ed.), *Equal Employment Policy for Women: Strategies for Implementation in the United States, Canada, and Western Europe* (Philadelphia: Temple University Press).

Dahlgren, L. (1985) 'Presentation of the EWA-Project: An Experimental Treatment Facility for Female Alcohol Abusers' (Working Paper).

Dahlström, E. and R. Liljeström (1983) 'The patriarchal heritage and the working-class woman', *Acta Sociologica*, vol. 26, no. 1.

Haavio-Mannila, E. (1986) 'Inequalities in health and gender', *Social Science Medicine*.

Hagnell, O. et al. (1982) 'Are we entering an age of melancholy? Depressive illnesses in a prospective epidemiological study over 25 years: The Lundby Study, Sweden', *Psychological Medicine*, vol. 12.

Heidenheimer, A. J. (1976) 'Professional unions, public sector growth, and the Swedish equality policy', *Comparative Politics*, vol. 9, October.

Jonung, C. (1984) 'Patterns of occupational segregation by sex in the labor market', in G. Schmid and R. Weitzel (eds), *Sex Discrimination and Equal Opportunity: The Labor Market and Employment Policy* (Berlin: WZB Publications).

Korpi, W. (1978) *The Working Class in Welfare Capitalism: Work, Unions and Politics in Sweden* (London: Routledge and Kegan Paul).

Leiniö, T.-L. (1985) 'Sex and ethnic segregation in the 1980 Swedish labor market', Paper presented at the International Sociological Association Conference, Research Committee on Migration, Yugoslavia.

Levi, L. et al. (1984) 'The psychological, social and biochemical impacts of unemployment in Sweden', *International Journal of Mental Health*, vol. 13.

LO (1981) *Fackligt-socialt Arbete I Praktiken, 1: Sa Här Jobbar Facket med Socialt Arbete* (Stockholm: Landsorganisationen).

LO (1983) *L0-Medlemmar I Välfärden, Rapport 3* (Stockholm: Landsorganisationen).

LO (1985) *LO-Medlemmar I Välfäreden, Rapport 4*, (Stockholm: Landsorganisationen).

Meijer, H. (1969) 'Bureaucracy and policy formulation in Sweden', *Scandinavian Political Studies*, vol. 4.

Meyer, D. (1987) *Sex and Power: The Rise of Women in America, Russia, Sweden and Italy* (Middletown, CT: Wesleyan University Press).

OECD (1980) *Women and Employment* (Paris: OECD).

OECD (1984) *Working Group on the Role of Women in the Economy: The Integration of Women into the Economy* (Paris: OECD).

Qvist, G. (1976) 'The *Landsorganisationen* (LO) in Sweden and Women on the Labor Market (1969–1973)', *International Journal of Sociology*, vol. 5, no. 4.

Rollen, B. (1980) 'Equality between men and women in the labor market: The Swedish National Labor Board', in R. Steinberg Ratner (ed.), *Equal Employment Policy for Women: Strategies for Implementation in the United States, Canada, and Western Europe* (Philadelphia: Temple University Press).

Ruggie, M. (1984) *The State and Working Women: A Comparative Study of Britain and Sweden* (Princeton: Princeton University Press).

Scott, H. (1982) *Sweden's "Right to be Human" Sex-Role Equality: The Goal and the Reality* (Armonk, New York: M. E. Sharpe).

Stephens, J. D. (1979) *The Transition from Capitalism to Socialism* (London: Macmillan Press).

Wheeler, C. (1975) *White-Collar Power: Changing Patterns of Interest Group Behavior in Sweden* (Chicago: University of Illinois Press).

11

The Unsubtle Revolution
Women, the State and Equal Employment

Ronnie Steinberg

Since World War II, a non-violent, even 'subtle' revolution has changed the economic life of the United States – the massive entry of women into the labor force.[1] At the same time that their labor force participation has been increasing dramatically, women have been channelled into a restricted range of work, which offers them, on average, lower pay than men, less job security, and little voice in their trade unions – in short, second-class status (Reskin and Hartmann, 1986). Moreover, until very recently, the problems associated with women's entry into paid employment were largely treated as individual concerns to be resolved by women and their families.

Nevertheless, there has been some state action directed against gender-based labor market inequality. Since World War II the Women's Bureau of the US Department of Labor, along with a handful of trade unions, has advocated federal equal pay standards (Klein, 1985; Gabin, 1985). But it was not until the Kennedy administration, and the establishment of the President's Commission on the Status of Women, that pressure from interest groups within government proved sufficient to move Congress into action, resulting in the 1963 Equal Pay Amendment to the Fair Labor Standards Act. Even so, in that amendment, federal pay standards were watered down to render all but the most narrow comparisons between jobs beyond the bounds of the law.

The record on other federal equal opportunity legislation and on employment and training programs reveals a concern primarily with male minorities and only secondarily with women workers. The addition of the category 'sex' to the list of protected classes in Title VII of the 1964 Civil Rights Act was intended as a deliberate maneuver to defeat the bill. Even

Kennedy's Commission on the Status of Women chose not to support the amendment, so as not to threaten the new rights for minorities by extending them to white women (Peterson, 1983). When the Equal Employment Opportunity Commission began to receive complaints from women, staff expressed indifference, if not anger, as many of them had joined the Commission to participate in the fight against racism. Sexism in employment was just not a serious concern.

The 1964 Executive Order prohibiting federal contracts to employers who discriminate in their employment policies and practices ignored 'sex' as a basis of discrimination until 1968, when the order was amended. Similarly, the take-off in the Manpower Development and Training Programs, also in the mid-1960s, occurred on the heels of widespread urban unrest compounded by the visible problem of youth unemployment. Although the rate of minority female youth unemployment had always been considerably higher than minority male youth unemployment, the programs targeted the latter group.

These reforms, however, unintentionally laid the foundation for federal intervention to correct female labor market inequality in the 1970s. They carried a potential somewhat realized in that decade, due in large measure to the emergence of the women's movement – itself a function of the changing consciousness about women's position – and its transformation into an interest group operating in mainstream political arenas (Costain, 1982; Katzenstein, 1987). The movement's gains were greatest in the extension of legal entitlements in the employment and education sectors, the same areas in which civil rights organizations achieved considerable success (Boneparth, 1982: 3-4). These included Congressional approval of the Equal Rights Amendment; federal legislation on educational equity and non-discrimination in credit; allocation of training resources for women, especially for non-traditional jobs; the strengthening of Title VII and Executive Orders applied to both women and minorities; and first initiatives on equal pay for work of comparable worth. In the 1970s, Congress alone passed 71 laws addressing the feminist political agenda (Klein, 1984: 30). Even the judiciary shaped policy; the courts proved sympathetic to broader definitions of discrimination, although they consistently applied more liberal standards in deciding race discrimination cases.[2]

The backlash, since Reagan's election in 1981, against those changes is itself a reflection of how far-reaching the gains of the 1970s were for women. It brought with it a decided shift in the structure of politics around government reforms for employed women. No longer did the legislature and the executive work in concert as they had during the Carter administration. Early in the Reagan administration, top executive staff developed a number of plans to dismantle Title VII and related reforms. In the face of strong political opposition, they shifted tactics to cutting appropriations, intentionally selecting ineffectual agency heads, and appointing judges who interpreted civil rights and labor legislation narrowly.

What the Reagan forces did not anticipate, however, was the quiet, but unsubtle, revolution in women's position in politics. By the 1980s, women had become state legislators, county officials, mayors and agency administrators at all levels of government. A National Women's Political Caucus survey reports that, between 1971 and 1983, there was a dramatic increase in the percentage of female state legislators from 5 per cent to 13 per cent and of female mayors from 1 per cent to 9 per cent, while between 1975 and 1980 the proportion of female county officials doubled (from three per cent to six per cent) and that of municipal officials tripled (Flammang, 1984).

Many local chapters and national offices of the League of Women Voters (LWV), National Organization of Women (NOW), National Abortion Rights Action League (NARAL), the National Women's Political Caucus (NWPC), and the Women's Equity Action League (WEAL) also had hired political staff, resulting in heightened visibility.[3] Fully 48 per cent of all the women's rights lobbying groups with offices in Washington in 1981 came into being after 1960 (Schlozman, 1986: 16). Along with a number of more traditional women's organizations that have been lobbying for some time, groups have registered political achievements at the same time as they have held the backlash somewhat at bay. Their presence, for example, has made it impossible to amend Title VII legislation, to stop the movement of comparable worth at the state and local level, or to dismantle many of the job training programs that prepare women for jobs historically held by males.

Women have become an institutionalized force in American politics, and because of this, there is a shift in *expectations*. Government is now viewed as the arena in which solutions can be found to the labor market problems of employed women.[4] Of course, these expectations have not been completely fulfilled; women still have a way to go to achieve political parity with other, more entrenched interest groups. None the less, women, on average, are currently much less likely to tolerate discriminatory treatment by employers than they would have been 20 years ago and politicians know this. Even employers pay lip-service to equal pay and equal opportunity rights, although they do so in the context of their strong opposition to comparable worth.

The political route traveled by liberal feminist women passed through three overlapping phases. Women's early achievements were the result of fairly conventional interest group politics. Individual women, women's organizations and, somewhat later, several trade unions lobbied Congress, pressured administrative agencies, and brought court cases.[5]

Not surprisingly, business groups, like the Equal Employment Advisory Council (a lobbying arm of the Business Roundtable with an annual budget of $1 million), the National Association of Manufacturers and local Chambers of Commerce, fought to constrain the scope of the new legislation and orders through limiting the guidelines and regulations that flowed from them. Opposing these efforts, women's groups learned how to operate as effective lobbyists at all levels of government in the 1970s. They also made good use of public opinion, electoral support and a climate generally favorable to their agenda in a way they had been unable to accomplish previously.

As liberal feminists matured politically, they shifted tactics. As indicated above, women sought elected office and appointments to high-level policy-making positions in unprecedented numbers. These women entered public service with considerable political savvy and an explicit liberal feminist agenda. They created policy networks among themselves and with a variety of supportive women's organizations (Meehan, 1985).[6] Women's organizations engaged in strategic political pressure, often working in concert with feminists inside government to redirect existing resources towards eliminating sex-based employment discrimination. They made good use of the gender gap, revealed in the 1982 mid-year elections and, which for a short time, convinced male politicians to be sensitive to the priorities of liberal women constituents and support feminist initiatives.

A second shift was ushered in with the Reagan administration. For the first time in two decades, central forces within government actively opposed the use of government resources to achieve fairness in employment for working women.[7] Control of job training programs is now in the hands of local private industry councils and sensitive to the needs of business as defined by business. A national campaign to discredit comparable worth has been mounted by high-level White House staff and major executive appointees, using tax monies for support. No longer do business groups even need to lobby actively over these reforms. Even women's groups have decreased the level of conventional lobbying that they do. Instead, they work closely with and often follow the lead of elected and appointed women in state and federal government.

Feminist politics over employment policy has thus gone through three stages. The first stage is best captured by an interest group model, while the second can be characterized as insider–outsider coalition-building. The third stage might be characterized as one of bureaucratic conflict, in which those agencies within branches, and levels of government fight for control over the definition and scope of reforms.

This chapter explores the nature and shift in strategies underlying reforms in employment policies for women workers. It does so by examining two reforms, each peaking at a different time. The first provided job training programs, culminating in the 1978 amendments to the Comprehensive Employment and Training Act. It represents a reform achieved through the combined use of interest group politics and, to a lesser extent, insider–outsider coalition-building.

The second reform is equal pay for work of comparable worth, also called pay equity. It is especially interesting to examine because it gained visibility right before the backlash against mainstream feminist reform emerged. Especially since 1983, it has been the focus of a fight *within* government over the proper role for achieving fairness for women workers. The dynamics of bureaucratic conflict over comparable worth will be explored primarily at the national level, with some discussion of the bureaucratic politics in New York State.

TRAINING WOMEN FOR NON-TRADITIONAL JOBS[8]

Employment and training programs have not always been associated with the goal of equal employment opportunity for women and minorities. In 1933, the incoming Roosevelt administration enacted the first federally-sponsored work relief and work training programs for unmarried men 18–25 years of age, the Civilian Conservation Corps (Clague, 1976: 3). While moving away from targeting the young and unmarried, later programs continued the male bias by limiting opportunities to one person per household.

Further training programs to combat unemployment and aid the economically disadvantaged grew under the Kennedy administration and have continued up to the present. As constituency groups showed their political muscle, new targeted groups were added to the legislation so that by 1967, there were 17 separate categorical programs.

The Comprehensive Employment and Training Act (CETA) was enacted in late 1973. It allowed the federal government to continue to provide funds (primarily in the form of block grants) but transferred the authority and responsibility for programs to state and local governments. Again the unemployed and the economically disadvantaged were targeted. The Act implied that those most in need should receive the most services but specified no criteria for establishing need. CETA followed its predecessors in giving no special priority to the employment problems of women. The consequence of this was that women made up more than 55 per cent of those who were to receive CETA benefits, but, until the late 1970s, represented fewer than one-half of those served by CETA.

Finally, in 1975, in response to direct pressure from several interest groups – including Wider Opportunities for Women, the Alliance for Displaced Homemakers, the Coalition on Women and Poverty (staffed by National Organization for Women and the National Women's Law Center), and the Women's Lobby – policy-makers began to pay more attention to the needs of women. Moreover, the Women's Bureau of the Department of Labor took on the role of internal lobbyist.

The changing orientation toward women was finally expressed legislatively in the 1978 CETA re-authorization, which contained more provisions favorable to women than any prior training policy (Harlan, 1985: 289). Training programs that receive government monies were required to provide equitable training opportunities to women, including affirmative action plans with goals and timetables. Corrective action was to be taken if the proportion of female program enrollees differed by more than 15 per cent from that in the eligible population. Non-traditional training for women was given specific mention, and the Department of Labor committed $5 million for fiscal year 1979–80 for displaced homemakers (Shields, 1981).

The CETA amendments provided seed money that helped create institutional change. Well over 100 programs were set up exclusively to train women to enter occupations historically dominated by males. One example cited by Harlan is the Women's Technical Institute in Boston, which, since the 1970s, has trained more women electronic technicians than the city's largest technical school has produced in its 75-year history (Harlan, 1985: 298). Firms subject to government consent decrees requiring them to employ women in historically male jobs according to a specified set of goals and timetables would turn to local CETA programs for potential recruits (see Deaux and Ullman, 1983 regarding the steel industry). This pressure solved the major problem of finding employment for women once they had completed their training. Other programs were developed solely to meet the distinctive training needs of displaced homemakers and the number of women enrolled increased dramatically.

What happened in the middle 1970s that resulted in this addition to CETA program priorities? As indicated above, the 1970s were a time of substantial and growing support for the goals of the Women's Movement, especially around employment policy. One can observe this evolution in sentiment in the public opinion polls between 1968 and 1980. In 1968, while 66 per cent of women favored giving women the same job opportunities as men, only 33 per cent believed that women's opportunities in business were more constrained than men's.

Then, as Ethel Klein notes:

> By 1980 the majority of women felt that they did not have an equal chance with men in becoming business executives (57 per cent), getting a top job in government (55 per cent), entering prestige professions (52 per cent), or obtaining loans and mortgages (51 per cent). More women felt that they were excluded from leadership responsibilities in 1980 (45 per cent) than in 1970 (31 per cent), and the sense that women had less access to skilled jobs grew from 40 per cent in 1970 to 48 per cent in 1980. (1984: 92–3)

In addition, the Carter administration was especially sympathetic to the labor and civil rights concerns of subordinate power groups. Secretary of

Labor Ray Marshall had longstanding ties to the civil rights and labor movements. The Department strengthened guidelines and regulations having to do with equal opportunity for women as well as minorities. It took an unprecedented number of cases to court attempting to push existing laws to their limit. The Department of Labor settled several cases out of court with women's organizations. As a result, more monies were allocated to programs directed at women's labor market equality. A number of cases involved programs to train women for non-traditional jobs.

In this favorable social and political climate – with a sympathetic administration and a Democrat-controlled Congress – two organizations spearheaded mobilization for the 1978 CETA amendments – Wider Opportunities for Women (WOW), and the Displaced Homemakers Alliance (DHA). WOW was started in the early 1960s by a group of volunteer women who believed that career advisory and job development services were all that was needed to create the conditions for women's equal employment. By the late 1960s, WOW had grown into a national organization encompassing both individual services and broader social change initiatives (Fleming, 1983). Quickly learning that employment and training programs were designed for men, and that most jobs for which women were trained kept them below the poverty lines, the organization shifted its focus to training for jobs historically held by males. Hampered by mediocre enforcement of inadequate laws, they successfully litigated against the government, forcing the Department of Labor to establish affirmative action standards in construction work.[9] When they were in turn sued for reverse discrimination and blocked from using CETA monies for non-traditional training programs, they, along with other women-run training programs and organizations like the Coalition of Labor Union Women, pressured Congress for explicit sex equity requirements (Meehan, 1985: chapter 3).

DHA grew out of the national NOW Task Force on Older Women, created in 1973. Displaced homemakers are middle-aged women with little paid employment experience, who have been left by their husbands with little money and even less ability to achieve economic self-sufficiency. The programs combine job training with broader employment skills to prepare these women to enter the labor market effectively – i.e. to achieve economic independence. In the early 1970s, the NOW Task Force had evolved into two separate organizations. The first was Jobs for Older Women and the second the Displaced Homemakers Alliance, both located in California. Under pressure from these organizations, California passed the first displaced homemaker law, establishing a two-year pilot project in Alameda County. Measures were also passed in Maryland, Oregon and Minnesota.[10] Thus, by the time the 1978 CETA amendments were being considered in Congress, there were several displaced homemaker programs operating throughout the country. This experience could be referred to by those lobbying for federal resources.

In 1977, at the instigation of DHA, Representative Yvonne Burke and Senator Birch Bayh filed identical bills, calling for the development of a minimum of 50 displaced homemaker centers, which would not only provide services but also coordinate available community resources. At the same time, a member of the legislative staff warned the group to persuade President Carter to include displaced homemakers as a targeted category in his CETA Re-authorization Bill. Through direct pressure on the White House, the category was added. Then, interest group energies shifted to the CETA amendments, as the simpler route to legislative reform.[11]

Hearings were held in both the House and the Senate, and DHA and WOW assisted in drafting the list of witnesses. The major source of resistance was not business interests, but Congressional reaction to the idea that so-called middle-class white women were needy. It was one thing to broaden the concept of economically disadvantaged from minority male youth to minority female youth. It was another thing to suggest that abandoned middle-class women were actually victims of poverty. Eventually, with considerable effort to educate members of Congress, the measure was passed, although appropriations were much smaller than originally hoped for.

Interestingly, the institutionalization of women in the political arena was deepened by this victory via the creation of a national network of local programs. One of them was the Women's Work Force Network, coordinated by WOW and composed of over 125 women's employment programs from across the country. In addition to offering technical assistance to new training programs, the Network monitors public policy in employment and training and works with Congressional staff and sympathetic members of Congress to retain as much equal opportunity language in training bills as is possible under the Reagan administration.

The Displaced Homemakers Network was also formed out of this experience and continues today. It works very much in concert with the Women's Work Force Network to keep as much job training activity for women alive as possible during the less receptive Reagan years. Both groups achieved their agendas using conventional pressure and lobbying tactics. As each has matured politically, they have established strong ties with several sympathetic members of Congress and their staffers as well as with relevant agency bureaucrats.

In October 1982 President Reagan signed the Job Training Partnership Act (JTPA), to take effect in late 1983. JTPA is, in most cases, less specific than CETA about non-traditional training programs for women. The legislation once again emphasizes training the population most in need, although it mentions a concern with providing services equitably. It prohibits discrimination, emphasizing the elimination of occupational segregation, but makes no mention of affirmative action. It does target young women, and women welfare recipients, but it does not target displaced homemakers. These changes suggest the limits of an interest group political strategy in a less hospitable political context, especially where the interest group is relatively new, and operating with few resources.

Not surprisingly, political pressure from women has shifted from the federal government to Private Industry Councils at state and local levels where program resources are controlled. The impact of JTPA on women's programs has been mixed. One study of displaced homemaker programs found that about half the programs were continuing to run at about the same level as in earlier, more favorable, times (Miller and Spero, 1986). In those states in which women's advocates have become insiders, programs have continued relatively undisturbed. Where women have been unable to gain sufficient political influence, programs have suffered greatly.

Even many suffering programs have survived, however, often on limited funding from other sources, such as the Vocational Education Act.[12] Since we know that federal government resources are crucial to the growth and effectiveness of programs of benefit to women, such efforts will only thrive again when federal initiatives are strengthened. This will only take place when advocates *within* government once again gain ascendency.

EQUAL PAY FOR WORK OF COMPARABLE WORTH: NATIONAL OVERVIEW[13]

The goal of equal pay for equal work, the precursor of the more recent comparable worth policy, was first introduced in the late nineteenth century by the socialist and suffrage movements, as well as by trade unions and women's rights organizations. Yet it only began to be taken seriously as a political goal during World War II, when several states, including New Jersey, Illinois and New York, passed Equal Pay Acts (Steinberg, 1982: chapter 4).[14] Responding to the likely deterioration of male wage rates resulting from women filling men's jobs, the War Labor Board established the principle of equal pay for equal work, although it provided only for voluntary compliance.

A pathbreaking case was brought before the War Labor Board in 1945 by the United Electrical Workers (UE) against both General Electric and Westinghouse. Identified as 'the first national-level case to establish the concept . . . known as "equal pay for comparable worth"', these UE complaints developed out of a decade-long union effort to narrow wage differentials between women's and men's work in the electrical industry (Milkman, 1981: 185). In deciding the General Electric and Westinghouse case on 29 November 1945, the Board noted that the issue was not equal pay, but was 'that the jobs customarily performed by women are paid less, on a comparative job content basis, than the jobs customarily performed by men' and 'that this relative underpayment constitutes a sex discrimination' (Milkman, 1981: 195).

On 17 December the Board issued a second ruling, which was never complied with. This comparable worth campaign culminated in 1946 labor–management contract settlements including across-the-board as opposed to percentage wage increases, the effect of which was to raise the wages of lower-paid, historically female jobs relative to wages for historically male jobs (ibid., 327).

The Women's Bureau of the US Department of Labor provided sustained support to proponents of equal pay legislation after the war (Cook, 1984: 271). In 1952, for example, the Bureau consolidated the activities of some 20 large national organizations into a united campaign for passage of a federal law. But these forces had to await a more conducive political climate to see their goal realized. That climate emerged in the early 1960s, with support from President Kennedy and direct pressure from the President's Commission on Women.

The 1962 federal equal pay amendment to the Fair Labor Standards Act was motivated by different concerns than the earlier equal pay acts. Unlike the earlier reforms, it was less concerned with protecting male wage rates than with raising the level of wages paid to women workers. To achieve this objective, the Bill originally considered by the House contained comparable worth standards and it carried the strong endorsement of the Kennedy administration and the support of women's and union groups. But due to strong business opposition, the Bill was amended several times to eliminate completely this comparable worth standard (Milkovich and Broderick, 1982). The final equal pay for equal work standard reflected the weak power position of partisan interest groups and the lack of systematic (as opposed to anecdotal) information supporting their arguments about the sources and consequences of labor market inequality.

Comparable worth did not surface again as a political demand until the early 1970s, when a number of isolated initiatives occurred. Two warrant mention. First, at the request of the government employees union, AFSCME, and in cooperation with the Commission on the Status of Women, the State of Washington undertook a comparable pay study which found that female jobs received on average approximately 20 per cent lower pay than equivalent male jobs. No action was taken to correct for the observed undervaluation (Remick, 1980). Second, beginning in 1972, the Electrical Workers Union (IUE) initiated a Title VII compliance program.[15] Westinghouse Electric Corporation was targeted by the union, and several Westinghouse plants eventually revised their contracts through out-of-court settlements to pay equivalent male-dominated and female-dominated jobs equal pay. One plant resisted but was forced to change its compensation structure when a US Court of Appeals upheld the union's claim of sex-based wage discrimination.

Early comparable worth initiatives bypassed the interest group model and followed instead an insider–outsider coalition approach.[16] Specifically, these reforms were initiated largely by state Commissions on the Status of Women, which found a natural ally in public sector unions engaged in organizing drives around the country (Johansen, 1984; Commission on the Economic Status of Women, 1985: Evans and Nelson, 1986; Flammang, 1987).[17]

But pay equity policy first became nationally visible in 1977 when Equal Employment Opportunity Commission (EEOC) Chair Eleanor Holmes Norton identified the issue as a priority of her administration. Among other activities, the Commission contracted with the prestigious National Research Council of the National Academy of Sciences to examine the feasibility of implementing comparable worth. Her selection of the Academy to carry out the investigation appeared to be strategic, because she wanted, if possible, 'organized science' to conclude that wage discrimination was pervasive and that implementing comparable worth was feasible. In April 1980, Norton organized hearings on the issue, seeking out experts and activists to testify (EEOC, 1980). While a number of representatives of working women's organizations testified, no representative of the more broadly based women's rights groups appeared.[18]

Nevertheless, Norton's actions served as the stimulus for forming a national network of groups and individuals working to achieve comparable worth at the state or municipal level in particular workplaces. Yet it was not until comparable worth became a visible, national demand around 1980 that broad-based women's rights groups like NOW, WEAL and even the National Women's Political Caucus added their support. Even so, these women's organizations initiated reform efforts in only a very few states and localities – most notably in West Virginia and, more indirectly through electoral politics, in New Mexico. This is not meant to be a critique of these women's organizations, but is offered instead to clarify the unique strategic route taken to achieve this reform.

Around 1980 as well, the opposition first stated the case against pay equity in *Comparable Worth: Issues and Alternatives*, published by the Equal Employment Advisory Council, a lobbying arm of the Business Roundtable with a $1 million annual budget (Livernash, 1980). The Business Roundtable viewed the volume as containing a set of definitive arguments that would undercut the momentum building around the reform. By then, however, it was simply too late to stop the reform: too many groups had begun initiatives around comparable worth.

Three events in 1981 contributed to the further legitimacy of the reform. In June, comparable worth took a small, but significant step forward in the courts with the Supreme Court ruling in *County of Washington* v. *Gunther* (49 USLW 4623). The court indicated in its decision that it would be willing to regard certain explicit inequities between dissimilar jobs as wage discrimination under Title VII, although not necessarily as comparable worth.[19]

Almost one month later, in San José, California, AFSCME Local 101 struck for one week over failure to implement a pay equity study. Although the (female) City Manager rapidly adjusted the salary of managerial positions as a result of a compensation study, she resisted AFSCME demands for a similar comparable pay compensation study of non-exempt jobs. The Manager and City Council finally agreed to do the study, largely in response to combined pressure from women inside city government and women's organizations (Flammang, 1987). While the study revealed undervaluation, labor and management made little headway, due to management obstruction. The union finally filed a complaint with the EEOC and, angered by this, the City Manager broke off negotiations. A strike vote was taken. The parties reached a tentative agreement one week later. The contract agreement did endorse the principle of comparable worth, and provided modest salary adjustments for undervalued female-dominated job titles (Farnquist et al., 1983).

Then, in fall 1981, the National Research Council committee issued its long overdue final report, *Women, Work and Wages: Equal Pay for Jobs of Equal Value* (Treiman & Hartmann, 1981).[20] The report remained focused on technical issues yet it provided strong evidence of the distributive injustices suffered by women and men who found themselves in historically female occupations. Moreover, by suggesting some possible modifications of job evaluation techniques, it undercut the opponents' arguments that such techniques could not be used to estimate wage discrimination. The study thus became a useful power resource for comparable worth proponents.

Many activities at the state and local level, begun in late 1981 and 1982, became visible in 1983 (Rothchild, 1984). Studies began in more than one dozen states between fall 1983 and the end of 1984, including Maine, Massachusetts, New York, Ohio, Illinois, Wisconsin, West Virginia and Oregon. Pay equity legislation was passed in California, Hawaii and Montana. New Mexico followed a different approach by first appropriating $3.3 million for increases for the 3000 lowest-paid state employees (86 per cent of whom are women) and then requiring a study to identify possible additional adjustments. While full case studies of each initiative could contribute greatly to our understanding of the political economy of reform initiatives for women, only a very brief overview of one state initiative is presented here.

THE NEW YORK STATE COMPARABLE WORTH INITIATIVE

New York State represents perhaps the best example of an initiative carried out almost totally within government by political elites. The pressure for the reform came not through grassroots mobilization, nor even through the pressure of conventional interest groups. Rather, it emerged as a result of the successful use of networks built within state government by a university-based advocacy organization seeking equal employment for women in state government, the Center for Women in Government.[21] The president of the Center's board was also a high-level appointee of the Governor, with strong ties to the Governor's Office of Employee Relations (GOER), responsible for collective bargaining in the public sector. The highest-ranking woman in the major state public employees union, the Civil Service Employees Association (CSEA), also sat on the Center board. Both had a longstanding interest in comparable worth, as did the Center's Executive Director and Research Director. An additional factor in the equation was that CSEA was worried that its administrative bargaining unit, comprised almost entirely of clerical workers, was dissatisfied with union efforts in their behalf. Several years earlier, CSEA had lost two of its bargaining units (and well over 60,000 members) to another union – the Professional Employees Federation – because of membership discontent.

1982 negotiations were affected by these larger forces, and the final contract set aside $1 million – $500,000 to do a comparable pay study and $500,000 to do a management classification study. Neither management nor labor had thought through the consequences of that settlement in advance. The pressure to do a study was being felt *within* each side, and it was easier to promise a study than to raise salaries in female jobs by 1 or 2 per cent at a cost of $15–20 million. It is unclear whether either side planned to implement the contract provision. Management, for instance, did not know what it wanted to do in its classification study. Labor leadership did not want to take on an issue that would create the necessity for bargaining higher percentage wage increases for its less powerful women members. The extra pot of money had originally been put in to achieve balance: pay equity for labor, something for management. One indicator of weak commitment was the 18-month delay between signing the contract and funding a study. During that time, there was a change in administration and a new Director of GOER. But to counteract all of this inertia, women's networks within government and within the union were mobilized, and in effect labor and management were forced, in the end, to follow through on the contract clause it had cavalierly bargained, primarily due to the pressure from high-level women appointees, especially on GOER and the Governor's Office.

During that period, the New York Assembly Task Force on Women's Issues held hearings on comparable worth, despite the fact that neither labor, management nor the Center for Women in Government wanted them. Yet each participated. Several women's organizations also testified, because they were asked by the Task Force chair to make a statement. These hearings had no effect on the direction of the reform. The Director of GOER begrudgingly testified that a study would be done.

Over their two-year duration, GOER monitored the studies closely. Especially with the Center for Women in Government's study, political struggles among different sectors of management to contain it continued unabated. CSEA leadership initially displayed considerable indifference to the study, but, as the study moved forward, labor and management did bargain over such technical issues as the percentage cut-off for female-dominated jobs and the pay policy lines that would be used as the basis for wage adjustments of female-dominated jobs. Each of these decisions would have considerable impact on the scope of the reform and cost of implementation. The Center for Women in Government, while providing technical expertise, also provided a liberal feminist voice in a sea of male leadership exhibiting a modest understanding of the technical study approach and an increasingly sophisticated understanding of the economic and political consequences of the study results.

The most interesting political battles occurred within the ranks of management. In one of its initial proposals, the Center for Women in Government proposed an advisory committee composed of representatives of labor, management, legislators, and women's and minority organizations. This suggestion was deleted by management, which felt that to participate in an advisory committee would be, in effect, to rubber stamp the study results. Instead, GOER assigned a contract monitor as a liaison between management and the study team. The union concurred with management's decision.

As the study evolved, and as the GOER staff person appointed as study monitor began to understand the financial and political implications of the study, he got increasingly concerned. At the same time, some within management had found by working with the Center that it was not out to destroy and discredit the state, but engaged in conducting a serious study of the scope of wage discrimination in New York State. The orientation of these managers changed, and they wanted not to separate themselves from the study but to control it more directly. Almost one year into the study, management organized an advisory committee, with representatives from the Civil Service Department, the Division of the Budget, the Governor's Office, and GOER.[22]

As the Center proceeded with the project, the Division of the Budget raised several highly technical methodological concerns, which effectively stopped the study for some time. The Budget Division was the only management group that had not played a key role in the reform initiative from the start. It appeared that its staff thought the whole enterprise reckless and even though the Governor had long since publicly endorsed the study; Budget was going to dismantle it. A battle ensued between GOER and the Budget Division. GOER won through the strong ties between its Director and the Governor's top staff. In late November, the Center was told it could continue its study as originally designed.

In September 1985, the final report of the New York State Comparable Pay study was submitted to labor and management (Steinberg et al., 1985). The study found that jobs with 100 per cent female incumbents paid, on average, two full salary grades less than those jobs with 100 per cent male incumbents, for no other reason than the job was performed entirely by women. The competing management consulting firm study reported an even higher estimate of wage discrimination. Not surprisingly, at a press conference on the study results organized by the GOER, management announced the Center's most conservative estimate of wage discrimination and was vague on the results of the management study.

Several months before the results of the two studies were released, CSEA and GOER negotiated as part of its two-year contract a 1 per cent set aside, or approximately $34 million, for pay equity adjustments. It also allowed for a one-year developmental phase during which the study results would be translated into a coherent implementation plan. Since classification is a management prerogative, a management task force would shape the plan, subject to labor review.

The New York State experience offers an extreme case of top-down policy change. While, narrowly speaking, one could argue that interest groups participated in the initiative, they did so only to the extent that their leaders were involved in pressuring management. The policy was initiated by women government insiders, who effectively used the *threat* of mobilization of women constituents in the electorate and in the union as a power resource. Most of the women who will benefit from pay equity adjustments will have little, if any, understanding of the nature of the gains made. Interest groups outside the collective bargaining arena also played almost no role in policy formulation. Instead, different interest groups within the state, and frequently within management, fought vigorously over the survival and scope of the reform.

FEDERAL PAY EQUITY INITIATIVES: AN OVERVIEW

Nowhere is the fight within the government clearer than in the battles at the federal level between 1983 and 1985. Following the Tanner decision in *AFSCME* v. *State of Washington*, several members of Congress introduced Bills. Most called for a pay equity study of federal employment, either of agencies under the control of Congress or of a sample of agencies under the Executive. This is especially interesting because national interest groups pressuring for comparable worth were *opposed* to federal legislation as a strategy for achieving national standards. The National Committee on Pay Equity, the League of Women Voters, and AFSCME, for example, preferred at that time to build precedents under Title VII of the 1964 Civil Rights Act through the courts, and through state and local collective bargaining and legislative initiatives. They regarded federal legislation as premature, too visible a target for opponents. None of these Bills went anywhere.

With one exception, the Reagan administration kept a low profile until its re-election in 1984. Although a handful of Justice Department officials and members of the Council of Economic Advisors individually threw darts at the reform, only the US Commission on Civil Rights took any organized action, with its Consultation on Comparable Worth on 6–7 June 1984. Ostensibly, the purpose of the consultation was information-gathering, and both proponents and opponents of the reform were invited to testify. There was virtually no press coverage. Yet one has only to read the Consultation Proceedings to gain a strong sense of the intensely political nature of the event (US Commission on Civil Rights, 1984). The majority of Reagan appointees were using these consultations as the basis for building, when the timing was right, the case against comparable worth. The two Carter-appointed Commissioners used their limited leverage to expose the contradictions of their opponents' positions.

Not two weeks after the election, before the Commission had discussed the report or voted on it, Clarence Pendleton, Chair of the Commission, began leaking what would become the majority position of the Commission on Civil Rights, calling comparable worth 'the looniest tune since "Looney Tunes" came on the screen'. For the next several months, Clarence Pendleton and Linda Chavez, the Commission Executive Director, traveled across the country attacking the reform. The media gave them considerable coverage wherever they went.

This second round of backlash was not organized by business interests directly, but by the Reagan administration operating in the interests of business. It has been responded to, not so much by women's organizations and trade unions directly, but by elected and appointed officials in Congress and in state and municipal governments.[23] Thus, the interest group model has, in the case of this reform, been replaced by an approach in which government insiders fight each other relatively independently of the interest groups that support them.

Proponents of pay equity at the federal level were largely found in Congress. While they continued to submit Bills, nothing took off until late 1984 when Senator Dan Evans and Congressman William Ford commissioned the Government Accounting Office (GAO) to examine the feasibility of carrying out a federal comparable pay study (US GAO, 1985). GAO was also charged with determining how such a study would best be conducted and providing an estimate of the cost of the study. GAO released its report to Congress in March 1985 proposing a $1.2 million study.

Also prominent was Congresswoman Mary Rose Oakar, Chair of the House Subcommittee on Compensation and Employee Benefits of the

Committee on Post Office and Civil Service. She organized over five days of hearings on the GAO report, spanning 3½ months. The list of witnesses included representatives from five states in which pay equity initiatives had been carried out, federal employees potentially affected by a study, and all the public sector unions affected by the study. The National Association of Manufacturers and the American Personnel Management Association spoke in opposition to the Bill, as did Clarence Pendleton and others of the Civil Rights Commission and the Director of the Office of Personnel Management. Even pro-Choice anti-feminist leader, Phyllis Schafly, testified, calling comparable worth further evidence of the 'rhetoric of envy' typical of feminist politics (US, Committee on Post Office and Civil Service, 1986: 453).

During this time, the Commission on Civil Rights finally issued its report, which was critical of comparable worth (US Commission on Civil Rights, 1985). Upon reading the Commission's report, several members of Congress were incensed that a number of the arguments were built on inaccuracies of fact and distorted treatment of expert testimony. They asked GAO to review the report, and a few weeks later, GAO concluded that:

> The Commission's report defines comparable worth differently from comparable worth advocates, and it is the report's definition of comparable worth that the Commission recommended be rejected. The report also contains internal inconsistencies and errors. (GAO, 1985)

Thus, government agencies were now fighting openly over this sensitive political issue. Although this appears to have been historically true over many reform issues, it seems to be a new way of conducting politics over women's reform – largely as a result of access to political resources previously denied them and the rise of the opposition within government.

In general, the political dynamics surrounding equity initiatives are different from early labor market reforms for women. Early reform efforts fit comfortably within an interest group model. That is no longer the case. Having entered the political arena – as elected officials, as appointed high-level administrators, and as leaders of mobilized interest groups – political elite women are using their new leverage to achieve their reforms in strategically different ways. Feminists and anti-feminists have now moved their conflict into government arenas, whether at the local, state or federal levels, they are using the resources of their positions to make or block change.

CONCLUSION

Thus far, the discussion has focused on three points: first, that the emergence of the contemporary women's movement has ushered in a 'revolution' in

American politics, resulting in a series of substantial reform initiatives. A second related point is that reforms initially intended for minorities laid the foundation for federal intervention to improve the unequal labor market position of women workers. A third point, developed most fully in this chapter, is that there has been a shift in the strategic *politics* of liberal feminist reform. There has thus not only been a revolution in substance but also a revolution in process. This encompasses the election and appointment of women into high-level positions, especially at the state and local level, and their increasingly sophisticated use of their positions to use public opinion, the gender gap and even, when necessary, mobilized groups to achieve political reforms. Women are now increasingly sitting behind those infamous closed doors participating in shaping the scope of policy.

These are profoundly optimistic arguments about the impact of the women's movement on employment reforms. And yet, my fourth and final point is less so. Although women's employment rights are indeed fuller in 1986 than in 1964 when Title VII was passed, the gains that have occurred have been minimal. The implementation of job training programs under the 1978 amendments to CETA fell short of the goal of fully integrating women into training programs. While 53 per cent of all enrollees in CETA Title II B programs in 1980 were women, women still remained under-represented in proportion to their eligible population. Women's enrollment was affected by such features as veterans preference, age limits in apprenticeship, and means tests based on family income as opposed to individual earnings. It was no doubt also affected by limited resources for childcare assistance. Women were also more likely to be trained in classrooms for low-paid traditionally female work. Non-traditional programs for women had difficulty competing with traditional programs in terms of cost-effectiveness. They also experienced problems with job placement, as few firms felt serious government pressure to hire women, even at the height of affirmative action under the Carter administration (Haignere and Steinberg, 1983). Of course, with JTPA, the whole initiative to train women took a step backward, primarily because strong federal standards and oversight and monitoring would be largely absent.

The scope of comparable worth policy has been equally restricted. It began as an attempt to value characteristics associated with women's work not done in men's jobs. This would have meant that the caring functions found in female-dominated health sector jobs, for instance, would be more highly compensated. Although proponents still push for a feminization of the job content values in wage structure, they rarely succeed. What generally happens is that historically female work is compensated at the same rate of return per job content characteristic as men's work. In other words, if a woman's job requires a college degree, that job is now compensated at a level equivalent to a male job requiring a college education. As the National Research Council put it:

Paying jobs according to their worth requires *only* that *whatever characteristics are regarded as worthy of compensation* by the employer should be equally so regarded irrespective of the sex, race or ethnicity of job incumbents. (Treiman and Hartmann, 1981: 70; emphasis added)

This consistency standard has yielded wage adjustments of 5–20 per cent, with most falling at the lower end. Feminizing workplace values would yield even higher adjustments but comparable worth has not revalued women's work. It only rewards women for what is already considered valuable in men's work. Thus, male values prevail.

Similarly, a number of technical decisions, including the definition of female-dominated jobs, which job evaluation system is used, and which pay policy line is selected as the basis for wage adjustments, regularly reduce pay equity implementation plans to little more than the appearance of change. Once the reform is implemented, there is little chance that the legislature or executive will move to examine wage discrimination in, for instance, job titles with 50–70 per cent female incumbents. By that time most of the momentum will be lost.

A profound change in the composition of the political arena has simultaneously ushered in significant labor market policies for women and reduced them to minimal reforms. In part, that is the nature of reform efforts for subordinate power groups in advanced capitalist democracies. After all, negotiation and compromise is the name of the game women have joined. Yet, there are degrees of compromise, and how much one party has to give up is often a function of its power position relative to the opposition. Women are now strong enough to get government to do something about the problem of pay equity but are not yet strong enough to achieve the revaluation of women's work that was intended by those who originated the reform.

Discussing the reasons underlying the subversion of liberal feminist reforms is beyond the scope of this chapter. Partly, it is a function of the fact that the women's movement has not adequately mobilized and educated its constituents around its agenda. As a result, women political elites can play politics without being accountable directly to the women who will benefit from the reform. Partly, however, it is a function of the liberal feminist strategy of attempting to achieve economic and political equality without social equality. Patriarchal relations are so deeply embedded in our institutions, and reproduced on a daily basis within our most intimate interactions in the family, that it would be hard to imagine all but formal equality, for example, in political and economic institutions while continuing to suffer such extreme inequality in the family.

That, of course, is the tension that has pushed and that will continue to push labor market equality for women ahead. Women are increasingly being expected to operate as equals in the labor market at the same time that they remain responsible for household duties. Not surprisingly, they are finding it difficult to balance work and family life. Their solution is not to leave the labor market (if only because families cannot afford them to do so), as many did after World War II, but increasingly to change the structure of the situation by attacking discrimination and lack of policies facilitating a balance between work and family life. As women continue to enter the political and economic arenas, they will provide a permanent constituency for equality policy. This dynamic creates the potential for realizing the substantive agenda of the unsubtle revolution that has, in the last few years, begun to take shape.

NOTES

1 Introductory material is drawn from Steinberg and Cook (1986).
2 'The shift in the definition of discrimination from intent to impact, embodied in the 1972 amendments to Title VII of the Civil Rights Act, was first made by the courts in *Griggs* v. *Duke Power Company*, 401 U.S. 424, 3 EPD 8137' (Robertson, 1980).
3 According to Costain (1982: 22–3), the road from social movement to interest group with paid lobbying staff was a rocky one, especially for NOW and the NWPC. The impetus for such change in the character of these organizations grew out of the Equal Rights Amendment (ERA) initiative.
4 It is interesting to note, however, that while government is viewed as an appropriate arena in which to claim labor market protection, most women still seek private solutions to claims and concerns involving their family responsibilities.
5 Klein points out that the new feminist organizations lobbying Washington did not have the finances, membership, expertise, or networks to mount a national campaign of their own. They relied heavily on the resources and experience of older, more traditional women's rights organizations, such as the Business and Professional Women's Foundations (Klein, 1984: 22–3).
6 This is not to say that women elected officials do not operate at a serious disadvantage, even when they transcend what Susan Carroll (1985) has called the 'barriers in the political opportunity structure'. Both NOW and the NWPC have invested considerable resources in the election of feminist candidates at all levels of government, especially since the defeat of the ERA.
7 Although President Nixon opposed equal employment and appointed rather weak commissioners to the Equal Employment Opportunity Commission, he did not actively try to dismantle the reform as the Reagan administration did.
8 Much of the first half of this section is drawn from Haignere and Steinberg (1983).
9 Despite winning the case, attempts to get women on construction sites were largely ineffective. Thus, in 1981, NOW began a special project to monitor

construction sites in four parts of the country.

10 In each subsequent case, a woman state legislator had contact with California groups for advice and information.

11 For several reasons, adding displaced homemakers as a targeted group under the general employment and training act eases the likelihood of obtaining results compared with drafting separate legislation addressed solely to the needs of that group. (Miller, Spero and Coles, 1987).

12 In addition to CETA and JTPA, women are trained through the Vocational Education system. Equity in vocational education was introduced as an amendment to the 1963 Vocational Education Act, a few years prior to the CETA amendments. Unlike the transition from CETA to JTPA, the 1984 Vocational Education Act included a new and expanded emphasis on sex equality.

13 Material for the first part of this section is drawn from Steinberg (1984; and 1986).

14 At that time, many of the same states passed Fair Employment Practices Acts, a few of which prohibited compensation on the basis of sex. In general, however, the emphasis of FEP laws was on race, while EPA was limited to sex-based comparisons within essentially the same jobs.

15 Because of what the union called 'initial assignment discrimination', women were assigned to traditional female jobs and paid less than men who were performing traditionally male jobs, even though both female and male jobs carried no entry requirements. Female jobs also had restricted career ladders (Newman and Wilson, 1981; Newman and Vonhof, 1981).

16 In a few instances, comparable worth was initiated by women workers through collective bargaining (see Blum, 1986 and Ladd-Taylor, 1985). Indeed, Blum points to tension between women workers and women political elites over control of the direction of the reform.

17 There are several other reasons why pay equity emerged first in the public sector. First, the public sector is a significant employer of women. Second, public sector personnel systems are more highly articulated than those in the private sector.

18 Specifically, in the 1970s, several organizations emerged representing the interests of specific categories of employed women. These organizations took an early interest in pay equity and worked – primarily through insider–outsider coalition building – to get the reform on the public agenda.

19 In general, the Courts have proven to be a barrier in furthering the development of comparable worth policy. Early decisions rejected the concept. A case involving tree trimmers and nurses in Denver, Colorado (in which the nurses demonstrated hospital collusion in salary setting for staff) was decided against the nurses. The judge declared that comparable worth was 'pregnant with the possibility' of destroying the free market system (*Lemons* v. *City and County of Denver*, 620 F.2d 228 (10th Cir. 1980). In the last few years, the courts again have decided against comparable worth in a number of cases, suggesting that a 'market defense', which has been unacceptable under the Equal Pay Act, is acceptable. In other words, if a business is able to demonstrate that the wage structure is based on market considerations and not on the gender of the employee, then employers need not meet comparable

worth standards.
20 The timing of the release of the NRC/NAS final report was unfortunate. Had it
    come out in 1979 as originally projected, Commissioner Norton would no
    doubt have drafted regulations before President Reagan took office and they
    might have put the new administration more on the defensive about compar-
    able worth.
21 The Center for Women in Government was founded in 1978 by two women
    formerly employed by AFSCME. Although it was university-based, and (in
    addition to a training component) conducted academic research, its primary
    objective was to eliminate sex discrimination in public employment.
22 The Governor's Commission on the Status of Women was not represented on
    the Management Advisory Committee. New York State is one of the few cases
    where the Commission played virtually no role in bringing the reform about.
23 There are important exceptions to this generalization, however. For example,
    the Philadelphia Pay Equity Coalition (PhilaPEC) organized an event sur-
    rounding a breakfast speech made by Clarence Pendleton to a business group.
    They met Pendleton as he arrived to give the speech, presenting him with the
    annual 'Looney Tunes' award and a balloon-sized figure of Daffey Duck. This
    received extensive media coverage and greatly embarrassed Pendleton and his
    business sponsors.

REFERENCES

Blum, L. (1986) 'Women and advancement: Possibilities and limits of the
    comparable worth movement', Paper presented at the American Sociological
    Association.
Boneparth, E. (1982) 'A framework for policy analysis', in E. Boneparth (ed.),
    Women, Power and Policy (New York: Pergamon).
Carroll, S. J. (1985) *Women as Candidates in American Politics* (Bloomington, IN:
    Indiana University Press).
Claque, E. (1976) *Manpower Policies and Programs – A Review, 1935–75*
    (Kalamazoo, MI: The WE Upjohn Institute for Employment Research),
    January.
Commission on the Economic Status of Women (1985) *Pay Equity: The Minnesota
    Experience* (St Paul, MN).
Cook, A. (1984) 'Development in selected states', in Helen Remick (ed.),
    Comparable Worth and Wage Discrimination (Philadelphia: Temple University
    Press).
Costain, A. N. (1982) 'Representing women: the transition from social movement
    to interest group', in E. Boneparth (ed.), *Women, Power and Policy* (New York:
    Pergamon).
Deaux, K. and J. C. Ullman (1983) *Women of Steel: Female Blue-Collar Workers in
    the Basic Steel Industry* (New York: Praeger Publishers).
Equal Employment Opportunity Commission (1980) *Hearings on Job Segregation
    and Wage Discrimination* (Washington, DC: Government Printing Office).
Evans, S. M. and B. J. Nelson (1986) 'Initiating a comparable worth wage policy in
    Minnesota: notes from the field', *Policy Studies Review*, vol. 5, no. 4.

Farnquist, R. L., D. R. Armstrong and R. P. Strausbaugh (1983) 'Pandora's worth: the San José experience', *Public Personnel Management*, vol. 12, no. 4, Winter.

Flammang, J. A. (ed.) (1984) *Political Women: Current Roles in State and Local Government* (Beverly Hills, CA: Sage Publications).

Flammang, J. A. (1987) 'Women made a difference: comparable worth in San José', in M. Katzenstein and C. Mueller (eds), *The Women's Movement of The United States and Western Europe: Consciousness, Political Opportunity, and Public Policy* (Philadelphia: Temple University Press).

Fleming, J.P. (1983) 'Wider opportunities for women: the search for equal employment', in I. Tinker (ed.), *Women in Washington: Advocates for Public Policy* (Beverly Hills, CA: Sage).

Gabin, N. (1985) 'Women and the United Auto Workers' Union in the 1950s', in R. Milkman (ed.), *Women, Work and Protest* (London: Routledge and Kegan Paul).

Haignere, L. and R. Steinberg (1983) *New Directions in Equal Employment Policy: CETA, Non-Traditional Jobs for Women and Equal Employment Opportunity*, Working Paper no. 13 (Albany, NY: Center for Women in Government).

Harlan, S. L. (1985) 'Federal job training policy and economically disadvantaged women', in L. Larwood, A. H. Stromberg and B. A. Gutek (eds), *Women and Work: An Annual Review* (Beverly Hills, CA: Sage Publications).

Johansen, E. (1984) *Comparable Worth: The Myth and the Movement* (Boulder, CO: Westview Press).

Katzenstein, M. (1987) 'Comparing the feminist movement of the United States and Western Europe: an overview', in M. Katzenstein and C. Mueller (eds), *The Women's Movement of The United States and Western Europe: Consciousness, Political Opportunity, and Public Policy* (Philadelphia: Temple University Press).

Klein, E. (1984) *Gender Politics* (Cambridge, MA: Harvard University Press).

Ladd-Taylor, M. (1985) 'Women workers and the Yale strike', *Feminist Studies*, vol. 11, no. 3, Fall.

Livernash, E. R. (ed.) (1980) *Comparable Worth: Issues and Alternatives* (Washington, DC: Equal Employment Advisory Council).

Meehan, E. M. (1985) *Women's Rights at Work: Campaign and Policy in Britain and the United States* (New York: St Martin's Press).

Milkovich, G. T. and A. Broderick (1982) 'Pay discrimination: legal issues and implications for research', *Industrial Relations*, 21.

Milkman, R. (1981) 'The reproduction of job segregation by sex: a study of the sexual division in the auto and electrical manufacturing industries in the 1960s', PhD dissertation (University of California at Berkeley).

Miller, J. and A. Spero (1986) 'Is the Job Training Partnership Act training displaced homemakers?', A Technical Report on Services to Displaced Homemakers Under JTPA, Displaced Homemakers Project.

Miller, J., A. Spero and R. Coles (1988) 'Displaced homemakers in the employment and training system', in S. Harlan and R. Steinberg (eds), *Job Training for Women: Research Perspectives and Policy Directions* (Philadelphia: Temple University Press).

Newman, W. and J. M. Vonhof (1981) 'Separate but equal – job segregation and pay equity in the wake of *Gunther*', *University of Illinois Law Review*, 269–331.

Newman, W. and C. W. Wilson (1981) 'The union role in affirmative action', *Labor Law Journal*, 323–42.

Peterson, E. (1983) 'The Kennedy Commission', in I. Tinker (ed.), *Women in Washington: Advocates for Public Policy* (Beverly Hills, CA: Sage Publications).

Remick, H. (1980) 'Beyond equal pay for equal work: comparable worth in the State of Washington', in R. Steinberg Ratner (ed.), *Equal Employment Policy for Women* (Philadelphia: Temple University Press).

Remick, H. (1986) 'Race-based wage discrimination in Washington State', in National Committee on Pay Equity, *Pay Equity and People of Color* (Washington, DC: National Committee on Pay Equity).

Reskin, B. F. and H. I. Hartmann (eds) (1986) *Women's Work, Men's Work: Sex Segregation on the Job* (Washington, DC: National Academy Press).

Robertson, P. (1980) 'Strategies for improving the economic situation of women in the United States: systematic thinking, systematic discrimination and systematic enforcement', in R. Steinberg Ratner (ed.), *Equal Employment Policy for Women* (Philadelphia: Temple University Press).

Rothchild, N. (1984) 'Overview of pay initiatives, 1974–1984', in US Commission on Civil Rights (ed.), *Comparable Worth: Issue for the 80s*, vol. 1 (Washington, DC: Government Printing Office).

Scholzman, K. L. (1987) 'Representing women in Washington: sisterhood and pressure politics', in P. Gurin and L. Tilly (eds), *Women in Twentieth Century American Politics* (New York: Russell Sage).

Shields, L. (1981) *Displaced Homemakers: Organizing for a New Life* (New York: McGraw Hill).

Steinberg, R. (1982) *Wages and Hours: Labor and Reform in Twentieth-Century America* (New Brunswick, NJ: Rutgers University Press).

Steinberg, R. (1984) 'A want of harmony: perspectives on wage discrimination and comparable worth', in H. Remick (ed.), *Comparable Worth and Wage Discrimination* (Philadelphia: Temple University Press).

Steinberg, R. (1986) 'The comparable worth debate', *New Politics*, vol. 1, no. 1.

Steinberg, R. and A. Cook (1986) 'Policies affecting women's work in other industrial countries', in A. Stromberg and S. Harkness (eds), *Women Working*, second edition (California: Mayfield Publishing Company).

Steinberg, R., L. Haignere, C. Possin, C. Chertos and D. Treiman (1985) *The New York State Comparable Pay Study Final Report* (Albany, NY: Center for Women in Government).

Treiman, D. J. and H. I. Hartmann (eds) (1981) *Women, Work, and Wages: Equal Pay for Jobs of Equal Value* (Washington, DC: National Academy Press).

US Commission on Civil Rights (1985) *Comparable Worth: Issue for the 1980s*, vol. 2 (Washington, DC: US Government Printing Office).

US Department of Labor (1980) 'CETA journey: a walk on the women's side', Pamphlet 19 (Washington, DC: US Government Printing Office).

US Department of Labor, Women's Bureau (1983) *Time of Change: 1983 Handbook on Women Workers* (Washington, DC: US Government Printing Office).

US General Accounting Office (1985) *Options for Conducting a Pay Equity Study of Federal Pay and Classification Systems*, March (Washington, DC: US

Government Printing Office).

US House of Representatives, Committee on Post Office and Civil Services, Subcommittee on Compensation and Employee Benefits (1985) *Hearings on Options for Conducting a Pay Equity Study of Federal Pay and Classification Systems* (Washington, DC: US Government Printing Office).

12

Wedded to the Welfare State
Women against Reaganite Retrenchment

Harold Brackman,
Steven P. Erie and Martin Rein

All public disturbances generally commence with the clamour of
women . . .

Leicester Journal, 1800[1]

Fear of losing Government benefits appears to be causing women to
oppose the Administration. Continued growth of the gender gap in its
current form could cause serious trouble for Republicans . . .

White House Pollster, Ronald H. Hinkley, 1982[2]

THE ENIGMATIC GENDER GAP

In the early 1980s a new phenomenon emerged in American politics – the
so-called gender gap. President Reagan's policies – domestic and foreign –
produced an unprecedented political polarization of women's and men's
electoral behavior. In the 1982 Congressional elections, women turned
against many candidates linked to Reagan, a move which prompted the
White House to launch a gender counter-offensive. At the urging of
presidential advisors who argued that the Republican Party's future was at
stake, a Working Group on Women was set up in the White House. The
Republicans also hired a 'gender gap specialist', drafted Transportation
Secretary Elizabeth Dole to serve as a spokesperson on women's issues,
and convinced the President to stop his saber-rattling after the Grenada
invasion. Combined with Congressional resistance to further domestic
budget cutbacks, which halted retrenchment of social spending, the
Republican strategy appeared to work. On election day 1984, the Reagan

landslide seemingly buried the gender gap; a majority of women supported the candidate many feminists called 'The Caveman'.[3]

1984 appeared, then, to be a replay of failed political hopes for American women and yet another indication that differences between women and men's political behavior had eroded. Of course, earlier studies had pointed to long-standing and striking gender differences. In their comparative study summing up two generations of conventional wisdom, Almond and Verba characterized women's political behavior as 'more frequently apathetic, parochial, conservative, and sensitive to the personality [aspects] . . . of electoral campaigns' (1963: 388). Their explanation: women's 'intra-mural family existence . . . outside the political system' (1963: 397).

This conventional wisdom is now under sustained attack, however. Feminist students of politics, for example, have shown that low female voter registration and turnout rates – relative to men – are the result of a generational lag in political socialization, not an intrinsic characteristic of women's behavior (Kleppner, 1983; Bourquet and Grossholtz, 1984: 117, 223n.). The turnout gap gradually declined and, in 1984, was reversed. Women are now more likely than men to vote in Presidential elections. Likewise, the conservatism of politically active women up through the mid-1960s has been discounted as an artifact of the early tendency for upper-class women to vote more (Goot and Reid, 1984; Clymer, 1985).

Politics may not be an 'unnatural practice' for women after all (Siltanen and Stanworth, 1984: 186–8). Yet, largely missing from the revisionist account, which focuses on electoral behavior, is the marriage of gender politics and the welfare state. Reagan's Panglossian 1984 campaign may have temporarily closed the gender gap, but any new attack on the welfare state, such as the Gramm–Rudman Bill's self-tightening fiscal straitjacket, may mobilize women into a new resistance movement. Women's combatant status is a product of structural changes in the domestic economy – the massive movement of women into the labor force, the feminization of poverty, and the expansion of the welfare state. All three are intertwined. The job market has channeled many working women into human services – health, education and welfare. And as the number of female-headed families has mushroomed, poverty – and government welfare programs – have also become 'women's issues'. Women *are* the welfare state, both as service providers and as welfare recipients. Although dormant in the 1984 campaign, social program retrenchment remains a political fault line dividing women and men. This chapter traces four stages in the relationship of American women to the welfare state: New Deal beginnings, the Great Society, Reaganite retrenchment, and women's resistance to social program cutbacks in the 1980s.

THE NEW DEAL: THE PAST AS PROLOGUE

The 1930s cemented the relationship between social programs and women, both as professionals and as clients of the growing welfare state. One might also term the bond between social programs and professional women an 'elective' affinity – in the sense that health, education and welfare were widely viewed as appropriate job extensions of women's traditional nurturing role in the home. Pragmatic professionals politically mobilized the country's 'forgotten women' as well as the new female elite to support the New Deal.[4] The new welfare programs assisted poor women. At a time when one-quarter of adult women worked or sought relief, the WPA maintained a clientele that was nearly one-fifth female (Ware, 1981: 107–10; Sealander, 1983: 97). Despite the invidious gender distinction between 'unemployment relief' for men and residual 'family relief' for women, a significantly higher proportion of women – one-third – were actually given white-collar WPA jobs than was true for the men who composed the program's 'shovel brigade' (Wandersee, 1981: 97; Ware, 1981: 61–5; Sealander, 1983: 63).

Yet the gains of the 'New Deal's women's network' were paradoxical. Eleanor Roosevelt's legions wanted to be treated 'just like the boys' in the army of social reform. They used their influence, however, to structure a welfare state which – even after the New Deal extended minimum wage, maximum hours and other work safeguards to men – encapsulated women within gender-specific protective legislation. The fixation of the New Deal reformers on 'for women only' protective legislation blinded them to the forms of sex discrimination being built into supposedly 'sex-neutral' New Deal legislation. The Fair Labor Standards Act 1938, for example, was explicitly sex-neutral; yet working women suffered from its sweeping exemption of many female-dominated job categories such as domestic service. Such laws, according to recent studies, ultimately fostered women's economic and social ghettoization (Wandersee, 1981: 95; Sealander, 1983: 159).

Equally paradoxical was the fact that the New Deal's female vanguard could not fashion a mass movement of middle-class or working-class women. These pragmatic reformers entered the rough-and-tumble world of politics but kept their potential followers safely domesticated on the 'protected' fringes of equal involvement. In part as a consequence, organized feminism all but disappeared in the 1940s as the daughters of female New Dealers settled into the complacent 1950s.[5] Ultimately, however, the New Deal pioneers found heirs among their granddaughters: a third generation committed to a new women's movement and to the welfare state's defense. Yet for this to happen the links between gender politics and social policy had to be more fully drawn. What was needed were the structural transformations ushered in by the 1960s.

THE GREAT SOCIETY AND THE FEMINIZATION OF THE WELFARE
STATE, 1960–80

The New Deal was a dress rehearsal for the Great Society. Despite the rise
of female professionals and program clientele in the 1930s, the New Deal
was a largely male affair. The Great Society was another matter. In the
1960s and 1970s, tens of millions of women were integrated into the
domestic political economy in ways fundamentally different from men.
Mushrooming federal social expenditure paved the way, rising from $11
billion in 1950 to $264 billion in 1980. The burgeoning welfare state became
intertwined with the lives of women in several ways.

Human services employment represents a key path of welfare state
'genderification'. Since 1960, social welfare employment has grown from
12 to 20 per cent of the US labor force, accounting for more than
one-quarter of the overall job increase. The federal budget generated up to
40 per cent of all new jobs in health, education and welfare (Thurow, 1981:
162–4; Erie and Rein, 1986: 8–13).

As the American welfare state was shifting into high gear in the 1960s,
record numbers of women were entering the labor force. In the years from
Kennedy's presidency to Reagan's, the number of female workers doubled
– from 20 million to over 40 million. By 1986, nearly 50 million American
women were employed, representing 53 per cent of all women over 16 and
45 per cent of the entire work force. Once a laggard among industrial
countries, the United States now has the second highest female labor force
participation rate in the world, surpassed only by Sweden.[6]

Working women moved in massive numbers into the federally-
subsidized human services sector. Since 1960 the fields of health, education
and welfare have generated new jobs for two out every five women,
compared with only one of five men. By the early 1980s nearly one-third of
all women worked in human services compared with only 10 per cent of
men (Erie and Rein, 1986: 8–13). Social welfare served as the major port
of entry in the labor force for middle-class women. From 1960 to the
mid-1970s the expanding human services industry accounted for 62 per
cent of all professional and managerial job gains for white women and 79
per cent for black women. In contrast, the social welfare sector generated
only 28 per cent of all professional and managerial job gains for white men
and 37 per cent for black men. Despite the much-touted move of women
into corporate America in the 1970s, nearly two-thirds of middle-class
women still worked in human services in the early 1980s (Erie and Rein,
1986: 14).

Historically the human service labor force has been heavily female;
under federal stimulus after 1960, it became even *more* feminized. In 1940
women comprised 59 per cent of the sector's 3 million workers. By 1980, 70

per cent of the nation's 17 million social welfare employees were women.

The growing representation of women in human services employment might be explained in terms of the interaction of job availability and gender socialization. Women entered the labor market in large numbers as welfare state employment was taking off. Many authors point to the similarity of the work performed in human services and women's traditional family roles. The family socializes women into nurturing and supportive roles, and as women moved into the paid labor force, many continued to perform the same functions, albeit in the 'public' sphere (Hartmann, 1976; Harkness, 1985).

The feminization of poverty and welfare   is in part a consequence of the social revolution which accompanied the 1960s economic revolution. New attitudes toward sexuality, marriage and divorce assaulted the traditional nuclear family. In the ensuing meltdown, the number of female-headed families mushroomed. Poverty became a female condition and the costs of raising poor children a public responsibility.

Over one-half of poor families in the 1980s were headed by women, up from one-quarter as late as 1960. Divorce is a primary culprit in the feminization of poverty. Of the nation's 10 million female-headed households, over 80 per cent are headed by divorced or separated mothers. During the first year after a divorce, women with small children experience a nearly 75 per cent drop in their standard of living. With only 4 per cent receiving alimony and only 2 per cent modest amounts of child support, divorced women turn up on the welfare rolls (Gough, 1979: 48–9; Scott, 1984: 19).

Casualties from the marital wars have turned to welfare programs such as Aid to Families with Dependent Children (AFDC), food stamps and Medicaid, which provides health insurance for the poor and elderly. AFDC alone absorbed a six-fold increase in female clientele after 1960. As the number of female-headed families doubled – from 2.2 million to 5.9 million – so did their welfare participation rate, from 29 per cent to 50 per cent. In benefit-rich states such as California, over 60 per cent of all families headed by women are on the AFDC rolls (Erie, Rein and Wiget, 1983: 95–100; California, 1985: 63).

Welfare policy helped propel the female caseload explosion. The AFDC program is a product of the New Deal and its 'for women only' protective ethos. Modeled on the Progressive era's Mother's Pension programs, Aid to Dependent Children (renamed AFDC in 1962) was designed as a cash relief program for non-employed women whose working spouses had been killed or disabled in industrial accidents. In an era when only one-quarter of women worked, AFDC was a surrogate 'family wage' for financially helpless women and children (Moynihan, 1968: 13; Steiner, 1974).

The tandem economic and social revolutions of the 1960s broke down the program's protective rationale. With rising illegitimacy and divorce rates, unmarried and divorced women crowded onto the welfare caseload. Nevertheless, as record numbers of women entered the labor force, public sentiment also scapegoated 'lazy welfare chiselers'. According to a growing number of critics, welfare now served the undeserving as well as deserving poor. Yet even as criticism mounted, the 1960s supplied a new – and old – program rationale: welfare became an entitlement rather than protection. In their campaign for entitlement, welfare rights organizations and anti-poverty lawyers resurrected an earlier rallying cry of women protesters, first used in the early nineteenth century (Piven and Cloward, 1971: 248–84; Patterson, 1981: 155–9; Randall, 1982: 41).

In response to the entitlement campaign, policy-makers fashioned incentives for women to go on – and stay on – welfare. During the 1960s, AFDC benefit levels rose faster than average earnings – 75 per cent versus 48 per cent. By linking medical coverage to welfare eligibility, the launching of Medicaid in the mid-1960s made AFDC more attractive. Congress also liberalized AFDC earnings rules, encouraging women to mix work and welfare (Ross and Sawhill, 1975: 98–106). Federal social programs in the 1960s thus became intertwined with the economic fortunes of millions of women, who were either human service providers or impoverished welfare recipients. In two important sectors – employment and welfare – women comprised over 70 per cent of the more than 20 million participants.

REAGANITE RETRENCHMENT, 1981–86

In the first years of his presidency, Ronald Reagan and the Republican Party moved to cut back the welfare state; in doing so, they threatened the link between women and the state which the previous two decades had established. The budgetary axe of the first administration was a two-edged affair for women, aimed at both impoverished welfare recipients and human service providers. For fiscal year 1982, the Republicans reduced social spending by $35 billion relative to the Carter administration's proposed budget. Two-thirds of the 1982 cutbacks were achieved in programs serving the poor and near poor.[7]

Aid to Families with Dependent Children was particularly targeted in the first round of welfare state pruning. Inspired by a punitive desire to root out 'welfare chiselers', the administration substituted workfare for work incentives. Recipients would now earn their welfare checks toiling in social service agencies at the minimum wage. At the same time, the administration penalized voluntary work effort. For anyone plucky enough to try the labor market rather than the workhouse, Reagan raised the marginal tax rate on earnings from an already high 67 per cent to a confiscatory 100 per cent (Erie and Rein, 1982: 71–86).

AFDC cutbacks were harsh medicine which poor women were forced to swallow because it was supposed to force them off the dole and reinvigorate their work ethic, as well as reduce the federal budget. As a cost-cutting measure, the Reagan plan backfired, however. Nationwide, 500,000 poor families headed by working women lost some or all of their AFDC benefits, and 100,000 families fell below the poverty line. The cutting edge of Reagan's welfare reductions gave affected women the cruel choice between dead-end, minimum-wage jobs with no supplemental income from government or total welfare dependence. Three-quarters chose low-wage work. Yet the one shirker in four who quit work in order to qualify for welfare was enough to cancel any program savings.

Thwarted in one direction, Reagan then squeezed budgetary savings from middle-class women. The President's budget for the 1983 fiscal year targeted discretionary social spending rather than entitlement programs. The second round of cutbacks took direct aim at Great Society service programs and their legion of providers. Of the $11 billion in 1983 cutbacks, three-fifths were in social services, education, and employment and training. The Brookings Institution's Henry Aaron warned that Reagan's 1983 budget represented '. . . the boldest and most controversial attempt in fifty years to roll back the place of the federal government as a guarantor of equal opportunity and provider of social services' (1982: 149–50).[8]

To the extent that unemployment checks, even in the generous District of Columbia, are only a fraction of government salaries, Reagan's firing of female human service providers paid off handsomely. The President's Office of Management and Budget projected that cutbacks for the fiscal years 1981–4 would produce a trimming of the federal domestic payroll of 8 per cent – 150,000 workers (Erie and Rein, 1986: 17). Federal retrenchment had a substantial ripple effect on state and local government payrolls, moreover, where it resulted in a loss of another 700,000 human service jobs. In private health and social service agencies, dependent upon public funding and employing one-half of the nation's 11 million female human services workers, the effect was also substantial (Bureau of National Affairs, 1982: 22–3). Women, in particular, walked Reagan's retrenchment plank. In Washington, DC, for example, female managers were laid off at a rate of 150 per cent higher than male administrators (Federal Government Task Force, 1981: tables 1–3).

With help from Congress, the first Reagan administration also heightened the fiscal crisis – the tendency for revenues to lag behind expenditures – in order to justify further welfare state retrenchment. As early as 1973 it was apparent that the 1960s fiscal surplus permitting Great Society funding was quickly disappearing. Sharply reducing federal revenues, Reagan's 1981 tax cut served social as well as economic ends. With federal revenues evaporating, defense outlays mounting, Social Security inviolate, and the deficit skyrocketing, the administration had placed an effective lid on domestic spending.

Yet Reagan's efforts backfired at the polls. Welfare recipients traditionally have been political non-combatants. Retrenchment in the 1982 and 1983 fiscal years, however, mobilized them as the linkage between voting and economic well-being became very clear. In the 1982 Congressional elections, Reagan paid a price for his budget-squeezing. Facing welfare and unemployment benefit cutbacks, AFDC recipients and the jobless registered the greatest turnout increases and sharpest shift away from Reagan-backed candidates of any group in the electorate.[9] Women helped send Democrats back to Congress, stiffening Congressional resistance to further social program cutbacks. The chastened White House conducted a post-mortem of the midterm election. White House pollster Ronald H. Hinkley conceded that women had voted out of 'astute self-interest': 'Among separated and divorced women, there is a view that Reagan is a threat to the supports originating with Government.'[10]

Given Reagan's re-election boast in 1984 that the best was yet to come, the prospects for women were obviously uncertain. Reagan's budget for fiscal year 1986 gave a hint but not a real taste of his prescription for women because the medicine he ordered was greatly watered down by Congress. The Good Doctor wanted $1.2 billion in further AFDC cutbacks, $375 million in food stamp reductions, elimination of Legal Services and the Work Incentive Program for welfare recipients and partial dismantling of his own Job Training and Partnership program for the unemployed (Coalition on Women and the Budget, 1985). Billions more were to be saved as Medicaid costs were shifted to the states. Perhaps the Doctor's greatest affront to women was his proposal to pare by one-fifth – from 3.1 million to 2.5 million – the number of pregnant and nursing mothers being served by a highly successful federal nutritional program.[11]

The 1986 cutbacks, in the words of House Budget Committee Chairman William Gray, were merely 'the appetizer' compared with 'the entrée' dished up by the administration the next year. Stealing a page from his 1982 playbook, Reagan proposed $38 billion in domestic program reductions, with nearly one-half coming from health, education, social services and income support programs (Blakely, 1986: 140; Hook, 1986: 222). Social safety net programs such as AFDC serving poor women were particularly targeted – on the ideological grounds that the poor would do better walking the economic tightrope without welfare's protective undergirding. Under the administration's new trapeze act without a safety net, the $10 billion squeezed from the poor in 1987 was supposed to grow to $107 billion by 1992.[12]

The massive proposed social program cutbacks would fall on the shoulders of middle-class women as well. Two-thirds of the first round of cutbacks for the Department of Housing and Urban Development, for example, were to come from salaries and related administrative expenses.

Democratic Congresswoman Pat Schroeder has called the 1987 budget a potential 'grim reaper for federal workers'. The 8 per cent across-the-board cut would produce nearly a 100,000 reduction in the federal workforce (mostly through attrition) equalling that already engineered in 1981.[13] As the cutbacks of the first administration demonstrated, even greater employment reductions promise to be felt in other heavily female sectors dependent upon the federal social program pipeline – state and local government, the non-profit sector and the for-profit health sector.

As the President intoned in his State of the Union Address in 1986, 'private values must remain at the heart of public policies'. The Reagan revolution demands regular sacrifices of the public sector at the altar of the marketplace.

Congress's ability to resist the draconian budget-cutting measures was further undermined by the Balanced Budget and Emergency Deficit Control Act 1985, otherwise known as Gramm–Rudman. Its self-tightening budgetary scissors mandated an amputation of as much as $55 billion in federal spending in order to meet the $144 billion deficit ceiling set by the Act for the 1987 fiscal year, which was the first full year covered by the new law. Thereafter, annual cutbacks of equal or greater magnitude were legislated, with the goal of balancing the federal books by 1991.[14]

Gramm–Rudman exempted Social Security from automatic cuts in the event of failure to meet deficit targets and limited cutbacks in indexed entitlement programs – such as federal pensions which had a substantial effect on the middle class – to the loss of cost-of-living adjustments. Certain key programs, including AFDC and supplemental security income, were also spared the axe. On the other hand, Medicare and four other health programs of special interest to the poor faced a budgetary amputation of $2 to $5 billion in the 1986 fiscal year plus additional cuts of 2 per cent per year beginning in 1987 (*Congressional Quarterly Weekly Review*, 1985: 2604, 2609–10; Rauch, 1986: 18–21).

Despite a Supreme Court decision in 1986 against the Act's 'automatic cut' provisions, Gramm–Rudman remained a potent constraint on Congressional behavior during the period of $200 billion deficits.[15] As of the spring of 1987, a compromise between the White House and Congress might or might not materialize, but either way the prospects are for continuing program deferral and recisions that could produce deadlock in funding for human service delivery systems. Among the certainties are that, if the Administration were to have its way, the 'Gramm–Rudman Diet Plan' (as one critic called it) would require even more belt-tightening by the poor (Kinsley, 1985: D5; Rauch, 1986: 15–21).

Clearly the efforts to close the gender gap undertaken in the 1984 election were no longer a top priority. When Reagan decided 'to be Reagan again' – and thus return to the more stringent plans for federal spending which had characterized his first term in office – it meant that the decision was made even if it meant estrangement from female voters on whom he had temporarily counted to win re-election. The 'new class war' had been renewed.

WOMEN'S RESISTANCE TO RETRENCHMENT DURING THE 1980s

Through its tenure, the Republican administration did its best to marshall Congressional and bipartisan blessing for a strategy of welfare state retrenchment. Yet this economic and political strategy, which means disproportionately targeting vulnerable women, is courting failure. The cosmetics of the 1984 Presidential campaign and the veneer of Congressional approval cannot provide an enduring face-lift. For deep-rooted economic and social reasons, women voters remain highly responsive to the issue of social program cutbacks. There are several major factors which are likely to produce future opposition by women to the United States' newest poor laws.

Social welfare attitudes

Disproportionate support by women for government social services has been evident at least since the first public opinion polls of the 1930s initially revealed the existence of such positive attitudes. Women's support for the welfare state has grown stronger in recent years. In the Presidential elections between 1972 and 1980, for example, there were significant gender differences in attitudes toward government as both service provider and job guarantor (Cook, 1979: 114–15; Klein, 1984: 147–637). Contradicting Reagan's supposed mandate in 1980, 72 per cent of women voters in that election opposed the reduction of social services; only 62 per cent of men did the same (Klein, 1984: 158).

Despite the decline in general self-identification as 'liberal' which occurred in the 1970s among both women and men, gender differences in support for 'safety net' programs remain high among all income and ethnic groups. In particular, the largest gender gap is among upper-income whites (Rossi, 1983: 729–32; Abzug and Kelber, 1984: 116–31; Gurin, 1985: 160). Given the endemic threat of marriage break-up which holds instant proletarianization over the heads of even affluent women, this should not come as a surprise. But black women – with the highest unemployment rate of any group – remain the United States' most committed feminists, unmatched in their support for the welfare state (Fulenwinder, 1980: 110–11, 124–5; Giddings, 1984: 344–52).

If 'the people' were more than semi-sovereign, and if politics were merely a matter of translating public opinion into policy, then the persisting enthusiasm for social welfare, especially among women, would have dramatic political consequences. The results would be not the withering away of the welfare state, but the unravelling of Reagan's retrenchment initiatives.

Electoral behavior

Reagan's 1984 election day landslide seemingly buried the gender gap. Yet all of the 1984 Presidential exit polls agreed there were statistically significant differences in voting between women and men. The gap ranged from 4 per cent (*New York Times*/CBS News) to 9 per cent (NBC News) with the *Washington Post*/ABC News poll offering an estimate of 8 per cent (*New York Times*, 9 November: A 11]. The *Times*/CBS results were particularly important support for the idea that the gap had been bridged, since their 1980 poll had shown an 8 per cent difference. In the rush to scoop their rivals in 1984, however, the *Times* and CBS hastily reported findings from only *one-half* of their sample of voters. The gender gap was alive and well among the missing half of the sample. Having contributed to the end-of-the-gap orthodoxy, the *Times* buried the complete results of its 1984 exit poll in the back pages of an issue nearly three months after the election. The real gap in their exit poll was 6 per cent – 56 per cent of women versus 62 per cent of men supporting Reagan (Mansbridge, 1985: 165–76). In fact, there was remarkable continuity in the *relative size* of the gender spread between 1980 and 1984. But the real change between 1980 and 1984 was that Reagan moved from minority to majority status among women voters.

How might we explain that Reagan won over a majority of women in 1984 after being spurned in 1980? One major factor was his considerable success in neutralizing the war-and-peace issue among women. Following the 1980 election, one observer estimated that two-thirds of the gender gap in voting was due to the greater fears of women that Reagan would be 'trigger-happy'. By her estimate, excluding the effect of the peace question, the gap in 1980 would have been only 3 per cent (Mansbridge, 1985: 168).

Up to the end of 1983 Reagan did little to win women's support by halting his saber-rattling. Polls showed his highest disapproval rating among women coincided with American intervention in Lebanon and with the invasion of Grenada (Elshtain, 1984: 22–4). Then, Reagan's less bellicose stance in the first half of 1984 was remarkably effective in removing the effects of foreign policy from the gender gap. Coupled with some economic recovery and a slowdown in welfare state retrenchment, Reagan's new-found non-interventionism contributed to his increased support among women voters in November.

Yet the President's considerable success in neutralizing the war-and-peace issue narrowed but did not close the gender gap. A gap of 10 per cent persisted throughout the pre-election polls, materializing in the 6–9 per cent range on election day. Reagan may have 'stolen the peace issue' but the remainder of the gap was increasingly filled with 'domestic policy content' (Cooper, 1984). Central to the gap's domestic content are the divergent social welfare agendas of women and men, reflecting the hard-won truths of immediate life experience which are less likely to be neutralized by seductive ad campaigns. Recognizing the domestic gender gap, the Republican Party campaigned in 1984 – without notable success – by claiming credit for new pension equity and child support legislation which Reagan had finally signed into law after giving only lukewarm support during their passage through Congress.

In social policy terms, the gender gap in Congressional voting may be even more important than in Presidential elections. In 1984 the gap between women and men's support for House candidates was important. Fully 50 per cent of women supported the Democratic Party, while 45 per cent supported the Republicans; exactly the reverse was the case for men (Abzug and Kelber, 1984). Except for this gender voting difference, both Houses of Congress might have been controlled by conservative Republicans.

For Democratic Party strategists, a persistent differential of 6–9 per cent in greater female support for Democratic candidates has been a fact of life since 1968. Minority women comprise the vanguard of the Democratic faithful. Before the 1984 election, a Reagan aide sneeringly reduced the gender gap to the 'anti-Republicanism of Jewish women, black women, and feminists' (quoted in Elshtain, 1984: 23). The only real 'rainbow' coalition that currently exists is among ethnic women. In 1984, 93 per cent of black women voted the Democratic ticket as did 73 per cent of Jewish women and 65 per cent of Hispanic women (Abzug and Kelber, 1984). The Hispanic electorate may serve as the crucial partisan battleground in future elections; here, the partisan gap between female and male voters consistently runs around 20 per cent.

The 1980s witnessed the emergence of another gender gap potentially benefiting the Democrats, this time in voter registration and turnout. The traditional double-digit gap in favor of men declined to single digits in the 1960s. In 1968, when women favored Humphrey over Nixon by 6 per cent, the lower voter participation rate of women was significant enough to tip the Presidential popular vote in favor of Nixon (Klein, 1984: 143). The 1980 election closed the turnout gap for the first time as 67.1 per cent of women reported voting compared with 66.6 per cent of men (*Women Today*, 8 February 1985). Between 1980 and 1984, female registration surged by 6.4 million. On election day, 60.8 per cent of eligible women voted compared with 59 per cent of men (*New York Times*, 28 January 1985). The turnout gap is greatest among minority groups. In 1984, while white women and men voted at an identical 60.9 per cent, black women voted 5.3 per cent more and Hispanic women 1.2 per cent more than their male counterparts (*Women Today*, 8 February, 1985).

In 1984 the gender gap failed to derail initiatives to cut back welfare spending in significant measure because of a conservative counter-mobilization in the name of 'pro-family' values. Reagan's pro-family policies are designed, in part, to divide women politically. On the one hand, they encourage middle-class women to remain within (or return to) a privatized family existence. Quoting her boss, White House assistant Faith Whittlesey said that as soon as Reaganomics restores prosperity, 'the rest . . . [will be] easy. Once men earn a family wage, all those women can go home and look after their own children the way they did when I was growing up' (Hewlett, 1986: 231–2). For Reagan, privatization yields political dividends. Unlike their counterparts in the workplace, full-time homemakers tend toward conservatism and lower levels of political efficacy. Yet they hold their own along one crucial dimension of involvement: voting (Sapiro, 1983: 123, 132, 151–2). On the other hand, social program cutbacks demoralize working-class women already doubly burdened with family and job responsibilities and lower-class women forced back on the welfare rolls. Contrary to liberal hopes, conservative policies often reinforce conservatism and voter apathy rather than militant involvement.[16]

Policy initiatives

For women to lead an anti-retrenchment coalition, policy initiatives must do more than promise relief for single and employed women. They must reach out to others in the name of a liberal conception of 'family values'. One potential bridge is the new 'economic equity' legislation. First floated in Congress in 1981, the Economic Equity Act demands pension equity, enforcement of child support payments, insurance policy fairness, Individual Retirement Accounts for homemakers, and bigger tax breaks for child care (Hewlett, 1986: 174). Merely by revising the formula for computing Social Security benefits to include 'earnings sharings', for example, the stake housewives have in social programs would be significantly increased.

Other promising bridges are maternity leave, daycare, and child welfare initiatives. The United States remains the only advanced industrial country without a national maternity policy, and 60 per cent of American working women have no rights to any kind of leave when they bear a child. Childcare also remains a critical unmet need as over half of women with pre-school-age children now work. In 1986, Republicans on the House Education and Labor Subcommittee on Human Resources rejected the new childcare proposals, calling instead for nebulous 'economic and social initiatives' that would give women the choice of staying at home. Democratic politicians would do well to support policies broadening the range of life choices opened to women by the welfare state.[17]

CONCLUSION

Currently there is no winning formula guaranteeing victory in the future battles American women will fight over the new poor laws. Missing from the formula are appropriate political vehicles – vehicles that lead beyond today's disarray in the women's movement and the Democratic Party. Yet if one believes that politics follows social structure, the question becomes when – not if – such vehicles will be found.

NOTES

1 Cited in Thomis and Grimmet (1982, 30).
2 Quoted in Adam Clymer (1982, A31).
3 For a fuller discussion of the gender gap's rollercoaster ride in the early 1980s, see Brackman and Erie (1986).
4 As head of the Democratic National Committee's Women's Division, Molly Dewson recruited 75,000 women to educate voters about New Deal legislation in the 1936 campaign (Gittel and Shtob, 1983: S72). Responding to an inquisitive reporter, Dewson said this about her political efforts: 'Don't you think that, for one not a feminist, I get in pretty good licks for the girls?' (Ware, 1981: 17).
5 Susan M. Hartmann summarizes the experience of 'Women in the Political Arena' during and after World War II (1982: 143–62). Despite the eclipse of organized feminism in the 1940s, women continued to support bread-and-butter liberal candidates. A small gender gap of 4 per cent favored Truman's Fair Deal in the 1948 Presidential election.
6 On the relationship of job growth and women's labor force participation, see Smith (1980: 358–62).
7 *Congressional Weekly Report* 39 (26 September 1982), 1833; *Congressional Record* 127 (2 April 1981), E. 1539–40, 1565–68.
8 For analyses of the impact on women of the Reagan cutbacks, see Rix and Stone (1982) and Coalition on Women and the Budget (1983).
9 Adam Clymer, 'Jobless Voted More Heavily in '82 Than in '78 Congressional Elections', *New York Times* (18 April, 1983), A1, A12; Clymer, 'Gap Between the Sexes in Voting Seen as Outlasting Recession', *New York Times* (22 May, 1983), A26.
10 Quoted in Adam Clymer, 'Warning on "Gender Gap" From the White House', *New York Times* (3 December, 1982), A26.
11 'Budget Anguish', *Wall Street Journal* (26 December 1984), 5.
12 Lena Williams, 'Civil Rights Leaders Assert Budget Will Hurt Minorities', *New York Times* (9 February 1986), A13.
13 Joann S. Lublin, 'Bureaucracy's Budget Officers Are Beleaguered By Spending Curbs in the Gramm–Rudman Law', *Wall Street Journal* (23 January 1986), 62; Cathy Trost, 'Federal Workers Again Will Be Facing Layoffs Unless Lawmakers Can Compromise on Budget', *Wall Street Journal* (6 February

1986), 46.
14 *Congressional Quarterly Weekly Report* (5 October 1985), 1975–7; *Congressional Quarterly Weekly Report* (19 October 1985), 2093–4; and 'Fiscal Challenge: Budget Struggle Gets Major Changes Due to Gramm–Rudman', *Wall Street Journal* (17 January 1986), 3.
15 'Waist Reduction', *Wall Street Journal* (2 February 1986); *Congressional Quarterly Weekly Review* (1986: 2880–2). Despite the projections for narrowing the deficits, the red ink reached $220.7 billion for the fiscal year ending 30 September, 1986. See 'Reagan, Congress gird for fight over need to meet the deficit target', *Wall Street Journal* (12 January 1987), 1.
16 Sapiro (1983: 133) offers a view of the politically inhibiting impact of the 'double burden' of job and family that qualifies the more positive findings of Kristi Anderson regarding the relationship of employment to political participation (Anderson, 1975).
17 For an argument parallel to ours, see Elshtain (1981: 298–354).

REFERENCES

Aaron, H. (1982) 'Nondefense programs', in J.A. Peckman (ed.), *Setting National Priorities: The 1983 Budget* (Washington, DC: Brookings Institution).
Abzug, B. and M. Kelber (1984) *Gender Gap* (Boston: Houghton Mifflin).
Almond, G. and S. Verba (1963) *The Civic Culture* (Princeton, NJ: Princeton University Press).
Anderson, K. (1975) 'Working women and political participation, 1952–1972', *American Journal of Political Science* (August).
Blakely, S. (1986) 'Local officials seek to shield urban aid from deficit cuts', *Congressional Quarterly Weekly Report* (25 January), 140.
Bourquet, S. and J. Grossholtz (1984) 'Politics as unnatural practice: political science looks at female participation', in J. Sintanen and M. Stanworth (eds), *Women and the Public Sphere: A Critique of Sociology and Politics* (New York: St Martin's Press).
Brackman, H. and S. P. Erie (1986) 'The future of the gender gap', *Social Policy* (Winter).
Bureau of National Affairs (1982) *Layoffs, RIFs, and EEO in the Public Sector* (Washington, DC: Bureau of National Affairs).
California Lieutenant Governor's Task Force (1985), *The Feminization of Poverty* (January).
Clymer, A. (1982) 'Warning on "gender gap" from the White House', *New York Times* (28 January), A9.
Coalition on Women and the Budget (1983) *Inequality of Sacrifice: The Impact of the Reagan (FY 1984) Budget on Women* (Washington, DC: Coalition on Women and the Budget).
Coalition on Women and the Budget (1985) *Inequality of Sacrifice: The Impact of the Reagan FY86 Budget on Women* (Washington, DC: Coalition on Women and the Budget).
Cook, F. L. (1979) *Who Should Be Helped? Public Support for Social Services* (Beverly Hills, CA: Sage Publications).

Cooper, A. (1984) 'Mondale has support of women's groups but not necessarily of female voters', *National Journal* (20 October).

Elshtain, J. B. (1981) 'Toward a critical theory of women and politics: reconstructing public and private', in *Public Man, Private Women* (Princeton: Princeton University Press).

Elshtain, J. B. (1984) 'The politics of gender', *Progressive* (February).

Erie, S. P. and M. Rein (1982) 'Welfare: the new Poor Laws', in A. Gartner et al (eds), *What Reagan is Doing to Us* (New York: Harper and Row).

Erie, S.P. and M. Rein (1986) 'Women and the welfare state: potential for a new progressive alliance', in C. Mueller (ed.), *The Politics of the Gender Gap* (Beverly Hills, CA: Sage).

Erie, S. P, M. Rein and B. Wiget (1983) 'Women and the Reagan Revolution: Thermidor for the social welfare economy', in I. Diamond (ed.) *Families, Politics, and Public Policy* (New York: Longman).

Federal Government Service Task Force (1981) *Impact of 1981 RIFs on Minorities and Women and Updated RIF Projections for FY82* (Washington, DC: Federal Government Service Task Force).

Gittell, M. and T. Shtob (1983) 'Changing Women's Roles in Political Volunteerism and Reform of the City', *Signs* (Spring Supplement).

Goot, M. and E. Reid (1984) 'Women: if not apolitical, then conservative', in J. Sintanen and M. Stanworth (eds), *Women and the Public Sphere: A Critique of Sociology and Politics* (New York: St Martin's Press).

Gough, I. (1979) *The Political Economy of the Welfare State* (London: Macmillan Press).

Gurin, P. (1985) 'Women's gender consciousness', *Public Opinion Quarterly* (Summer).

Harkness, S. (1985) 'Women's occupational experiences in the 1970s: sociology and economics', *Signs* (Spring).

Hartmann, H. (1976) 'Capitalism, patriarchy and job segregation by sex', *Signs* (Spring).

Hartmann, S. M. (1982) *The Home Front and Beyond: American Women in the 1940s* (Boston: Twayne Publishers).

Hewlett, S. A. (1986) *A Lesser Life: The Myth of Women's Liberation in America* (New York: William Morrow).

Hook, J. (1986) 'Deep new cuts in social spending proposed', *Congressional Quarterly Weekly Report* (8 February), 222.

Kinsley, M. (1985) 'The Gramm–Rudman plan: a shameful scam', *Los Angeles Times* (20 October).

Klein, E. (1984) *Gender Politics: From Consciousness to Mass Politics* (Cambridge, MA: Harvard University Press).

Kleppner, P. (1983) 'Were women to blame? Female suffrage and voter turnout', *Journal of Interdisciplinary History* (Spring).

Mansbridge, J. J. (1985) 'Myth and reality: the ERA and the gender gap in the 1980 election', *Public Opinion Quarterly* (Winter).

Moynihan, D. P. (1968) 'The crisis in welfare', *The Public Interest* (Winter).

Patterson, J. T. (1981) *America's Struggle Against Poverty, 1900–80* (Cambridge, MA: Harvard University Press).

Piven, F. F. and R. A. Cloward (1971) *Regulating the Poor: The Functions of*

Public Welfare (New York: Vintage Books).

Randall, V. (1982) *Women and Politics* (New York: St Martin's Press).

Rauch, J. (1986) 'Politics of deficit reduction remains deadlocked despite balanced Budget Act', *National Journal* (4 January).

Rix, S. and A. J. Stone (1982) *Impact on Women of the Administration's Proposed (FY 1983) Budget* (Washington, DC: The Women's Research and Education Institute).

Ross, H. L. and I. V. Sawhill (1975) *Time of Transition* (Washington, DC: Urban Institute).

Rossi, A. S. (1983) 'Beyond the gender gap: women's bid for political power', *Social Science Quarterly* (December).

Sapiro, V. (1983) *The Political Integration of Women: Roles, Socialization, and Politics* (Urbana, IL: University of Illinois Press).

Scott, H. (1984) *Working Your Way to the Bottom* (London: Pandora Press).

Sealander, J. (1983) *As Minority Becomes Majority: Federal Reaction to the Phenomenon of Women in the Work Force, 1920–1963* (Westport, CT: Greenwood Press).

Smith, R. E. (1980) 'Women's stake in a high-growth economy in the United States', in R. Steinberg Ratner (ed.), *Equal Employment Policy for Women* (Philadelphia: Temple University Press).

Steiner, G. Y. (1979) 'Reform follows reality: the growth of welfare', *The Public Interest* (Winter).

Thomis, M. I. and J. Grimmett (1982) *Women in Protest, 1800–1850* (London: Croom Holm).

Thurow, L. (1981) *The Zero-Sum Society* (New York: Penguin Books).

Wandersee, W. D. (1981) *Women's Work and Family Values, 1920–1940* (Cambridge, MA: Harvard University Press).

Ware, S. (1981) *Beyond Suffrage: Women in the New Deal* (Cambridge, MA: Harvard University Press).

13

The German Paradox

Non-feminization of the Labor Force and Post-industrial Social Policies

Gisela Erler

THE PRESENT DILEMMA OF SOCIAL POLICY FOR WOMEN: EQUAL
VALUE FOR CARING WORK OR EQUAL EMPLOYMENT
STRATEGIES?

As in many other countries, social policy in the Federal Republic of
Germany (FRG) is not particularly supportive of women. Women are
more likely to live in poverty than are men and many of their social security
rights are defined by reference to male achievements as well as being
controlled by men. Recently, many people have objected to this lack of
support and its real effects on women. There is a basic issue underlying all
discussions about improving the effects of social policies on women. It
involves the matter of caring work and the issue of how society will in the
future structure the tasks involved in reproducing the labor force. If the
traditional sexual division of labor in the home is being replaced and if the
employment paths of women and men are increasingly converging, the
concept of what is fair in social policy must be modified. If patterns do not
alter and female and male work lives remain at variance, or if they are
changing too slowly to be of immediate political relevance, the implications
for social policy will be quite different.

Presently, social policy in FRG is primarily geared to women who stay at
home and have a husband working full-time. If the husband is regularly
employed and the family unit is maintained, the wife is completely insured
(as are the children) while the husband is working, and she will receive a
pension, making her fairly well-off in her old age. The expectation that this
pattern is the norm clearly has become outdated, however, since it makes
no allowances for new social realities and for new sets of ideas. The notion

that women will have personal autonomy, whether it is sought for personal reasons or because it is forced upon them by divorce or death of their spouse, does not always fit well within the present arrangement. Developments like the 1977 divorce laws do assume that women should and will have access to the labor market in the same way that men do, and that this access will offer them independence and security. On the other hand, other social policies – like the law granting parental leave or the debate about allowing people to withdraw from the labor force for care work, with pension rights, health insurance and re-entry guarantees – are based on the assumption that women's participation in the labor force will be more discontinuous and responsive to family needs than will men's.

The argument developed here claims it is necessary to build a social policy which both acknowledges women's possibilities for autonomy and independence from individual men and at the same time safeguards some important elements of the old system which protected those people – primarily women – who have non-traditional (i.e. non-male) biographies in their work lives. Social policy should recognize that many women organize their working lives around the care they give their families. They may either give up employment, take part-time work or accept work considered to be of lower status because it is 'for women'.

Social policy has been an indirect way of paying for reproductive work. The debate about social policy is, then, very much a debate about equal value not just for women's work in the workplace but also in the home. Moreover, while it may seem to be primarily a debate about gender roles, it is even more a debate about the values of a late or post-industrial society. It is about the structures that will shape individuals' lives as paid work becomes scarcer, thus being at the same time more important for status and less important in terms of the time and energy necessarily spent at it.

WHERE WOMEN ARE NOT GOING: FACING THE REALITY OF A CLOSED LABOR MARKET

In 1960, the Federal Republic of Germany had a larger percentage of women working outside the home than did several other industrial countries (Sengerberger, 1984). This pattern has since been reversed. The FRG rate of female labor force participation is fairly low by comparison with other advanced industrialized nations; only the Netherlands has a smaller percentage of women participating in the labor force. The relatively low employment rate of women in such a highly industrialized nation with a highly educated female population often seems puzzling and somehow not to fit with the overall trends of other similar societies. Germany's 'poor performance' in this respect is sometimes considered to be a sign of social retardation. Before exploring these issues, and before assessing the contribution of social policies to the relatively low female employment rate, it is helpful to discuss the situation and perspectives of the German labor market. Despite an improved economic performance after the recession of the early 1980s, there are few signs that (in the short run) employment can be expanded significantly for women or for any other group of workers (Haller et al., 1985). A shorter working week, which over the next years will be reduced to about 35 hours, will create some new jobs. In the best of all scenarios, this job creation will be sufficient to reduce the present rate of unemployment only if GNP grows on a yearly average increase of 3.5 per cent. A growth rate of this size, however, could have dramatically negative consequences for the ecology of such a densely populated country, and therefore many politicians and economists are now stressing the need for 'qualitative growth', a term which indicates growth in industries which are less harmful to the environment. But there are very serious limits to the applicability of this concept, and the reasons for the difficulties are partly the same ones that make it difficult for German women to find jobs. Germany has an *atypical* economic structure compared to other modern economies because the contribution of manufacturing to the Gross National Product is greater than the norm. In 1980, 44 per cent of all people employed were working in this sector, as opposed to only 30 per cent in the US or 35 per cent in Japan. This atypical structure has meant that the service and communication industries – the principal job creators for women – have not grown to the same extent in Germany that they have in other countries (Haller et al., 1985).

The present strength and restructuring of the German economy is not based on the expansion of the service sector. The driving force of the strongly export-oriented economy is, besides luxury cars, highly specialized tool-making and machine-building industries which are based on the craft skills of male workers. Where employment for women is available, it is most often in the jobs which are least secure, since the women are not part of the skilled labor force. As Piore and Sabel point out, the small and medium-sized, highly specialized companies – which are the core of present industrial success stories – are likely to be controlled by specific subcultural patterns which are more likely to resist the incorporation of female labor (1985). Large enterprises like car manufacturers or the post office are more easily persuaded to take on female apprentices in traditionally male jobs than are small and medium-sized firms where personalized relations are more the rule than bureaucratized ones.[1]

The educational system also imposes certain barriers to extending and diversifying women's employment. Girls tend to stay in formal education longer, while boys leave school and take up apprenticeships for skilled craft jobs. These are more likely to lead to well-paid jobs in the manufacturing sector. At the same time, women everywhere display a preference for office and interpersonal work. Therefore, at this point in history it seems unlikely that large numbers of German women will suddenly become motivated or trained to take up highly-qualified and well-paid technical jobs. Whatever the deeper reasons for this relative disadvantage of women in the technical fields, it is certainly the case that the educational system, which is based on apprenticeships for more than half of all school-leavers in Germany, offers a much greater variety of jobs for boys.

Beyond the unfavorable economic and educational structures, there are other factors working against any improvement in women's position in the labor market. Of major importance are cutbacks in state employment. The burgeoning postwar welfare state provided a large number of well-paid professional and semi-professional jobs for women in teaching, health care, social services and administration. Then, in the 1970s, the state adopted a freeze on hiring which virtually eliminated any new employment for a long time to come. This cut off one of the few areas of employment possibilities and promise for both educated and less-skilled women workers.

Finally, in office work, even though computerization is taking over at a much slower rate than many experts had anticipated, many jobs formerly done by women are being replaced by computerized equipment. Moreover, the impact of the new technology differs for women and men. Trends toward recomposition and requalification of work which creates new skilled workers overseeing and manipulating the technology, have tended to create jobs which have gone to men. Moreover, sectors of high female employment have seen little recomposition or requalification. Instead, in office work and service-sector jobs like sales, old-fashioned Taylorized models have predominated, along with other technological changes which remove responsibilities from jobs. The much-heralded 'end to the division of labor' has failed to reach many female jobs (Kern and Schumann, 1984).

In summary, if an additional 20–30 per cent of women must be employed in order to give women financial and social autonomy through employment alone, we cannot conclude that the near future promises the changes needed to bring that about. In addition, over 60 per cent of the women presently employed earn less than DM 1200 per month, which means they earn less than they need to be even moderately independent. Female wages derive from the fact that work done by women in Germany, as everywhere else, is grossly underpaid. A contributory factor is the traditional work biography of many women, which is less continuous than men's because it is linked to the sexual division of labor in the home.

A MYSTIQUE OF PARTNERSHIP: THE UNACKNOWLEDGED STABILITY OF TRADITIONAL PATTERNS IN THE HOME

Profiles of the psychological state of German women show them to be quite dissatisfied, depressed and ambivalent (Erler et al., 1983). Any deeper analysis of this mass depression, especially among younger women, shows it to result from the clash of contradictory values. Most women wish to be part of the labor force and to hold qualified jobs, appropriate to their high educational levels. But at the same time, most of them wish to be able either to interrupt their careers for a period of time once they have children, or at least not to be completely job-oriented while they have dependent children. In addition, women in general, regardless of their family responsibilities, define their career-orientations differently from the ways men do and adopt unfamiliar social strategies in the workplace. Often, this behavior, because it is different, is valued less and women experience a sense of failure or at least frustration.

These patterns could be seen to result from the fact that German women have not adjusted their identities to the needs of a fully industrialized lifestyle. Alternatively it could be interpreted as the result of the relatively strong position of German women. Due to the country's wealth, more women than elsewhere can still afford to choose among different lifestyles and many can still opt to interrupt their work-life for childrearing. Only 32 per cent of mothers with children under three continue working. Women's decisions are also linked to the fact that men, contrary to current mythology, have not become more significantly involved in housework and childcare than they have been over the last 60 years (Kruger, 1985). While some men among younger couples now accept more childcare responsibility, progress is very slow indeed. In addition, any such progress is more than offset by the growing number of divorced women who have exclusive childcare responsibility. Genuine role-sharing or reversal seems to take place only among couples where it was always traditionally found – where the women have a higher status in the labor market. Finally, certain fields, like care for the elderly, remain exclusively female. There is no trend toward even marginal male involvement in this very important area, except on a professional basis (Trojan, 1984). It can be demonstrated that much as German women wish to be relieved and supported by their male partners in all these reproductive areas, they themselves usually place high value on these tasks. Given a choice, they try to combine their reproductive and job identities in a new mix rather than simply to adapt to patterns which would very much reduce their involvement with caring.

Any new strategies for social policy must evaluate these attitudes and assess their relative legitimacy as well as advantages and disadvantages for society as a whole and for women themselves. If a concern for quality makes the specific mix of values which women maintain seem useful, then strategies are needed which do not penalize women for adopting and living these values. If greater emphasis, however, is placed on overcoming such 'outdated' strategies of privacy, then other roads are feasible. In all cases, however, it is essential not to mystify the reality of the sexual division of labor in the home; it has been quite resistant to fundamental change, for many and complex reasons on the part of women and men (Trojan, 1984). No valid strategy can be based on the assumption that the sexual division of labor will be easily abandoned in the near future.

CARE: THE MAJOR UNRESOLVED ISSUE OF POST-INDUSTRIAL SOCIAL STRATEGIES

For more than 100 years, two basic concepts have determined the fantasies and strategies of social policy-makers: either the family was viewed as the only plausible and legitimate source of providing care for dependants of all ages or there would be a gradual dissolution of familiy ties. The proponents of family care pointed to the negative effects of a reality which allowed nursery schools, schools, hospitals, old people's homes to intervene in the family network and make care less family-centered. According to those who looked for the dissolution of the family, communal and societal structures made parental or familial ties secondary to other sources of support and responsible care. Thus, proponents of both concepts predicted that family-based care would decline. However, both groups were wrong. Family input remains a basic and important ingredient of care in all advanced industrial societies. Yet, the implications of this fact for society as a whole and for caregivers (mostly women) are not well analysed or understood in many theories of social policy.

In Germany the wealth of the present adult generation is to some degree acquired at the social expense of the next generation. The current very low birthrate encourages immediate consumption of goods but burdens the coming generation with care problems. By 2030, each adult worker in Germany will have to pay for one person on old-age pension. Also, the number of persons needing care will increase immensely, both in absolute numbers and relative to the numbers able to support such care. This future results not only from one of the lowest birthrates in the world, but also because many more people now live into their eighties and nineties and they are, of course, much more likely to need care than younger people. At the moment, over 80 per cent of all elderly and chronically ill people are cared for by their families, or, more specifically, by their daughters and daughters-in-law. The 'sandwich' phenomenon – women who are still responsible for children of their own and already responsible for their mothers or even grandmothers – is increasing rapidly (Riedmüller, 1984).[2] These demographic trends have grave consequences for the lives of innumerable women, yet they are often ignored or suppressed in debates about social policy, even women-centered ones.

Analysts often stress that elderly people frequently prefer to live on their own, to share feelings and intimacy with their children at a distance (Fogarty, 1984; Klipstein and Strümpel, 1984). While it can be shown that three-generation households often have increased levels of stress and sometimes very conflicting and negative attitudes toward the elderly living there, the problem of care for chronically ill people is not solved by these arguments. Moreover, it is clear that for most elderly sick people, the very interest in life and basic motivation to continue living is based on contact with people to whom they feel close and in whom they are interested.[3] For sick and old people, a close relationship to the family is vital, in a very literal sense. The crucial question becomes, then, whether autonomy of the potential caregivers – the adult woman in her middle years – can be achieved only by fully institutional solutions or whether other ways are conceivable, ways which do not sacrifice one generation's well-being to another's.

The issue is in some ways the same for the care of children, even though it is less dramatic. For children, a mix of home and outside settings can easily be created, and children benefit from such institutions early on, even though the question of 'minimal' parental involvement remains open. In Germany, many women and men have come to prefer a life pattern which does not isolate children, which does not separate adults from children; rather, they look for a new mix of private and public activities for themselves and their children.

In order to develop a meaningful discussion of caring – both for the elderly and for children – it is important to recognize that there has been a reorientation of values in German society. It can be argued that the relatively lower levels of feminization of the German labor force as well as the conflicts many women feel about entering it at all, or on terms other than their own, coincides with a new framework of political and social thought. This framework can be described by the notion *Wertewandel*, change of values. Having experienced this change to a new framework, the attitude of the German public is very different from that of other nations (Blanke and Evers, 1984; Evers, 1986).

At the core of these values is a very skeptical attitude toward progress in general, technical progress in particular, and a very critical attitude toward work as it is structured and defined presently. This thinking is linked in some ways to the rise of the Green Party, but it is not limited to traditionally 'left' parts of the population. It is one of the off-shoots of the many grassroots groups, citizen groups, or self-help groups that have grown up in the past fifteen years. In many ways, all these efforts can be seen as an attempt to create an intermediate social structure which could exist between the large public institutions and the individual. People holding these new values redefine political issues and oppose the loss of autonomy and sense of self which most institutions have imposed on their workers or clients over the past decades. The issue of care under humane circumstances, care which does not work according to the industrial logic of arbitrary exchange but leaves room for continuity, mutuality, human interest, and community and not society, has found a new legitimacy in the context of the *Wertewandel* discussion. The time lag in the 'modernization' of female biographies in Germany may turn out to have been a great opportunity for an alternative modernization, corresponding to the needs of the emerging post-industrial society.

THE NEW WELFARE MIX

An ecological perspective on society requires a better understanding of stability and change, of basic human needs and options. It has become clear through all of this that a certain continuity of structures and contacts is vital when human well-being is threatened and that it requires a social framework which allows for such continuity. Industrial society has eliminated the space for such basics and things have reached a critical level. The discussion about a 'new welfare mix' in Germany aims at recreating or maintaining some of the necessary space, while still taking account of the contemporary labor market situation.

Such a *new* welfare mix would be composed of some or all of a number of ingredients. First, it would have to include family-support systems for caregiving families, to provide relief during vacations, on weekends, evenings, etc. This might also involve medical assistance from professionals or help with household chores, especially if the recipients were living alone or if the caregiver were overburdened. In a very literal sense, the families or individuals would receive support from public funding in full or in part in order to be able to manage on their own. Helpers might be recruited among a variety of groups from professionals in the fields of social work or medicine, or from community members (for example, housewives looking for an additional income, or youngsters, including young men, who are exploring their potential and need to earn some money).

Even though there are many people willing to do semi-professional care work and even though there is a need for it, nevertheless, there are still many reservations about it. One of the major issues is that social welfare professionals fear unfair competition. This conflict is a difficult one since the welfare labor market is indeed crucial for educated women and they are rightly anxious that their employment possibilities will decrease if intermediate, semi-professional and voluntary structures are granted too much importance. This remains a real dilemma, especially since volunteers and semi-professionals may ultimately begin looking for regular jobs in the welfare labor market as well. On the other hand, considering quality and cost, it is important to allow a well-balanced use of these new sources of care, which give possibilities to people who by their own choice or unvoluntarily are not full members of the labor market. Much will depend on the creative response of institutions to these intermediate workers. Institutions may integrate them and use them as an opportunity for much-needed innovation or, on the contrary, institutions may see them as an instrument to put negative pressure on the regular labor force. There is some evidence that in union-dominated social-democratic administration– such as Hamburg – attempts to use the 'second labor force' creatively have turned out less successfully than under more conservative governments which respect the needs of the already employed without carrying this to the point of excluding new options, which has come to mean, in reality, excluding new workers. In any case, the semi-professional support sector must expand dramatically over the next decades if quality of life is to be maintained or improved for caregivers and people cared for privately.

A second element of the new welfare mix involves community self-help. Most countries with high levels of female employment have seen the virtual death of neighborhoods. In FRG, this process has not been completed yet and it has become clear that by investing in neighborhoods, by offering free space and equipment to the women and children remaining there, the quality of life and self-esteem can be dramatically improved.[4] The informal opening of the nuclear family to public space, without superimposing alien structures, is an important part of helping women (and some men) to create a promising life-style for themselves. It helps to make the transition from private to public a less painful, intimidating or hopeless event, and helps to keep women in touch with a larger reality and with job opportunities. Any future social policy for women which plans to leave room and time for family responsibilities needs to invest heavily in such neighborhood structures. Nor do these need to be controlled by professionals, because experience shows that women running such centers on a non-professional basis with some state funding for pay create the most effective structures.

Thirdly, the new welfare mix must provide independent financial security for family caregivers. Here, we are entering the classical field of social policy. The respected Catholic Family Union demands a full secretarial wage (including pension rights and health insurance) for a parent staying at home with three children for twelve years. This is presently the most radical demand. The Green Party demands a medium salary for 18 months per child. Despite the differences, the general idea of paying for care is becoming very popular in Germany. While concern with women's participation in the labor force differs greatly, all parties have now adopted a rhetorical commitment to protecting family absences from work financially. Ultimately this will mean that pension rights will have to be to some degree separated from individuals' work records.[5] It might also be assumed that greater financial protection and higher status for reproductive work could induce men to take on a share of it.[6]

Finally, in the new welfare mix, any strategy supporting women in the home or in part-time work needs to be fully balanced by support structures for women who work full-time. First, since the present provision of infant care is very limited and public crèches are not very popular, their quality must be improved and their fees reduced. There is now a clear disincentive for parents to put children under three into any kind of public institution because the rates are very high. Moreover, public institutions, considered to be rigid, professional and beyond the influence of users, are being challenged by self-help groups in the childcare sector and the conflict will need to be resolved by mediating innovation. Future policy will have both to expand public institutional all-day services for pre-school and school-age children as well as to give support to the growing number of infant and toddler groups set up by parents who want an environment for their children which they can control themselves.

For the elderly, two major revisions of the institutional sector are needed. One is to reinstate citizen rights to many residents of homes for the elderly. These were often unnecessarily taken from them and the decision deprived these people of the right to choose where to live and curtailed their mobility and freedom of choice in many ways. The other revision is the introduction of *day-care for seniors*, so they can spend the day away from home in an environment which will take care of their special needs. This could be an important in-between solution, especially when the caregivers are working women and the older person is not bedridden.

The basic logic of all these changes in the structure of social services is to give all concerned actors more options to solve a crisis situation. In the labor market more options could mean sharing the available salaried work in a more intelligent way, by allowing those who want a break, for particular reasons, as much protection as possible and giving realistic options for returning to the labor force. In this way, more room will be provided for those who, in the future just as now, find it difficult to enter the labor market. Without such expanded protection, women will increasinly retreat from care work in the private field and men will not enter this area at all. Such avoidance will lead to all the well-known problems for society as a whole. What is needed is an adequate social concept which avoids the major mistake of most theories of social progress – to wit, that housework and care work will either magically disappear, be shared by everyone, or be done by institutions in a satisfactory manner. Maintaining real space for these tasks will mean overcoming the false alternatives of paid work or care work. A new welfare mix, a new social policy for women and men, depends on an alternative and attractive mix of employment and other social tasks. The tradition of the welfare state and of social transfer payments makes such an option at least conceivable for Germany; free-market solutions have little acceptance and are generally not regarded as effective tools for maintaining social responsibility. The only question is whether both conservative and progressive policy-makers will overcome their own traditional adherence to either an outdated family model or to an equally anachronistic and rigid full-employment goal.

NOTES

1 See *Frauen und Arbeit* (Bundesanstalt für Arbeit, 1985).
2 See also, Vierter Familienbericht (1986).
3 While for childcare it can be argued that group involvement is highly beneficial for the children, because their social and cognitive development can be improved by early group settings, the pychosocial reality of the sick and old person is very different. New ties are not easily formed, new interests cannot be artificially created.
4 *Mutter im Zentrum/Mutterzentrum* (1985).
5 This perspective is also linked to the emerging debate about a guaranteed income. See Schmid (1984).
6 Even though Sweden shows clearly that presently only a minority of men are eligible for such a perspective even under very positive circumstances.

REFERENCES

Blanke, B. and A. Evers (1984) *Die Zweite Stadt. Unkonventionelle Formen des Umgangs mit Arbeit und Sozialen Diensten in der lokalen Politik* (Vienna).
Erler, G., M. Jaeckel and J. Sass (1983) *Mütterzwischen Beruf und Familie. Familienpolitik mit Mutterschaftsurlaub, Elternurlaub oder Erziehungsgeld? Modelle und Meinungen aus fünf Europaischen Landern* (Munich).
Evers, A. (1986) *Zwischen Arbeitsamt und Ehrenamt. Unkonventionelle lokale Initiation im Schnittpunkt von Arbeit und sozialen Diensten* (Vienna).
Fogarty, M. et al. (1984) *Irish Values and Attitudes: The Irish Report of the European Value Systems Study* (Dublin).
Haller, W. and K. Lauck (1985) *Arbeit für alle, Grundlagen der Arbeitsumverteilung zur Losung der Arbeitslosigkeit* (Neuthart).
Kern, H. and M. Schumann (1984) *Das Ende der Arbeitsteilung. Rationalisierung in der Industriellen Produktion. Bestandsaufnahme, Trendbestimmung* (Munich).
Klipstein, M. and B. Strumpel (1984) *Der Uberflus am Uberdruss. Die Deutschen nach dem Wirtschaftswunder* (Munich).
Kruger, D. (1985) 'Trends und Tendenzen in der Hauslichen Arbeitsteilung unter Rollentheoretischer Perspektive', in R. Nave-Herz, *Familiare Veränderungen seit 1950. Eine Empirische Studie* (Oldenburg).
Piore, M. and C. Sabel (1985) *The Second Industrial Divide* (New York: Basic Books).
Riedmuller, B. (1984) 'Frauen haben keine Rechte. Zur Stellung der Frau im System Sozialer Sicherheit', in I. Kickbusch and B. Riedmuller et al., *Die Armen Frauen. Frauen und Sozialpolitik* (Frankfurt).

Schmid, T. (1984) *Befreiung von falscher Arbeit. Thesen zum Garantierten Mindesteinkommen* (Berlin).

Sengenberger, W. (1984) *Wirtschafs und Arbeitmarktpolitische Entwicklungen und Tendenzen in den USA, Grossbritanien und in der BRD*, unpublished (Munich).

Trojan, A. (1984) *Professionalisiergung und Laiisierung in der sozial- und ge-sundheitspflegerischen Versorgung alter Menschen*, Vortragsmanuskript (Kassel).

Vierter Familienbericht (1986) *Die Situation der Alteren Menschen in der Familie*, Sachverstandigenkommission der Bundesregierung (Bonn).

PART IV

Women's Identities: Into the Future

14

When a Strike Comes Marching Home

Anni Borzeix and
Margaret Maruani

A STRIKE BY WOMEN IN THE LAND OF *GERMINAL*

The development of class consciousness and feminist consciousness are complex processes which have confounded observers for years. The ways in which individuals take up collective identities linking them to others in workplaces and communities can be studied in various ways. This chapter examines the processes by observing a strike staged about ten years ago by women working in a clothing factory in northern France – the locale of *Germinal*, Emile Zola's famous novel of mining life.[1] While much has changed in the mining country since Zola wrote, legacies of that time are still passed on. This strike is evidence of both the longevity of some traditions and the appearance of new ones. Despite the obvious methodological limits involved in founding a general argument upon a case study (as is done here), none the less, this case deserves attention because many of its characteristics are pertinent to the theme of this book.

A few words about the strike itself. The strike at CIP (Confection Industrielle du Pas-de-Calais) was a 'women's strike': 117 women out of 118 strikers with only one union, the Confédération Française et Démocratique du Travail (CFDT). The CIP strike lasted three years altogether. For 18 months, from July 1975 to January 1977, the striking women occupied their factory day and night; they continued making shirts without a boss, without supervisors, without production quotas. They undertook these actions in opposition to collective dismissal. In some ways, the CIP labor dispute resembled other strikes (especially the famous one at LIP) at that time, in which workers occupied factories and controlled production.[2] In the mid-1970s, strike banners often carried the slogan, 'We Produce, We

Sell, We Pay Ourselves'. Despite the existence of similar strikes, however, CIP was an epic that struck the imagination. In a little truck without headlights or a horn, CIP strikers drove all over France publicizing their actions. Wearing their highly visible red and yellow capes, they paraded and demonstrated in the streets; they invaded local TV studios, unemployment offices, and local government offices (*préfectures*). They even put on a play. When force was used against them, they made their case heard by alerting politicians, including future ministers,[3] and unionists throughout the area. On foot, by bicycle, or by truck, they lugged all over the country the shirts that their factory made. They did not 'sell' these shirts but 'exchanged' them for solidarity, for support, and for the money they needed. In this way, they managed to hold out for three years – and win. A Belgian manufacturer finally bought the factory, transformed it into furniture production, and rehired almost all the women.

This strike, then, while being a single case, does demonstrate many things about the effects of the feminization of the labor force. First, this strike involved a *category of women* – married women with children – whose participation in the labor force has, in nearly all industrialized countries, increased immensely over the past 20 years. The labor force participation rate of 30-year-old women, for example, rose in France from 40 per cent in 1962 to 69 per cent in 1982. Seven out of ten women in the 25–40 year age band are now paid workers. In this sense, women strikers of CIP are quite representative of this general trend. But their strike is also quite remarkable because the strikers belonged to the first generation of women in the mining region of the Nord and Pas-de-Calais to remain in the labor force after marriage. Even though the clothing industry had traditionally hired women, local norms had prescribed that wives withdraw from the labor force.[4]

Another reason to scrutinize this labor dispute is that it centered on the issue of *women's employment*. The women strikers occupied their factory day and night for 18 months; they put production under worker control and continued making shirts. They did not do all this in order to demand higher wages or less toilsome working conditions. Rather, their major demand was to save jobs and prevent the company from shutting down. They voiced a demand which was new for the region and this generation of wage-earners – the right to jobs for all, including married women with children.

Women working is not, in itself, anything new.[5] Almost as many French women were employed at the beginning of this century as now; in 1911, as in 1975, eight million women were in the paid labor force in France. What is novel about the situation today is that women have continued to work during a full-blown economic recession, and that they have not given up their jobs as easily or frequently as before.[6] The result is that although men's employment has decreased overall, female employment rates have increased. Men's labor force participation rate has declined (from 72 per cent in 1975 to 67 per cent in 1985); women's has mounted (from 41 per cent in 1975 to 45 per cent in 1985). Almost all of the increase in the size of the French labor force is due to jobs taken up by women – from 1975 to 1982, the labor force increased by 1.7 million people, of which 1.5 million were women. Considering this general trend, what happened in the mining country where the CIP strike took place is all the more relevant. In the 1960s while the coal industry was in the midst of a massive recession, the clothing industry expanded; with this expansion, a new category of workers appeared in the local labor market: ex-miners' wives now ready to work. Then, the economic crisis of the 1970s hit the region dramatically, especially in the clothing and textile sectors. Employment fell by half and the CIP strike was only one case out of hundreds where workers tried to oppose collective dismissal.

CIP is interesting beyond its own narrow history because it provides a case study, albeit one perhaps seen as if through a magnifying glass, somewhat distorted and exacerbated owing to the intensity of the labor dispute. This case study can address two questions. The first asks about the meaning and scope of the demand to the right to employment for all women, including those with children. The subversiveness of this demand can be seen through the CIP strike. As long as it stayed within the realm of everyday routine, married women's work was accepted as an economic necessity. When, however, it sparked a long, fierce labor dispute that was outrageous according to norms in the local setting, the principle of the right of women to work caused a controversy. This happened perhaps because behind the front of economic necessity lay one of the touchiest aspects of gender relations. When work is not just a necessity but becomes a demand or even the claim to a right, the balance of power between women and men is upset.

The second question addressed is women's motivations for work and involvement in union actions. When these unskilled workers – daughters and granddaughters of miners – went on strike, where did they find their inspiration, their collective identity, their models? Did the strike itself generate a collective identity new in the mining country? In other words, in a cultural setting where the consciousness of belonging to the working class is almost automatic, what can be said about the 'consciousness of being a woman'? This strike offers an opportunity to reflect upon the interaction between class and gender consciousness among unskilled women workers and, more generally, upon the question of feminism within the working class.

STRIKES AS A HERITAGE

The CIP strike has left marks on the working class hereabouts, as much as the miners' strike in 1963.

local CFDT unionist

Labor disputes in the mining country are more than reference marks that successively stake out the local history of the working class and of labor unions. Nowadays, workers – including women workers – still draw inspiration for their social identity from the principal miners' strikes of the past. History remains a powerful frame of reference, a source of ideas and identity that is continually updated and corroborated by each new episode in the class struggle.

The miners' culture is a heritage that was handed down in direct line to the women at CIP. They talked about brothers, fathers, grandfathers, all of whom were miners and most of whom were communists belonging to the CGT (Confédération Générale du Travail). The 'nursery stories' on which these women had been raised centered on the Popular Front of 1936 and the major strikes by miners in the Nord and Pas-de-Calais.[7] This political heritage is, we should not forget, essentially masculine. Yet, whether they had lived through this past or not, the women referred to it in order to explain and interpret their own conflict.

Although it might sound like a cliché to write that the keys to the present lie buried in the past, history was essential for the CIP strikers. Nevertheless, this return to their roots was paradoxical in that the CIP labor dispute at first glance seemed to have nothing in common with the miners' strike. In almost every way this small, long strike by working women in a clothing factory differed profoundly from the massive, spectacular, virile strikes by hundreds of thousands of miners. Not only were the scope, length and gender of these strikes different, but their demands and actions as well. The miners could never have imagined occupying the pits and taking over production.

In spite of these differences, however, earlier labor disputes continued to set the frame of reference; they shaped the collective memory, suffused actions, infused meaning into the CIP strike and thus helped reproduce local culture. Like a founding cosmology, they provided – and still do, in spite of social and economic changes – the power to explain contemporary social relationships. A class consciousness on which the working-class community was founded had been passed on and kept alive through labor disputes, those special occasions that touch the quick, as class antagonisms are laid bare, exacerbated, and seen for what they are.

In this sense, every new strike is suffused with all previous strikes. Whereas near-sighted observers might tend to see the local history of the working class as a yellowed picture that has been brought down from the attic, a daguerreotype from a bygone age, actors in the struggles do feel the continuity between present and past. The interviews themselves placed this reference mark in our research. In order to understand fully this labor dispute involving unskilled women working in a clothing factory, we had to go back to the local mine with its legends, its accidents, and its traditions of class struggle, union actions and political affiliations, despite the fact that the mine had been shut down 20 years ago. Miners' jobs had vanished in the region, but their culture was still alive. Labor disputes in the mines constituted the founding myth behind the CIP strike. Beneath the immediate community wherein the CIP strike broke out was buried another community, a historical frame of reference: the culture of the mines.

Becaue of this link to the past, class antagonism dominated the strike. The deepest sense of identity felt by these women has to be sought within the working class. It was experienced as the ever strongly felt opposition between the small and the large, between those who drudge and those who profit, between those who wear themselves out and those who dress themselves up. While strikers at CIP never talked about 'capitalists' or 'proletarians' and they never mentioned the 'class struggle', they lived it from day to day. Their stories, though about class antagonism, were not spangled with key words borrowed from the traditional militant vocabulary.

The CIP strike reinvigorated convictions grounded in history; it was a corroboration, not a discovery. The women did not make a show of their membership in the working class. When referring to the working class, interviewees simply said 'working people' or 'workers'. That they felt a class identity and solidarity was one of those truths felt but not analysed, a certitude so natural that it did not have to be put into words. Moreover, for all the women whom we met, class struggle and class solidarity involved the unions. To join a union – whether the CDFT or CGT – was a natural, normal act because 'the unions defend workers'. You are a worker, you join a union. There was never any question about that.

PRE-EMPTING THE HERITAGE

A strike like the one at CIP could not have happened twenty years ago. Women, alone, doing what they did! Never! There were strikes by women in the wool companies, but that wasn't the same. There were miners' strikes too, but they were not the same either.

The town mayor

Up to this point, we have emphasized the continuity with the past, the recurrence of what was lasting. In this sense, the history of local labor disputes was a heritage bequeathed to all workers, a dowry bestowed upon women who entered the labor force. Looking at it from the opposite angle, this example also shows how group consciousness – the feeling of belonging to a social community – is constructed not only by borrowing materials from the past but also by rejecting and displacing some of these materials.

It consists of both continuous lines and breaking points.

Three things were original about the CIP strike. It was a strike by women in a region with a masculine tradition of class struggle; it was a labor dispute over protecting the jobs of married women in an environment where the notion of married women working was far from accepted; and it was the beginning, within a deeply patriarchal culture, of values that have to do with feminism.

Women at CIP broke with the past when they stepped onto a stage that, until then, had been occupied by male miners who played their roles according to the masculine norms of the mining culture. This culture had drawn an idealized picture of women as housewives who held the purse strings, ran the household economy and boosted morale whenever there was a strike. Women always had a place in the working-class culture of northern France, but it was 'their' place, not as main actors, but as wives and daughters of miners, workers, strikers. This held true even if women were employed. The 'second sex' always played secondary roles in local history, roles defined in relation to husbands, fathers, brothers.

Given this situation, women entering local history as main actors meant commotion. Not only were they determined to go on working after marriage, but they were ready to go on strike for their jobs, become active union members, and assume political responsibilities. Public order was upset. Wives with jobs also disturbed the peace at home by upsetting the balance of power within the couple. These two disturbances shook one of the pillars of miners' culture, namely, the traditional, patriarchal, working-class family. In all these respects, then, the CIP strike did not perpetuate a tradition; it marked a rupture. It heralded the eruption of disorder in the relationships between women and men at the factory, at the town hall, and at home.

The CIP strike would never had occurred had it not drawn inspiration from the masculine tradition of the mining country but on the other hand, these women, by striking for jobs, were pre-empting a masculine heritage. This pre-emption seemed to undermine the pre-eminence of men in society. The CIP strike was loyal to the past that it betrayed. To claim a job for everyone was part of the tradition, but to include married women in the 'everyone' implied adapting the tradition and, in particular, putting an end to the male monopoly over the job market and labor unions. The CIP women inherited the right to strike, to fight for jobs, but renounced their obligation as wives to be submissive. In other words, they pre-empted what was intended for men and refused to accept the lot that had been willed to their mothers. The strikers took from the past only what could be of help to them. Grounded as it was in an inherited class consciousness, what effect could this strike have on feminist consciousness?

WHEN THE STRIKE, AND STRIKERS, COME HOME

We were locked in a fight ['On etait un rapport de force'] . . . We learned
to fight like the devil . . . For *everything*.

A striker

Comments such as this were made by the CIP workers to describes the
side-effects of their action.[8] In these words, they declared that the spirit of
rebellion which had carried them through the strike did not fall away as
they went beyond the factory gates. It imbued their everyday lives,
suffused all their social relationships. More importantly, it did not vanish
when they stepped across the traditional boundaries separating work from
home, the factory from the kitchen, production on the assembly line from
'reproduction' in the domestic world.[9] This spirit of rebellion which
infused their whole life was proof that the usual image of a passive,
submissive female labor force was false, that intensive exploitation does
not always imply extensive docility among workers.

Our survey method[10] also helped break down boundaries because
inquiries into personal biographies[11] make it meaningless to compartment-
alize the spheres of private and public life. The two obviously overlap and
act upon each other. Postulating this interaction at the start made it
possible, among other things, to observe transfers between spheres –
transfers of learning processes, behaviors, aptitudes, attitudes, knowledge
and know-how.

Much has already been written about transfers from home toward the
world of work, from the family to the factory or office, from patriarchy
toward capitalism. Among the qualities that women learn within the family
and that are appreciated by employers are tractability, endurance, precision in their work and submission to authority. This strike, however,
throws light upon transfers in the reverse direction, from the workplace to
the household, from the job (and strike) to home life. What happens
whenever a strike, this momentous event in the world of work, comes
home? During their strike, the CIP workers learned to fight for their
dignity, independence, and autonomy. The interviews show how, thanks to
this labor dispute, negotiating became an ongoing process within families,
how the strength felt and generated in the occupied factory upset for years
afterwards the balance of power between spouses, how the 'bargaining
power' acquired during the conflict was exported into family life.

This example is undoubtedly too specific. After all, a strike is an extreme
case that brackets a period of time. None the less, can the results of this
survey be extended to working women in general? If it can, then a strike
brackets more than a phase of life, a span of personal history. By opening a

window of understanding, it exposes the broader, deeper processes of transfers from the workplace to the household, processes that normally lie invisible during everyday life, under the double cover of the economic exploitation and gender domination of working women.

THE RIGHT TO JOBS FOR ALL: A SUBVERSIVE CLAIM?

– Do you remember the CIP strike?
– The strike was logical. They no longer had work. It's logical to go on strike when they take your job away . . .
– And women working?
– I'm against that. The husband should earn enough. I don't like it, women with jobs, because now, when they come home from work in the evening, they say, 'To each his own.' They wear the pants. I wouldn't stand for that.

Interview with an old miner living next door to the factory

The local politicians and male unionists of the locality backed the strike. They did so actively and warm-heartedly, resolutely and decisively. However, the women strikers did not receive the support of their own families! Most of their husbands were opposed to the strike, and some went so far as to use blackmail: 'It's me or your strike, me or your job.' At best, husbands were indifferent. How can these attitudes be understood?

The combination of a strike by women for their right to jobs seemed against nature in this working-class region of France. It was freakish. In the land of *Germinal*, the wives of strikers and mothers of miners just did not hold jobs because throughout the mining region, women ceased working at marriage. The working conditions and social system of the mines created a tradition, a model of women as housewives. This model has outlasted the mines, however. As already mentioned, the CIP workers were the first generation of married women to stay at work. Therefore, whereas in the sphere of work, men might think it logical that workers (even women) should claim the right to employment, within the sphere of family life, this claim was no longer normal but suspicious. It became a menace to the patriarchy on which the family was based. During the CIP strike, the 'logic' of working-class solidarity came into contradiction with the ideology underlying the power relationship between women and men. The old miner's reaction quoted above demonstrates this contradiction clearly.

The husbands' opposition did not arise, then, from economic motives, since the wives' wages were indispensable to the households' financial survival. It was ideologically motivated instead. Their wives working disturbed the peace at home; it called authority into question. This irksome fact, especially when generated by economic necessity, exposed the new bonds of dependency within the family. These women were fighting to impose ideologically what had been accepted as an economic necessity.

Whereas, for men, the right to a job leads to conflict only within the world of work, demanding this right for women opens up two fronts of fighting: on the one hand, facing up to the boss and fighting at the workplace to keep a job and, on the other hand, facing up to one's family and fighting at home for the right to strike for a job. In the CIP strike, one dispute led to another. In most cases, striking for a job broke the peace at home. When the strike, and strikers, came home, the claim to the right to a job dealt a blow to the familial order. Husbands felt that both their supremacy in the family and their hegemony over work were threatened. By clinging to their jobs, the CIP workers were undermining the foundations of social relationships within the family. The authority of the male head of household and bread-winner could not hold up against the wife who decided that her job was an absolute necessity, important enough to spend three years persistently struggling for it.

WORK AND EMPLOYMENT

This case study helps to distinguish two notions that are usually combined: work and employment or, more specifically, the relation a person has to each of these. The relation to work refers to the ways that individuals experience their job, especially how they react to the conditions under which they have been hired and actually work. This relation involves wages, authority relations, promotions, qualifications and working conditions, among other things. The relation to employment, on the other hand, involves access to the labor market and to jobs. It refers not only to oppositions such as working/non-working, employed/unemployed or precarious/steady employment, but also to the opinions, attitudes and behaviors that a person adopts when losing a job or looking for one.

In the case of CIP, women spent three years struggling obstinately and with determination in order to be employed again as they had been. But they were also fighting for work that they did not like. Most of them had not chosen their activity; they sewed because there were no better jobs available. All of them were unskilled and worked for minimum wages. Moreover, they all hated the working conditions – the assembly-line, production quotas, the work speed, the authority hierarchy and controls. None the less, all of them clung to their employment.

The accounts given in our interviews revealed the contradictions between work and employment. What interviewees said could not be used to draw a pretty picture of work. Their comments were a far cry from the exaltation of well-done work, of satisfied workmanship, or of love for one's job. Instead, work was discussed in contradictory terms. It was life and death. As one of them said, time was 'dead' before, when she was a housewife. However, 'death' also brought to mind their fathers, grand-fathers and brothers – miners who died of silicosis. Work was, quite literally, a liberation: 'I work; therefore, I am . . . a free woman.' But it was also alienation: work was 'hell'. To be more exact, having employment can help free a woman even if she has to do 'alienating' work.

The distinction between the relations toward work and toward employ-ment helps explain a simple, perhaps obvious, phenomenon of immense importance – not liking one's job does not constitute a refusal to be employed. Work can be both bondage and liberation, evil and good. Researchers who study male participation in the labor force do not mix up notions as fundamental as these two. However, confusion begins when women are studied. Many, many women work in very bad conditions, whether in terms of wages, skills or the repetitiveness of tasks. Therefore they have a so-called 'negative relation' to work and, logically, one claims, they would like to cease working. This reasoning often leads directly to a simplistic conclusion that only privileged women – those who have a positive relation to work, who hold interesting, pleasant and well-paid jobs – want to work. All the others – in other words, the large majority of women – have only one dream: to stop working. Accordingly, work is defined, for women, as a luxury or else a dire necessity. How many debates about women working have been trapped in the false dilemmas of either liberation or alienation through work?

Work is, undeniably, alienation for everyone, woman or man. If it alienates men, why would it not do so to women? But for employment, the situation is different. There are two lessons to be learned from this strike, which exacerbated certain fundamental social processes having to do with women's participation in the labor force, processes that are less visible during everyday life. First of all, the subversiveness of the demand for women's right to employment can be explained only in relation to both life on the job and life at home. Secondly, a clear distinction between employment and work might help us to understand why women have decided to stay in the labor market during a period of economic recession, although the conditions under which they participate in the labor force are not improving and, indeed, are often worsening.

BEYOND THE OUTER APPEARANCES OF FEMINISM

– We've said it more than once among ourselves: our husbands should see us working.
– They wouldn't do it. I'm sure they wouldn't do it.
– . . . I use a drill.

– We've got everything, everything like men.
– . . . Maybe there're jobs where you have to have a whole lot of strength and then . . . but anyway, there are strong women.
– Obviously.
– People always tend to say the 'weaker sex', but instead it's the sex that can endure more.
– More enduring, that's true.
– That's for sure. In a way, we are the stronger sex.
   Conversation between two ex-strikers, now working at the furniture factory

During the strike, the women never discussed their action in such terms. When we carried out our first series of interviews during the heat of events,[12] there was talk about 'workers on strike', not about a 'women's strike'. The trade unions followed the academic rules of French grammar: 117 female workers (*ouvrières*) + 1 male worker (*ouvrier*) = 118 workers (*ouvriers*) in the masculine gender! Five years later, when we came back, the feminine gender was being used. How did speech slip from resorting to the generic masculine to asserting a feminine identity? This semantic metamorphosis can perhaps be interpreted as the result of a lapse of time that can be measured by the difference between first-hand, on-the-scene accounts and a subsequently reconstructed story. Group memory had worked over the grammar.

While they were occupying their factory, the CIP workers were asked about the 'sex' of their strike. At that time, the question seemed to them out of line and out of place. They even objected to the idea that their labor dispute could be seen as a 'women's strike'. They were 'workers' – whether women or men mattered little – engaged in a fight against collective dismissal. More basically, what they replied was, 'forget the fact that we are women.' If a strike were to be attributed lofty aims, in their eyes, it had to be described in the masculine gender.

When, a few years later, we attempted to retrace with them the history of this strike, their story followed another line; we were told about a strike *by women*. Words and labels had changed. The 'workers on strike' had cleared the stage for 'We the women who led this strike, publicized it, made it last for over three years and, finally, won it.' This 'we the women' stood in contrast to 'they the men' who 'have never done as well, might have been less willing, or would have been carried away and have become too violent'. These too were stereotypes, but they had an obvious symbolic function. The assertion of this difference meant that the women had finally laid claim to their strike. Thenceforth, the labor dispute could, without being discredited, be ascribed to women. The heritage of the miners' struggle had become their own and their strike was proof of this. Although it was not fully noticed right away, this discovery of gender would, by analogy, lead to other revelations, particularly in relations within the family.

None the less, the word 'feminism' was never mentioned during interviews. It belonged neither to the vocabulary nor to the history of these women. They would even have objected to the label. Although during the strike, no feminist slogan broke the usual rules of trade union rhetoric, all these themes later permeated actors' accounts, and did so with the tranquil force of convictions revealed during the strike but grounded in everyday life. Therefore, whenever they were asked about the effects of the strike on their personal and workplace lives, they provided an abundance of anecdotes, stories, examples, images, practices, words, facts and gestures that had to do – regardless of what interviewees thought – with feminism in the broadest sense of the word.[13] They rejected women's exclusive responsibility for housework and raising children. They demanded that birth control no longer be taboo; they refused maternity as the fate from which no women could escape. They fought for their autonomy which, for many among them, entailed the right to hold a job, join a union and lead their own lives in a realm of freedom outside the home.

All interviewees confidently stated that they had won. Their victory had called for boldness and self-confidence. A major conquest was over their own previous timidity toward society[14] as well as toward their husbands. They had dared stand their ground, hold out and speak out where before they would have held their peace. The change came about during the long strike, but the conquest outlasted the strike. Although family structures did not change much, and no divorces occurred, the power relationship within the couple was redefined. Step by step, these women moved the bounds of what was 'right'. What is natural today was unthinkable yesterday. There was no sudden break between the two, but nothing is like it used to be. These women transgressed the norm not by breaking it overtly, but by sidestepping obstacles and diverting their behavior from its normal course. Their weapon was a force that corroded inner reality more than outer appearances.

Another feminist theme ran through their accounts: the questioning of men's supposed superiority. This was not proclaimed in tirades against patriarchy, the established order and the domination of women by men. Rather it was clearly expressed through practices and ideas. The CIP women played with feminine and masculine roles by making a game of stereotypes and role models. Their humor, irony and mockery reversed several symbolic oppositions:

- Inside/outside: women demonstrating in the street, men sitting at home, waiting for their return, and even preparing meals.
- Passive/active: women leading a labor action, men dragging their feet; feminine rebellion, masculine submissiveness. Still today, the women but not their husbands belong to unions.
- Weak/strong: what if the weaker sex has more fortitude? More

force? More forcefulness? Besides, in their new jobs, some of these women have everything that men are supposed to have: hammers, nails, pliers, drills . . .

Interviewees did not declare themselves to be feminists, but their actions and attitudes, their symbols and reference marks, their way of thinking had to do with feminism. This remark can be generalized beyond the case under study so as to open discussion about the emergence of feminism in the working class. The union movement quite naturally provides women workers with a political culture but it is not a feminist one, in spite of official speeches about women's liberation, or emancipation.[15] During this survey, we were surprised to notice how much difference there was between what was said and what was done. This observation led us to the following hypothesis: unlike some intellectual or middle-class feminists, working-class women do not speak louder than they act. The lag between words and deeds still exists but in the reverse direction: between deeds and words.

In effect, the ways feminism is lived in speech or action depend upon women's social class. Words and deeds differ because the ways in which women are dominated vary across classes and since the forms of domination vary, there are multiple indicators of change. Different indicators or breaking points exist, which erupt into the consciousness of working class women and it leaves different marks on the working class. The 'feminine condition' is not one and the same throughout society. We are not all alike regardless of what some feminists pretend. Therefore, 'feminism' should take the plural form, even though all feminisms are tackling problems arising from a common source.

NOTES

This chapter was translated by Noal Mellot, CNRS, Paris.

1 On the strike itself – its circumstances, goals and effects – and the method used for its analysis, see Borzeix and Maruani (1982).
2 See 'Les Enfants de LIP', *CFDT Aujoud'hui*, September 1975.
3 Two local politicians became ministers in the Left government after 1981: Pierre Mauroy (Prime Minister) and André Delelis (Minister of Trade).
4 For an historical perspective on women and work in the mining country in nineteenth-century France, see Tilly (1985a; 1985b).
5 About the significance of the so-called novelty of women working, see Maruani (1985); Maruani and Nicole (1985). An interesting interpretation of what happened to the idea of women's work during the nineteenth century is developed in Blunden (1982).
6 Recent reference to the intensification of women's participation in the paid

labor force in France can be found in Bouillaguet-Bernard et al. (1981); Huet (1982).

7   In 1948 and 1963.

8   Actually this was our purpose when we decided to interview the ex-strikers five years after their conflict ended. Our main interest then was not the strike itself but its consequences. What marks were left by such an experience on the workers' family, work and political lives? What had changed for them?

9   On the concept of 'reproduction' and the theoretical debate around the interaction between production and reproduction as discussed in recent work in France, see *Le Sexe du travail* (1984).

10 A series of lengthy interviews was carried out over a year with the strikers themselves (30 out of 100) and with the main local witnesses and actors (political or union representatives), from which we reconstructed four biographical narrations representative of the social group formed by the strikers. For more details about the method see Borzeix and Maruani (1982). On the biographical approach and its use in analysing the female labor force, see APRE (1985).

11 For another discussion of the impact of workplace relations on gender relations see Beechey (Chapter 3).

12 We first met the CIP women in 1977 at the time of their strike. We were engaged in two different research projects: one on unions' labor process and one on unions and feminism. See Borzeix (1980) and Maruani (1979).

13 When speaking of feminism one must distinguish its established or organized forms from its more informal manifestations. In the first case one refers to different movements, groups or organizations. In the second case it is to a mixture of ideas, social practices and/or forms of contestation. It is in the second sense that the term is used here.

14 Two of the ex-strikers have, since then, accepted political responsibilities in the local Municipal Council.

15 On women in French labor unions see Maruani (1979) and Jenson (1984). For historical references see Guilbert (1966) and Zylberberg-Hocquard (1981).

REFERENCES

APRE (1985) *Temps sociaux. Trajectoires selon le sexe*, Cahier no. 2, May.

Blunden, C. (1982) *Le Travail et la vertu* (Paris: Payot).

Borzeix, A. (1980) *Syndicalisme et organisation du travail* (Paris: CNAM).

Borzeix, A. and M. Maruani (1982) *Le Temps des chemises* (Paris: Syros).

Bouillaguet-Bernard, P. et al. (1981) *Femmes au travail: Prospérité et crise* (Paris: Economica).

Guilbert, M. (1966) *Les Femmes et l'organisation syndicale avant 1914* (Paris: CNRS).

Huet, M. (1982) 'La progression de l'activité féminine est-elle irréversible?', *Economie et Statistique*, no. 145.

Jenson, J. (1984) 'The "problem" of women', in M. Kesselman and G. Groux (eds), *The French Workers' Movement* (London: Allen and Unwin).

Le Sexe du travail (1984) (Grenoble: PUG).

Maruani, M. (1979) *Les Syndicats à l'épreuve du féminisme* (Paris: Syros).

Maruani, M. (1985) *Mais qui a peur du travail des femmes?* (Paris: Syros).

Maruani, M. and C. Nicole (1985) 'Quelques reserves sur l'armée de reserve', *Revue Française des Affaires Sociales*, no. 2.

Tilly, L. (1985a) 'Coping with company paternalism', *Theory and Society*, 14.

Tilly, L. (1985b) 'Family, gender and occupation in industrial France: Past and Present', in A. S. Rossi (ed.), *Gender and the Life Course* (New York: Aldin Publishing).

Zylberberg-Hocquart, M. H. (1981) *Femmes et féminisme dans le mouvement ouvrier français* (Paris: Editions Ouvrières).

15

Gender Relations and Female Labor

A Consideration of Sociological Categories

Anne-Marie Daune-Richard

Until recently women's work has generally been analysed in terms of economic concepts appropriate to a market economy dominated by relationships of commodity exchange, in which men's behavior was the norm. Now, in the wake of the feminist movements of the 1970s, many studies have made visible the contribution of domestic labor – which is outside the sphere of commodity exchange relations – to social production. But the importance of these studies is not limited to their quantification of this non-market labor, of this 'shadow-work'. By questioning the ways in which social theories conceptualize work, these studies cast doubt on the very capacity of such gender-based theories to provide a complete understanding of the role of women as genuine social agents in production relations and thus to provide an adequate understanding of women's social identity.

We propose here, on the basis of our own research, to contribute to this reconceptualization of labor. Using a problematic of gender relations, this chapter shows how we constructed a heuristic category labelled 'women's work'. This category, as we have elaborated it, usefully explicates the structural dimension of the sexual division of labor between women and men, as well as the actions of women and men who make these structures happen.

The chapter begins with a short critical survey of different theoretical conceptualizations of women's labor force participation. Using a problematic of gender relations, it then proposes the heuristic category 'women's work' that intersects two social fields: the space where commodities are produced and the space where individuals are produced and reproduced. This is founded on the articulation of practices and their meanings. Finally, in using the category 'women's work' we can see how to analyse within kinship networks which link women cross-generationally.

'WOMEN'S WORK': AT THE INTERSECTION OF PRODUCTION AND REPRODUCTION

Existing approaches to theorizing women's labor force participation all have severe limitations, which can be overcome only if the category 'women's work' incorporates the duality of female activity – paid labor, within the sphere of market relations, and domestic labor, within the sphere of the reproduction of individuals.

The most common approach has been *essentialist*, in which gender differences derive from biology. Such studies base their understanding of women's labor on a notion of the *female condition*. This notion assigns all women a place in social relations which is ahistorical, since it relies on biology as the determining factor. This 'condition', determined solely by biological difference, designates that women's primary social responsibility is for biological reproduction – childbearing and rearing as well as domestic labor. Hence these studies presume that women's labor market activities must be shaped by prior and priority duties as wives and/or mothers. According to this theoretical approach, women suffer from the 'social handicap' of biology. This supposed handicap then becomes the explanation for women's marginalization in the labor force. Wage-earning women are studied as a particular subset of the general category of wage labor, a categorization based only through the observation of male behavior. What women do is then a deviation from the norm, and explained as a consequence of the supposed essential differences which biology makes.[1]

Another approach to women's participation in the labor force which makes an essentialist distinction is that which conceptualizes 'sex as a variable'. In the first instance, sex is taken as a classificatory model. The classic models here are sociological and demographic studies in which the variable 'sex' is introduced at a certain point in the analysis although it may just as well be excluded since the units of observation are not initially constructed on the basis of gender. In other cases, the variable is treated as a *subordinate* one (Passerson and de Singly, 1984). This kind of treatment is very common in the sociology of work, where consideration of the variable 'sex' – if it is taken into account at all – is limited to those women whose family situation interferes with 'normal' labor market activity. Once again, of course, male behavior constitutes the model of what is normal.

Contemporary feminists have encouraged the abandonment of an essentialism that privileged (more or less explicitly) biological attributes and they have sought more social conceptualizations of gender differences.

As a result, several different efforts to understand gender as a social construction emerged. These new approaches defined 'sex' categories (or classes) in terms of a social relation understood as a gender system (Mathieu, 1971). They often used the notion of 'patriarchy'.[2] With reference to work, these studies focused on domestic labor to the virtual exclusion of paid labor, because they identified the family as the site where the domination – and exploitation – of women by men takes place. But giving little attention to women's participation in the labor force meant they could not account for something which was a major aspect of real women's lives.[3]

A third major approach for understanding the labor force participation of women appears within neo-Marxism. Studies from this perspective explicitly dealt with the issue of the *articulation* – or interconnection – of production and reproduction.

One type of neo-Marxism explored the links between the spheres of commodity production and reproduction of the labor force in a capitalist system. Such studies identified a presumed relative autonomy of the spheres of production and reproduction in traditional Marxist understandings of wage relations which incorporated the assumption that workers arrived in the labor market 'fully formed' (Lautier, 1977). Instead, these neo-Marxist analyses demonstrated that the separation and exclusion of reproduction functions from the sphere of production actually brought about a marginalization of reproduction. Moreover, at the time that the 'public' (production) and the 'private' (reproduction) were cleaved, women were designated responsible for the sphere of reproduction. The consequence was, of course, that women experienced social marginalization. In accordance with this insight, then, such studies see the labor market situation of women in direct relation to their responsibilities for domestic labor, although these are, of course, socially and not biologically designed relations.

A second mode of analysis (largely derived from the first one) no longer locates women's work solely in the context of relations between production and reproduction of labor. Rather it focuses on the articulation of the sphere of commodity production and the sphere of reproduction of individuals. This research stream, characterized by both its feminism and its Marxism, incorporates the notion of 'reproduction', by extending its definition to cover all activities that *socially* organize the reproduction of individuals.[4]

Thus, this last perspective proposes a new heuristically-constituted configuration of the social which enables researchers to do three things. The first is to account for the primary (but not exclusive) assignment of women to the sphere of reproduction and of men to the realm of production. The second is to recognize the structural character of this sex-based assignment of individuals to one or the other of these two spheres and to conceive of the relation between spheres as one of articulation and not one of causal determination. In other words, the sexual division of labor is treated as a social division (Daune-Richard, 1985a). Thus, researchers may construct a category which captures the intersection of individuals' participation in both of these two social fields. Within this category, such studies reopen the question of the validity of certain concepts (work, class, social mobility) and disciplinary divides (Sociology of Work, Sociology of the Family, Economics and Sociology).

To this point, we have outlined the different ways women's labor force participation has been conceptualized in several theoretical approaches. By way of a preliminary conclusion, a typology of problematics emerges. Two major kinds of approaches base their notions of gender on the essentialism of biology. The first one is *deterministic*, deriving women's labor force behavior from their biologically-based so-called 'condition'. It makes the argument that there is a causal relation of determination between the biological and the social, with social relations following directly from biological differences. The second approach limits itself to analysing *correlations* between biological characteristics and social behaviors. While deterministic assumptions are not normally incorporated at the outset, usually by the end of the study biology has emerged as an important variable explaining women's deviation from the 'norm' of (men's) labor force participation. Another approach which makes frequent use – although without acknowledging it does so – of an essentialist construction of gender is found principally, in its more or less elaborated versions, in traditional Marxist analyses. Here the subordination of gender to relations of production is a part of the paradigm.

Feminist analyses utilize these terms like *exploitation* and *appropriation*. However, these problematics deal almost exclusively with domestic labor, since they concentrate on the family as the site of the exploitation of women by men. Women's paid work is frequently not directly included in such studies, and even more rarely dealt with theoretically.

Finally, with respect to neo-Marxism, we can distinguish two major approaches. One stresses the transfer of domestic characteristics onto the terrain of paid work. The other, derived from the principle of transversality of gender relations, proposes a conceptualization based on the interconnectedness of domestic and paid labor. This chapter now explores the implication of the latter line of argument in more detail.

Toward the end of the 1970s, several themes converged in the study of gender relations. First, it became clearer that domestic labor is of decisive importance for the continuation of the productive sector in all societies. Moreover, there was a simultaneous recognition that such 'invisible' labor was predominantly performed by women. Thus, the question of domestic labor became the focus of a large debate which occurred at the crossroads of two types of preoccupations, those of feminists focusing on relations between women and men and those of analysts concerned with the reproduction of the labor force and, more generally, with social reproduction.

Secondly, it became obvious that attempts to deal with waged labor and domestic labor separately and to ignore gendered social practices in the workplace were a fundamental obstacle to any valid analysis of female labor. Even a cursory examination of the labor market reveals a rapid and considerable increase in the labor force participation rates of women, especially married women under 35 with one or two children. Thus, empirical observation shows that marriage and children act less as a brake on women's labor force participation than in the past. In the same vein, several studies found, without being able to explain their findings, that women, in their strategies for combining career and family, make choices that are not easily explicable in terms of any simple reference to only one of their fields of activity. For example, women who continuously participate in the labor force behave quite differently both in their family and their work life strategies from women who have never worked or who have broken off their careers from time to time (Labourie-Racape et al., 1977).

Therefore, a first influence on the work reported here is the body of literature which recognizes that we must rethink theorizations of labor. Propositions focusing on the articulation of relations of production and reproduction are formalized in this context. They begin from the hypothesis that individuals' locations in the family and in production must be considered simultaneously. Failing to take both aspects into account will mean a failure to come to grips with the nature of gender relations in society as a whole and in work in particular.

A second influence comes from studies based on the notion of gender relations. A first point they make is that, beyond the diversity of form and content which cloaks them, there is a relation of socially-constructed genders. The principle of this relation is continuously produced and reproduced. A second important point is that this relation cross-cuts all other sectors and social fields, even if the ways it affects them in any one instance are differentiated.[5] With these theoretical propositions in place, the sexual division of labor emerges at the intersection of all social forms and spaces which organize the production of goods and services.

We have tried to construct a heuristic category, 'women's work', which refers both to domestic and paid labor, by situating ourselves at the junction of these two theoretical formulations, namely the articulation of relations of production and reproduction and the transversality of gender relations. Our argument is the following: if gender relations cross-cut all social domains and if labor includes both the production of commodities (paid labor) and the reproduction of individuals (domestic labor), then we have to envisage *women's work* as a category which permits the simultaneous examination of both paid and domestic labor. In this way, the category is situated at the intersection of a sphere of commodity production and a sphere of reproduction of individuals.

Our empirical research has shown the extent to which this way of proceeding provides a better understanding of the linkages between women's career paths and the details of their domestic responsibilities. In a survey of women without training and of female industrial workers and clerical staff, we were able to show how, from a very early age, their family situation structured their places in the production process. Indeed, their original modest family situation shaped in several ways the career paths and destinies of these women (Daune-Richard, 1983a; Barrère-Maurisson et al., 1983). Many women in the sample had broken off their primary school education or had been compelled to abandon any prospects for vocational preparation in order to help or even replace their mothers who could not carry out their own domestic duties. When they did receive some sort of training their families had directed these women into particular channels, whose common features were that they were highly feminized and that they were popularly considered 'useful' to a married woman and mother. In certain cases, some of the women failed to fulfill their goals for training because such plans would have involved leaving the family home and moving to another city. In all such cases their families were adamantly opposed.

When faced with the burdens of motherhood, the management of their own time and space was fundamentally marked by their search for ways to improve the conditions of domestic labor (Haicault, 1984; Chabaud-Rychter, 1985). These efforts reduced further their chances to upgrade their qualifications or, in a general sense, 'to have a career'. Thus, the criteria that guided their choice of employment were primarily related to time limitations and the constraints of distance, stemming from their domestic role. The large majority of women in the survey lived in the same district as they worked and this situation resulted from a strategy of trying 'to be away from the house the shortest time possible', as one participant put it.

The constraints of distance and time pushed women as far as to accept jobs requiring less skill and training than they had before or might have aspired to. For example, a woman who was a supervisor for eight years before quitting for the birth of her last child was willing to accept a job as an unskilled worker. Her rationale was that in this way she could 'avoid the transportation costs and be away for the shortest possible time'. In the same way, the question of work schedules is very important in the way these women assess a job. They seek a maximum concentration of work hours during the day and/or the week, in order to liberate chunks of time – which they call 'free' – to perform the major part of their domestic duties. In this sense, a continuous day without large breaks, split shifts, a 40-hour week in 4½ days, are all formulas that are appreciated, particularly by the mothers of young children.

Finally, we would like to indicate here – without discussing it since we shall return to this point later – another aspect of the linkage between work and household in women's life-cycles. The extended family and kinship networks, by functioning as a route to job recruitment and by lightening the load of housewives, facilitated (always within limits) these women's access to employment. They were especially important in permitting mothers with children at home to continue their careers. It was, in fact, the extended family itself that put into practice the specific articulation of relations of production and reproduction.

These examples demonstrate that the social construction of a trajectory for women and of their workplace identities can only be understood via an appreciation of women's double lives – both at work and at home. In the sexual division of labor, societies' designation of women's responsibility for the sphere of reproduction – and in particular reproduction of the family – leads to the domination of paid labor by domestic situations. Nevertheless, the actual mechanisms of the domination and the channels which it follows are infinitely more complex – even contradictory – than they may appear at first glance, or have appeared in earlier theoretical formulations. The importance of this complexity will emerge more clearly when we move beyond an examination of practices and deal with the articulation of practices and their meanings.

PRACTICES AND THEIR MEANINGS: AN ANALYSIS OF WOMEN'S WORK

Only when the gender of individuals is no longer accepted as a simple biological datum can we conceive of gendered individuals as social actors. And only then can we explore the relationship between action and thought, practice and meaning.

Constructing analyses which are founded on the concept of a *social relation* implies that we make use of analytical categories that are sociologically constructed. The epistemological implication of this notion is that analytic categories can have no simple function; they do not merely classify actions as 'facts' or constellations of 'facts'. Categories do not rest merely on an empiricist observation of behavior. Working with sociologically-constructed categories means that the analyst recognizes the need to take *social actors* into account, as well as realizing that the 'meaning' of any 'action' must be understood. In other words, social facts cannot be taken as 'givens'; the meanings of practices are as important for our understanding of events as the practices themselves.

In the past, sociology has frequently theorized the relationship between practices and meanings within paradigms which assume a hierarchical ordering. Either primacy is given to thought (idealism) or to matter (materialism) (Daune-Richard and Haicault, 1985). The Marxist paradigm underpinned most analyses of gender relations in France in the 1970s. This paradigmatic root meant that materialist formulations of the oppression of women dominated. Only Colette Guillaumin tried to escape from a simplistic materialism with the proposition that the social construction of sexual differences has two aspects. There is both a physical appropriation – which objectifies women in the material world – and an appropriation in thought – which, via a mental construction, objectifies them as 'things' in thought itself (Guillaumin, 1978). However, even for Guillaumin, this was a sort of intuition which has not led – even in her more recent studies – to the elaboration of workable methodological tools.

In a recent book Maurice Godelier (1984) undertakes a rethinking of Marxist social theory, focusing in particular on the 'thought' and 'matter' aspects of social relations. Criticizing the Marxist notion of the relative autonomy of instances or of levels (base/superstructure), Godelier argues that 'thought does not exist as a superstructure where other constitutive elements of social reality are reflected in a distorted way and with a time lag' (1984: 22). For him,

> in all social relations there is an ideational (*idéelle*) component which appears simultaneously as one of the very conditions of emergence and reproduction of this relation and as its internal organizing schema, as part of its structure, like the part of this relation which exists in thought, and consequently, is thought. (1984: 21)

In sum, for Godelier, 'the distinction between base and superstructure is not a distinction of levels or of instances, nor is it a distinction between institutions, though it may appear as such in certain cases'. As a principle, it is a 'distinction of functions' (1984: 171). He claims that the 'real' contains both an ideational and a material component that are inextricably linked, with the former consisting of a production of meaning or signification.[6]

Godelier's approach is useful to us because it is a major reconceptualization of the intimate connection between the material and the mental in any theory of social relations.[7] In this way, practices become inseparable from their meanings. To inquire about their articulation at the theoretical and methodological levels is to attempt to move beyond the eternal opposition of structures and actors. It is also to try to grasp the moving and contradictory dynamic of social relations, as they evolve and reproduce themselves.

If the construction of any sociological category must incorporate the assumption that practices and meanings are inseparable, any objectification of practice and meaning can be no more than analytic, a heuristic decomposition of the category for purposes of study. It is this preoccupation which has guided the several stages of our construction of the concept 'women's work'. A first step systematically delineated the described practices and the meaning given to them. We then identified any contradictions existing between practices and meanings, within a given meaning system. In this way we could then construct a system of meaning which, linked to a system of practices, permitted the sociological definition of 'women's work'. In this way, we were able to clarify our understanding of the ways women are situated, not only as subjects but also as actors in the sexual division of labor.

In this first step of the analysis our study reveals a strong correlation between practices which were described and the meaning given to them. While a majority of women surveyed said that they were very attached to their employment, their evaluation of their jobs in the main was based on how they saw them interacting with their domestic activities. It has been shown elsewhere that housework requires that women be available to the family (Chabaud-Rychter et al., 1985). Moreover, other studies document that housework is – and has to be – an invisible, disguised work, essentially performed away from other members of the family, especially men (Dalla Costa et al., 1973). The women in our sample profoundly integrated these social norms about the conditions of domestic labor, allowing them to shape their view of their jobs as well as the characteristics of their whole professional careers.

Consequently, they geared their strategies or organized their schedules toward liberating some time alone at home to perform most of their domestic tasks. Hence, many preferred swing shifts and even women who did not have such schedules tended to organize their time along similar lines. Either they got up in the mornings earlier than the rest of the family in order to do some housework, or they used the time between departure of their husbands and children and the start of their own job for domestic tasks. Often, too, Saturday morning was a half-day devoted to housework, most frequently in the absence of the family, either because school and husbands' schedules made it possible or because they 'kicked everybody out of the house' in order to do household tasks by themselves.

In general, their evaluation of their work schedule was shaped by the 'availability to the family' dimension of their domestic work. Once the problem of getting the children to school was resolved satisfactorily, there was a strong tendency to prefer morning shifts (especially the 7.00 a.m. to 3.00 p.m. one) since these allowed them to take care of most of their domestic tasks before the return of husbands and children and to be present at dinner. Their efforts to limit the distance between home and work also contributed to the same process. Limited commuting time enabled them to use the slices of time before or after work, which coincided with the absence of different members of the family. There were also, however, frequent and important contradictions between practices and the discourses about them. The example used here is the issue of pay (Daune-Richard, 1983b). In quite a few interviews, women used the money they earned as a rationale for their participation in the paid labor force. They reasoned that their wage, added to their husband's, allowed the family to enjoy·a higher standard of living which they very often represented as absolutely essential. Irrespective of the actual size of the family income or the gap between wives' and husbands' salaries, women insisted that their earnings were indispensable. More often than not, this insistence did not correspond to any 'objective' assessment of the contribution which the wives' earnings represented in the family budget.

Our examination of the total context showed that this kind of rationale of necessity emerged in the situations in which women wished to justify their work outside the home. This was particularly the case in families whose resources – and especially the husbands' earnings – made this 'necessity' less than evident to the observer.

All in all, the notion that a second income was indispensable was most linked to women's ideas of autonomy and personal independence from the family in general and the husband in particular. Therefore, we found arguments which contradicted the practical situation. At times, some women spent their wages on themselves while avowing elsewhere in the interview that they were spent on the whole family. In effect, more than just the issue of finance, it was the total relationship between men and women – in the past, present and future – which was involved. The ways women spent their money made visible their desire to alter their position within the family and to achieve a space in which they might construct an alternative social identity. Thus, in a discourse which could be seen as 'symbolically' in contradiction with 'reality', the dynamic of gender relations appeared.

To clarify further the way that the meaning of work develops, we can use the example of the way the women interviewed described their relationships to their jobs (Daune-Richard, 1985b). We found that the evaluations of paid labor were directly linked to those of domestic labor. In other words, the constitution of women's relationship to work simultaneously involved the domain of domestic and paid labor; the process can be described in the following way. Women sought paid jobs in order to escape the constraints and the isolation of housework, yet they chose employment which still allowed them to meet their domestic responsibilities, which they had no intention of reducing. In this way, the relationship to paid work is largely determined by the workplace. And for that reason also, contradictions emerge within the discourse of both domestic and paid labor.

In a context in which the links between practice and meaning simultaneously shape the space of domestic and paid labor, by giving equal importance in the constitution of this category, 'women's work', to practices and meanings, we were able to analyse both coherence and contradictions between the two. In doing so we could home in on the elements of the sexual division of labor, parallel to the effects of structure, which women bear. We could also identify the spaces in which resistance could emerge.

ANALYSING WOMEN'S LABOR WITHIN KINSHIP NETWORKS

Analysts of gender relations denounce studies which take the concept of 'man' as the point of comparison for women's behavior. Instead, they claim that it is essential to show how *each* gender – in the relationship which binds them – specifically constitutes its social relations. The operation of a system of gender relations, at the level both of structures and of individuals, created the sexual division of labor within the family (housework) and within production (paid labor). Therefore, the constitution of the category 'female labor' required that we identify how the category of 'labor' functions, fragments, changes and, eventually, is transmitted among women. But, to understand female labor force participation, it seemed that we needed to start by examining social connections *within* a single gender.

With regard to housework, many studies have shown the importance of the family as the site of circulation and transmission of domestic practices. Chaubaud-Rychter et al. (1985) documented that, within a single family, women are relatively interchangeable for domestic labor. Other studies explain that women's specialization in housework, as well as the familial context in which such work is done, tends to transform kinship networks into privileged channels for the transmission of domestic know-how and practices (Young and Willmott, 1957; Bott, 1970; Pitrou, 1976; Luxton, 1980). Extending these insights we hypothesized that mother–daughter relations affected not only housework but also the modes of integration into the system of production. Hence, in studying women's labor, rather than simply studying 'women' as a whole, it is helpful to specify the focus more and look at kinship networks among women.

According to our findings, the family network provided a great deal of support to the women interviewed, who were all mothers. Nevertheless, this support was not gender-neutral; it was provided above all by female members of the kinship group, and especially by women in the working women's family. The most common kind of help provided was childcare, either full-time (which was not common) or as a stopgap around the parents' daily schedules, on half-day school holidays or other school vacations, or during children's illnesses. Help also involved preparation of meals. Often a mother brought a cooked evening meal to her daughter's house or regularly invited the daughter's family to a meal. Mothers of working women also often took care – either completely or at least in part –

of the laundry (washing and ironing) and other tasks like mending and alterations in clothing. To a lesser extent grandmothers sewed and knitted for their grandchildren. Other female members of a woman's family (sisters, aunts) would occasionally provide help; this was almost always childcare.

Help from the husband's family, in particular from a mother-in-law, was much less common. It was supplied if the working woman's own mother was not available because she lived too far away, if she was ill, or if the mother and daughter did not get along. In our sample this last reason was very unimportant.

In sum, the circulation of domestic labor among mothers and daughters is a factor which shapes the supply of women's labor in the productive sphere.[8] Families develop strategies which depend on spatial proximity of the nuclear family, the extended family and the workplace. The goal of these strategies is to facilitate women's participation in the paid labor force after they have children. But these strategies also severely limit working women's mobility, since their notion of a 'good job' involves 'family' criteria. Once they have achieved an organization of space and time which enables them to combine domestic and paid labor, they are reluctant to change jobs unless forced by external changes, like the departure of the workplace or family events.

This lack of ability or desire to change jobs reinforces the initial effects of women's location in the labor force – their lack of training and participation in feminized sectors – and keeps them in job ladders without a future. Despite this, however, having a 'good' family network does give even women with few qualifications and training (the kind of women on which this survey concentrated) better 'chances' in their careers. Women cut off from their kinship group had more discontinuous employment histories and higher risk of job loss.[9] The stronger situation of women linked to their kinship group was due both to the better resolution of conflicts between domestic and paid labor and to the fact that kinship networks also served as networks for the acquisition of jobs.[10]

In sum, the circulation of housework among mothers and daughters is important for two reasons. First, it provided real support which allowed these working women to keep their jobs. But secondly, because domestic labor was exchanged between women of the same kinship group, the fact that mothers took charge of it meant that women did not see these arrangements as a break from their primary responsibility for domestic labor.

A third way that female kinship networks played an important role was in the constitution of women's relationships to their jobs. Our study shows that women's labor force participation is constituted both as a continuation and as a break from the model provided by their mothers. In the majority of cases there is an important continuity between the discourse of mothers and that of daughters about how to do housework.[11] At the same time, there is a convergence of the meanings which mothers and daughters give to women's participation in the paid labor force, despite the fact that most of the mothers did not do paid work or did so only irregularly.[12]

In conclusion, these findings suggest that the social assignment of women to reproduction and their responsibility for housework make female kinship networks – and especially the role of the mother of the working woman – an essential reference point for understanding both labor force participation and family roles.

CONCLUSION

This chapter began with a critique of the existing approaches available to understand women's social activities in all their complexity. To move beyond the deficiencies of such studies we tried to work out a new way of defining the social and a new category of analysis, 'women's work'. The conclusion of these efforts is that a complete understanding of female labor requires a categorization which captures women's dual roles, in domestic and paid labor. It also requires an appreciation of the interconnections of practices and meanings for fully comprehending socially constructed – as opposed to biologically-determined – gender systems. Finally, by conducting analyses within single-sex groups – female kinship groups – we have demonstrated the complicated way in which family situation structures involvement in production. This analysis has all been directed toward the rejection of the false dichotomy of structures/actors. It shows that another perspective can reconceptualize the sexual division of labor to illuminate the practices and meanings within which women live, as well as the spaces for resistance against those practices and meanings which reproduce long-standing unequal systems of gender relations.

NOTES

Translated by Tahsin Corat and Jane Jenson.

1 This is a very common approach to studying women's labor force participation (Sullerot, 1968; 1978). Even Marxist researchers make use of it, although they envisage improvements in the female condition once transformations of productive forces occur and new techniques of human reproduction appear (CERM, 1978; Bleitrach, 1984).

2 See, in particular, Delphy (1970) who uses the term 'patriarchal class'.

3 This gap was primarily a theoretical one, since numerous empirical studies from 1975 on provoked important research sessions. See, for example, the following reports: 'Institution familiale et travail des femmes', at the Annual Meeting of the Société Française de Sociologie, Nantes, June 1980; 'Les

Femmes et la question de travail', organized by the Centre Lyonnais d'Etudes Féministes, December 1980; and 'Femmes, féminisme et recherche', national meeting organized by Association Femmes, Féminisme et Recherche, Toulouse, 1982.

4 For an example of such studies see *Le Sexe du travail (1984)* and *Les Cahiers de l'Atelier Production/REproduction* listed in the references.

5 This relations expresses itself more or less directly in terms of power. Thus, in the 'private' realm, within the European family, it operates as 'love' (Haicault, 1980). The form in urban African families is not the same (Vidal, 1977).

6 Godelier indicates this interconnection in a chapter titled 'La Part idéelle du réel' (1984).

7 In effect, this discussion links back to the issue of the reproduction of social relations. It is also important to acknowledge Mathieu's point that for women there is 'une part réelle de l'idéel' (1985: 186-223). She argues that women's consciousness is constrained and mediated by the fact that they are oppressed by men.

8 The use of the notion 'circulation' suggests a system of duties and obligations of which the form and content which those involved activate are socially codified and defined. Ethnographers often use the notion.

9 Pernot-Escourrou (1981) made similar observations.

10 The difficulties were both material and psychological. Among the working women surveyed, health problems – especially those of a psychological sort – plagued almost only those respondents cut off from their family networks, and especially from their mothers. With regard to job searches, it was almost always the female members of the kinship group who intervened, just as the responsibility for support in housework came from the female part of the group.

11 It should be noted that we do not speak of the 'transmission' of models. Learning is a continuous process of construction and deconstruction of the mother's model by daughters. It occurs throughout the relationship, from childhood through adolescence and adulthood. To see mothers take up and support the model which their daughters' paid work implies suggests that learning can go 'backwards', from daughters to mothers. This possibility calls into question the idea that there is only one way that intergenerational transmission can occur.

12 In the rare cases where there is a break with the maternal model, almost invariably there is something unusual about the training opportunities given to the daughter. And it is the mother alone – not both parents – who is considered responsible for this break if for some reason it has turned out badly.

REFERENCES

'Actes du colloque Femmes, Féminisme et Recherches' (1982) (Toulouse: AFFER).

Barrère-Maurisson, M. A., F. Battagliola and A.-M. Daune-Richard (1983) 'Trajectoires professionnelles des femmes et vie familiale', *Consommation – Revue de socioéconomie* (Paris).

Battagliola, F. et al. *(1986) A propos des rapports sociaux de sexe, Parcours épistémologiques* (Paris: CNRS), October.

Bleitrach, D. (1984) 'Contribution à une analyse de la condition féminine', *La Pensée*.

Bott, E. (1970) *Family and Social Networks* (New York: Shenckman Publishing Company).

Cahiers de L'Apre (1985–6) (Paris: CNRS–PIRTTEM)
   no. 1 – 'Crise et emploi des femmes', February 1985
   no. 2 – 'Temps sociaux. Trajectoires selon le sexe', May 1985
   no. 3 – 'Production/reproduction et rapports sociaux de sexe', September 1985
   no. 4 – 'La famille comme unité de production', February 1986
   no. 5 – 'Rapports intrafamiliaux et rapports sociaux de sexe', May 1986
   no. 6 – 'Division sexuelle du travail, famille et rapport salarial', September 1986

centre d'Etudes et de Recherches Marxistes (CERM) (1978) *La Condition féminine* (Paris: Editions Sociales).

Chabaud-Rychter, D., D. Fougeyrollas-Schwebel and F. Sonthonnax (1985) *Espace et temps du travail domestique* (Paris: Librairie des méridiens).

Dalla-Costa, M. R. and S. James (1973) *Pouvoir des femmes et subversion sociale* (Geneva: Librairie Adversaire).

Daune-Richard, A.-M. (1983a) 'Travail professionnel et travail domestique. Le travail et ses représentations au sein de lignées féminines', *Travail et Emploi*, no. 17.

Daune-Richard, A.-M. (1983b) 'Salaire, nécessité et fantasie', *BIEF*, no. 13, *Les femmes et l'argent*, II, (Aix-en-Provence: CEFUP, Université de Provence), December.

Daune-Richard, A.-M. (1984a) 'Travail professionnel et travail domestique. Etude exploratoire sur le travail et ses représentations au sein des lignées féminines' (Aix-en-Provence/Paris: CEFUP/Document Travail et Emploi (Copublication CEFUP/Ministère du Travail).

Daune-Richard, A.-M. (1984b) 'Activité professionnelle, travail domestique et lignées féminines', *Le sexe du travail* (Grenoble: PUG).

Daune-Richard, A.-M. (1985a) 'Division sexuelle, division sociale du travail: présentations du travail et catégories de sexe', *BIEF*, no. 16 (Aix-en-Provence: Centre d'Etudes Féminine de l'Université de Provence), Spring.

Daune-Richard, A.-M. (1985b) 'Travail salarié, travail domestique: de la construction d'un rapport au travail au sein de lignées féminines', *Dialogue*, no. 90.

Daune-Richard, A.-M. and M. Haicault (1985) 'Le poids de l'idéel dans les rapports sociaux de sexe', *Cahiers de l'APRE*, no. 3: *Production/reproduction et rapports sociaux de sexe* (Paris: PIRTTEM–CNRS).

Delphy, C. (1970) 'L'Ennemi principal', *Partisans*, no. spécial, libération des femmes, November.

Delphy, C. (1975) 'Pour un féminisme matérialiste', *l'Arc*, no. 61.

Les femmes et la question du travail (1984) (Lyon: Presses Universitaires de Lyon).

Godelier, M. (1984) *L'idéel et le matériel* (Paris: Fayard).

Guillaumin, C. (1978) 'Pratique du pouvoir et idée de nature: l'appropriation des femmes', *Questions féministes*, no. 2, February.

Guillaumin, C. (1981) 'Femmes et théories de la société. Remarques sur les effets théoriques de la colère des opprimées', *Sociologie et Sociétés*, vol. XIII, no. 2, October.

Haicault, M. (1980) 'Sexes, salaire, famille', *Sociétés, Annales de l'Université de Toulouse*, vol. XVI.

Haicault, M. (1984) 'La gestion ordinaire de la vie en deux', *Sociologie du Travail*, no. 3.

Labourie-Racape, A., M.-T. Letablier and A. M. Vasseur (1977) 'L'activité féminine', *Cahiers du Centre d'Etudes de l'Emploi*, no. 11 (Paris: PUF).

Lautier, B. (1977) 'Forme de production et procès du travail domestique', *Critiques de l'Economie Politique*, no. 4, October/December.

Luxton, M. (1980) *More Than a Labour of Love* (Toronto: The Women's Press).

Mathieu, N. C. (1971) 'Notes pour une définition sociologique des catégories de sexe', *Epistémologie Sociologique*, no. 11.

Mathieu, N. C. (1973) 'Homme-culture et femme-nature', *L'Homme*, XIII, no. 3.

Mathieu, N. C. (1985) 'L'arraisonnement des femmes. Essais en anthropologie des sexes', *Cahiers de l'Homme*, new series XXIV (Paris: Ecole des Hautes Etudes en Science Sociales).

Passeron, J.-C. and F. de Singly (1984) 'Différences dans la différence: socialisation de classe et socialisation sexuelle', *Revue Française de Science Politique*, vol. 34, no. 1, February.

Pernot-Escourrou, F. (1981) 'Liens entre histoire professionnelle et familiale des ouvrières de la télémécanique dans deux établissements en Haute Normandie', Thesis, University of Paris V.

Pitrou, A. (1976) *Relations entre générations et insertion sociale* (Aix en-Provence: LEST/CNRS).

Pitrou, A. (1979) *Vivre sans famille* (Toulouse: Privat).

Le sexe du travail (Grenoble: Presses Universitaires de Grenoble).

Sullerot, E. (1968) *Histoire et sociologie du travail féminin* (Paris: Gauthier).

Sullerot, E. (1978) *Le Fait féminin, qu'est-ce qu'une femme?* (Paris: Fayard).

Vidal, C. (1977) 'Guerre des sexes à Abidjan, masculin, féminin, CFA', *Cahiers d'Etudes Africaines*, vol. XVII, no. 65.

Young, M. and P. Willmott (1957) *Family and Kinship in East London* (London: Routledge and Kegan Paul).

16

The Conflict Between Housework and Employment

Some Notes on Women's Identity

Barbara Sichtermann

Twenty years ago when I had just left school to begin my professional training, the different futures available to a woman could be described in very simple terms: either she stayed at home or she took a job. The choice would make her either a housewife or a worker. The forced choice which women have long faced has had important consequences not only for their identities but also for the construction of spaces for resistance to capitalism's norms in bourgeois society. Here I offer a short outline of the ways in which present and future possibilities might be considered.

The alternative of 'staying home' or 'taking a job' was based on the assumption that women who 'stay at home' do not work. It was this assumption which the women's movement in the Federal Republic of Germany fought against in a heated debate which began in the early 1970s and is still going on today. Feminists asked how it was possible to overlook the mountains of hard work associated with housekeeping and motherhood, work that was being done every day by millions of women all over the world, and to refuse to accept it as 'legitimate work'. From Marxism came the term 'socially required' work, which would treat as 'true' work the efforts which non-employed women made every day in their homes and neighborhoods, at the nursery table and the school gates, in kitchens and supermarkets, and indeed even in the beds of their husbands. Of course the women's movement was not interested in terminological sophistry but rather in the appreciation, acknowledgement and re-evaluation of what most women all over the world did every day: that is, housework and caring for their families.

The traditional alternative is still presented to women but no longer as candidly nor as frequently as twenty years ago. Instead, more people now say 'a woman either works in the home or outside the home. She does housework or she has a job.' Contemporary usage reflects efforts to make up for past mistakes and to acknowledge women's work in the home as a valuable contribution to society. Housewives, too, are coming to regard themselves as accepted for the work they do. Nevertheless, the debate continues and has become even more complex with the changed situation of the last twenty years.

As long as only a paid job was regarded as actual work, the debate followed fairly simple lines. Women demanded equal opportunities in education and employment as well as reduction of household chores. Soon, however, the sluggishness of the situation *and* of the men who did not even dream of getting out the vacuum cleaner when they got home from work forced women to make modifications and differentiations which today make the debate very complex and difficult. Women discovered that when they took a job they could not really count on help with the housework from their husbands or support for childcare from public institutions. Responsibility for reproductive work stuck to women like a curse, restricting their mobility and availability for paid work and determining their ambitions and qualifications (Ostner, 1978). The 'double burden' of working women began to afflict middle-class women, as more of them took up paid employment. When women came home from work, they had to do the usual ironing and cleaning, which could be done only at the cost of forgoing all leisure time. The work of taking care of the family began to show a face that was by no means its only but certainly its most ugly one: that of unrelenting toil. And of course it was the women alone who were subjected to it

That working life represents an element of burden and stress – regardless of its merits and the satisfaction that it can bring – was generally recognized with the concept and reality of 'leisure time' (in German, *feierabend*) Every working man, whether proletarian or middle-class, had a right to leisure time and he also had his good fairy-godmother to provide it – if he were married. Employed women could not hope for a fairy-godmother to help them; on the contrary, they had to play this part themselves. After leaving work to go home, women went to another job because they, unlike men, had no 'time off'. Women had neither leisure time nor the recreation and relaxation which are essential preconditions for work and, in particular, for the enjoyment of work. In this race, work is the permanent winner: as fast as a woman may run, work is always there waiting for her (Beck-Gernsheim, 1980).

Because women have a double responsibility for job and home, which are both areas of work, they bear a *third* burden. The third area of stress is that *tour-de-force* that represents the only way the different and indeed often conflicting demands of the two spheres can be combined and met. In many cases it is not possible to reconcile them, and women are forced to hold together and maintain, within themselves and in their work, things which are functionally incompatible. It is as if they had to offer the same kind of resistance as the force which repels the two equal poles of a magnet (Becker-Schmidt et al., 1985). In reality, then, women who are crushed between job and housework and who exhaust themselves in their effort to unite the two are subject to a triple burden.

Let us return to our original alternative: 'The woman stays home, or she takes a job.' The women's movement has taught us or forced us to see that the housewife also works very hard, particularly when she has children. But *why* was such a forceful objection, indeed such a struggle, needed to bring our working society to recognize this fact? *Why* is it that men and women alike have not agreed from the very beginning that the housewife is also 'working'? What is more, how was it possible that this obvious fact came to be suppressed, ignored and denied? What did one think that housewives actually did, when the role of housewife was not associated with work? The context which hides the answer to these questions is not easy to identify and outline. Nor is the universal concept of 'patriarchy' or 'sexism' sufficient to explain it. Rather, it is necessary to explore the very roots of ideas of the 'modern' in the development of capitalist society.

In Leo Tolstoy's *Anna Karenina* there is a beautiful passage in which the newly-married landlord Lewin expresses his dissatisfaction with the fact that his young wife Kitty does 'absolutely nothing' all day long. Himself untiring in running his estate, Lewin has an antipathy for idleness and reproaches Kitty for her 'laziness'. He has not yet understood – so Tolstoy tells us – that she knows instinctively what is in store for her once she grows used to her roles as lady of the manor and mother. Her husband does not understand that Kitty is a little afraid of her future tasks with their (as Tolstoy puts it) 'immense burden of work' and she is trying to rest, free from care, for one last moment, and at the same time trying to accumulate strength for the future.

Tolstoy was situated particularly well for providing some insight into the history of what we today call 'housework' or 'the lot of the housewife'. He describes, a full hundred years before our time, a situation in which women had almost no alternative to family and housework, while the quest for individual happiness that characterizes modern times had already begun. We learn that Russians at that time understood that woman bore an immense workload in the home. At the same time Tolstoy makes it unmistakably clear (although not apparent from the above quotation) that the work which women devote to their families and the country was very highly respected and recognized. In Tolstoy's writings the minor nobility and – whenever they appear – the peasants show an almost religious reverence for their mothers and housewives. Of course, all power rests in the hands of men who also have prestige, glory and honor, while the women (who, for Tolstoy, are absolutely equal to the men in terms of intelligence and temperament) almost never leave their familiar surroundings. Despite all this, one never gets the impression that women felt underrated, insufficiently recognized and respected, or generally suppressed.

Tolstoy's work reveals an earlier society to us. Studies of pre-bourgeois, corporative societies where tradition, religion and biological determination dominated much more strongly than today, demonstrate that women and men did not see themselves competing with one another, for each had her or his private world (Illich, 1983). They experienced each other as strangers between whom intimacy and love were possible, although detachment and lack of understanding were much more natural and widespread. At the same time they needed each other and depended upon each other for the continued existence and well-being of the family and the people as a whole. Most importantly, the glue that held this fragile gender coalition together was respect for the unfamiliar but important achievements and abilities of the other. Women looked to men in admiration of their military and civic roles, while men regarded women with tenderness and piety because of their fruitfulness. Needless to say there was also a lot of infamy between the sexes, but the ideal of a concordance based on the respect and admiration of the opposite sex (without whose presence and efforts either one of the partners would have been lost and lonely) was achieved.

This situation can also be described by saying that in pre-bourgeois times women and men had reached a compromise or an accord, based on as assertion of the others' otherness and the impossibility of either resembling or even completely understanding the other. This arrangement implied that women could move in their realm – the home – with relatively great autonomy and did not have to beg for recognition for services and achievements. Of course, housework included a great number of activities, ranging from crafts to agriculture and even teaching, and thus offering a wide spectrum of opportunities to prove oneself and to find satisfaction. That women worked was as accepted as any sunrise, and that men did a completely different kind of work and thus did not compete with women was as self-evident as the fact that the sun also set.

The came a time when the things that women did in the house no longer were called 'work'. The period in which the women were finally deprived of the term 'work' for their activities was of course when the form of paid labor – of abstract labor as Marx correctly identified it – became widespread. This type of labor became the *tertium comparationis* for all elements and aspects of the new, commodity-based economy. 'Work' became identified with paid labor, with labor sold on the labor market, and with socialized (*vergesellschafteter*) labor. This dominating trait of capitalist society became so powerful as a category as well as a fact that it successfully displaced from its terminological purview all other forms of activity that were not mediated by the market (*vergesellschaftet*).

Not only did the labor of housewives lose status, but also that of the peasant farmers who worked their own land and the self-employed craftsmen. They all did a little of everything – they fed the children, plowed the earth or made their clothes, but 'work' was something else again, something that could be specifically measured, compared, paid for, something that was simultaneously free and at the same time forced, shared and alienated. In short, work became something quite complex. It was labor at the front-line of progress, in the factories, mines and mills, wherever something was produced for the market and – following this mode – wherever the state with its mechanisms of administration and control accompanied and supplemented the 'socializing' function of the market. It was thought that any form of labor not mediated by the market did not create value. The care and caretaking women performed in the home was first among these 'valueless' labors. Despite having been highly respected for thousands of years both as hard labor and as forms of self-expression, non-market activities could no longer be conceptualized in terms of the new labor theory of value. These activities had no definition in market terms and were subsumed under the *differentia specifica* of market societies.

My guess is that bourgeois society let out a sigh of relief when it turned out that, at least in certain central aspects, housework proved resistant to capitalist organization of labor. By that time, society recognized the first symptoms of horror from the new forces unleashed. Some nostalgic voices began to warn against any further acceleration of the pace of progress. How many romantics have there been since early nineteenth-century Romanticism? Every romantic has been concerned about women, sometimes warmly, sometimes hatefully, always passionately. The reason is simple enough. Women are the largest social group who have not pawned their brains and nerves to the moloch of capitalism and who are still doing what the majority of people have done since the dawn of time – taking care of their kin.

Whereas it was primarily bourgeois women who were privileged enough to remain outside the market sphere, proletarian women could rarely sustain a traditional pre-industrial female role. And in entering the paid labor force, these women became caught in an historical incompatibility. Working *in* the home, women were fulfilling the expectations of parents, children, neighbors, the clergy and even their own wishes; *outside* the home, they were doing something inappropriate for women, even if need left them no choice. A hundred years ago these two forms of labor were worlds apart, not only in their content and different degree of commodification but also in terms of morality. They constituted two entirely different modes of existence, two worlds as alien to each other as capitalism and the inertia of village life or, for that matter, as alien as the sexes once were to each other with their different, mutually impenetrable life-spheres. A proletarian woman in the factory was actually part of man's world. In terms of the traditional organization of social tasks, this seemed as reprehensible as blasphemy itself (Jurszyk and Tatschmurat, 1985).

Throughout history women have, of course, performed work outside the house (Ennen, 1985). Since time immemorial, women have mastered a broad spectrum of extramural activities and it would be wrong, then, to blame modern capitalism for absorbing women into the process of commodity production. The difference is, however, that it is not until late into modern times that we find massive resistance against paid labor for women in an historically new way, and cutting across all class lines. The expressed need for a 'home' seems to be on the rise and is often expressed with a sense of urgency, at times rising to the level of hysteria. The after-effects still trouble us today.

The reason for this expression of need can be found in the overall disorientation following structural revolutions in rural areas in the wake of industrial capitalism, in the sometimes rather sudden urbanization of communities and the breathless incorporation of hitherto self-contained institutions and individuals into larger networks. These developments caused a kind of dizzy spell and, in panic, people sought something to hold on to. The family at least seemed exempt and protected from the centripetal powers of accumulation and its corollaries, technology and abstract labor.

Reports of philanthropists, doctors or clergymen about labor issues demonstrate much less concern or horror about the negative physical effects than about the deplorable *moral* effects of paid labor on working women. Given the principles of the capitalist labor market, assigning women to the home was probably less an indication of animosity toward women or a display of male superiority than it was an indication of a diffuse desire felt by the entire society (including most women) to prevent capitalist de-personification from becoming universal. Women and home symbolized a barrier, a sphere of human relations free from determination or mediation by the rules of the market. Women who had been the traditional adminstrators of such elementary relations seemed predestined to the task of defending this barrier.

To cut a long story short, the barricade did not hold. The capitalist economy soon began to penetrate the walls of the home and to reshape the identity structures of women and mothers. For a considerable time, critical social research has been collecting material on this process: on the transition from motherly 'care for an entire house' (including the potential for a productive, creative and satisfying existence) to a functional discipline adapted to the schedule of the capitalist work day; from impeccable adminstrator and faithful and caring mother figure to part and parcel of a fully-automated kitchen, life-plan and educational strategy (Bock and Diden, 1977). Today we know that housework performed under the tyranny of the clock, of detergent ads and in the isolation of a secluded apartment can hardly be considered a point of resistance against capitalist co-operation, as it may have been in the past. None the less, there are ineradicable residues of human immediacy which are resistant to becoming simple exchange values. Capitalism cannot but leave these enclaves and vestiges intact and responsive to the needs of labor reproduction. Childrearing continues successfully to withstand any analogies to factory work, despite all attempts to make it so on the part of baby food industries, official educational programs, public health organizations, and the like.

If this analysis is correct, and if the 'home' has been defended against society's inherent evolutionary thrust – a defence which was, of course, unorganized, spontaneous and at a gut level – then it remains difficult to understand why housework received so little recognition during the bourgeois era. The reason for the anomaly lies in capitalism's power to plunder, exploit and transform such traditions, which soon lose their voice along with their independence. The housewife who saw her husband disappear every day into an alien social system fell silent. The term 'work' henceforth belonged to him who used it as a living resource; it was he who kept that formidable machinery running which patterned the entire life of society. Every day as men went through the factory gate to exchange their labor for wages, they performed their own initiation into modernity. The 'freedom' of the wage-laborer meant not only that he was freed from ownership of the means of production, but also that he had the freedom of a new mobility and flexible use. The vision of progress intoxicated even the workers; in spite of occasional resistance, the grandeur of that vision infected the mood of the productive classes and silenced the weak and disoriented voices of tradition. The momentum of bourgeois society was so powerful that it bulldozed any dissenting traditions, traditions that none the less were the psychological pillars on which that society rested.

On the whole, the ideal for women was simply to *stay* in the house. In the context of an achievement-oriented bourgeois society, this meant to be *and* stay there *for her children and her husband*. The norm, borrowed from the image of aristocratic leisure life, has remained attractive to this day. Whereas the middle classes now permit women, married and unmarried alike, to develop a self-definition based on a profession, the rural poor and the small-town working classes by and large maintain the ideal of the 'non-working' mother at home. In these social circles that early bourgeois image of women remains the one sought after. It is the woman who 'simply stays home' (even though 'simply staying' may mean hard labor) for her husband, for sons and daughters, and for God.

This idea does not represent an attempt to keep women down nor is it political calculation in Christian disguise which accounts for the strength and vitality of the image to this day. It is the expression of a subconscious need to protect society from the powers unleashed by the process of capital accumulation. The notion of the woman who 'stayed home' – who existed for the family – still carries the tang of resistance against capitalism's efforts to affect every fibre of our life; it also rings with a popular yearning for a kind of human enclave, embodying, like a mother's smile, the needs and wishes which the capitalist organization of labor, constructed around the great machine, leaves unfulfilled.

It is ironic, then, that the bourgeois housewife *qua* mistress of her servants was basically abolished by the labor movement, albeit in an indirect way. As wages rose, even the bourgeoisie could no longer afford to maintain servants. Domestic service disappeared from the list of proletarian occupations, and the houses and apartments of the upper-middle classes shrunk to the familiar size of the one-family unit. Even ladies of the upper strata resigned themselves to what the lower strata had been doing for quite a while: taking the children to school, shopping, even cooking and getting upset about an inefficient cleaning aid. The occupation of housewife lost almost the last vestiges of art and leisure and implied little but repetitive, empty and tedious chores. Housework had turned barren just like any other work and it came to be called just that: work.

None the less, for structural reasons, housework never linked up completely to the *differentia specifica*, to labor-producing 'value' in the context of a market. Therefore, the mother at home remains the focus of all sorts of projections which cannot be incorporated into the normal work life – visions, desires, forms of self-expression (Friedan, 1977). They all draw their substance from the vision of an alternative life where no one is defined exclusively in functional terms. These visions are translated into hopes of being cared for, nurtured, warmed and tucked in at night, all those things which cannot be defined in exchange value terms. But today, 'reproduction' and private life – demanding all that space for personal development, for trying out the heart, the senses, emotions and sexuality – have to make do without the tacit vision of a mother at the center of that space for the regeneration we call 'home'. The realm of paid labor has proven more attractive than the home, which in turn shriveled away and became socially less interesting as factories grew.

At the same time, the egalitarianism of money, of compulsory education, and of the capitalist market showed their effects. Enlightened women completed what capitalist transformation had left unfinished – they proclaimed equal rights for everyone and demanded equal access to education, professions, income, and independence. Women too wanted to be able and entitled to build a life of their own. They wanted the choice to exist, to be there for their own benefit. These aspirations required paid work which, in turn, precluded 'being there', staying at home. Even if they could only partially be there for others, and even if no one was going to be there for them, women demanded the right to work. This represented the death-blow to the ancient alliance of the sexes around a sex-specific division of labor. As the alliance began to dissolve, so did society, as it became increasingly 'atomized'.

It took quite a while, as we know, to secure these gains for enlightened women, and to this day not much progress has been made beyond the first steps; but the road is wide open ahead of us. Capitalism does not object to full equality, including even some potential special rights recognizing maternity. There is no logical objection to a substantive equality, but could there be historical objections?

The result of my deliberations on the conflict between housework and employment is that assigning women to the home may well be a form of objecting to, even of resisting, the totalizing tendencies of capitalism. Practically all of society once shared in this resistance, up to the advent about 100 years ago of the so-called first-wave women's movement. When our foremothers demanded equal rights it had already become obvious that lullabies and apple-pies were insufficient to stop the onslaught of capitalism. The symbols of resistance had turned into symbols of subjugation, of adaptation. The most pious intentions were powerless against the structural causes of the housewives' misery. In their homes women had become lonely outposts; there was little choice for them but to make way for their freedom, albeit the freedom of paid labor.

That universally convertible currency of social exchange – money – had advanced to an absolute power; only those owning it could hope to keep up. Like fossils, housewives still acted in the sphere of use-value while, at the same time, living amidst bourgeois (i.e. capitalist) society and preparing their children for a life in that very society. Obviously, this location entailed an ongoing conflict between norms – whether in terms of the meaning and goal of life in general, or in terms of feelings, morality, achievement or self-esteem. Moreover, depending on their husbands meant being at their mercy; never before had women found themselves in such a vulnerable position. Women could no longer withdraw to a sphere of their own, at least not without getting even more deeply entangled; housework had ceased to be a legitimate complement or counterweight to the man's world. Housework and making or mending shoes, rearing children and tilling the land could not compete; the age of money-making was clearly dominant.

All the housewife had to counter the world of money was her heart – and she was soon to find out that she had better hold on to that. Modern times not only withheld the honor and dignity that had been her traditional title; they mocked and scoffed her. A household now was defined in terms of commodities that could be bought; it was not the housewife who controlled the household but money and its owner. She herself could easily be replaced by hired help.

Men had themselves absconded with the help of a double standard. Surrendering to the temptations of a new era, they appeased their consciences by consecrating their wives and daughters to the old powers. They paid their dues to religion and conventions with pious and home-based/domestic women. The men went to work and transformed the old world but then when morality and fear of God came knocking at their door, someone would be there to open it.

This strategy succeeded reasonably well as long as women perceived their lives had meaning, that is to say as long as they did not experience them as a sacrifice. To the extent that the home lost its designation as an enclave of human concerns, women began to find it intolerable that they were supposed to keep on with their identity being curators of a museum, so to speak. Uprooted and disoriented, they wandered along a kind of anti-progressive frontier which was beginning to look more like occupied territory than like a refuge. Were the women to blame that the rest of society was showing symptoms of indigestion in the face of its own progress? Were they supposed to foot the bill and yet remain exiled from the scenes of modernity, from the marketplace and the workplace, from all those rewards and positions to be attained? The more society became streamlined and the norms of capitalist labor shaped its general outlook, woman's identity as a structural weakling became more and more mortifying for her and her position in relation to her partner more and more untenable. Not only was he physically stronger and socially superior, he was even epochs ahead of her. Not only could he withhold tenderness and money but he could block her access to the age in which she lived. Slowly, very slowly – the process took about a century and is still going on – women began to understand and to leave home, to stop *staying* (home) and to go *working*.

Meanwhile the *tertium comparationis* between the sexes has been firmly established: wage labor. Competition is pushing mightily against traditional barriers which once regulated access to the various segments of the labor market along sex lines. Women, mothers included, have entered the labor force in increasing numbers. At the same time, reproductive activities become more and more defeminized. The number of single-parent households is on the rise. Men can easily take care of themselves and being married to a housewife has ceased to be the natural goal. Men are discovering (and women are suspending) their inclination and ability for traditional 'caring'. The trends still do not describe the majority, but they are observable among those minorities as are traditionally open to social experiments. In overall terms, wage labor and housework balance out in terms of genders; the capitalist labor market purges more and more traditional residues from its mechanism.

At the same time, a virulent discussion has flared up about the meaning of life and labor; consuming seems to be losing in importance, while creativity and personalized work are gaining. There is a renewed emphasis on finding what remains as the gratifications of housework. Private pleasures and family life are being increasingly defended against the inroads of industrially prefabricated pleasures, and men are expected to contribute equally to them. More and more, wage labor is reduced in status, as it is assigned a mere instrumental value, regardless of whether it is skilled or unskilled labor. No longer can it define the whole identity and social position of workers, whether male or female, and no longer can it be invested with excessive pride or be the only basis for their self-esteem.

As traditional motives, habits and practices dissolve, and as new norms, goals and roles take shape, women have suddenly found themselves in the position of an avantgarde, given their long-standing dual orientation toward home and the labor market. At the same time, men are discovering and accepting reproduction and conjugal life as enclaves protected from the 'lies' of capitalism. In this sense we can speak of a 'feminization' of labor in Germany. In the feminist press and literature, we witness attempts to introduce norms and ideals of private life into the realm of work in order to defeat its notorious alienation not simply by 'humanizing' it but also by 'feminizing' labor-force activites, especially as far as work schedules are concerned.

There can be no doubt, then, that the worlds of home and of labor are moving closer. They are beginning to exchange attributes, including some gender-specific ones, and they imitate each other and compete with each other. At their respective cores, however, they are still alien and even hostile, resistant to change and, for the most part, still gender-specific. Things have begun to move but amidst all the commotion, shuffle and confusion it is obvious that certain complexes are not moving at all. In the workplace, the top-level jobs are still male; in the family, childrearing remains largely a female task. There are exceptions here and there, a few more perhaps than ten years ago, but nothing really significant.

Finally, in reassessing the split between paid work and housework, the moral of the story is *not* that women should move back into the deserted house, surrendering all claims to an independent job. There is no alternative for women except to step beyond the threshold of the home. But that is only *half* the moral. The other half begins from curiosity about the deserted house. The home represents a potential locale for resistance against capitalist atrophy of humane forms of life. Housework has been rightly thought to conserve this resistance since the origins of capitalism and can do so into the future.

The implication is that we should treasure and preserve the vision that housework and family life can evade capitalism's effects. With this vision we could devise a strategy which defines the private sphere (whether in family terms or not) as a fortress against universal commodification. Within that sphere women could expand, confirm, cultivate and modify the abilities they acquired during their long history in the home. The vision of the home as a barrier to the reduction of all life to abstract functions was not mistaken; it should be extended beyond women to protect all people. This cannot be, then, women's task alone. Rebuilding the home from the ruins and rubble of capitalist commodification requires the efforts of both women and men.

At the same time, it is important to remember that the abstract functions we perform outside the home always contain a certain 'human surplus'; rarely, if ever, can we describe them exclusively in functional terms. The reality of outside is attractive precisely because its criteria are different from those that apply in the family circle. It is honorable to succeed in the work world; it is disgraceful to fail (Strümpel, 1982). Achievement norms may change their content, but they will survive. Most likely they will always differ from the norms of private life, and there is nothing wrong with that. As a social being, everyone secretly wishes to be judged by the average standard of necessary social labor – and to pass. No adult wants to be judged solely on the basis of his or her good intentions. In short, quite apart from monetary rewards (without which no emancipation could occur today), even wage labor offers some psychological gratifications. These are indispensable for women today, and women not only have a claim to them, but the *right* to redeem that claim as well.

REFERENCES

Beck-Gernsheim, E. (1980) *Das Halbeirte Leben. Männerwelt Beruf, Frauenwelt Familie* (Fischer Verlag).
Becker-Schmidt et al. (1985) *Nicht wir haben die Minuten, die Minuten haben uns. Qeitprobleme und Zeiterfahrungen von Arbeitermuttern in Fabrik und Familie* (Verlag Neue Gesellschaft).
Bock, G. and B. Diden (1977) 'Zur Entstahung der Hausarbeit im Kapitalismus', in *Frauen und Wissenschaft* (Courage Verlag).
Ennen, E. (1985) *Frauen im Mittelalter* (Beck Verlag).
Friedan, B. (1977) *Der Weiblichkeitswahn* (Reinbek).
Illich, I. (1983) *Genus. Zu einer historischen Kritik der Gleichheit* (Reinbeck).
Jurszyk, K. and C. Tatschmurat (1985) 'Leben und Arbeiten der Industriearbeiter- innen, ein Struck Frauenforschungsgeschichte', in *Frauenforschung, Beitrage zum 22 Deutschen Soziologenta Dortmund 1984* (Campus Verlag).
Ostner, I. (1978) *Beruf und Hausarbeit* (Campus Verlag).
Strümpel, F. (1982) 'Wertveranderung und Arbeitsmotivation', in C. Offe et al. (eds), *Arbeitszeitpolitik* (Campus Verlag).

Index

Italics indicate references to tables or figures; 'n' (eg 41n) indicates a reference to a note at the end of a chapter.

Abbreviations:
Can. = Canada
Fr. = France
FRG = Federal Republic of Germany
It. = Italy
Sw. = Sweden
UK = United Kingdom
US = United States

Index by Mandy Crook